THE CAMBRIDGE COMPANION TO
JOHN WESLEY

A leading figure in the Evangelical Revival in eighteenth-century England, John Wesley (1703–1791) is the founding father of Methodism and, by extension, of the holiness and Pentecostal movements. This Cambridge Companion offers a general, comprehensive introduction to Wesley's life and work, and to his theological and ecclesiastical legacy. Written from various disciplinary perspectives, including history, literature, theology, and religious studies, this volume will be an invaluable aid to scholars and students, including those encountering the work and thought of Wesley for the first time.

Randy L. Maddox is Professor of Theology and Wesleyan Studies at the Divinity School, Duke University. A leading scholar of the theology of John and Charles Wesley and of theological developments in the later Methodist or Wesleyan tradition, he is the author of *Responsible Grace: John Wesley's Practical Theology* and editor of *Aldersgate Reconsidered* and *Rethinking Wesley's Theology for Contemporary Methodism*.

Jason E. Vickers is Associate Professor of Theology and Wesleyan Studies and Director of the Center for Evangelical United Brethren Heritage at United Theological Seminary, Dayton, Ohio. He is the author or editor of numerous books, including *Wesley: A Guide for the Perplexed, Invocation and Assent: The Making and Remaking of Trinitarian Theology*, and *Immersed in the Life of God: The Healing Resources of the Christian Faith*.

CAMBRIDGE COMPANIONS TO RELIGION
This is a series of companions to major topics and key figures in theology and
religious studies. Each volume contains specially commissioned chapters by
international scholars, which provide an accessible and stimulating
introduction to the subject for new readers and non-specialists.

Continued after the Index

THE CAMBRIDGE COMPANION TO

JOHN WESLEY

Edited by Randy L. Maddox
Duke University, Durham, North Carolina

Jason E. Vickers
United Theological Seminary, Dayton, Ohio

Ron –

GOD'S RICHEST BLESSINGS!

JSVickers

CAMBRIDGE
UNIVERSITY PRESS

CAMBRIDGE UNIVERSITY PRESS
Cambridge, New York, Melbourne, Madrid, Cape Town, Singapore,
São Paulo, Delhi, Dubai, Tokyo

Cambridge University Press
32 Avenue of the Americas, New York, NY 10013-2473, USA

www.cambridge.org
Information on this title: www.cambridge.org/9780521714037

© Cambridge University Press 2010

This publication is in copyright. Subject to statutory exception
and to the provisions of relevant collective licensing agreements,
no reproduction of any part may take place without the written
permission of Cambridge University Press.

First published 2010

Printed in the United States of America

A catalog record for this publication is available from the British Library.

Library of Congress Cataloging in Publication data

The Cambridge companion to John Wesley / edited by Randy L. Maddox, Jason E. Vickers.
    p.   cm. – (Cambridge companions to religion)
Includes bibliographical references and index.
ISBN 978-0-521-88653-6 (hardback) – ISBN 978-0-521-71403-7 (pbk.)
    1. Wesley, John, 1703–1791.   I. Maddox, Randy L.   II. Vickers, Jason E.   III. Title:
Companion to John Wesley.   IV. Series.
BX8495.W5C24   2010
287.092 – dc22   [B]   2009026768

ISBN 978-0-521-88653-6 Hardback
ISBN 978-0-521-71403-7 Paperback

Cambridge University Press has no responsibility for the persistence
or accuracy of URLs for external or third-party Internet Web sites
referred to in this publication and does not guarantee that any content
on such Web sites is, or will remain, accurate or appropriate.

FOR

Richard P. Heitzenrater

Exemplary Wesley Scholar and Generous Colleague

Contents

List of illustrations

We want to express our appreciation to Dr. Peter Forsaith, Research Fellow at the Oxford Centre for Methodism and Church History, Oxford Brookes University, for his assistance in obtaining these illustrations.

Contributors

William J. Abraham is Albert Cook Outler Professor of Wesley Studies and Altshuler Distinguished Teaching Professor, Southern Methodist University, Dallas, Texas. He is the author of *Divine Revelation and the Limits of Historical Criticism* (1982), *Wesley for Armchair Theologians* (2005), *Canon and Criterion in Christian Theology* (1998), and several other books and articles.

Ted A. Campbell is Associate Professor of Church History, Southern Methodist University, Dallas, Texas. He is the author of *The Gospel in Christian Traditions* (2009), *Methodist Doctrine: The Essentials* (1999), *Christian Confessions: A Historical Introduction* (1996), *The Religion of the Heart: A Study of European Religious Life in the Seventeenth and Eighteenth Centuries* (1991), and *John Wesley and Christian Antiquity* (1991).

Kenneth J. Collins is Professor of Historical Theology and Wesley Studies, Asbury Theological Seminary, Wilmore, Kentucky. He is the author of *The Theology of John Wesley: Holy Love and the Shape of Grace* (2007), *A Real Christian: The Life of John Wesley* (1999), *The Scripture Way of Salvation: The Heart of John Wesley's Theology* (1997), and several other books and articles.

Kenneth Cracknell is President Emeritus of the Cambridge Federation, where he was Senior Tutor at Wesley House. A British Methodist Minister, he has served as missionary in Nigeria and in two Methodist circuits in England. He was, for ten years, director of interfaith relations for the British Council of Churches and acted as a Consultant to the World Council of Churches for a further twenty years. Most recently he has been Distinguished Professor in Residence at the Brite Divinity School, Texas Christian University in Fort Worth. Now retired, he lives in Vermont. He is the author of numerous articles and books, including *Our Doctrines: Methodist Theology as Classical Christianity* (1998) and, with Susan White, *An Introduction to World Methodism* (2005).

Dennis C. Dickerson is James M. Lawson, Jr., Professor of History, Vanderbilt University, Nashville, Tennessee. He is the historiographer of the African Methodist Episcopal Church and author of *A Liberated Past: Explorations in A.M.E. Church History* (2003); *Religion, Race, and Region: Research Notes on A.M.E. Church History* (1995); and *Militant Mediator: Whitney M. Young, Jr.* (1998). He has also published several articles on the Wesleyan dimensions of African American Methodist communities.

Jeremy Gregory is Senior Lecturer in the History of Modern Christianity at the University of Manchester. He is the author of *Restoration, Reformation and Reform, 1660–1828: Archbishops of Canterbury and Their Diocese* (2000) and (with John Stevenson) *The Companion to Britain in the Eighteenth Century, 1688–1820* (revised edition, 2007). He edited *The Speculum of Archbishop Thomas Secker, 1759–68* (1995), and *John Wesley: Tercentenary Essays* (2005), and he has written numerous essays and journal articles on religion and culture in the long eighteenth century.

David N. Hempton is Alonzo L. McDonald Family Professor of Evangelical Theological Studies, Harvard Divinity School, Cambridge, Massachusetts. He is a social historian of religion with particular expertise in populist traditions of evangelicalism in Europe and North America. He is the author of many articles and books, including *Methodism and Politics in British Society, 1750–1850* (1984), winner of the Whitfield prize of the Royal Historical Society, and *Methodism: Empire of the Spirit* (2005), winner of the Jesse Lee prize.

Sarah H. Lancaster is Professor of Theology in the Hazen G. Werner Chair of Theology, Methodist Theological School of Ohio, Columbus. She is author of *Women and the Authority of Scripture: A Narrative Approach* (2002), as well as numerous articles on John Wesley and Wesleyan theology. She has been co-chair of the Wesley Studies Group of the American Academy of Religion.

Deborah Madden is a Research Fellow in the Theology Faculty of the University of Oxford. She has published several articles on Wesley's interest in health and healing, as well as a monograph, *'A Cheap, Safe and Natural Medicine': Religion, Medicine and Culture in John Wesley's 'Primitive Physic'* (2007). More recently, she has edited and contributed to a collection of scholarly essays, *'Inward and Outward Health': John Wesley's Holistic Concept of Medical Science, the Environment and Holy Living* (2008).

Randy L. Maddox is Professor of Theology and Wesleyan Studies, Duke University, Durham, North Carolina. He is the author of *Responsible Grace: John Wesley's Practical Theology* (1994), a contributor to *Wesley and the Quadrilateral* (1997), and editor of *Aldersgate Reconsidered* (1990) and *Rethinking Wesley's Theology for Contemporary Methodism* (1998). He also serves as Institute Secretary of the Oxford Institute of Methodist Theological Studies and as Associate General Editor of the Wesley Works Editorial Project. He is a past president of the Wesleyan Theological Society, past co-chair of the Wesley Studies Group of the American Academy of Religion, and past General Editor of Kingswood Books.

Rebekah L. Miles is Associate Professor of Ethics, Southern Methodist University, Dallas, Texas. She is the author of *The Bonds of Freedom: Feminist Theology and Christian Realism* (2001) and *The Pastor as Moral Guide* (1999). She is a contributing author to *Wesley and the Quadrilateral: Renewing the Conversation* (1997) and has published several other articles on Wesley's significance for current issues in theology and ethics.

Isabel Rivers is Professor of Eighteenth-Century English Literature and Culture at Queen Mary, University of London, and co-director of the Dr Williams Centre for Dissenting Studies. She is author of *Reason, Grace, and Sentiment: A*

Study of the Language of Religion and Ethics in England, 1660–1780, 2 vols. (1991–2000); editor of *Books and Their Readers in Eighteenth-Century England* (1982) and *Books and Their Readers in Eighteenth-Century England: New Essays* (2001); and has published a number of articles on seventeenth- and eighteenth-century literature, religion, and thought. She is currently writing *Vanity Fair and the Celestial City: Dissenting, Methodist and Evangelical Literary Culture in England, 1720–1800*.

Randall J. Stephens is Associate Professor of History, Eastern Nazarene College, Quincy, Massachusetts. He is author of *The Fire Spreads: The Origins of Holiness and Pentecostalism in the American South* (2008), an editor of the *Journal of Southern Religion*, and editor of *Historically Speaking*.

Karen B. Westerfield Tucker is Professor of Worship, Boston University, Boston, Massachusetts. She is the author of *American Methodist Worship* (2001), editor of *The Sunday Service of the Methodists: Twentieth-Century Worship in Worldwide Methodism* (1996), and co-editor of *Oxford History of Christian Worship* (2005). She has also published several articles and book chapters on the contributions of the Wesleyan tradition to worship.

Jason E. Vickers is Associate Professor of Theology and Wesleyan Studies and Director of the Center for Evangelical United Brethren Heritage, United Theological Seminary, Dayton, Ohio. He is the author of *Wesley: A Guide for the Perplexed* (2009) and *Invocation and Assent: The Making and Remaking of Trinitarian Theology* (2008), as well as several book chapters and journal articles on John and Charles Wesley's theology.

Robert W. Wall is the Paul T. Walls Professor of Scripture and Wesleyan Studies, Seattle Pacific University, Seattle, Washington. He is the author of several books, including *The Catholic Epistles and Apostolic Traditions* (2009) and *Called to Be Church: The Book of Acts for a New Day* (2006). He has been a major contributor to the recent emphasis on reclaiming a theological reading of scripture, with a particular concern for the characteristic emphases of a Wesleyan reading of scripture.

Charles I. Wallace Jr. is Chaplain and Associate Professor of Religious Studies, Willamette University, Salem, Oregon. He is the editor of *Susanna Wesley: The Complete Writings* (1997). He is also the author of numerous articles and essays on the Wesley family.

Acknowledgments

The editors wish to thank their colleagues at the Divinity School at Duke University and at United Theological Seminary for encouraging and supporting their work on this project. In addition, we would like to say a special word of appreciation to Julia Abla for creating the index and to Evan Abla for proofreading. Finally, we would be remiss if we did not thank Andrew Beck for sharing and supporting our vision for this volume from the beginning.

Chronology of John Wesley

1703	born June 28 (June 17 by the Julian calendar then in use) at Epworth
1707	brother Charles born December 18 at Epworth
1709	rescued from burning parsonage in Epworth, February 9
1714–20	student at London's Charterhouse School
1721–24	student at Christ Church, Oxford
1725	began keeping spiritual journal, while studying for Master's degree
1726	elected Fellow (in Greek) at Lincoln College, Oxford, on March 17
1727	awarded Master of Arts degree, February 14 becomes curate at Epworth and Wroot, under father
1728	ordained Anglican priest on September 22
1729	in March Charles initiates small gathering of students at Oxford (first "society") John called back to duties at Lincoln College in October; became leader of the small student group
1735	father Samuel Wesley Sr. dies on April 25; after April 25, John and Charles Wesley sail for Georgia (under auspices of SPCK), October 14
1736	Charles Wesley leaves Georgia in July, returning to England
1737	John Wesley leaves Georgia on December 22, returning to England
1738	experience of assurance at Aldersgate on May 24
1739	first "open-air" preaching in Bristol, beginning of Methodist revival; brother Samuel Wesley Jr. dies on November 8
1740	starts Kingswood School for coal-miners' children
1742	mother Susanna Wesley dies on July 30
1744	begins annual meetings with traveling preachers
1749	Charles Wesley marries Sarah Gwynne on April 8
1751	marries Mary Vazeille in February
1760–62	controversies over Christian perfection
1763	Model Deed adopted
1765	sermon "The Scripture Way of Salvation" (his mature position)
1769	sends first lay preachers to North America
1771	issues first set of collected works
1775	questions legitimacy of American colonists' complaints
1784	"blesses" new American church, sending *Sunday Service*, Articles, and newly ordained ministers (Thomas Vasey and Richard Whatcoat) with Thomas Coke
1788	brother Charles dies on March 29
1791	dies on March 2

Abbreviations

Letters (Telford) *The Letters of the Rev. John Wesley, A.M.*, edited by John Telford, 8 vols. (London: Epworth, 1931) [NB: Use only for letters dated after 1755].

NT Notes *Explanatory Notes Upon the New Testament*, 3rd corrected edition (Bristol: Graham and Pine, 1760–62; many later reprints).

Works *The Works of John Wesley*; begun as "The Oxford Edition of The Works of John Wesley" (Oxford: Clarendon Press, 1975–1983); continued as "The Bicentennial Edition of The Works of John Wesley" (Nashville: Abingdon, 1984–); 16 of 35 vols. published to date.

Works (Jackson) *The Works of John Wesley*, ed. Thomas Jackson, 14 vols. (London, 1872; Grand Rapids: Zondervan, 1958).

Introduction

RANDY L. MADDOX AND JASON E. VICKERS

John Wesley (1703–91) is a prominent figure in the history of Western Christianity. Educated at Oxford University and ordained a priest in the Church of England, Wesley became one of the leading architects of the Evangelical Revival in eighteenth-century England. The "Methodist" wing of the revival that he led became known for their rigorous spiritual practices, their personal piety, and their concern for the poor, the imprisoned, and the uneducated. Although these traits were ridiculed by some in the early years, by the end of his life, Wesley had emerged as one of the most significant religious figures in England.

Wesley's significance within broader Western Christianity is grounded, in part, in the phenomenal growth and spread of Methodism after his death. What began as a meeting of a few students at Oxford who were seeking spiritual accountability has blossomed into a worldwide movement consisting of more than 100 denominations, which minister to more than 75 million people.[1] When one adds to this the Pentecostal and Charismatic churches that trace their heritage from Methodist roots, the number of Christians who can be regarded as Wesley's spiritual or ecclesiastical descendants is staggering. These descendants have made Wesley part of the physical landscape in churches, private homes, and on university and seminary campuses around the world – preserving his memory in the form of paintings, busts, and life-sized statues (see cover and Figure 1). They have also named churches, schools, coffeehouses, campgrounds, retreat centers, and even their children after him.

Transcending this role as founder of a significant Christian movement, John Wesley has come to be regarded widely as a saint of the church. Already in 1769, upon hearing Wesley preach, a visitor to England from the University of Uppsala in Sweden described him as "the personification of piety" and as "a living representation of the loving

---

[1] Figures given on the website of the World Methodist Council.

Figure 1. John Wesley, ca. 1784, bust by Enoch Wood. This bust was crafted at a live setting in 1781 or 1784. Nearly fifty years later, the artist told Adam Clarke that Wesley had thought this likeness "much the best" that anyone had attempted. Clarke himself considered this bust "the only proper likeness of this illustrious man." Photograph by Richard P. Heitzenrater.

Apostle John."[2] Numerous Christian believers have been similarly inspired over the past two centuries by Wesley's writings and accounts of his life and ministry. His Methodist heirs eventually adopted an annual liturgical commemoration of both John and his brother Charles.[3] In recent years, the Wesley brothers have been added as well to the liturgical calendars of their own Church of England and some other Protestant communions. Less formally, tens of thousands of Wesley's heirs have gone on pilgrimage to see the places where he lived and carried out his ministry.

This veneration of John Wesley has fostered an abundance of hagiographic literature. In addition to book-length lives of Wesley, there are

[2] The visitor was Professor Johan Henrik Liden; recorded in Heitzenrater, *Elusive Mr. Wesley*, 280–81.
[3] On the history of such commemorations, see Randy L. Maddox, "Celebrating Wesley – When?" *Methodist History* 29 (1991): 63–75.

Figure 2. Wesleyan Centenary picture, representing the rescue of the Founder of Methodism from the fire at the Parsonage House at Epworth, by Henry Perlee Parker (1840). Shown as an etching, courtesy of the Oxford Centre for Methodism and Church History, Oxford Brookes University, Oxford, England.

countless pamphlets, magazine articles, and even theatrical and video presentations of his life and ministry. Add to this the frequent re-telling of (often mythical) Wesley stories and quotes in sermons, books, and – more recently – online blogs. Although such materials have kept Wesley's memory alive, they generally adopt a highly selective and uncritical focus on Wesley as spiritual exemplar or model religious orga-nizer. This tendency can be illustrated by two of the best-known paint-ings of John Wesley's life: the depiction of his childhood rescue from the burning rectory in Epworth by Henry Perlee Parker (Figure 2); and the depiction of his final moments by Marshall Claxton, titled "Holy Tri-umph, The Death of John Wesley" (Figure 3). These are idealized scenes, which reveal as much about the sensibilities of their nineteenth-century artists as they do about the events they depict.[4] They also obscure as much about Wesley as they reveal. The first suggests that Wesley's sense of religious vocation was owed largely to a providential rescue,

4   See the analysis in Peter S. Forsaith, *John Wesley – Religious Hero?* (2004).

Figure 3. "Holy Triumph, The Death of John Wesley," by Marshall Claxton (1844). Original painting in the Museum of Methodism, Wesley's Chapel, City Road, London, England. Copyrighted photograph by Graham Portlock, with permission.

invoking the biblical text "Is not this a brand plucked from the burning" (Zech. 3:2). The second epitomizes the Methodist ideal as a "good death," surrounded by family and fellow believers, in anticipation of heavenly blessing. Although there is an element of truth in each, these paintings portray Wesley in isolation from the broader social and religious forces that shaped his life and ministry. Likewise, they neglect many dimensions of Wesley's impact upon his contemporary context and later history.

A central goal of this *Cambridge Companion to John Wesley* is to counter such selective and uncritical presentations of his life and work, by introducing readers to the range of Wesley's writings and activities, placed in historical context. One implication of this goal is that we could not begin directly with Wesley. Instead, the opening chapter (by Jeremy Gregory) is devoted to a summary of recent scholarship – and some significant new emphases in this scholarship – about Wesley's context: the "long eighteenth century" in Britain. Against this backdrop we turn to a brief survey of Wesley's life and ministry, by Kenneth J. Collins. This is followed by David Hempton's analysis of Wesley's stance, and the impact of early Methodism, on some of the central dynamics of eighteenth-century British life. The core of this *Companion* is then devoted to surveying major dimensions of Wesley's activity and writings. In each case, there is a joint concern to place Wesley's practice in context and to note the impact of his engagement upon the broader context. The focus of each chapter is readily apparent from the titles in the Table of Contents. Perhaps the main thing worth commenting on at this point is the range of the activities included – from the long standard consideration of Wesley as revivalist to the analysis of his lesser known (but equally passionate!) concern to offer medical advice. The final section of the volume provides a sense of the global range of Wesley's impact and some of the current debates over his legacy among his progeny.

HISTORY OF WESLEY STUDIES

The dedication of a *Cambridge Companion* to John Wesley reflects not only a positive estimation of his significance for understanding religious and cultural life in eighteenth-century Britain and beyond, but also recognition of the academic field of Wesley Studies. Popular hagiographic literature related to Wesley has flourished ever since the commemoration of his death in 1791. Scholarly and critical studies have been much rarer. Through the nineteenth century, even those scattered studies that rose above the popular level remained largely parochial in nature – by Methodists, for Methodists. With the transition to the twentieth century, biographical, historical, and theological studies of Wesley tended to become a little more critical, moving beyond reverential recounting of the founder's life or teachings. Moreover, whereas most remained internal studies for Wesleyan traditions, they began to view Wesley within the larger context of Christian history.[5] But, through mid-century, serious study of Wesley continued to be the occasional avocation of a few isolated scholars. This changed dramatically through the second half of the twentieth century.[6]

---

[5] See the survey of these earlier periods in Heitzenrater, *Elusive Mr. Wesley*, 344–86; and Randy L. Maddox, *Rethinking Wesley's Theology for Contemporary Methodism* (1998), 213–26.

[6] Cf. Albert C. Outler, "A New Future for 'Wesley Studies': An Agenda for 'Phase III'," in M. D. Meeks (ed.), *The Future of the Methodist Theological Traditions* (1985),

An important marker of this emerging change was the volume on *John Wesley* that Albert C. Outler published in 1964, as part of Oxford University Press's Library of Protestant Thought. The book was mainly a representative sampling of Wesley's writings, but it contained critical introductions and notes, which were more advanced than anything that had preceded it. It also sold more copies than any other volume in the series. These combined attributes demonstrated strong interest in rigorous Wesley scholarship, in Methodist circles and beyond. The importance of the volume is underscored by the fact that it remains in print today.

Several other strands contributed to the maturation of Wesley Studies as a scholarly field through the second half of the twentieth century. The Oxford Institute of Methodist Theological Studies began gathering scholars for periodic conferences in 1958.[7] A new scholarly journal on *Methodist History* was launched in 1962. The Wesleyan Theological Society was formed in 1965, issuing its own *Wesleyan Theological Journal*. A Wesleyan Studies Group was organized at the American Academy of Religion in 1982. And, in 1988, Abingdon Press launched the Kingswood Book series, dedicated to Wesleyan and Methodist scholarship. Chairs of Wesley Studies have also been established at such universities as Duke, Southern Methodist, and Vanderbilt, as well as several research centers.[8] In short, the structures of a scholarly field have been put in place.

With this growing network of supportive structures, the field of Wesley Studies has come of age. Over the last two decades, an average of ten new scholarly books or dissertations have appeared annually, as well as numerous journal articles.[9] These studies have covered everything from Wesley's politics and theology to his dietary habits and family life. They have witnessed a number of debates about and increasing sophistication in interpretation of Wesley's writings.[10] Most importantly, there has been an increase in interdisciplinary and contextual studies, as well as a growing interest in Wesley on the part of non-Methodist scholars.[11]

34–52; Henry Derman Rack, "Some Recent Trends in Wesley Scholarship," *Wesleyan Theological Journal* 41.2 (2006): 182–99; and Heitzenrater, *Elusive Mr. Wesley*, 387–94.

[7] For the history and archives of this group see http://www.oxford-institute.org/.

[8] A convenient list of these centers can be found on the web site of the Duke Center for Studies in the Wesleyan tradition: http://www.divinity.duke.edu/wesleyan/research/index.html.

[9] Cf. http://www.divinity.duke.edu/wesleyan/docs/Recent_Dissertations.pdf.

[10] See Randy L. Maddox, "Reading Wesley as Theologian," *Wesleyan Theological Journal* 30.1 (1995): 7–54.

[11] For example, Wesley featured prominently in J. C. D. Clark's landmark work, *English Society: 1660–1832.*

The present *Companion* draws upon and is intended to contribute to this interest.

EDITIONS OF JOHN WESLEY'S WRITINGS

The long standard, and still broadly used, collection of Wesley's *Works* was edited by Thomas Jackson, and released in 1829–31. There are many limitations to this edition. In the first place, it is not complete. Not only was Jackson unaware of some of Wesley's writings, he omitted portions that might reflect badly on Wesley. For example, in the setting after Methodism had separated from the Church of England, Jackson omitted items where Wesley stressed his connection to the Church (such as his extract from the *Homilies*). Secondly, Jackson is not consistent in which edition of various Wesley publications he prints, nor does he indicate variants between editions. Thirdly, Jackson only rarely indicates the sources from which Wesley drew many of his publications. Finally, Jackson's edition provides little introductory material or annotations to set Wesley's writings in context.

One of the most significant expressions of increased scholarly focus on John Wesley in the last half century was the launch in 1960 of the Wesley Works Project, dedicated to producing the first truly critical edition of his writings.[12] It addresses all of the shortcomings of the Jackson edition, and much more. Sixteen of the projected thirty-five volumes are now in print as *The Bicentennial Edition of the Works of John Wesley* (detailed listing in the Select Bibliography). They have become the clear standard for scholarly study of John Wesley.

Until the *Bicentennial Edition* is complete, however, it will be necessary for students to draw as well on the Jackson edition of Wesley's *Works*, as well as some other resources listed in the Select Bibliography. Readers should be aware that there is a CD-ROM version of the major sections of the *Bicentennial Edition* that are in print.[13] For convenience, this CD-ROM also includes the complete Jackson edition, but in a format that is not paginated. Providence House Publishers sells a CD-ROM of the Jackson edition that reflects the pagination of the print format. Readers can also find the Jackson edition online in several locations.[14]

---

[12] See Frank Baker, "The Oxford Edition of Wesley's Works and Its Text," in K. E. Rowe (ed.), *The Place of Wesley in the Christian Tradition* (1976), 117–33.

[13] The current CD-ROM does not include every volume published, only completed sections, so it contains the four volumes of *Sermons*, the seven volumes of *Journals*, and the *Collection of Hymns* (vol. 7).

[14] The best organized site for this and other public-domain Wesley texts is the Wesley Center at Northwest Nazarene University: http://wesley.nnu.edu/.

JOHN AND CHARLES WESLEY

One of the challenges of this project has been to avoid extended treatments of Charles Wesley (1707–88) in this study of his brother John. The brothers were personally close, and worked together closely in the Methodist branch of the Evangelical Revival, particularly from 1739 to 1749 (when Charles married and restricted his traveling).[15] There were also broad areas of agreement between the brothers on matters of doctrine, so that hymns of Charles are often the best illustrations of theological points that John makes in sermons.

Precisely because they were so close, consideration of Charles is particularly helpful on points where the brothers stood in some tension. A good example is their difference concerning the potential of a split between Methodists and the Church of England. Charles was clearly the stronger "Church Methodist."[16] He was committed to the revival of *the Church of England*, whereas John was committed to the *revival* of the Church of England. This difference played over into their disagreements on other topics, such as the use of lay preachers.[17] Another area of growing difference between the brothers was their reaction to claims of instantaneous Christian Perfection or entire sanctification, particularly after the controversy of the 1760s.[18]

Given these important points of agreement and tension, readers will find many passing references to Charles Wesley in this volume. But, we have resisted extended treatment, precisely because Charles deserves study in his own right. For too long he has been reduced to John's sidekick. This is turning around, with the organization of the Charles Wesley Society (in 1990) and growing publication of his writings in scholarly editions.[19] We look forward to the day when a similar *Companion* to Charles Wesley is produced.

[15] See John A. Newton, "Brothers in Arms: The Partnership of John And Charles Wesley," in K. G. C. Newport & T. A. Campbell (eds.), *Charles Wesley: Life, Literature, and Legacy* (2007), 58–69.

[16] This is the thesis of Gareth Lloyd, *Charles Wesley and the Struggle for Methodist Identity* (2007).

[17] Richard P. Heitzenrater, "Purge the Preachers: The Wesleys and Quality Control," in Newport & Campbell, *Charles Wesley*, 486–514.

[18] See particularly John R. Tyson, *Charles Wesley on Sanctification* (Grand Rapids: Zondervan, 1986); and S. T. Kimbrough, Jr., "Charles Wesley and the Journey of Sanctification," *Evangelical Journal* 16 (1998): 49–75.

[19] Kenneth G. C. Newport. (ed.), *The Sermons of Charles Wesley: A Critical Edition with Introduction and Notes* (2001); and S T Kimbrough, Jr. & Kenneth G. C. Newport (eds.), *The Manuscript Journal of the Rev. Charles Wesley, M.A.*, 2 vols. (2008). For an online critical edition of his poetry, see: http://www.divinity.duke.edu/wesleyan/texts/index.html.

THE CONTRIBUTION OF RICHARD P. HEITZENRATER
TO WESLEY STUDIES

It remains only for us to explain the dedication of this book to Richard P. Heitzenrater. Readers will find his name recurring in discussion and notes throughout the volume. This is because no one in the present generation has contributed more to the rigorous study of John or Charles Wesley, or the establishment of the field of Wesley Studies. It is no accident that Dick (as all soon learn to call him) has held the chairs in Wesley Studies at both Southern Methodist University and Duke University.

Heitzenrater is perhaps best known for "breaking the code" of Wesley's private diaries, opening this rich resource to scholars. His textual expertise is reflected in his selection as general editor of the Wesley Works Project. His networking and organization skills are reflected in his roles as the organizing chair of the Wesleyan Studies Working Group of the AAR and as a co-convener of the Wesley Studies working group of the Oxford Institute for Methodist Theological Studies. These skills are also appreciated more broadly, as reflected in his election in 2009 as President of the American Society of Church History.

In addition to his editorial contribution to *John Wesley's Sermons: An Anthology* (with Albert C. Outler) and the seven volumes of Wesley's *Journal & Diaries* in the *Bicentennial Edition* (with W. Reginald Ward), Heitzenrater has published several influential secondary studies of John Wesley and early Methodism, including *Wesley and the People Called Methodists*, *The Elusive Mr. Wesley*, *Diary of an Oxford Methodist*, *Mirror and Memory*, and *The Poor and the People Called Methodists*.

The specific occasion for this dedication is Dick's seventieth birthday and retirement as a William Kellon Quick Professor of Church History and Wesley Studies at the Divinity School, Duke University. All students of Wesley will join us in celebrating his career and his contribution.

Part I

Wesley's context

1 The long eighteenth century

JEREMY GREGORY

John Wesley's long life (1703–91) almost spanned the eighteenth century. Any *Companion* to him needs to provide some sense of this period. Scholarly biographies of Wesley have provided some attention to this topic, of which the most impressive and successful to date is Henry Rack's *Reasonable Enthusiast: John Wesley and the Rise of Methodism*.[1] Extended treatments of his age by Wesley scholars have been rare and rather unsatisfactory. For example, in 1938, the amateur historian J.H. Whiteley published *Wesley's England: A Survey of XVIIIth Century Social and Cultural Conditions*, as part of the celebrations marking the bicentenary of Wesley's conversion. The book is drawn from secondary sources, aimed at a Methodist readership, and fails to give a coherent sense of the period. However, Whiteley astutely recognized that "the difficulties of the project are manifold, for this is a century of England's story whose details are surprisingly contradictory and elusive."[2]

Eighty years later, this characterization holds. There is no consensus among professional historians about Wesley's context. Indeed, at present they are probably more divided than they have ever been about how to conceptualize the period in which he lived. Their debates (in which some of the contributors to this *Companion* have made vital interventions)[3] are critical because they have a crucial bearing on how we should judge Wesley's significance, what he stood for, and what he achieved. For example, did Wesley "revive" religion at a time when, as many historians have asserted (and Methodist scholars have often assumed), spiritual and religious concerns were ebbing away?[4] Or rather, did he build on and develop

---

[1] I am grateful to Henry Rack and Geordan Hammond for their comments on this chapter.
[2] J.H. Whiteley, *Wesley's England*, 11.
[3] See David Hempton, *Religion and Political Culture in Britain and Ireland*; and Isabel Rivers, *Reason, Grace and Sentiment*.
[4] John Kent, *Wesley and the Wesleyans* (2002).

what some more recent scholars see as an existing vibrant and pastorally dynamic religious culture?[5] Should he be viewed as opposing or extending the Church of England?[6] Was he "anti-Enlightenment"?[7] Or was he actually part of a wider enlightenment trend?[8] Answers to questions such as these (let alone questions about whether Wesleyan Methodism saved England from having a French-style revolution[9]) are only possible if we have as full an understanding as possible of the period in which Wesley lived.

As this *Companion* will show, Wesley's life and works offer insights for potentially reconciling or reconfiguring the current rival views of the eighteenth century. As someone who lived as long as he did; who traveled, wrote, and said so much (he has perhaps left more of a written record than any other person who lived in the eighteenth century); and who had views and opinions about almost all aspects of his times, Wesley can cast significant light on his context.[10] Thus, whereas studies of Wesley should take account of his context seriously, studies of his age should also pay attention to Wesley. He is of value to a wider group of historians than those associated with the movement he founded.

SCHOLARLY DEBATE OVER THE NATURE OF THE EIGHTEENTH CENTURY

The central difference between the rival views of Wesley's context can be framed sharply by a simple question: Did the eighteenth century mark the founding of modern England/Britain? Stated a bit more elaborately: Did the forces of change signposted by the Glorious, the Agricultural, the Industrial, and the French Revolutions help to transform the time in which Wesley lived into the modern era?

---

[5] Inter alia, Jeremy Gregory, "The Making of a Protestant Nation: 'Success' and 'Failure' in England's Long Reformation," in Nicholas Tyacke, ed., *England's Long Reformation, 1500–1800* (1998), 307–33.

[6] Frank Baker, *John Wesley and the Church of England.*

[7] E.P. Thompson, *The Making of the English Working Class* (1963); and Roy Porter, *The Creation of the Modern World* (2000).

[8] Bernard Semmel, *The Methodist Revolution* (1973); David Bebbington, *Evangelicalism in Modern Britain* (1989), 20–74; and David Hempton, *Methodism: The Empire of the Spirit*, chapter 2.

[9] Elie Halevy, *The Birth of Methodism in England* (1971); and Halevey, *England in 1815* (1949). For an overview of the debates his work has engendered, see *Religion and Revolution in Early Industrial England: the Halevy Thesis and its Critics*, edited by G.W. Olsen (1990). See also John Walsh, "Elie Halevy and the Birth of Methodism," *Transactions of the Royal Historical Society* 25 (1975): 1–20.

[10] Maldwyn Edwards, *John Wesley and the Eighteenth Century* (1933).

On one side of the debate are historians who affirm the transformative nature of the eighteenth century. In making this case, they have emphasized such topics as the rise of parliamentary government and the development of political parties,[11] agricultural change,[12] urbanization and industrialization,[13] the growth of the middling sort,[14] the birth of a consumer society,[15] and new kinds of print culture.[16] They have also drawn attention to the advance of progressive ways of seeing the world, represented variously as a scientific outlook,[17] the Enlightenment, and the Age of Reason.[18] Stressing how these advancing emphases would marginalize the role of religion and the churches in political, cultural, and social life, some scholars have characterized the period as the start of secularization in modern Britain/England.[19] This view of the eighteenth century as one dominated by modernizing change was shared by most historians who wrote through the nineteenth and the first three quarters of the twentieth centuries, whatever their own political and religious standpoints.[20]

This reigning view influenced strongly the way that Methodist scholars have understood Wesley's context. In 1909, for example, W.J. Townsend contrasted the period when Wesley was born (which, Townsend said, "was so different... from the England of today as to be scarcely recognizable"[21]) with that when he died, emphasizing progress in economic, social, political, and cultural life from around 1760 that

---

[11] B.W. Hill, *The Growth of Parliamentary Politics in England, 1689–1742* (1976). See also his later, *The Early Parties and Politics in Britain, 1688–1832* (1996).

[12] J.D. Chambers and G.E. Mingay, *The Agricultural Revolution, 1750–1880* (1966).

[13] Peter Mathias, *The First Industrial Nation: An Economic History of Britain, 1700–1914* (1969).

[14] Paul Langford, *A Polite and Commercial People: England, 1727–1783* (1989).

[15] Neil McKendrick, John Brewer, and J.H. Plumb, eds., *The Birth of a Consumer Society* (1982).

[16] G.A. Cranfield, *The Development of the Provincial Newspaper, 1700–1760* (1962).

[17] R.E. Schofield, *Mechanism and Materialism: British Natural Philosophy in an Age of Reason* (1970).

[18] Roy Porter, *The Enlightenment* (1990).

[19] Alan D. Gilbert, *Religion and Society in Industrial England* (1976); and Roy Porter, *English Society in the Eighteenth Century* (1982).

[20] This view implicitly owed much to Thomas Babington Macaulay, *History of England from the accession of James II* (1849–61), in particular the famous third chapter, which measured the social improvements in England in the early nineteenth century against the situation in 1685, and which influenced other classic Whig interpretations of the age such as W.H. Lecky, *A History of England in the Eighteenth Century*, 3 vols. (1904–13), which was cited by Townsend.

[21] W.J. Townsend, "The Times and Conditions," in Townsend, Workman, and Eayres, *A New History of Methodism*, 2 vols. (1909), 1:77–133; and "English Life and Society, and the Condition of Methodism at the Death of Wesley," 1:335–78; quote on p. 82.

anticipated something like the modern world – with Methodism intimately responding to, and helping to create, the agents of change.
In Townsend's view, for example, the Methodist connexion could not
have developed without a better road network, while improvements
in lighting allowed Methodist evening services to flourish. Conversely,
Townsend maintained that Methodism helped to transform social, cultural, and economic attitudes and behavior.[22] Similarly, in 1965, in the
first volume of *A History of the Methodist Church in Great Britain*, Sir
Herbert Butterfield, Regius Professor of Modern History at Cambridge
and an authority on the period, as well as being a Methodist (and for much
of his life a lay preacher), contributed an essay on "England in the Eighteenth Century."[23] For someone who had risen to fame with his icon-
oclastic *The Whig Interpretation of History* (1931), Butterfield's essay
offered a very Whiggish reading of the age, seeing the eighteenth century
as increasingly more like the twentieth (whereas the seventeenth century was "a strange, violent, fantastic, baroque world"[24]), emphasizing
"modern" developments in a wide range of spheres and activities, from
the creation of the Bank of England to new technologies, better transport
links, the rise of political consciousness, and precursors to the theory of
evolution. Perhaps above all, and of consequence in a book on Methodism, Butterfield emphasized that this was *the* significant period in what
he termed "the Great Secularisation."[25]

Those historians who came to similar conclusions did so from a
variety of perspectives. Some have viewed these as generally positive
developments,[26] whereas others have bemoaned what they have considered the loss of an organic community (something on which historians
from both the left and the right have concurred).[27] And – of import for
Wesley studies – most historians have tended to agree that religion (for
better or worse) was, by and large, of less importance in the eighteenth
century than it had been in previous periods.[28]

---

[22] Ibid., 80, 342, 370–74.
[23] Herbert Butterfield, "England in the Eighteenth Century," in *A History of the
Methodist Church in Great Britain*, edited by R.E. Davies and E.G. Rupp (1965), 1:3–33.
[24] Ibid., 4.
[25] Ibid., 6.
[26] Porter, *Creation of the Modern World*. Actually Porter's attitude to the place of religion
in the Enlightenment was more complex than some of his publications suggest. For
a more nuanced picture see his "The Enlightenment in England," in Porter and M.
Teich, eds., *The Enlightenment in National Context* (1981), 1–18.
[27] See E.P. Thompson, "The Moral Economy of the English Crowd in the Eighteenth
Century," *Past & Present* 50 (1971): 76–136; and Peter Laslett, *The World We have
Lost* (1965).
[28] See C. J. Sommerville, *The Secularization of Early Modern England* (1992).

Turning to the other pole of the current debate, a growing number of scholars have begun to challenge this long reigning view of the eighteenth century as witnessing the birth of modernity and secularization, and as most like the nineteenth and twentieth centuries. These scholars contend that the period in which Wesley lived was more marked by continuities with the sixteenth and seventeenth centuries, where religion, the churches, and traditional orders such as the crown[29] and aristocracy[30] still dominated, and where older ways of seeing the world, influenced by Reformation paradigms and ways of thought, still controlled habits of mind and patterns of behavior.[31] A number of historians have also argued that the social and economic developments of the time were less transformative than was once thought, and that, in most regards, these changes were accommodated within long-established forms of organization and behavior.[32] Although there were undoubted advances in agriculture and industry, and a marked population growth, these were more evolutionary than revolutionary in character. Indeed, many of the qualitative changes relating to quantitative growth, these scholars contend, happened in the nineteenth rather than in the eighteenth century.[33] Other historians have reassessed our understanding of the "Enlightenment," demonstrating that, in England at least, enlightenment values could go hand in hand with religion.[34] Most specifically, the "secularization thesis," which could be taken for granted even by someone as interested in religion as Butterfield,[35] and where the eighteenth century was deemed the crucial step on the ladder, has now been criticized from several directions: its start has been delayed until the nineteenth or even

[29] Ian Christie, *Stress and Stability in late Eighteenth-Century Britain* (1984).

[30] John Cannon, *Aristocratic Century: the Peerage of Eighteenth-Century England* (1984).

[31] See, above all, J.C. D Clark, *English Society: 1688–1832*; but also Tony Claydon, *Europe and the Making of England, 1660–1760* (2007); and Gregory, "Long Reformation."

[32] Ann Kussmaul, *A General View of the Rural Economy of England, 1538–1840* (1990); and Mark Overton, *Agricultural Revolution in England* (1996).

[33] Roderick Floud and Donald McCloskey, eds., *The Economic History of Britain since 1700*, 2 vols. (1981); N. F. C. Crafts, *British Economic Growth during the Industrial Revolution* (1985); and Maxine Berg, *The Age of Manufactures, 1700–1820* (1985).

[34] Porter, "England"; and Bebbington, *Evangelicalism*. See also Bebbington, "Revival and Enlightenment in Eighteenth-Century England," in Andrew Walker and Kristin Aune, eds., *On Revival. A Critical Examination* (2003), 71–86; and Hempton, *Empire of the Spirit*, 32–54. My take on this is that rather than seeing Enlightenment and Evangelicalism/Enthusiasm as polarities, we should acknowledge that what we might term "Enlightenment" includes certain "Evangelical" qualities and vice versa.

[35] See his *Christianity and History* (1949); *Christianity in European History* (1951); *Christianity, Diplomacy, and War* (1953); and *Writings on Christianity and History*, edited by C.T. McIntire (1979).

the twentieth centuries.[36] Some have argued that in England this only occurred in the 1960s (ironically at just the time when Butterfield was writing);[37] others have denied that it has happened at all.[38] What was once assumed to be the inevitable trajectory, not only of Western European but of world history, looks less convincing in the early twenty-first century, when religion can be viewed as being at the center of world affairs. Taken together, these re-assessments of the period in which Wesley lived amount to a thorough revisionism of the modernizing and secularizing view of the age (although, of course, not all historians who subscribe to one part of the revisionist program necessarily agree with all of it, and they might be surprised to see their names linked together here).

Although a number of historians, writing on different topics, have contributed to this revised view of the period, the most overt and comprehensive revisionist statement continues to be J.C.D. Clark's highly influential *English Society, 1688–1832: Ideology, Social Structure and Political Practice during the Ancien Regime* (1985).[39] This made a powerful case for a wholesale rejection of the modernizing agenda, stressing the central role of the monarchy, the aristocracy, and the Church of England throughout Wesley's lifetime and beyond. Clark applied the concept of "the confessional state" to England between the Restoration of 1660 and the constitutional changes of 1828–32.[40] In particular, he argued that the political and hegemonic power of orthodox Anglicanism meant that real political radicalism in the period could only be expressed through heterodox theology (thereby challenging the idea of secular political advances). For Clark, the Church's dominant place within the political and social life of the country was strengthened by the Test Acts of 1673 and 1678, which ensured that to hold political

---

[36] Owen Chadwick, *The Secularisation of the European Mind in the Nineteenth Century* (1975).

[37] Callum Brown, *The Death of Christian Britain* (2001).

[38] David Nash, "Reconnecting Religion with Social and Cultural History: Secularization's Failure as a Meta-narrative," *Cultural and Social History* 1 (2004): 302–25.

[39] Revised in 2000, with an amended chronology extending backwards to 1660 and a new subtitle: *Religion, Ideology and Politics during the Ancien Regime.*

[40] J.C.D. Clark, "England's Ancien Regime as a Confessional State," *Albion* 21 (1989): 450–74. This term had been used by historians of early modern Europe, particularly Germany, to denote the interplay of religion and state building from the sixteenth to the eighteenth centuries. For an analysis of the comparison, see Andrew C. Thompson, "Early Eighteenth-Century Britain as a Confessional State," in Hamish Scott and Brendan Simms, eds., *Cultures of Power in Europe during the Long Eighteenth Century* (2007), 86–109.

office or to be a Minister of Parliament it was necessary to be a member of the Church of England.

Although, as some of Clark's critics have emphasized, sections of the English population did not conform to the Church,[41] he is surely right to argue that the centrality of the Church's legal position had a profound impact on political and social life. The State, the English universities, the army, and the civil service were Anglican strongholds; and, in the localities, clergy were often the Justice of the Peace, making them responsible for the administration of local government. But, it is perhaps more accurate to describe this position of the Church as an Anglican hegemony (another phrase Clark has used) than as a "confessional state." This alternative description is indicative of the ways in which, although its position was contested, the Church effectively dominated and sought to marginalize those who challenged its social and political role. Many Churchmen believed that the interests of Church and State were in fact inseparable and interdependent, and that enemies of the Church were also enemies of the State.

Clark might have also emphasized that those who see the eighteenth century as forward-looking do not always appreciate how the memory of the 1640s and 1650s when "the world was turned upside down" continued to frighten the majority of the political nation for a century and half after 1660. Not for nothing did Wesley's opponents accuse him of reviving civil war "enthusiasm," particularly as his grandfather had been a supporter of regicide.[42] A good indication of the interdependence of Church and State can be seen in the Church's response to the Jacobite rebellions of 1715 and 1745, when the vast bulk of the clergy and the Church's hierarchy supported the Hanoverian regime. In 1745, Archbishop Thomas Herring of York (later archbishop of Canterbury) played a crucial role in forming the Yorkshire association to defend the regime and to raise money for the government. Countering the accusations of his opponents, Wesley too took a strong pro-Hanoverian stand.[43]

---

[41] Penelope Corfield, "Georgian England: One State, Many Faiths," *History Today* (April, 1995): 14–21.

[42] See *Enthusiasm no Novelty; or the Spirit of the Methodists in 1641 and 1642* (London: T. Cooper, 1739); George Lavington, *The Enthusiasm of Methodists and Papists compared*, 3 parts (London, J. and P. Knapton, 1749–51); A.T. Blacksmith (sometimes attributed to John Witherspoon), *Enthusiasm Delineated: or, the Absurd Conduct of the Methodists Displayed in a Letter to the Rev. Messieurs Whitefield and Wesley* (Bristol: T. Cadell, 1764); and S. Roe, *Enthusiasm Detected, Defeated; with Previous Considerations concerning Regeneration, the Omnipresence of God, and Divine Grace, &c* (Cambridge, England, 1768).

[43] Wesley, *Journal* (18 September–9 October 1745), *Works*, 20:90–94.

This temper continued into the decade after Wesley's death, where the Church was a staunch defender of the government during the French Revolution,[44] believing that threats to the State would also be destructive to the Church and to true religion generally (leading one to wonder whether it was the Church, rather than Methodism that saved England from having a revolution along French lines).

The revisionist interpretation, particularly Clark's full-blown statement, has provoked continuing debate since the mid-1980s.[45] Scholars who remain convinced of emerging modernity in the period have expanded their fields of enquiry, authoring exciting studies on the concepts of sociability and politeness, the periodical press, clubs and coffee houses, cultural history, popular politics, crime, sexuality, the body and medicine, consumerism, and women's history and gender history.[46] Many of these topics are studied within the paradigm of "the public sphere," and most have important bearings on early Methodism, given Wesley's alertness to consumerist techniques, his use of printed media, his interest in science and medicine, the role of Methodist societies as

---

[44] Robert Hole, *Pulpits, Politics, and Public Order in England, 1760–1832* (1990).

[45] For some discussion and criticisms, see Joanna Innes, "Jonathan Clark, Social History, and England's Ancien Regime," *Past & Present* 115 (1987): 165–200; the reply by Clark 117 (1989): 195–207; the special number of *Albion* 21 (1989) which was devoted to Clark's interpretation; G.S. Rousseau, "Revisionist Polemics; J.C.D. Clark, and the Collapse of Modernity in the Age of Johnson," in *The Age of Johnson* 3 (1989), 421–50; Roy Porter, "English Society in the Eighteenth Century Revisited," in Jeremy Black, ed., *British Politics and Society from Walpole to Pitt* (1990), 29–52; the articles by Clark, Porter, and Black in the *British Journal for Eighteenth-Century Studies* 15 (1992): 131–149; and Frank O'Gorman, "Eighteenth Century England as an Ancien Regime," in Stephen Taylor, Richard Connors, and Clyve Jones, eds., *Hanoverian Britain and Empire* (1998), 21–36.

[46] See respectively: Clive T. Probyn, *The Sociable Humanist: the Life and Works of James Harris 1709–1780* (1991); and Lawrence E. Klein, *Shaftesbury and the Culture of Politeness* (1994). Hannah Barker, *Newspapers, Politics, and Public Opinion in late Eighteenth-Century England* (1998). Peter Clark, *British Clubs and Societies 1580–1800* (2000); Markman Ellis, *The Coffee-House: a Cultural History* (2004); Brian Cowan, *The Social Life of Coffee* (2005). John Brewer, *The Pleasures of the Imagination: English Culture in the Eighteenth Century* (1997). Douglas Hay and Nicholas Rogers, *Eighteenth-Century English Society* (1997). Robert Shoemaker, *Prosecution and Punishment* (1991). Karen Harvey, *Reading Sex in the Eighteenth Century* (2004). For example, Roy Porter, *Flesh in the Age of Reason* (2003); and Porter, *Disease, Medicine and Society in England, 1550–1860* (1987). John Brewer and Roy Porter, eds., *Consumption and the World of Goods* (1993) John Brewer and Ann Bermingham, eds., *The Consumption of Culture, 1660–1800* (1995); and John Brewer and Susan Staves, eds., *Early Modern Conceptions of Property* (1995). Hannah Barker and Elaine Chalus, eds., *Gender in Eighteenth-Century England* (1997); Michele Cohen and Tim Hitchcock, eds., *English Masculinities, 1660–1800* (1999); and Hannah Barker and Elaine Chalus, eds., *Women's History, Britain, 1700–1850* (2005).

religious clubs, and the prominence of women in early Methodism. Historians of Methodism are only now beginning to take these findings on board.[47]

On the other hand, a number of publications over the last two decades have confirmed aspects of Clark's interpretation of the age, if not necessarily agreeing with all his conclusions.[48] Reviewing some of this seemingly contradictory scholarship over fifteen years ago with a question that has not yet been resolved, W.A. Speck not surprisingly asked: "Will the real eighteenth century stand up?"[49] How far, he wondered, was it a period of secularization and change, anticipating the modern world; or how far was it a more traditional and religious society, with links to the early modern period.

Reflections of the debate in standard assessments of Wesley

These different interpretations of the eighteenth century affect how historians have viewed Wesley himself and early Methodism. Despite the advances of the revisionist viewpoints, the understanding of the eighteenth century as both modernizing and secularizing has had the strongest influence in this regard. In broad terms, it has encouraged scholars to see Wesley and Methodism as counter-cultural – going against the dominant Enlightenment, this-worldly, and a-religious (if not irreligious) trajectories of the day.[50] Townsend set the precedent in 1909, portraying Wesley as a heroic individual who stood outside the degeneracy of the age.[51] But, within this framework, historians have differed over

---

[47] But, see Henry Abelove, *The Evangelist of Desire. John Wesley and the Methodists* (1990) for Wesley and consumerism; Deborah Madden, *"A Cheap, Safe and Natural Medicine"*, for Wesley and medicine; Phyllis Mack, *Heart Religion in the British Enlightenment. Gender and Emotion in Early Methodism* (2008) for Methodism and gender; and Barbara Prosser, *"'An arrow from a quiver'. Written Instruction for a Reading People: John Wesley's Arminian Magazine (January 1778–February 1791)"* (University of Manchester Ph.D. thesis, 2008) for Wesley and print culture.

[48] See *The Church of England, c. 1689–c. 1833*, J. Walsh, C. Haydon and S. Taylor, eds., (1993); Mark Smith, *Religion in Industrial Society: Oldham and Saddleworth, 1740–1865* (1994); Judith Jago, *Aspects of the Georgian Church* (1996); Jeremy Gregory, *Restoration, Reformation, and Reform, 1660–1828: Archbishops of Canterbury and their Diocese* (2000); J. Gregory and J.S. Chamberlain, eds., *The National Church in Local Perspective: the Church of England and the Regions, 1660–1800* (2003); W.M. Jacob, *The Clerical Profession in the Long Eighteenth Century, 1680–1840* (2007); and Robert G. Ingram, *Religion, Reform and Modernity in the Eighteenth Century. Thomas Secker and the Church of England* (2007).

[49] W.A Speck, "Will the Real Eighteenth Century stand up?" *Historical Journal* 34 (1991): 203–206.

[50] Mark Noll, *The Rise of Evangelicalism* (2003).

[51] Townsend, "The Times and Condition," 80.

whether Wesley and early Methodism represented a backward-looking force, a throw-back to an age of faith,[52] or whether he was more forward looking, encouraging new social communities (such as the development of a working class[53]) and, with his stress on "the religion of the heart," anticipating movements like Romanticism.[54]

By contrast, the emphases of the revisionist standpoint make it possible to understand Wesley as part of, rather than apart from, the dominant habits of thought and behavior of his era. If religion was much more central to the age than the secularization hypothesis would have it, then Wesley looks less like a reaction to his context, and more like a child of his time. Indeed, Clark underlined Wesley's Tory politics and pro-establishment views as part of his argument for the strengths of the confessional state. He highlighted the fact that, whereas Wesley attacked the spiritual and pastoral shortcomings of the established Church, he shared many of its social and political assumptions.[55]

In reaching their various conclusions about the nature of the eighteenth century, historians have sometimes used evidence from Wesley to underpin and support their interpretations. They have drawn particularly on his *Journals*, which offer apparent eyewitness commentary over a period of fifty-five years on the age in which he was living. The *Journals* provide us with a variety of information about Wesley's world, as evidenced by the extraordinarily rich, 160-plus page general index to the *Works* edition.[56] We find here Wesley's comments on such topics as the state of the roads, the landscape, the weather, the villages and towns he visited, agricultural and industrial changes of his time, as well as comments on the religious temper of the day.

Wesley's *Journals* are so crammed with information about eighteenth-century life that they ought to be mandatory reading for all historians of the period. This wealth of information might tempt one to see Wesley's comments and observations almost as a neutral documentary on his times, furnishing the historian with clear-cut evidence about

---

[52] This seems to be the thrust of Kent's *Wesley and the Wesleyans*.

[53] R. F. Wearmouth, *Methodism and the Common People of the Eighteenth Century* (1945); and Gilbert, *Religion and Society in Industrial England*.

[54] Frederick C. Gill, *The Romantic Movement and Methodism: a Study of English Romanticism and the Evangelical Revival* (1937).

[55] Clark, *English Society*, 235–39. To be sure, Clark's view of Wesley as an insider within the confessional state has been criticized by David Hempton, who emphasizes Wesley's radicalism and the conditional nature of his submission to the Georgian polity; Hempton, "John Wesley and England's *Ancien Régime*," in his *The Religion of the People*, 77–90.

[56] The comprehensive general index, compiled by John Vickers, is in *Works* 24:546–711.

what the eighteenth century "was really like." However, the fact that Wesley's words have been used to bolster rival interpretations of the period indicates that this very abundance of detail in the *Journals* makes it possible to find almost anything in them. And, of course, the *Journals* are not unbiased evidence. Like any other source, they come from a particular perspective (often with an axe to grind and a point to make). They were generally written up some time after the events Wesley describes.[57] Moreover, as in other areas of his word and deed, Wesley's commentary on his times can seem somewhat contradictory. At least it seems so when pressed into an either/or dialectic – such as either "modern" or "traditional." By contrast, John Walsh has suggested a more nuanced reading, portraying Wesley as a both/and personality, who was able to accommodate and combine some of the apparent conflicting tendencies in his context.[58]

Reflections of Wesley's example in a more nuanced understanding of his context

We can find in Wesley aspects of both the "traditional" and the "modernizing" eighteenth centuries. Arguably, he was influenced by, and furthered, both the Reformation and the Enlightenment. This fact should help us recognize that the binary polarities with which we have been inclined to discuss the eighteenth century in Britain/England are rather misleading. We need a more complicated and nuanced account. In particular, we need to resist the inclination (perhaps encouraged by Clark's revisionist manifesto) to align religion one-sidedly with the forces of tradition and continuity. As Roy Porter has suggested, we should not view those perennial concerns of the historian, continuity and change, as being necessarily in antagonism.[59] Traditional priorities, such as religion, can be agents of change and innovation, as evidenced by the rise of Methodism.[60] Likewise, new genres and ways of behaving, such as periodicals and clubs (as in the *Arminian Magazine* and the "Holy Club"), can be vehicles for older concerns.

RECOGNIZING THE LONG EIGHTEENTH CENTURY

Disagreement among historians about the period in which Wesley lived has not been limited to alternative assessments of its defining

---

[57] See W.R Ward's insightful introduction in *Works*, 18:1–119.

[58] John Walsh, *John Wesley, 1703–1791: a Bicentennial Tribute* (1993), 12.

[59] Porter, "English Society . . . revisited," 32–33.

[60] See Robert Ingram, *Religion, Reform and Modernity in the Eighteenth Century* (2007).

features. There is divergence even over when it began and ended. Recognizing the artificial nature of defining historical periods by the century marks of a calendar, scholarly accounts of the "eighteenth century" in Britain often start with 1714,[61] 1760,[62] or even as late as somewhere in the 1780s, as in Vic Gatrell's unabashedly modernist study of eighteenth-century satire.[63] Particularly in the latter case, these accounts often run on long past 1800. The result is that the eighteenth century (reckoned by calendar) is split between two historical periods – dividing before and after 1760, or c. 1780.

To take a relevant example, in his contribution to *A History of the Methodist Church*, Herbert Butterfield saw changes on most fronts accelerating with increasing velocity after about 1780, using the metaphor of a tidal wave to indicate that the world after 1780 was qualitatively different from the world before.[64] But stopping, or starting, the period then (or in 1760) makes little sense when considering someone like Wesley, who lived through these divides.

In part to avoid these difficulties and ambiguities, and to make sense of the eighteenth century as a whole, historians have increasingly found the concept of the "long eighteenth century" useful. This approach has the eighteenth century beginning in 1688/9 (or even 1660), and sees it continuing well into the nineteenth century, to c. 1832 and beyond.[65] It has the merit of encouraging scholars of the period to encompass both late seventeenth-century and early nineteenth-century developments. Although the validity of this periodization will no doubt continue to be debated, it seems to make sense for someone like Wesley – whose parents, both central figures in his life, were born in the 1660s; whose own wide-ranging theological and religious authorities often came from the last decades of the seventeenth century; and whose immediate followers, as well as some of the practices he advocated (such as dual allegiance to the Church and the Methodist societies[66]) continued for several decades after his death.

---

[61] For example, W.A Speck, *Stability and Strife: England, 1714–1760* (1977).

[62] I. R. Christie, *Wars and Revolutions: Britain, 1760–1815* (1982).

[63] Vic Gatrell, *City of Laughter: Sex and Satire in Eighteenth Century* (2006).

[64] Butterfield, "England in the Eighteenth Century," 22–23.

[65] Frank O'Gorman, *The Long Eighteenth Century: British Political and Social History, 1688–1832* (1997) has enshrined the concept in a book title. See also, Wilfrid Prest, *Albion Ascendant: English History, 1660–1815* (1998).

[66] See Gareth Lloyd, *Charles Wesley and the Struggle for Methodist Identity* (2007); idem, "'Croakers and Busybodies': the Extent and Influence of Church Methodism in the late 18th and early 19th Centuries," *Methodist History* 42 (2003): 20–32; Frances Knight, *The Nineteenth-Century Church and English Society* (1995), 23; and the discussion of the 1851 census by John Wolffe, *The Religious Census of 1851 in Yorkshire* (2005).

IMPLICATIONS OF RECENT SCHOLARSHIP
FOR WESLEY STUDIES

Whether historians accept the implications of the revisionist approach to the eighteenth century or not, our knowledge of eighteenth-century Britain has clearly deepened and become more nuanced over the past two decades. Many of our conventional understandings of the period (on which some Wesley scholarship is still premised) have been challenged or modified. The rest of this chapter will highlight three areas where recent research has made significant alterations to the ways in which Wesley's England has been understood: the state of the Church of England; the relationship between Anglicanism and dissent; and the nature of the British Enlightenment.

State of the Church of England

The most obvious change in our knowledge of Wesley's context is the transformation in our understanding of the eighteenth-century Church of England, and the place of religion more broadly in the period.[67] Older histories not only viewed this as an age of secularization (as we noted earlier), they portrayed it as a nadir in the history of the Anglican Church.[68] The ills most often flagged for adverse comment (and which have frequently been cited as explanatory factors in the rise of Methodism) include pluralism, which meant that the clergy were frequently non-resident in their parishes; the issue of tithes, which led to disputes between clergy and those who were not members of the church, and antagonism from parishioners who resented clergy gaining from improvements in agricultural production; the increasing gentrification of the clergy, which supposedly distanced clergy from the great majority of their parishioners; and a slothful attitude to pastoral work, which left their parishioners bereft of pastoral care.[69] Cathedrals received particularly bad press as being centers of torpor, if not scandal. At the level of high politics, bishops have been blamed for slavishly following the priorities of government ministers (even sacrificing the Church's own

---

[67] See note 48.

[68] See in particular, C.J. Abbey and J.H. Overton, *The English Church in the Eighteenth Century*, 2 vols. (London, 1878); John Stoughton, *Religion in England under Queen Anne and the Georges, 1702–1800*, 2 vols. (London, 1878); and J.H. Overton and F.C. Relton, *The English Church from the Accession of George I to the End of the Eighteenth Century, 1714–1800* (London, 1906).

[69] For modern restatements of these ills, see E. J. Evans, "Some Reasons for the Growth of English Rural Anti-clericalism, c. 1750–c. 1830," *Past & Present* 66 (1975): 84–109; and W.R. Ward, "The Tithe Question in England in the early Nineteenth Century," *Journal of Ecclesiastical History* 16 (1965): 67–81.

interests if necessary), and of being voting fodder for the government in the hopes of securing ever more lucrative preferment. At the local level, parish clergy have been criticized for bowing to the requirements of the local elite.

In short, the eighteenth-century Church of England has frequently been a byword for lax standards and pastoral negligence, indicating an institution that had fallen far short of the ideals of the Church of the sixteenth and seventeenth centuries or of the nineteenth century.[70] In this scenario, Wesley (and Methodism) has been seen as a backlash against the pastoral stagnation of the established Church, as well as a counter-cultural throwback to an age of religious fervor and excitement. It is, however, worth stressing that many of the ways in which the pessimistic history of the eighteenth-century Church of England has been written, in both the nineteenth and much of the twentieth centuries, was from what has been called a "Methodist perspective," with Wesley's criticisms of the Anglican Church being cited as proof of the shortcomings of that institution.[71]

For many nineteenth-century Churchmen, keen to dwell on the inadequacies of the eighteenth-century Church against which they measured their own successes, Wesley's Methodism was seen as an explicable, if regrettable, reaction against the prevailing lethargy of the age.[72] In the first half of the twentieth century, Norman Sykes, an Anglican cleric and later dean of Winchester, developed a more positive portrayal of the eighteenth-century Church.[73] Sykes pointed out that the Church was more efficient as an organization, and its clergy more hardworking as individuals, than had previously been recognized. To a certain extent the criticism of earlier historians could be shown to be based on the biased opinions of the Church's opponents, or the result of anachronistic expectations, judging the eighteenth-century Church by late nineteenth-century standards.

Building on Sykes, a revisionist school of historians has emerged whose detailed work, particularly on what the eighteenth-century Church was doing at the local and diocesan level, has modified and in

---

[70] Peter Virgin, *The Church of England in an Age of Negligence* (1989).

[71] The phrase is J.H. Plumb's, *In the Light Of History* (1972), 37. Wesley's negative comments were often taken out of context, and generally were not balanced by the affection that Wesley could feel towards the Church, and in particular its liturgy; cf. Jeremy Gregory, "'In the Church I will live and die': John Wesley, the Church of England, and Methodism," in William Gibson and Robert Ingram, eds., *Religious Identities in Britain, 1660–1832* (2005), 147–78.

[72] For example, Abbey and Overton, *English Church*, 2:57–58.

[73] Sykes, *Church and State*.

some cases reversed the more negative opinions of some of their prede-cessors. They have highlighted the Church's successes and its strengths, arguing that in many respects it was more effective in the eighteenth century than at any time since the Reformation.[74] Perhaps surprisingly for someone who is often seen among the Church's sternest critics, they could cite Wesley in their defense. As late as 1787, Wesley could preach: "It must be allowed that ever since the Reformation, and particularly in the present century, the behavior of the clergy in general is greatly altered for the better. . . . Insomuch that the English and Irish clergy are generally allowed to be not inferior to any in Europe, for piety as well as for knowledge."[75]

Yet, as might be expected with historical fashions, revisionism has been followed by a post-revisionism, which is wary of some of the up-beat claims of the revisionists and is concerned that they are ironing out some of the real structural and pastoral problems faced by the Church in this period.[76] W.R. Ward (himself a Methodist), for instance, warned over fifteen years ago that the fashionable rehabilitation of the eighteenth-century Church was going much farther than the evidence warranted.[77] There is at the moment, then, a debate between optimists and pessimists about the state of the Church in the eighteenth century.

Some recent scholars have maintained that, far from being a cor-rupt and inefficient institution, the Church had begun to reform itself long before the administrative reforms of the nineteenth century got underway, already clamping down on abuses such as pluralism and non-residence. Other scholars have suggested that the Church of England clergy remained more in tune with popular mores than has often been supposed.[78]

Although historians used to argue that industrialization and urban-ization were twin problems for a Church that supposedly did better in a rural context,[79] we can certainly exaggerate the ways in which these two developments were necessarily detrimental to the life of the Church. For example, it is often suggested that the Church in the eighteenth century failed to build new churches to meet the growth of the towns, and the

[74] See the works cited under footnote 48.
[75] Sermon 104, "On Attending the Church Service," §16, Works 3:470. This sermon is a defense of the efficacy of the Church, even when clergy might be deemed unworthy.
[76] M. F. Snape, *The Church of England in Industrialising Society* (2003); Donald A. Spaeth, *The Church in an Age of Danger: Parsons and Parishioners, 1660–1740* (2000).
[77] W.R. Ward, "Review of John Gascoigne, *Cambridge in the Age of the Enlightenment*," *History* 73 (1990): 497.
[78] Smith, *Religion in Industrial Society*.
[79] Gilbert, *Religion and Society*.

impression is sometimes given that apart from the fifty new churches act of 1711, which attempted to build new places of worship in newly populated districts of London (with only ten being built), little was done until the church-building explosion of the nineteenth century. In fact, some of the new urban centers like Bath, Warwick, York, and Newcastle provided a rich environment for the Church. In all these towns, and in many others, churches were either recently built or refurbished, congregations were large, and clergy benefited from the pleasures of urban society.[80] In parts of Lancashire (the area that witnessed the greatest upsurge in population and where industrialization was furthest developed, placing the greatest strain on its resources) the Church, through its use of newly built chapels of ease, was able to accommodate a greater percentage of the population at the time of Wesley's death than it had in 1740.[81] Even in Manchester, whose population growth in the last thirty years of the century astounded contemporaries, the Church was not negligent in providing new places of worship – eight new churches were built in the city, including St Peter's designed by the architect James Wyatt.[82]

Wesley sometimes blamed the pastoral failings of the Church on the bishops.[83] Others have echoed the charge, asserting that bishops were frequently out of touch with their dioceses, being more involved with the House of Lords than with their diocesan clergy. But, this image of bishops as negligent is misleading in many ways. Despite their involvement in politics, it is clear that the Church had many conscientious diocesans, who took care to monitor the clergy under their control and to provide pastoral oversight. Of course there were exceptions, and because there was no system for retirement, elderly bishops might lose a grip on their task, but modern research at the diocesan and local level has revealed much more active leadership than previous historians assumed.[84] For instance, despite the often-held view that the archbishops of Canterbury in the eighteenth century were by and large unconcerned with the well-being of the Church, several of them during Wesley's lifetime were outstanding administrators, such as Thomas Tenison (1695–1715), William

---

[80] Peter Borsay, *The English Urban Renaissance: Culture and Society in the Provincial Town 1660–1770* (1989).

[81] Smith, *Religion in Industrial Society.*

[82] Chris Ford, Michael Powell, and Terry Wyk, eds. *The Church in Cottonopolis: Essays to Mark the 150th Anniversary of the Diocese of Manchester* (1997).

[83] *Arminian Magazine* (1781): 492–93 for slurs on some of the people they ordained.

[84] See in particular, Jago, *Aspects of the Georgian Church;* Gregory, *Restoration, Reformation, and Reform;* and the essays in Gregory and Chamberlain, eds., *National Church in Local Perspective.*

Wake (1715–1737), Thomas Secker (1758–68), and John Moore (1783–1805).[85] Throughout the period, a number of diligent bishops can be found. Research into the diocesan archives has uncovered correspondence between bishops (or their officials) and the parish clergy, which indicates that bishops were more in contact with their subordinates than used to be supposed. Of particular interest in recent research are the extensive replies written by clergy to the questions asked by the bishops as part of their (usually) triennial visitation of their diocese. These not only provide us with remarkable information concerning the Church's role in individual parishes (such as its personnel, the number of services offered and who attended, and how often children were catechized), they also provide information concerning the numbers of Catholics and Protestant dissenters in the parish, and the number of inhabitants.[86] As yet, no one has attempted to collate the evidence from all the dioceses over the century, but some preliminary conclusions can be attempted.

What do we know about the parish clergy in this period (about whom, as individuals, Wesley could be both scathing and admiring)? Much of the writing about the parish clergy in the eighteenth century has been based on literary evidence and has focused on the stereotypes of a clergy divided into the extremes of the fox-hunting parson or the woefully poor curate. But, modern studies have indicated that most clergy fell well between these extremes. By and large, the clergy were a graduate profession, and the vast bulk of those who were ordained had either been to Oxford (as had Wesley), Cambridge, Trinity College in Dublin, or one of the Scottish universities. This matched the Church's desire to have a learned ministry, and in its propaganda it liked to contrast this fact with the supposedly unlettered status of its dissenting rivals (a criticism leveled at Wesley's lay preachers too, which explains in part why Wesley

---

[85] Gregory, *Restoration, Reformation and Reform*.

[86] For examples of published visitation returns, and related material, on which much of the following paragraphs are based, see Patricia Bell, ed., *Episcopal Visitations in Bedfordshire, 1706–1720* (2002); John Fendley, ed., *Bishop Benson's Survey of the diocese of Gloucester, 1730–50* (2000); K. Wyn Ford, *Chichester Diocesan Surveys, 1686 and 1724* (1994); Jeremy Gregory, ed., *The Speculum of Archbishop Thomas Secker* (1995); John Guy, ed., The *Diocese of Llandaff in 1763* (1991); S.L. Ollard and P.C. Walker, eds., *Archbishop Herring's Visitation Returns, 1743* (1928–30); Elizabeth Ralph, "Bishop Secker's Diocesan Book," in *A Bristol Miscellany*, edited by Patrick McGrath (1985); Mary Ransome, ed., *The State of the Bishopric of Worcester, 1782–1808* (1968); Mary Ransome, ed., *Wiltshire Returns to the Bishop's Visitation Queries, 1783* (1971); W.R. Ward, ed., *Parson and Parish in Eighteenth-Century Surrey* (1994); and W.R. Ward, ed., *Parson and People in Eighteenth-Century Hampshire* (1995).

was so keen to stress that his preachers should undergo rigorous programs of reading and study). It is true that, as the century progressed, an
increasing percentage of clergy came from what might be broadly called
the gentry ranks, but the wholesale gentrification of the clergy can be
exaggerated. Even at the time of Wesley's death, a significant number of
clergy (perhaps well over a quarter) came from more humble origins and
were less likely to have been out of touch with ordinary parishioners
than the pessimistic interpretation suggests. Moreover, an increasing
number had fathers (as had Wesley) who had also been clergy.

Certainly a large number of parishes, as a consequence of pluralism,
were staffed by curates. Some of these lived up to the image of the poorly
paid *lumpen proletariat*, but many were at the early stages of their career
and would move on to more settled and more lucrative employment.
Beneficed clergy (those in permanent employment) were either vicars or
rectors: the distinction being that rectors (since they received the tithes
on all produce within the parish) were likely to be richer than vicars
who only received "small" tithes (usually just on the minor products of
the parish). The lot of those who were most poorly remunerated was
somewhat alleviated during the course of the century through Queen
Anne's Bounty (established in 1704) which, through funds diverted from
government resources and by raising extra money, was able to make a
significant improvement to the less well endowed parishes.[87]

As far as the pastoral work of the clergy is concerned it is of course
impossible to generalize, depending as it did on the inclinations of individuals (although it is clear that bishops were not content with the most
minimal pastoral cover). There are examples of negligent clergy, but by
and large, the pastoral dedication of the parish clergy is more impressive
than the traditionally hostile picture would suggest. The broad results of
the visitation surveys indicate that services were regularly given on Sundays, and that the laity were generally happy to attend, as long as there
was a sermon.[88] The furnishings of many eighteenth-century churches,
and especially those that were refurbished or newly built in the period,
confirmed the ascendant place of the pulpit (and sermon) within the
interior of the church. For example, St Ann's, Manchester (built in 1711
from a donation by Lady Ann Bland) had a massive fifteen foot high pulpit, from which Wesley preached in 1738.[89] The dominance of the pulpit

[87] For an up to date discussion of the clerical profession, which synthesizes much of the
available research, see Jacob, *The Clerical Profession*.

[88] See F.C. Mather, "Georgian Churchmanship Reconsidered: Some Variations in Anglican Public Worship, 1714–1830," *Journal of Ecclesiastical History* 36 (1985): 268–69.

[89] Wesley, *Journal* (19 March 1738), *Works*, 18:230.

within the church, and especially the three-decker pulpit (which figured prominently in Hogarth's satirical prints, but who also, of course, satirized the Methodist preacher), was much derided by nineteenth-century Church reformers who accused their forebears of neglecting the sacrament. But, it is indicative of the central role given to the sermon, and of "the word" more generally within eighteenth-century religious life. To a large extent this reflects the influence of the Reformation on the piety of the eighteenth-century Church, and, indeed, a number of scholars have argued that the chief pastoral aim of eighteenth-century clergy was to continue the work of the Reformers, initiating parishioners into the fundamental message of the Reformation and educating them out of popery and superstition.[90]

The visitation returns indicate that clergy were involved in catechizing children, although this was usually only for part of the year, and clergy admitted to their superiors that sometimes parents were reluctant to send their children.[91] Another common complaint made by the clergy was the reluctance parishioners had in taking Holy Communion, but whether this was because they devalued the sacrament or they felt unworthy to receive it is not clear. The returns also show a broad difference between rural and urban parishes. In the towns, it was much more common to find weekday services being offered and attended. Some of the larger urban centers had communion once a month and occasionally every Sunday. In rural parishes, by contrast, clergy found it hard to take parishioners away from the agricultural routine. In many rural parishes, weekday services had long since died out. The visitation returns additionally demonstrate the wider role of the Church and the clergy in the life of the parish. Clergy frequently had the role of supervising the local school, managing charitable funds, and organizing poor relief, and as such played a vital role within the parish community. Within these patterns of pastoral provision, Wesley, during his only period as a parish priest while in Savannah, Georgia, can be regarded as something of a model incumbent. He held three services each Sunday, offered the sacrament on a weekly basis and on holy days, held two weekday services, and catechized as a regular part of his pastoral practice.[92]

---

[90] See Jeremy Gregory, "The Eighteenth-Century Reformation: the Pastoral Task of Anglican Clergy after 1689," in Walsh, Haydon and Taylor, *Church of England*, 67–85; idem, "The Making of a Protestant Nation: 'Success' and 'Failure' in England's Long Reformation," in Tyacke, *England's Long Reformation*, 307–33; Jonathan Barry, "Bristol as a Reformation City, c. 1640–c. 1780," in Tyacke, *Long Reformation*, 261–84; and Gregory, *Restoration, Reformation, and Reform*.

[91] Gregory, *Restoration, Reformation, and Reform*, 223–26.

[92] Hammond, "Restoring Primitive Christianity," 104, 161–64, 171–73, 351–58.

Recent scholarship has also emphasized the ways in which, long before Wesley's "conversion" in May 1738, Anglicanism had itself been undergoing a movement of renewal and reform. This was witnessed most obviously by the creation of the religious societies (from about 1678, first in London, then elsewhere), the societies for the reformation of manners (flourishing from the 1690s), the Society for the Promotion of Christian Knowledge (SPCK) in 1698, and the Society for the Propagation of the Gospel in Foreign Parts (SPG) in 1701 (all of which Wesley was influenced by and drew on), but can also be seen in efforts at Church reform.[93] The SPCK fostered a range of activities, including establishing a corresponding society for pooling and collecting information on the Church's work in the localities, encouraging the development of parish libraries, and, increasingly, publishing and disseminating religious tracts and pamphlets as a way of spreading religious education (something which Wesley would also do). During its first thirty years, it also had a special role in encouraging the establishment of charity schools.[94] The SPG reveals the extent to which the Church in the eighteenth century can be considered to be a missionary Church; recognizing that its mission was not only to its English parishioners, but also to those in its colonies.[95] Another example of the Church's links with religious groups outside the British isles were the various funds organized by the Church for the support of protestants in Europe who were suffering from persecution by Roman Catholics.[96] Wesley himself, of course, had contacts and links with a broader European religious context – as revealed, for

[93] J. Spurr, "The Church, the Societies, and the Moral Revolution of 1688," in Walsh, Haydon and Taylor, *Church of England*, 127–42; Craig Rose, "The Origins and Ideals of the SPCK, 1699–1716," ibid., 172–90; Tina Isaacs, "The Anglican Hierarchy and the Reformation of Manners, 1688–1738," *Journal of Ecclesiastical History* 33 (1982): 391–411; Gillian Wagner, "Spreading the Word: the Church and SPG in North America," *Journal of the Canadian Church Historical Society* 45 (2003): 65–76; S. Taylor, "Bishop Edmund Gibson's Proposals for Church Reform," in S. Taylor, ed., *From Cranmer to Davidson* (1999), 172–186; R.A. Burns, "A Hanoverian Legacy? Diocesan Reform in the Church of England, c. 1800–c. 1833," in Walsh, Haydon, and Taylor, *Church of England*, 265–82; and idem, "English 'Church Reform' Revisited, 1780–1840," in Arthur Burns and Joanna Innes, eds., *Rethinking the Age of Reform* (2003), 136–62. For ways in which some of these influenced Wesley, see Rack, *Reasonable Enthusiast*, 119, 239, 354, 361, 362.

[94] Craig Rose, "'Seminaries of Faction and Rebellion': Jacobites, Whigs, and the London Charity Schools, 1716–1724," *Historical Journal* 34 (1991): 831–55.

[95] See Hammond, "Restoring primitive Christianity." Although the SPG paid Wesley's salary, he was not a typical SPG missionary under the authority of the bishop of London and the Society. He was licensed by the Georgia Trustees and served as a volunteer missionary; cf. Hammond, "Restoring Primitive Christianity," 324–26.

[96] Sugiko Nishikawa, "The SPCK in Defence of Protestant Minorities in Early Eighteenth-Century Europe," *Journal of Ecclesiastical History* 56 (2005): 730–48.

example, by his visit to the Moravian community at Herrnhut within a few weeks of his "conversion" experience.[97]

In all of these areas of concern, the Church proved rather adept at raising funds for its activities and was particularly successful in getting money from the laity for its ventures.[98] The SPG and the Corporation for the Sons of the Clergy (which supported the widows and the children of deceased clergy) elicited money through annual concerts and services at St Paul's cathedral.[99] The ability of the Church to extract money from the laity points to one of the most important developments within the Church of England in this period, what has been termed the "laicization of religion."[100] It is this feature, rather than the conventional stress on this being an age of secularization, which is the hallmark of Anglican history of the time. Most histories of the Church concentrate on either the Church as an institution or on the clergy, but it needs to be recognized that (in part as a consequence of the Reformation) a considerable emphasis was placed by clergy on the role of the laity. It could be argued that Wesley's use of lay preachers was extending this to its logical conclusion.

Although as yet there are only a few studies of lay piety, it is clear that a considerable body of people not only attended the services provided by the Church, but also wanted to help the Church in other ways and to participate in debates about religion more generally.[101] Several members of the aristocracy, such as the Duke of Newcastle, the Earl of Dartmouth, and Lady Betty Hastings were pious defenders of the Church. Not many lay people joined Samuel Johnson in writing sermons, but the general support for the Church is impressive. The fund raising activities just mentioned, alongside regular payment of tithes and donations to individual parish churches (most of which dated from the medieval period and were increasingly in need of repair), certainly challenge the view that the Church was increasingly marginal to the life of parishioners.

It has been an axiom of much writing on the Church in the eighteenth century that it had lost its hold over the lower orders (who were

---

[97] On wider European links see W.R Ward, *The Protestant Evangelical Awakening* (1992).

[98] W.M. Jacob, *Lay People and Religion in the Early Eighteenth Century* (1996), 155–85.

[99] Jeremy Gregory, "Preaching Anglicanism at St Paul's, 1688–1800," in *St Paul's: the Cathedral Church of London, 604–2004*, edited by Derek Keene, Arthur Burns and Andrew Saint (2004).

[100] Sykes, *Church and State*, 379.

[101] Jacob, *Lay People*; Mark Goldie, "Voluntary Anglicans," *The Historical Journal* 46 (2003): 977–90.

thus ready to follow Wesley).[102] Certainly in this – as perhaps in all periods – signs of disaffection can be shown, particularly towards individual clergy and over particular grievances. But, this did not mean that the Church as an institution had lost its place in the hearts and minds of ordinary parishioners. The famous Church-and-King riots of the early 1790s, which among other things mobbed the dissenter and radical political thinker Joseph Priestley's house in Birmingham and burned his laboratory, were not very edifying, but they indicate that the Church could still inspire popular loyalties.

This review of the scholarship on the Church of England suggests that we should view Wesley's relationship to the Church in which he was born, ordained (by John Potter, then bishop of Oxford, and later archbishop of Canterbury), and, so he claimed, lived and died, in more subtle ways than traditional accounts of the rise of Methodism would have it.[103] Methodist scholarship is usually premised on the given fact of a moribund and ineffective established Church, but it may be that John Wesley and his brother Charles are evidence of a lively Anglican culture, and that much of what has been considered Methodist innovations should be seen as emerging from within an Anglican Church which was itself experimenting with developments in pastoral care.[104]

Relationship between Anglicanism and dissent

It is often said that one of the clearest testimonies to the failure of the Church in the eighteenth century in the pastoral sphere was the existence of dissent, especially of Methodism (sometimes labeled "new dissent"). If the Church was as successful as some of the more optimistic judgments would have us believe, it can reasonably be asked: Why did nonconformity exist? And why did Methodism develop?

It is worth stressing that these factors in themselves are not necessarily a useful guide to the successes or failures of the eighteenth-century Church. In the first place, by the 1730s, several contemporaries were noticing a decline in "old dissent" (Presbyterians, Congregationalists, Baptists, and Quakers) as many erstwhile dissenters conformed to the Church of England – including some, like Thomas Secker, a future archbishop of Canterbury, who had initially contemplated becoming nonconformist ministers.[105] The reasons given for the decline in old dissent were varied: some held the internecine wrangling over doctrine

---

[102] Gilbert, *Religion*; and Snape, *The Church*, 195.
[103] See Baker, *John Wesley and the Church of England.*
[104] Gregory, "In the Church I will live and die," 162–64.
[105] See Michael Watts, *The Dissenters*, vol.1 (1978).

responsible; some pointed to the ways in which the confessional State severely limited opportunities for nonconformists to have significant political, social, and educational positions if they remained outside the Church; and others blamed the decline of old dissent on the effects of the Toleration Act (see below) which supposedly weakened the backbone of nonconformity.[106] Whatever the reason, it is clear that the Church gained from winning over some former dissenters and, as a consequence, the challenge of nonconformity weakened.

Secondly, it is necessary to emphasize that Methodism should be seen, at least in the first instance, as a movement *within* the Church of England, rather than as a dissenting movement outside it. Wesley, the son of the rector of Epworth, remained a member of the Church of England throughout his life (as did George Whitefield and Howell Harris). Although he could be sharply critical of contemporary practice, his energies were devoted to reforming the Church. Moreover, he strove to keep the movement he founded within the Church, by encouraging his followers to attend both Church services and the Methodist meeting, and insisting that Methodist meetings should not clash with the times of church services. While these direction were not universally respected, or put into practice, by his followers, Methodism was more of an Anglican than a dissenting phenomenon at least until Wesley's death in 1791.[107]

In this light, it is curious that the current lively scholarship on the Church and the prolific research into Wesley have been kept remarkably separate. For example, the revisionist approach to the Church has seldom brought Methodism into its purview, except to argue that Wesley's criticisms of the shortcomings of that institution were frequently exaggerated, and to suggest that, in many parts of the country, the emergence of Methodism was rather later, and the number of adherents rather smaller, than a triumphalist Methodist reading would have it.[108] Future study, perhaps encouraged by this *Companion*, would benefit from bringing these research strands together.

If recent scholarship has provided a much more up-beat picture of the state of the Church of England, what can be said about the relationship between the Church and dissent? One feature of Wesley's context, which

---

[106] Richard Brown, *Church and State in Modern Britain, 1700–1850* (1991).

[107] On this, see the forthcoming University of Manchester Ph.D. thesis by David Wilson, "Church *and* Chapel: Parish Ministry and Methodism in Madeley, c. 1760–1815, with Special Reference to the Ministry of John and Mary Fletcher."

[108] See, for example the essays by Jeremy Gregory, William Gibson, Colin Haydon, and William Jacob in Gregory and Chamberlain, eds., *The National Church in Local Perspective*.

needs to be highlighted here is the "Toleration Act" of 1689. This act is often seen as a concomitant of the Glorious Revolution, maintaining the establishment position of the Church while giving limited concessions to nonconformists. Whereas some clergy sought to have the act repealed and others lobbied to extend its concessions, it served throughout the eighteenth century to sum up the position of the Church of England as established, yet broadly tolerant of at least some of its rivals.[109] Although commonly known as the "Toleration Act" by contemporaries and later historians, this legislation was originally entitled an "act for exempting their majesties' Protestant subjects dissenting from the Church of England from the penalties of certain laws," which indicates that it was less tolerant than has sometimes been suggested. Protestant dissenters could legally worship only in unlocked meeting houses, which had to be properly licensed, and which were served by ministers who subscribed to all of the Thirty-Nine Articles of the Church of England except those concerning baptism and Church government. The act clearly proscribed Roman Catholic worship, as well as that of Unitarians.

One of the issues which Wesley faced was whether Methodist meetings should be registered under the act. He strongly resisted this move, arguing that his followers were not dissenters, even though a number of clergy insisted on calling them such. To support his point, Wesley liked to boast that he brought his Methodist people to Church for communion.[110] The Toleration Act became important for the self-definition of the Church as one which was charitable and enlightened, at least compared with its competitors. Persecution of dissent was contrasted as a hallmark of popery. Although evidence can be found of mobs stoning and harrying dissenters (including early Methodists), and pulling down their meeting houses, clergy were expected to work within a framework where they persuaded rather than persecuted nonconformists back into the fold. This frame of mind explains in part why clergy were so eager to publish their views in print, as a way of competing with, rather than persecuting nonconformists. Clergy do seem to have generally treated Protestant dissenters with respect. The vicar of St. Lawrence, Thanet, for instance, reported to Archbishop Moore in 1786, with some pride: "I must do all my parishioners, both the Church of England, and likewise the Dissenters, the justice to say that they attend they public worship of God on the lord's day, at the Church and at the meeting house, with

---

[109] See James Bradley, "Toleration and Movements of Christian Reunion, 1660–1789," in *Enlightenment, Reawakening and Revolution, 1660–1825*, edited by Stewart J. Brown and Timothy Tackett (2006), 348–70.

[110] Wesley, *Journal* (28 November 1750), *Works*, 20:370; (9 April 1775), *Works*, 22:447.

great punctuality, regularity and decency."[111] Note how this particular clergyman not only had a positive view of dissenters, he saw both Anglicans and nonconformists as his parishioners – a lingering suggestion of the view that the Church of England had a responsibility for the entire nation.

Of more concern to Anglican clergy was the apparently growing sector of the population who did not attend any form of religious worship. Many suspected that the Toleration Act contributed to this problem; by not insisting that parishioners went to the Church of England services, it may have encouraged them to attend no place of worship at all. Whatever the cause, the growing presence of this group offered a place where the Church might join in with the dissenters. This shared pastoral purpose can be witnessed by Anglicans working with dissenters in the societies for the reformation of manners (in the 1690s and early eighteenth century) and in educational projects such as charity schools.

Nature of the British Enlightenment

If scholars of John Wesley could benefit from giving greater attention to the Church of England, there are other ways in which Wesley can be placed more centrally into recent eighteenth-century scholarship with profit. One of the most significant historiographical developments during the past twenty years has been to widen and complicate what might be meant by "the Enlightenment." Traditional scholarship, heavily based on a French model of the Enlightenment, viewed it as an anti-religious force.[112] On this reading, Wesley and Methodism more generally could be portrayed as a counter-Enlightenment backlash.[113] More lately, scholars working on British history have contested the notion that the Enlightenment was necessarily anti-religious. Roy Porter, in particular, has argued that in the English Enlightenment piety and reason could work in tandem.[114] Concurring, other researchers have shown that it is simplistic to place English Enlightenment figures like John Toland

---

[111] Quoted in Gregory, *Restoration, Reformation, and Reform*, 232.

[112] Classic studies of the Enlightenment include Paul Hazard, *European Thought in the Eighteenth Century* (1965); and Peter Gay, *The Enlightenment* (1967).

[113] See Thompson, *Making of the English Working Class*.

[114] Roy Porter, "The Enlightenment in England," in R. Porter and M. Teich, eds., *The Enlightenment in National Context* (1981), 1–18. In some of Porter's later and more extended considerations of the themes, he tends to see the Enlightenment as a secularizing force: R. Porter, *The Enlightenment* (1990); idem, *Enlightenment: Britain and the Creation of the Modern World* (2001). See also Sheridan Gilley's pioneering article: "Christianity and the Enlightenment: An Historical Survey," *History of European Ideas* 1 (1981): 103–21.

within an anti-religious camp. Although Toland was certainly critical of the Church and the clergy, his attacks were based on what he considered to be religious principles.[115]

Conversely, central religious figures like Wesley fit well in an English Enlightenment framework, complicating the view of him as anti- or counter-Enlightenment. The lynchpin of Wesley's theology was Arminianism and universal redemption – endlessly reiterated in his correspondence, his *Journals*, and his sermons. This was not only the dominant theology of the Church of England (again indicative of the fact that we need to understand Wesley as an Anglican), but its central premises can be understood as chiming in with the Enlightenment emphasis on optimism, human potential, perfectibility, and the essential equality of humankind.[116] Wesley's emphasis on evidence and experience can also be seen as echoing Enlightenment traits. This is not to say that Wesley was directly influenced by Enlightenment thought; he was frequently hostile to those classically labeled as Enlightenment figures, such as Voltaire, and there has been a long-standing debate about how far he was Lockean.[117] But, there does appear to be at least an elective affinity between his central concerns and those usually viewed as belonging to the Enlightenment.

Going further, it can be argued that the whole thrust of Wesley's religious message was – in Enlightenment fashion – the centrality of experience and feeling. But, if Wesley put great emphasis on sensation and empiricism, he was – again in Enlightenment fashion – keen to ensure that the experience was a genuine one, that the convert was neither deluded nor fabricating their feelings. It also needed to be tempered by Scripture and by reason, in a characteristically eighteenth-century balance.[118] In any case, Wesley's concern with experience and feeling should be understood as part of an eighteenth-century English emphasis

---

[115] Justin Champion, *Republican Learning: John Toland and the Crisis of Christian Culture, 1696–1722* (2003). See also his *The Pillars of Priestcraft Shaken* (1992).

[116] For suggestions of the links between Arminianism, Methodist theology, and Enlightenment thought see Semmel, *Methodist Revolution*, 87–109. Semmel, however, argued that Wesleyanism should be seen as a liberalizing force. I think we can agree that there are affinities between Methodism and the Enlightenment without forcing it into a liberalizing framework.

[117] See Frederick Dreyer, "Faith and Experience in the Thought of John Wesley," *American Historical Review* 88 (1983): 21–50; and John C. English, "John Wesley and the Anglican Moderates of the Seventeenth Century," *Anglican Theological Review* 51 (1969): 203–20.

[118] Rex Dale Matthews, "'Religion and Reason Joined': a Study in the Theology of John Wesley" (Harvard University Ph.D. thesis, 1986).

on empiricism and sentiment (seen in such a typically eighteenth-century virtue as benevolence) rather than as what might be thought to be a full-blooded Romanticism.[119] Equally typical was Wesley's fascination with developments in natural philosophy and medicine, which led him to keep abreast of the latest research and to disseminate it to his followers.[120]

More broadly, and crucially for our understanding of Wesley's context, his seeming ability to hold together faith and reason (although how far he did so in synthesis or in tension is a matter for debate) can be seen as part of a wider pattern of the age.[121] Jane Shaw in her *Miracles in Enlightenment England* has demonstrated how a larger range of commentators were able to balance "religious enthusiasm" with "reason." Her reading incorporates elements of the supernatural into an enlightenment worldview, challenging older models of an enlightenment hostile to religious sensibilities.[122] Studies such as this are beginning to uncover a religious eighteenth century, which makes it clear that characterizations of this as the "age of reason" have led to an unwarranted neglect of the religious impulses and drivers of the period. Recent research into all manner of topics, ranging from the art, literature, travel writing, and even the foreign policy of the time have argued for the need to bring back the religious framework and imperatives that have been marginalized by conventional scholarship.[123] It may have been that Wesley made such an impact on his age, not because his context was irreligious, but because it was already suffused with religious concerns.

[119] Even "romantic" writers may have placed more stress on reason than is sometimes suggested; see Jon Mee, *Romanticism, Enthusiasm and Regulation* (2003).

[120] See Laura Bartels Felleman, "The Evidence of Things Not Seen: John Wesley's Use of Natural Philosophy," (Drew University Ph.D. thesis, 2004); Madden, *Cheap, Safe and Natural Medicine*; and Prosser, "Arminian Magazine."

[121] See Henry Rack, "A Man of Reason and Religion? John Wesley and the Enlightenment," *Wesley and Methodist Studies* 1 (2009, forthcoming).

[122] Jane Shaw, *Miracles in Enlightenment England* (2006). See also Robert Webster, "Methodism and the Miraculous: John Wesley's Contribution to the *Historia Miraculorum*" (Oxford University D.Phil. thesis, 2006).

[123] See Clare Haynes, *Pictures and Popery: Art and Religion in England, 1660–1760* (2006); and Claydon, *Europe and the Making of England*.

Part II
Wesley's life

2 Wesley's life and ministry[1]

KENNETH J. COLLINS

The parents of John Wesley, Samuel and Susanna (nee Annesley), were raised in Puritan dissent, although both made their way back to the Church of England as young people. Deeply principled in many respects, Samuel and Susanna created a family environment at the Epworth rectory in Lincolnshire that eventually produced three priests for the church they so loved. John Wesley was born in Epworth on June 17, 1703 (according to the Julian calendar), and was the fifteenth of eighteen or nineteen children.

Something of a disciplinarian, Susanna Wesley believed that conquering the will of her children was the only strong foundation for a religious education. When this was done properly, the child could then be governed by the reason and piety of its parents until its own understanding came to fruition. Susanna had many opportunities to exercise strong leadership in the family and she cared for her children according to rule and method. Six hours a day were spent at school where instruction was serious and thorough and where loud talking and boisterous playing were strictly forbidden.

EARLY YEARS

Although the Epworth rectory played a salient role in Wesley's spiritual formation, it was relatively short lived. Nominated for the Charterhouse school in London by the Duke of Buckingham, Wesley studied at this institution from 1714 to 1720, at which point he matriculated at Christ Church, Oxford, where he received his baccalaureate degree in 1724. The following year brought a number of changes: Wesley's religious interests grew more serious; he was ordained a deacon by Bishop

[1] Some of the material for this essay is drawn from my book, *John Wesley: A Theological Journey* (2003) and is used by permission.

John Potter (ca. 1674–1747) of Oxford, who eventually became the arch-bishop of Canterbury; he read Jeremy Taylor's *Rules and Exercises of Holy Living and Holy Dying*, whereby he came to understand the end or goal of religion as holy love; he mastered the medieval spiritual classic *The Imitation of Christ* by Thomas à Kempis, which helped him to see the nature and extent of inward religion for the first time; and he encoun-tered a religious friend (perhaps Sally Kirkham or Robin Griffiths) who helped him to alter his whole manner of living.

Although Catholic scholarship on Wesley has tended to claim that the year 1725 marked his conversion, more recent readings of Wesley's life and thought have noted several factors of this period that challenge such an assumption. Thus, not only did Wesley, by his own admission, fail to lay a proper foundation of repentance and believing the gospel in his preaching, but he also had a limited, largely rationalistic, understand-ing of the nature of faith. Again, even though Wesley did indeed at this time comprehend the point of it all as holiness manifested in the love of God and neighbor, he nevertheless had yet to realize the nature of saving faith in his own life along with the two fruits that ever accompany it – namely, peace from a sense of forgiveness and power from the presence of the Holy Spirit within. Despite his difficulties, the following year on March 17, Wesley was elected Fellow of Lincoln College (an institution founded in 1427 to combat Lollardy). In 1727, he received his Master of Arts degree. The following year he was ordained a priest by the same bishop, John Potter, who had earlier ordained him a deacon.

Although a teaching fellow and an Oxford don, Wesley actually spent much time away from the university, in the parishes of Epworth and Wroot, assisting his elderly father during the period between August 1727 and November 1729. In this pastoral setting, Wesley saw little fruit to his ministry, but he continued to read spiritual and devotional literature. In 1729 (or perhaps in 1730) Wesley read William Law's *Christian Perfection* and *Serious Call to a Devout and Holy Life*. Whereas the works of à Kempis and Taylor had shown Wesley the importance of purity of intention and of entire consecration to God, William Law's writings introduced him to the height, breadth, and depth of the law of God. Having a keen sense of the difference between the letter and the spirit, Wesley now understood the law of God not as a lifeless code, but as a life-giving gift that reflected the excellence of the divine being. Wesley's studies in this pastoral setting were interrupted when he was called back to Oxford in 1729, by Dr. Morley, the rector of Lincoln College, who maintained that the interests of the College and the obligation of the statutes necessitated his return to tutorial duties.

THE RISE OF OXFORD METHODISM

Prior to John's return, his younger brother Charles (1707–88) had experienced a religious reformation in Spring 1729, which resulted in serious study and regular church attendance with another student, William Morgan. When John joined Charles at Oxford in the fall of 1729, Robert Kirkham also began associating with this emerging group, whose visible activities resulted in a variety of names given briefly such as the Holy Club, Bible Moths, Sacramentarians – and, by 1732, the name that eventually stuck, Methodists. Over the next two or three years as many as four dozen persons participated in the activities of various related cell groups throughout the university, including James Hervey (1714–58) and George Whitefield (1714–70).

From the very beginning, this little religious society at Oxford had focused on works of piety such as prayer, reading the Scriptures, and receiving the Lord's Supper as important means of grace. But, with the addition of John Clayton to the group, an increasing emphasis was placed on keeping the fasts (on Wednesdays and Fridays) of the ancient church. In terms of works of mercy, a constant concern as well, William Morgan added to the Methodist practice by enjoining the Wesleys and others to visit the Oxford prisons, the Castle and the Bocardo, for instance, as well as to work among the poor. As a part of their discipline and steward-ship, the Methodists cut off all needless expense so that they could be of greater service to the poor. In fact, Wesley noted that it was the practice of the early members to give away all that they had after they had provided for their own necessities.

Wesley's later reflections on the rise of Oxford Methodism are sig-nificant because in them he underscores the importance he attached to being a scriptural Christian, where the Bible constitutes the basic stan-dard or norm of the Christian life. In his *Plain Account of Christian Perfection*, for example, he stated: "In the year 1729, I began not only to read, but to study, the Bible, as the one, the only standard of truth, and the only model of pure religion."[2] Elsewhere, in his sermon "On God's Vineyard," Wesley pointed out: "From the very beginning, from the time that four young men united together, each of them was *homo unius libri* – 'A man of one book.' . . . They had one, and only one, rule of judgment. . . . They were one and all determined to be Bible-Christians."[3] Much of the theological substance of Oxford Methodism was revealed in

---

[2] *Plain Account of Christian Perfection*, §5, *Works* (Jackson), 11:367.
[3] Sermon 107, "On God's Vineyard," I.1, *Works*, 3:504.

Wesley's sermon "The Circumcision of the Heart," which was preached before the University at St. Mary's in 1733. This key sermon, as Wesley himself later put it, contained all that he taught concerning salvation from sin and loving God with an undivided heart.

GEORGIA

The second rise of Methodism occurred not at Oxford but in Georgia. Shortly after the death of their father in 1735, John and Charles Wesley, along with Benjamin Ingham and Charles Delamotte, embarked on a missionary journey to this British colony in North America. John later confessed to a friend that his chief motivation for undertaking this arduous task was to save his own soul: "I hope to learn the true sense of the gospel of Christ by preaching it to the heathen."[4] En route to Georgia their ship, *The Simmonds*, was buffeted by powerful Atlantic storms. Wesley, who was quite fearful, even admitting his reluctance to die, marveled at the serenity of the Moravian community on board, who calmly sang on in the midst of such terror. That evening Wesley recorded in his journal: "This was the most glorious day which I have ever hitherto seen."[5]

Shortly after he arrived in Georgia in February 1736, Wesley sought advice regarding his own moral and spiritual affairs from August Spangenberg, a Moravian leader. Before he would answer, however, Spangenberg posed two pointed questions to Wesley: first, "Have you the witness within yourself?" And second, "Does the Spirit of God bear witness with your spirit that you are a child of God?" Wesley was surprised by such probing questions and did not know quite how to answer. Spangenberg nevertheless continued his queries, "Do you know Jesus Christ?" Wesley paused and related, "I know he is the Saviour of the world." "True," Spangenberg replied, "but do you know he has saved you?" Wesley's response was once again both weak and indecisive: "I hope he has died to save me." The kindly Moravian leader then brought matters to a head in a very pastoral way and asked, "Do you know yourself?" Wesley responded, "I do." But, he later noted in his journal that he feared these were "vain words." Spangenberg had asked specific questions; Wesley offered general, even vague, replies.

This interview with Spangenberg, important in many respects, revealed to Wesley on one level that he lacked the witness of the Holy Spirit that he was a child of God. Indeed, Wesley marveled at the

---

4 Letter to John Burton (10 Oct. 1735), *Works*, 25:439.
5 *Journal* (25 Jan. 1735), *Works* 18:143.

assurance, the confidence, that Spangenberg seemed to have in matters of faith. This was the same sort of steady confidence that he had observed among the broader Moravian community on board the *Simmonds*. In the face of all this, Wesley was, of course, intrigued and naturally wanted to learn more from these German-speaking people.

ALDERSGATE

When John Wesley returned to England in 1738 (Charles had already preceded him), he continued his contacts with the Moravian community and formed a religious society, first at the home of James Hutton and then at Fetter Lane in London, with the help of Peter Böhler (1712–75), a young Moravian leader. This represents the third rise of Methodism. Under Böhler's spiritual direction, on May 24, 1738, Wesley experienced – while listening to Martin Luther's "Preface to the Epistle to Romans" being read at a religious society meeting in Aldersgate Street – the power and peace, the happiness and holiness, for which he had so longed: justification with its forgiveness of past sins, the new birth with its accompanying freedom from the power or dominion of sin, as well as the assurance that that he was no longer a servant but a child of God. In his journal on that day Wesley wrote: "I felt I did trust in Christ, Christ alone for salvation, and an assurance was given me that he had taken away *my* sins, even *mine*, and saved *me* from the law of sin and death."[6]

Wesley, himself, underscored the significance of his Aldersgate experience in two key ways. First of all, for his journal entry on May 24, 1738, Wesley composed a spiritual summary of his Christian walk up to that point. He pointed out, among other things, that while he was at Savannah he was "beating the air," being ignorant of the righteousness which comes from Christ with the result that he sought to establish his own righteousness or justification "under the law." "In this state," Wesley observed, "I was indeed fighting continually, but not conquering. Before, I had willingly served sin: now it was unwillingly, but still I served it." In this path marked by repeated spiritual defeat, by the continual dominance of sin, Wesley remained. In his own words, he "fell and rose and fell again." Aldersgate, then, represented an important actualization of saving grace, even if it was less grace than Wesley had originally expected.

Second, so significant was the date of May 24, 1738, that it specifically emerged a couple of more times in Wesley's writings as he continued to reflect on his spiritual journey. To illustrate, during the latter

---

[6] *Journal* (24 May 1738), *Works*, 18:249–50.

part of October 1738 and following, Wesley corresponded with his older brother, Samuel Jr., who had objected to his understanding of salvation and his new-found faith. In his letter, John reaffirmed his definition of a Christian in the following way: "By a Christian I mean one who so believes in Christ as that sin hath no more dominion over him, and in this obvious sense of the work I was not a Christian till May 24th last past."[7] Over seven years later, Wesley once again specifically referred to the date of his evangelical conversion, this time in a letter to "John Smith" in which he observed: "For it is true that from May 24, 1738, 'whenever I was desired to preach, *salvation by faith* was my only theme.'"[8]

Although Wesley later distinguished the faith of a servant from the faith of a child of God, and even though he also appended a number of disclaimers to the 1775 *Journal* account of his Aldersgate experience, he never repudiated the standard of the new birth and the assurance that commonly accompanies it, an assurance that marked his own conversion to the proper Christian faith.

MORAVIANISM

Clearly, Wesley had profited much from his acquaintance with the Moravians, Peter Böhler in particular. But, some of his theological and spiritual malaise *after* his Aldersgate experience resulted, in large measure, from their erroneous teaching. For one thing, some of the English Moravians had likely led Wesley to believe that justification, and the new birth that necessarily accompanies it, would eliminate not simply the power of sin (which was accurate), but the *being* of sin as well (which was not). Either that or Wesley had simply misunderstood them. Moreover, Wesley had also expected to receive the full assurance of faith at Aldersgate and was therefore surprised to learn that instead he currently had a *measure* of assurance occasionally marked by doubt and fear. This naturally perplexed and troubled him. Therefore, the following year Wesley began to articulate *degrees* of assurance in a very careful way and by the second Methodist Conference in 1745, Wesley indicated that in the case of a few exceptions assurance may not always accompany justifying faith. However, the reasons for this failure to realize the "common privilege" of a child of God were not revealed until much later: ignorance of the gospel promises and bodily disorder.

---

[7]   Letter to Samuel Wesley Jr. (30 Oct. 1738), *Works*, 25:575.
[8]   Letter to John Smith (30 Dec. 1745), §16, *Works*, 26:183.

Not yet realizing the full "legacy" that the Moravians had bequeathed to him, both the good and the bad, Wesley desired still greater contact with this people. To this end, Wesley set out for Herrnhut, a Moravian settlement about thirty miles from Dresden, in the early summer of 1738. By July 4th, Wesley had reached Marienborn where he conversed with Count Zinzendorf, the leader of the Moravians. At Herrnhut, itself, Wesley became acquainted with the testimonies of Christian David, Michael Linner, and Arvid Gradin, among others, all of which helped him to modify his understanding of Christian assurance and to reflect upon his doctrine of sin. Such witness also demonstrated to him the difference between the teaching of the English and German Moravians.

By September 16, 1738, Wesley was back in England, and he was pleased to learn that the society at Fetter Lane had increased from ten to thirty-two members in his absence. However, during this same month, some of Wesley's naiveté concerning the Moravians was beginning to wear off, for on September 27 or 28 he drafted a letter, which contained numerous criticisms in light of his recent visit. Among other things, Wesley noted the Moravian neglect of fasting, their levity in behavior, their failure to redeem the time, and their use of "cunning, guile, or dissimulation." Nevertheless, because Wesley still had some doubt about the accuracy of these judgments, he quietly put this letter aside. The substance of the letter eventually became a part of a later more lengthy one (August 8, 1740) – which Wesley did indeed send – in which he criticized the Moravians for their numerous excesses.

Wesley's relations with the Moravians were further strained because of different conceptions of ministry and pastoral care that were playing out at Fetter Lane. To illustrate, in November 1739, Philipp Heinrich Molther, who had been introduced to the Fetter Lane Society by James Hutton, began to teach society members, Jenny Chambers among them, that until they had justifying and regenerating faith, they should be "still" and leave off the means of grace. John Bray, a layperson and friend of the Wesley brothers, added his voice to Molther's teaching, such that by the time John Wesley came back to London in December 1739 he found that "scarce one in ten retained his first love."

Concerned about the effect of such preaching on the Fetter Lane Society, Wesley met with Molther in late December 1739. Two issues divided these men. First, Molther contended that there are no degrees in faith and that no person has any degree of it before all things have become new. Wesley, for his part, maintained that a person may have some degree of faith before all things become new; before one has "the full assurance of faith." Second, Molther taught that the way to saving faith was to be "still," that is, not to use the means of grace such as attending church, receiving the Lord's Supper, fasting, praying, reading Scripture, and undertaking temporal and spiritual good. Wesley, in contrast, affirmed the importance of all these means of grace as conducive to the reception of (initially) sanctifying grace, that grace that makes one *holy*.

Tensions within the Fetter Lane society increased in the months ahead. Finally, on July 16, 1740, Wesley was actually prohibited from preaching at this society any longer. Frustrated with this turn of events, as well as with the larger issues entailed, Wesley issued an ultimatum at Fetter Lane four days later, at which point he, along with eighteen or nineteen others, mostly women, the Countess of Huntingdon among them, left the society and began to meet at the Foundery. In his ultimatum Wesley not only criticized the "stillness" of the society, as expected, but he also impugned the notion that justifying faith excludes all doubt and fear. That is, Wesley now understood that justifying (as well as regenerating) faith does not imply the full assurance of faith, as he had once mistakenly believed. This teaching, part of the inheritance that Wesley had received from the English Moravians, was appropriately put aside.

THE METHODIST INFRASTRUCTURE

Toward the end of 1739, eight or ten persons, who were deeply convinced of their sins, approached Wesley in London and desired that he would spend some time with them in prayer and advise them how they could "flee the wrath to come." This group became the first United Society, a structure that soon defined the Methodist movement. These societies, Wesley observed, were companies of people having the form and seeking the power of godliness.

To determine whether the members were indeed working out their own salvation, local Methodist societies was divided into smaller companies called "classes," which were composed of about twelve persons, one of whom was the leader. Although the only requirement to join a Methodist society was a "desire to flee the wrath to come," to *remain* in a class aspirants had to evidence their desire for salvation by adhering to the General Rules: (1) avoiding evil, (2) doing good, and (3) employing the means of grace. These same three rules, the first two of which form the basic precepts of natural law, emerged elsewhere in Wesley's writings, often in the context of repentance. Open, willful sinners, those who refused to repent and to forsake their unholy ways, were not tolerated in the Methodist classes, lest the entire body be corrupted.

Although it was impossible to be a part of a Methodist society and not be a member of a class, one did not have to participate in a "band," a more rigorous form of corporate discipleship. The bands, an inheritance from the Moravians, were distinguished from the Methodist classes in that they had no designated leaders. Because participation was restricted to persons who had at least some measure of the assurance of the forgiveness of sins, accountability and care was shared mutually, with Wesley offering some guidance in the form of the "Directions given to the Band Societies," composed in 1744. Although the classes and bands met separately, they were united at least once a quarter (as the "society") for the love feast, yet another Moravian contribution.

For those distinct members who continually walked in the light of God, Wesley created the "select society." Wesley hoped that this select gathering would provide a group of earnest and mature Christians to whom he "might unbosom [himself] on all occasions," and one that he could also offer as an example to others as a pattern of love, holiness, and good works. Because many of these members were on the threshold of Christian perfection, and were an example to both the classes and bands, Wesley maintained that they need not be encumbered with many rules, nor did they have any stated leader. This highest level of the Methodist infrastructure, then, reveals that as grace increases so too does responsible liberty.

If classes, bands, and select societies comprised the entirety of the structure of Methodism in eighteenth-century England, the movement would have been far less likely to clash as it did with the Anglican mother church. But, Wesley went beyond his pietist and Moravian colleagues in his extensive use of lay preachers (John Cennick, Joseph Humphries, and Thomas Maxfield among them), often referred to as "helpers," as well as a number of "assistants" who aided in the superintending of these preachers. Wesley justified the employment of such preachers by making a distinction between an "ordinary" call and an "extraordinary" one. The Church of England, however, did not see the matter quite this way. Several priests, and even a few bishops, repeatedly criticized the lay preachers for their lack of education and for their habit of violating parish boundaries. In 1744, Wesley organized these preachers into a Conference, seeking to insure that the substance of Methodism preached by these lay people was none other than the doctrines of repentance, faith, and holiness – that is, the porch of religion, the door, and then religion itself.

Employing the Methodist infrastructure to full effect, Wesley created the office of steward to raise money on behalf of the poor and to meet the expenses of the Methodist societies. With an eye on many of the social reforms practiced by Lutheran pietists at Halle, Wesley sought money from the rich for the poor, collected clothing on their behalf, established a medical dispensary, gave loans to those in need, visited the sick and dying, helped to provide housing for widows and orphans, supported education at the Kingswood school and elsewhere, preached against the dangers of riches, and wrote forcefully against the horrible institution of American slavery, "the vilest that ever saw the sun."

Drawing from both pietist and Moravian models, Methodism quickly became an evangelical order within the Church of England that was personally relevant, theologically focused, and socially active. In other words, Methodism from its inception was never intended to be a church, but a *reforming order* within the larger communion of faith. This purpose was clearly evident in Wesley's last sermon before Oxford University in 1744 entitled, "Scriptural Christianity." As such, Methodism required an environment of "catholicity" in which to function. This is one of the reasons why Wesley was so strongly opposed to separation from the Church of England. "But whenever the Methodists leave the Church," he warned, "God will leave them."[9] They will have the form of religion, but lack the power thereof.

TENSIONS WITH CALVINISTS

During the early days of the revival Wesley distinguished the Methodism under his leadership and care not only from Moravianism, but from Calvinism as well. Thus in April 1739, Wesley published the sermon *Free Grace*, to which his brother Charles appended a hymn on universal redemption. In these works, which helped to split the Bristol societies, the Wesleys criticized the notions, so dear to Calvinists, of unconditional election, irresistible grace, and the final perseverance of the saints. Naturally, both pieces upset Whitefield, who responded to these publications over a period of a year and a half. On September 25, 1740, for example, Whitefield wrote a letter in Boston that was eventually published in England under the title *The Perfectionist Examined*. Among other things, Whitefield accused Wesley of making salvation dependent not on God's free grace, but on human free will. Copies of this letter were distributed to Wesley's congregation at the Foundery on

---

[9] Sermon 112, *On Laying the Foundation of the New Chapel*, II.14, *Works*, 3:589.

February 1, 1741. After preaching on that day, Wesley noted from the pulpit that the letter was a private one, published without Whitefield's permission, and so Wesley told the congregation that he would do just what Mr. Whitefield would do; that is, tear up the letter, which Wesley proceeded to do and the congregation followed suit.

Upon learning that Wesley and his congregation had torn up his letter that championed Calvinist distinctives, Whitefield decided to publish a reply. The correspondence entitled *A Letter to the Rev. Mr. John Wesley in Answer to his Sermon entitled 'Free Grace'* was originally written on December 24, 1740, but did not emerge publicly – Whitefield at the time had not wanted to aggravate an already difficult situation – until March 31, 1741. A few days earlier, Wesley had visited Whitefield to see for himself if the reports of his increasingly unkind behavior were true. Sure enough, Whitefield now seemed hardened in his opposition. He told Wesley quite plainly that they preached "two different gospels" and that he, therefore, would not give Wesley "the right hand of fellowship." To make matters worse, Whitefield declared that he was resolved to preach against John and Charles Wesley whenever he preached at all.

The division caused by the publication of the sermon *Free Grace* eventually led to the organization of Lady Huntingdon's Connection, an association of Calvinist preachers, as well as to the founding of the Calvinistic Methodists in Wales. In fact, the controversy surrounding Whitefield and the Wesleys became so difficult and intense at points that even some of Wesley's early lay preachers, such as John Cennick and Joseph Humphreys, were persuaded to break ranks and to depart from their "father in the gospel." However, Howel Harris, noted for his great work of evangelism in Wales, played a mediating role between the two parties during 1741 and 1742, and this led to the re-establishment of friendship between Whitefield and Wesley. In 1748, the Wesleys, Harris, and Whitefield held a special conference to improve relations. The key question before them was "How far can we unite with each other?" Despite the good intentions, only little progress was made.

Meanwhile, James Hervey, a former student of Wesley's at Oxford, had decided to be more forthright concerning the truths of predestination, election, and imputation. To that end he drafted a work entitled *Theron and Aspasio* and asked Wesley for his comments. When Wesley returned the manuscript with his suggestions, Hervey encouraged him to be more free in his criticisms since he was a friend. Wesley complied, offering more serious objections, which deeply offended his former student. Among other things, Wesley suggested that some of Hervey's notions were not scriptural. He took particular exception to

Hervey's idea of imputation, as it could render believers content, even self-satisfied, without holiness. Deeply concerned, Wesley published a brief rebuttal in *A Preservative Against Unsettled Notions of Religion* in 1758, followed after Hervey's death by *Thoughts on the Imputed Righteousness of Christ* (1762).

Chaffing under Wesley's censure, Hervey wrote a number of private letters that were very critical of the views of his former teacher. As his health began to fail in 1758, Hervey had second thoughts about publishing this material. On his death bed, he specifically ordered his brother *not* to print these letters. Somehow a surreptitious edition of these letters appeared in 1764. Hervey's brother, William, noticed a number of errors in this edition that reflected badly on his brother James, and so violating his previous promise not to publish; he came forward with a "corrected" edition of the work the following year entitled *Eleven Letters from the late Rev. Mr. Hervey to the Rev. Mr. John Wesley; containing an Answer to that Gentleman's Remarks on Theron and Aspasio*. The sermon *The Lord Our Righteousness* was Wesley's quick response. In this piece, Wesley maintained that the work of Christ was the meritorious rather than the formal cause of salvation, a view that allowed for prevenience, free will, and universal redemption and which consequently undermined the Calvinist notions of predestination and irresistible grace. So significant was the publication of this sermon that Albert Outler used it to mark the beginning of the "later Wesley."

Wesley's relationship with the Calvinists took a turn for the worse when George Whitefield died in September 1770 at Newburyport, Massachusetts on his seventh preaching tour of the colonies. The trustees of the Tabernacle at Greenwich in England invited Wesley to preach the funeral sermon there on November 23rd of that year. Accepting this opportunity to praise his colleague in ministry, and perhaps also to put a good face on what had been at times a difficult relationship, Wesley chose as his text Numbers 23:10, "Let me die the death of the righteous, and let my end be like his." In the third part of his sermon Wesley underscored the fundamental doctrines that Whitefield had proclaimed, focusing on justification by faith and the new birth, while never mentioning the "eternal covenant" or absolute predestination. This omission naturally roiled Whitefield's Calvinist friends, planting the seeds for the fierce controversy that was soon to come.

At the Methodist Conference in August 1770, Wesley and his preachers concluded that they had leaned too much towards Calvinism. This observation had already been made in 1744, but now it was offered with more force and with even less guarded language in eight propositions. Lady Huntingdon, who was the patron of many of the Calvinist Methodists and who had also founded a college at Trevecca, referred to the published *Minutes* of the 1770 Conference as "popery unmasked." In January 1771, Lady Huntingdon dismissed Joseph Benson from Trevecca for what amounted to adherence to Wesley's "popish" views. The saintly John Fletcher, confidant of Wesley and president of the college, resigned in support of Benson, his protégé.

Somewhat surprised by the energy of the Calvinist reaction, in particular the criticism that he had received in the first half of 1771 at the hands of William Romaine in the *Gospel Magazine*, Wesley reviewed the whole affair in a letter to Mary Bishop that same year and concluded with respect to the infamous eight propositions that they contained truths of the deepest importance. Walter Shirley, a cousin of Selina Lady Huntingdon, was not convinced. Sensing that the Conference *Minutes* of 1770 evidenced a "dreadful heresy," Shirley issued a circular letter that proposed that a rival conference be held in August 1771, the same time as Wesley's upcoming meeting in Bristol. In addition, the letter recommended that the rival conference go as a body to Wesley's assembly and insist on a formal recantation of the *Minutes* of the previous year.

As promised, on August 8, 1771, Shirley and nine or ten others attended the conference at Bristol. In an irenic move, Wesley and his preachers issued what in Wesley's eyes was simply a clarifying statement, but in Shirley's eyes constituted a retraction of the earlier minutes. The statement quelled the flames of controversy for a time, and a letter was circulated (supposedly in Shirley's own hand) acknowledging that he had been too hasty in his judgment of Wesley's sentiments. But, all was not well. For no sooner had the ink fully dried on Wesley's declaration that he sent off John Fletcher's *Vindication* of the Minutes of 1770 for publication, notwithstanding Walter Shirley's earnest request not to do so. Fletcher, who at times was referred to as Wesley's "vindicator," had been associated with the father of Methodism for several years. So confident was Wesley in Fletcher's ability, in his carefully reasoned arguments, that he wrote to the Countess of Huntingdon less than a week after the 1771 Conference: "The principles established in the [1770] *Minutes* I apprehend to be no way contrary to this, or to that faith, that consistent plan of doctrine, which was once delivered to the saints. I believe, whoever calmly considers Mr. Fletcher's *Letters* will be convinced of this."[10] Fletcher's reply to the Calvinists in his *Checks to Antinomianism*, which brought Richard and Rowland Hill into the fray,

---

[10] Letter to the Countess of Huntingdon (14 Aug. 1771), *Letters* (Telford), 5:274.

convinced Wesley that he had finally found a suitable successor to lead the Methodists after he was gone. But, such an honor was not to be, for John Fletcher, who had suffered ill health from time to time, died about six years prior to John Wesley.

THE PERFECTIONIST CONTROVERSY

All along many Calvinists, George Whitefield included, had taken exception to Wesley's teaching on Christian Perfection. And those from the Reformed wing of the revival were well aware of the fanaticism of the likes of George Bell and Thomas Maxfield during the 1760s with respect to this important doctrine. Indeed, Wesley's example of preaching Christian perfection in a tempered and judicious way was unfortunately not followed by all of his preachers. Bell, for instance, who had been converted in 1758 and was subsequently associated with Thomas Maxfield and John Wesley at the Foundery, preached Christian perfection in London and peppered his sermons with screaming and wild gesticulations from the pulpit. His "perfection," if that's even the proper term, was frankly antinomian: free from rule, precept, and good judgment. Indeed, so fanatical was Bell that he actually believed he had a miraculous power to discern the spirits, and he sharply condemned his opponents – mistaking them for the enemies of God – on this basis. Hearing several disturbing reports, Wesley investigated the whole matter. After meeting with Mr. Bell in December 1762, and realizing that there would be no change in his behavior, Wesley expelled this ranting preacher from his leadership role in the London societies of West Street and the Foundery.

Thomas Maxfield was similarly caught up in this controversy. Susanna Wesley had originally recommended him to her son in 1740. Now, more than twenty years later, Wesley was no longer satisfied with Maxfield's ministry, in particular his deprecation of justification (teaching a justified person is not born of God) and his repudiation of instantaneous entire sanctification. In a stinging letter, drafted in October 1762, Wesley rebuked his erring disciple: "You have over and over denied instantaneous sanctification to *me*. But I have known and taught it (and so has my brother, as our writings show) above these twenty years."[11]

The Bell-Maxfield fiasco convinced Wesley that greater care and discipline had to be exercised in terms of what was preached from a Methodist pulpit. To that end, the Methodist Conference, which met in

---

[11] *Journal* (29 Oct. 1762), *Works*, 21:394.

1763 adopted the Model Deed and inserted it into the *Minutes*. This document was important for two reasons. First, it established a standard of doctrine for preachers in accordance with John Wesley's *Explanatory Notes upon the New Testament* and his four volumes of his *Sermons*. Second, the Deed created a line of succession, so to speak. That is, the right to appoint preachers after the deaths of John and Charles Wesley and William Grimshaw, a trusted associate, was guaranteed to the Conference. In this way Wesley hoped to bring greater order and stability to the ongoing life of Methodism.

THE AMERICAN, SCOTTISH, AND ENGLISH ORDINATIONS

In 1769, Wesley sent his first missionaries to America, Joseph Pilmore and Richard Boardman. Upon realizing that these preachers had departed from Methodist doctrine and discipline, Wesley sent Thomas Rankin to the colonies as his General Assistant in 1773 to bring about greater regulation and control.

Sensing that the pastoral need in America was great, Wesley was determined to act decisively, especially in terms of the ongoing indifference on the part of the Anglican hierarchy. Exercising the role of a bishop at the 1784 Conference, Wesley set apart Thomas Coke as superintendent by the imposition of hands and by prayer. Once in America, Thomas Coke, who brought a copy of Wesley's *Sunday Service* with him, had instructions to consecrate Francis Asbury as general superintendent, a ceremony which took place at the Christmas Conference of 1784, the founding conference of The Methodist Episcopal Church. Beyond this, Wesley ordained Richard Whatcoat and Thomas Vasey as elders to foster the work of the Methodists in America. In justification of these irregular actions, Wesley claimed he knew himself to be as much a bishop as the Archbishop of Canterbury. His brother Charles, however, was not impressed.

Although Wesley repeatedly affirmed that he had no desire for Methodism to leave the Church of England, he was realistic enough to prepare for just such a possibility. Indeed, the Deed of Declaration in 1784 must not be viewed simply as the way in which Wesley provided for the institutional structure of Methodism beyond his death, but must also be seen as a structure which could, if necessary, provide order for Methodism independent of the mother church. Among other things, the Deed of Declaration defined the Methodist Conference for the Trust Deeds, established a connection throughout England, appointed a hundred preachers as the legal Conference (thereby providing the basis for future annual Conferences), and laid down guidelines for the reception of preachers into full connection.

Emboldened by his American ordinations, Wesley began to consecrate ministers for Scotland in 1785. Wesley justified this action by noting that the Church of England was not the established church in that land. But, Wesley did not stop there. Having ordained for America and now for Scotland, he finally crossed the Rubicon, so to speak, in 1788, and set apart ministers for work in England itself. Thus, Alexander Mather was ordained deacon and presbyter on August 6 and August 7, respectively. And, in a similar fashion, Henry Moore and Thomas Rankin were ordained the following year on February 26 and 27. Indeed, by the end of his career, Wesley had actually ordained more than twenty-five ministers for work in Scotland, England, America, and even for such places as Nova Scotia, Newfoundland, and the West Indies. That Wesley was not censured for such action by his own church indicates something of the lax and indulgent standards of the time. If he had been called to task, Wesley would likely have replied that the work of the gospel necessitated such actions, that it was far better to send in laborers to the field than to watch the harvest rot on the ground.

WESLEY'S LEGACY

Shortly before his death, holding together once again the importance of both personal and social ministry, Wesley wrote to William Wilberforce, who was a member of Parliament at the time, and urged him to continue his reforming, abolitionist efforts: "O be not weary of well doing! Go on, in the name of God and in the power of His might, till even American slavery (the vilest that ever saw the sun) shall vanish away before it."[12] A few years earlier, Wesley had corresponded with Granville Sharp, who had founded a society for abolition of slavery in 1787, and noted that "ever since I heard of it...I felt a perfect detestation of the horrid slave trade, but more particularly since I had the pleasure of reading what you have published upon the subject."[13] The substance of Methodism expressed in these reforming efforts consisted in the realization that loving one's neighbor, especially the oppressed, was one of the very best ways to demonstrate the love of God.

[12] Letter to William Wilberforce (24 Feb. 1791), *Letters* (Telford), 8:265.
[13] Letter to Granville Sharp (11 Oct. 1787), *Letters* (Telford), 8:17.

Leaving behind nearly 75,000 Methodists in England, Scotland, Wales, and Ireland; having traveled over 250,000 miles in ministry, and having preached more than 40,000 sermons that displayed the hope and promise of scriptural Christianity; John Wesley died in his 88th year on March 2, 1791, in London, exclaiming to the faithful beside his bed a truth that had characterized his entire ministry, "The best of all is, God is with us!"

3 Wesley in context

DAVID N. HEMPTON

The civil wars and constitutional dislocations of the mid-seventeenth century exercised an enduring influence over British politics and religion from which neither John Wesley nor his progenitors were exempt. Wesley's great grandfather (Bartholomew Westley) and grandfather (John Westley) were victims of the great ejection of nonconforming clergy in 1662; his father Samuel was an ex-Dissenter turned "high church" Anglican priest; and his mother Susanna, the daughter of an eminent Dissenting minister, also turned tables when she became a "high church" Anglican with thinly disguised Jacobite sympathies. Although both of John Wesley's parents were high church Tories, they fell out over William, Prince of Orange's legitimacy as king, which his father accepted and his mother rejected.[1] The seriousness of their disagreement, which was anything but a mere marital spat, indicates how profoundly divided Anglicans were over their increasingly incompatible devotion to divine right monarchy on the one hand and their hostility to Roman Catholicism on the other. The Catholicism of the later Stuart monarchs forced Anglicans to make a most unwelcome choice, which could bifurcate consciences, friends, and families.

In this way, the vicissitudes of the Stuart dynasty played out in family squabbles within the Wesley household – with its large number of children, variously estimated between seventeen and nineteen, the great majority female. Most scholars agree that whereas John Wesley's father Samuel was impetuous, theatrical, and a poor manager, his mother Susanna had remarkable powers of organization and resilience as she coped with near annual pregnancies, crippling debts (Samuel was once imprisoned for debt), and the child-rearing demands of a large and talented family. Both parents had high, if sometimes competing, ideals

---

[1] For fuller treatment of Wesley's family tree in rich religious and political context, see Henry D. Rack, *Reasonable Enthusiast*.

for parish ministry and of the usefulness of religious societies, including the Society for the Promotion of Christian Knowledge formed in 1698 and local Anglican parish societies for promoting a more disciplined piety within the Church of England. In short, John Wesley and his younger brother Charles inherited a family tradition with deep roots in both Puritanism and high church Anglicanism, grew up in a family where the strongest influences were female, and lived in a household poised uneasily between gentlemanly privileges and incipient poverty. These assorted shapers and tensions deeply affected John's life in his various capacities as son and brother, Anglican priest, itinerant evangelist, Methodist founder, authoritarian leader, unsuccessful husband, prickly controversialist, energetic educator, facilitator of female leadership, and relentless activist and disciplinarian.[2]

Unsurprisingly for someone from such a rich lineage of ambiguity and controversy, both John Wesley's public and private life and the wider impact of Methodism on eighteenth-century British religion and society have been subjects of keen debate. In fact, setting Wesley in his context is a surprisingly controversial task. I propose to look at these debates within the framework of five of the most hotly debated controversies about Wesleyan Methodism's impact on British society in the long eighteenth century: What was the relationship between Wesley's Methodism and the Anglican Established Church within which it took root? How did John Wesley and Methodism relate to eighteenth-century popular culture? What were Wesley's economic views and how did they shape the economic behavior of his followers? What were John Wesley's political views and how did they shape Methodist political culture? And finally, what truth, if any, is there in Élie Halévy's well-known thesis that Methodism helped save Britain from revolution?[3]

Before turning to these important questions, it is good to be reminded about the strength, geographical distribution, gender proportions, and occupational structure of the Methodist movement by the end of the eighteenth century. Although Methodist growth rates between 1740 and 1840 were remarkable, the Methodist membership (as defined

---

[2] For an expert delineation of John Wesley's early life and the formation of Methodism, see Richard P. Heitzenrater, *Wesley and the People Called Methodists*. For his relationship to his brother Charles Wesley, see John R. Tyson, *Assist Me to Proclaim: The Life and Hymns of Charles Wesley* (2007).

[3] Some of these questions, and others, are dealt with more comprehensively in David Hempton, *The Religion of the People: Methodism and Popular Religion c. 1750–1900* (1996).

by those with class tickets) in the British Isles was only just over 70,000 when John Wesley died in 1791 (56,605 in England), and it never accounted for more than 5 percent of the total English population. Historians conventionally multiply Methodist membership numbers by a factor of around three to discover the number of adherents or loose followers, but, even after that computation is made, Methodists never comprised anything other than a substantial religious minority of the total English population. In terms of gender, the history of Methodism, as with many other religious traditions, is also a history of female preponderance. Extensive surveys of Methodist membership lists before 1830 (some 80,361 members) has shown a female mean of 57.7 percent. Although this percentage varied considerably from one circuit to another, it was remarkably consistent over time and from region to region, and reflects a larger female preponderance than was true of the population as a whole.

In terms of geographical location, by the end of the eighteenth century Methodism had been particularly successful in the emerging manufacturing regions of the north-east, the north Midlands, the West Riding of Yorkshire, and the Potteries. It was strong too in mining areas (especially Cornwall), in seaports and fishing villages, and in those rural areas where the social control of Anglican squires and parsons was weakest. As England's industrial pace quickened in the early nineteenth century, Methodism grew quickly in factory villages and areas in which economic expansion attracted a migratory labor force. It is, however, too easily forgotten that Methodism also thrived in rural areas, especially where the Anglican parochial structure was weakest and where arable farming was practiced. By the time of the Census of Religious Worship in 1851, which allows for more statistical precision, Methodists were found in greatest numbers in the counties of Cornwall, Yorkshire, Lincolnshire, Derbyshire, Durham, and Nottinghamshire. Finally, in terms of social structure, class, and occupations Methodism made little impact on those at the top and very bottom of the social scale: the aristocracy, landed gentry, professional classes, wealthier trading communities, unskilled laborers, and paupers. Its greatest gains were among artisans, craftsmen, small farmers, miners, sailors, and soldiers. With this social context in mind, it is now time to turn to the five questions identified earlier.

WESLEY'S METHODISM AND THE CHURCH OF ENGLAND

As is well known, John Wesley lived and died within the Established Church, and maintained a profound veneration for its forms, liturgies, and doctrines throughout his life.[4] It was, after all, as an Anglican society that Methodism was first launched and sustained. Indeed, Wesley's conception of Methodism was extremely simple: "The official devotional system of the Church was to be supplemented by a network of private religious societies; revitalizing cells which would regenerate the Church from within," and equip it to be a more effective," instrument for reclaiming the irreligious and the unchurched.[5] In brief, Wesley wanted to reform the Church to make it more effective, not erode the Church to make it more vulnerable. It is nevertheless clear from his actions that by engaging in field preaching, practicing extempore prayer and house communions, disregarding parochial boundaries, and effectively disobeying Episcopal injunctions, Wesley effectively separated himself from the ecclesiastical discipline and regular routines of the Church.[6] In truth, Wesley's support of the Church of England was always more impressive in thought than in deed, and was neither static nor entirely unconditional. Indeed, there is a profound ambiguity at the heart of his opinions on religious establishments. On the one hand, he valued the ecclesiastical discipline, historical traditions (including the writings of the great Anglican churchmen), and social utility of the Church of England, whereas on the other, he regarded state patronage of religion as one of the "mysteries of iniquity" that destroyed the spirituality of the early church. The greatest blow against "the whole essence of true religion" he wrote, "was struck in the fourth century by Constantine the Great, when he called himself a Christian, and poured in a flood of riches, honours, and power upon the Christians; more especially upon the clergy."[7] The connection between establishment, wealth, and corruption was never far from Wesley's mind and he reserved his severest remarks for those "indolent, pleasure-taking, money-loving, praise-loving, preferment-seeking clergymen" whom he regarded "as the pests of the Christian world; a stink in the nostrils of God."[8] To overcome the inconvenience of devotion to the Established Church while disapproving of many of its bishops and priests, Wesley stated that the essence of the church was to be found in its articles and homilies, not in its personnel. Consequently, he rejected the divine right of episcopacy as a Tudor innovation and the doctrine of apostolic succession as historically unsustainable. His

---

4 See Frank Baker, *John Wesley and the Church of England*.
5 John Walsh, *John Wesley 1703–1791: A Bicentennial Tribute* (1993), 5.
6 W. M. Jacob, "John Wesley and the Church of England, 1736–40," *Bulletin of the John Rylands University Library of Manchester* 85.2 (2003): 57–71.
7 Sermon 61, "The Mystery of Iniquity," §27, *Works*, 2:462–63.
8 Sermon 125, "On a Single Eye," II.5, *Works*, 4:128.

defense of Anglicanism was, therefore, essentially devotional and pragmatic, leading one scholar to the conclusion that Wesley was "a rebel
in thought as well as in action, and only a sleepy, loosely disciplined
Church would have tolerated his shock tactics so long."[9]

Because Wesley viewed the Church of England as primarily an instrument of the gospel to redeem humankind, not a divine right institution of state to reinforce privilege, he worked out quite early on what
his sticking point would be if ecclesiastical discipline was used against
his nascent Methodist movement. In 1755, he told the Cornish evangelical, Samuel Walker, that he meant no separation from the Church,
but, if the Church interfered with itinerant preaching, extempore prayer,
Methodist societies, or lay-preaching, he would have no alternative but
to move out and accept the consequences. Henry Rack has suggested
that whereas Charles Wesley's self-declared "chief concern on earth was
the prosperity of the Church of England; my next, that of the Methodists;
my third, that of the preachers," his brother's priorities were almost the
reverse.[10] For John Wesley, the cause of vital religion and the need to sus-
tain his mission of holiness took precedence over the laws, forms, and
discipline of the Church of England. He was, nevertheless, constantly
aware that Methodist connexionalism might easily degenerate into con-
gregationalism and that the Anglican underpinning of the English state
was much better than no religious establishment at all, so he used
Methodism's position within the Church as a way of maintaining discipline, avoiding the legal disabilities of Dissent, and keeping out of trou-
ble. His pragmatic advice to his followers was to continue to pay their
tithes and church rates, attend on Anglican services and sacraments, and
avoid needless controversies.

Such an ambiguous position did not always sit well with Anglican
bishops and clergy or with the Anglican justices of the peace in the
English localities. Nor did it always grant Methodists protection from
the license of the mob. But, it worked tolerably well at least until the
1780s, when Wesley began to take steps that would soon make it impossible for the majority of Methodists across the North Atlantic region to
remain within the communion of the Anglican Church. The fact that
an erstwhile Oxford high churchman like Wesley could bring himself,
as a mere priest, to ordain preachers for America and Scotland in 1784–
85 (much to the chagrin of his brother Charles) shows how far he was
prepared to break the rules of the Church to fulfill his mission.

[9] Maldwyn Edwards, "John Wesley," in Rupert Davies and Gordon Rupp, eds., *A History
of the Methodist Church in Great Britain*, vol. 1 (1965), 71–72.
[10] Rack, *Reasonable Enthusiast*, 302.

Wesley's typically pragmatic acceptance of the fact that the American Revolution had effectively sundered Methodist connections to colonial Anglicanism forced the pace of separation between Methodism and Anglicanism in the United States. The equivalent separation in England had to wait until after Wesley's death, when the Plan of Pacification (1795) and the Form of Discipline (1797) supplied the necessary foundations for Methodism to emerge as an independent religious tradition outside the confines of, if not explicitly hostile to, the Established Church.

Given Wesley's driving ambition to spread scriptural holiness across the land and his willingness to play fast and loose with Anglican forms and discipline, it was perhaps inevitable that Wesley's Methodism would separate from the institution that hosted its early growth and development. Wesley's flouting of the rules and the Anglican Church's fear of populist enthusiasm made it difficult for Methodism to operate forever as a mere religious society within the Church of England. It is of course possible to conceive of other outcomes than eventual separation, but, given the realities of English social and political life in the eighteenth century, separation was the most likely scenario. Anglican bishops more often feared Methodism's capacity for ecclesiastical indiscipline than admired its potential for revitalizing the Church. In that regard, John Walsh has drawn attention to an essay by Macaulay on Ranke's *Popes* in which he stated that if Wesley had been a Roman Catholic the church would have known how to use his energies as it did those of Francis Xavier and Ignatius of Loyola, perhaps to found a great preaching order, whereas if Loyola had been Anglican he would inevitably have become the "head of a formidable secession."[11] This playful inversion of ecclesiastical traditions contains just enough truth to illustrate how the Church of England was as much frustrated by one of its most enthusiastic but errant sons as he was by it.

WESLEY, METHODISM, AND POPULAR CULTURE

The debates about the relationship between Methodism and popular culture have operated around two main propositions. The first is that Wesley, as an Oxford educated scholar/priest and as a field-preaching enthusiast, was uniquely able to build a bridge across the chasm between elite and popular culture. The second is that Methodism, as a recrudescence of populist Puritanism, was at loggerheads with those aspects of English popular culture that operated around alehouses, blood

---

[11] Walsh, *John Wesley*, 4–5.

sports, rough music, sexual bawdiness, and traditional festivals. Each proposition is more complicated than it first appears. In support of the first, E. P. Thompson, the great Marxist hammer of Methodism, described "the true character of Wesleyanism as explicitly a movement of counter-enlightenment" in which Wesley reaffirmed scores of superstitions, among which were "bibliomancy, old wives' medical remedies, the casting of lots, the belief in diabolical possession and in exorcism by prayer, in the hand of providence, in the punishment (by lightning-stroke, or epilepsy, or cholera) of ill-livers and reprobates."[12] In this scheme, it was Wesley's capacity to match Methodist superstition with the superstitions of the English lower classes that allowed Methodism to make such fast gains among them. This perspective has received some recent support from John Kent, who suggests that Methodism grew because it successfully tapped into a pre-existing tradition of "primary religion" from which urbane Anglicanism had already distanced itself.[13] Wesley was, therefore, largely a credulous and overbearing enthusiast whose devotion to biblicism and perfectionism shielded him from practical realities even in his own life. Ironically, there is now an equally lively tradition of scholarship interpreting Wesley as a son of the Enlightenment, which only goes to show what a complex figure he was.

The second proposition that Methodism was a populist puritan movement seeking to reform English morals as well as revive its religion also has some plausibility, especially as Wesley's desire to spread scriptural holiness was appropriately holistic in its aspiration. One of the many intriguing aspects of this topic is the gap that exists between some of the anti-Methodist rhetoric of the eighteenth century and the conclusions of modern historians. For example, early Methodism was frequently viewed as a religious cloak for sexual orgies. Methodist love-feasts, holy kisses, spiritual trances, and private meetings at night were easily misunderstood, but there were also allegations of pre nuptial fornication, bastardy, debauching of maids (even against Wesley himself), and of sexually active preachers on the move. Only a fraction of such allegations yielded enough evidence for prosecutions in church courts or quarter sessions, but the rumors were sufficiently persistent to create a receptive climate of anti-Methodist opinion in small communities. One sworn affidavit can stand for all:

> That at some Meeting he hath known & been present when
> woman [sic] have been taken from the Rooms where they

---

[12] E. P. Thompson, "Anthropology and the Discipline of Historical Context," *Midland History* 1, no. 3 (1972): 41–55.
[13] John Kent, *Wesley and the Wesleyans* (2002).

met & carried them into Bedchambers & thrown upon Beds
where they have lain in fits or swoons, & the preacher has cried
at the same time that they should let them alone for the Spirit
was entring them. And that he hath known several of them
leave their Work & labour by which they & their Family where
[sic] to be supported to attend the runnagate preachers, & that in
the Yard many of them have drawn Workmen from their Labour
to preach to them to the great Hindrance of the King's Works.
That he hath frequently himself contributed to their Collection
but knows not how the Money is disposed of.[14]

As well as allegations of appropriating money for undeclared and scur-
rilous purposes, rumors abounded of Methodists inducing madness and
displays of paranormal behavior, of practicing witchcraft and cunning
arts, of maliciously circulating prophecies of misfortune, and of inducing miscarriages and serious illnesses. Most rumors, as seems to be the
case with many new religious movements, concentrated on four main
areas: exclusivity and community fragmentation, hypocrisy and sexual
irregularities, maladministration of money and widespread corruption,
and the erosion of traditional values by introducing new and more rigorous standards of behavior. Although Methodism was viewed from one
perspective as a succession of highly charged sexual encounters, it was
more realistically feared as a revival of religious enthusiasm militating
against a consensual and convivial village culture (insofar as such a rosy
picture of village life ever really existed). Nevertheless, pretending to be
better than other people and driving a wedge between the "saved" and
the "lost" were criticisms of Methodism that survived in rural communities at least until the end of the nineteenth century.

Methodism's relationship to popular culture was clearly complex
and multi faceted. There is no doubt that in its strict disciplines and
condemnation of some of the more lewd and licentious aspects of
eighteenth-century life, Methodism was perceived to be a threat to traditional customs and values, but as Thompson and others have pointed
out, Methodism did not so much replace ancient folk beliefs and customs as it helped translate them into new and more acceptable kinds of
religious idioms. Methodism was neither at war with all aspects of popular beliefs and customs nor did it tamely adapt to conventional social
norms. By establishing standards of behavior appropriate for redeemed

---

[14] O. A. Beckerlegge, "The Lavington Correspondence," *Proceedings of the Wesley Historical Society* 42 (1980): 145.

and serious people, Wesley and his followers cut across many aspects of popular culture, which of course made Methodism more appealing for some, but also much less appealing for many others.

WESLEY'S ECONOMIC VIEWS AND METHODIST WORK DISCIPLINE

Most interpretations of Wesley's economic teaching have drawn attention to his emphasis on thrift and hard work. It has been suggested that Methodist discipline and acquisitiveness were symbiotically linked to the early development of industrial capitalism. Wesley and his followers are thus portrayed as exemplars of the Protestant ethic as described by Max Weber. Whatever the validity of these ideas in a more general sense, they do not accurately reflect Wesley's own teaching on economic matters, which was scarcely a model of acquisitive capitalism. After providing for necessities, Wesley repeatedly urged Methodists to give away the rest, otherwise they would be guilty of robbing God and the poor, corrupting their own souls, wronging the widow and the fatherless, and of making themselves accountable for the good they chose not to do. In addition, Wesley encouraged his followers to think nothing of the future, to demand no more than a fair price, and to make sure that their children were not burdened with excessive inherited wealth. He also experimented briefly with the primitive church's practice of the community of goods, until he discovered that Christian fellowship was no match for personal acquisitiveness. He was then forced to retreat into the medieval solution of voluntary poverty for a self-denying spiritual elite. Even so, his sermons never lost their anti-materialistic urgency as he viewed with dismay evidence of Methodism's upward spiritual mobility and its effects on the pursuit of holiness.

Wesley's challenging teaching to his followers on the spiritual dangers of acquisitiveness and conspicuous consumption was carried over into his general attitudes to economy and society in eighteenth-century England. He was a remorseless critic of the theatrical materialism of the rich and railed against luxury, waste, and the evils of inherited wealth. He also repudiated Adam Smith's view that surplus accumulation was the foundation of economic well-being. Wesley's intensely ethical and biblicist stance, combined with the conviction that all great spiritual movements in the history of the church surged from the poor, made him impatient with the manners and ideals of Britain's emerging consumer society. Wesley's disdain for the values of England's social elite grew only more marked as he got older. In general, he found it "much more comfortable to address the masses than win the souls of his social superiors."[15]

If Wesley's economic teaching cannot be matched too neatly with Weber's views about the Protestant ethic, a similar point could be made about the relationship between Methodism and work in the eighteenth century. Under the influence of E. P. Thompson's *Making of the English Working Class*, it has become axiomatic to assume that Methodism was the inculcator of a fierce work discipline among its converts. Yet, as John Walsh has shown, nothing was more ubiquitous in eighteenth-century anti-Methodist literature than the idea that Methodism was "the bane of industry." To support this allegation, critics of Methodism drew attention to the economically disrupting effects of field preaching, "sermon gadding," and various intense religious exercises. Similarly, Methodist emphases on faith, hope, and charity were not regarded as firm foundations for economic productivity. Although there is plenty of evidence to suggest that Methodism's emphasis on the disciplined life brought many of its converts within range of moderate prosperity, it is good to be reminded that the movement's charismatic enthusiasm also contained economically disruptive elements, which were noted more often by contemporaries than they are by social historians.[16]

WESLEY'S POLITICAL THEOLOGY AND METHODIST POLITICAL CULTURE

In an important book called *English Society 1688–1832*, Jonathan Clark has made a stimulating attempt to place John Wesley's theological and political views in their eighteenth-century context.[17] As part of his wider scheme of presenting eighteenth-century English society as largely pre-industrial, hierarchic, aristocratic, and confessional, he suggests that Wesley inherited almost intact the political theology of mainstream Anglicanism. As against those who regard Wesleyan Methodism as an essentially liberal, egalitarian, or progressive movement helping to usher in a new kind of society, Clark draws attention to Wesley's belief that God, not the people, was the origin and sustainer of all civil power and that obedience to the king was the mandatory responsibility of all subjects of Britain and her colonies. There is certainly some merit

[15] Nigel Aston, "John Wesley and the Social Elite of Georgian Britain, *Bulletin of the John Rylands University Library of Manchester* 85.2 (2003): 123–36.
[16] John Walsh, "'The Bane of Industry'? Popular Evangelicalism and Work in the Eighteenth Century'" *Studies in Church History* 37 (2003): 223–42.
[17] J. C. D. Clark, *English Society 1688–1832*.

in these arguments. Not only did Wesley inherit a strong Tory tradition from his parents, who were nevertheless divided on the legitimacy of the Hanoverian regime, but he clearly flirted with Jacobitism (later vigorously denied) in his early Oxford days and in the surprisingly Jacobite circles in which some of the early leaders of the evangelical revival were located. Wesley kept up his Jacobite sentiment far down the eighteenth century and united it with country-party principles to form a wide-ranging critique of British government and society, especially in the years of Robert Walpole's premiership (1721–42), when it seemed that the nation's Church and morality were being subjected to the mere whims of Whig party advantage.[18] As with many erstwhile Jacobites, Wesley slowly made his peace with the Hanoverian regime (as his father had done), largely because he came to believe that the Glorious Revolution of 1689 had ushered in an unprecedented era of civil and religious liberty. By the 1770s, Wesley had come to the conclusion that the threat to those liberties came not from king or parliament, but from radicals, mobs, miscreants, and misguided patriots. That is the main reason for Wesley's increased output of political writings in the 1770s.

In that decade, John Wesley, who mostly urged his followers to avoid political issues, published a range of opinions on controversial issues that helped chart the political course for his followers over the next half century and beyond. In 1772, he published *Thoughts Upon Liberty*, in which he criticized John Wilkes and the bawdy, ale-house tradition of metropolitan radicalism; in 1773, he published *Thoughts on the Scarcity of Provisions*, which was a vigorous attack on the greed and waste of the rich; in 1774, he published *Thoughts Upon Slavery*, which was a comprehensive attack on slavery and the slave trade based heavily on the work of the Quaker abolitionist, Anthony Benezet; in 1775, he published his *Thoughts on the American Colonies*, which was largely plagiarized from Samuel Johnson and, therefore, shared his view about the illegitimacy of the American cause; and, in 1780, he wrote "A Letter to the Printer of the *Public Advertiser* occasioned by the Late Act Passed in Favour of Popery," in which he defended a publication of Lord George Gordon's Protestant Association against the Catholic Relief Act of 1778.[19] Throughout this decade, Wesley, as an elderly man who suffered bouts of serious illness, was also preoccupied with securing the future of Methodism by protecting its distinctive connectional structure and itinerant ministry.

---

[18] W. R. Ward, *The Protestant Evangelical Awakening*, 300.

[19] For a more extensive treatment of John Wesley's political attitudes than is possible here see David Hempton, *Methodism and Politics in British Society 1750–1850* (1984), 20–54.

In a nutshell, by the 1770s, Wesley had set the Methodist political compass to point to anti-radicalism, anti-materialism, antislavery,
anti-Catholicism, anti-corruption, and anti theological heterodoxy, all
laced with a strong emphasis on Methodism's need to establish itself
as a self-organizing religious movement independent of coercion from
Church and State. He wanted more tolerance for his own movement
and less political freedoms for some others, especially Roman Catholics
(although he was not against *religious tolerance* for Catholics); he
enjoined obedience to the established order, but hated the conspicuous
consumption of the rich at the top of English society; and he opposed
slavery but spoke against the wider political mobilization of his movement lest it become deflected from its religious mission, which was his
top priority. Above all, he wanted to spread scriptural holiness across the
land, and to other lands for that matter, without restrictions imposed by
governments, churches, or local officials.

As this list of writings and positions makes clear, Wesley wanted
to urge his followers away from political partisanship and disaffection,
but he also saw no incongruity between that stance and his willingness
to speak out on a whole range of moral and religious issues, which had
political ramifications. One important issue that attracted his attention,
and the eventual support of large numbers of Methodists, was slavery.
Wesley, who had encountered some of the baleful effects of slavery during
his time in North America in 1735–37, issued *Thoughts Upon Slavery*
in 1774, the remarkable ethical dimensions of which are discussed in
another chapter.

In terms of the dissemination of antislavery ideas, however, not
much was achieved within Methodism between the publication of
Wesley's pamphlet in 1774 and 1787. At first, it looked as if Wesley's
pronounced antislavery views would determine the future policy not
only of the British but also the American branch of Methodism. But, the
decade of the 1780s witnessed a slow retreat in North America from an
absolutist position to one that took pragmatic account of evangelistic
exigencies and southern sensibilities.[20] In Britain, the widely dissemi-
nated Methodist periodical the *Arminian Magazine* was largely silent on
the issue of slavery. But the formation of the Society for the Abolition
of the Slave Trade in May 1787 led to another gear shift in Methodist
mobilization. Given Wesley's traditional hostility to pressure from without, it was no small step for him when he wrote to Granville Sharp

---

[20] For an excellent account of how and why American Methodism, especially in the
South, slowly capitulated to an acceptance of slavery see Cynthia Lynn Lyerly, *Methodism and the Southern Mind 1770–1810* (1998).

supporting the new society, and he quickly re-issued his *Thoughts Upon Slavery*. In 1788, the volume of antislavery materials in the *Arminian Magazine* increased. In April and May, the resolutions of the Society for the Abolition of the Slave Trade were published; in July and August, Wesley printed "A Summary View of the Slave Trade"; and, in October and November, Hannah More's influential poem against slavery was reproduced. Only days before he died, John Wesley, in a letter charged with emotion and with the gravity of age, gave his paternal blessing to a youthful Wilberforce's campaign against "that execrable villany, which is the scandal of religion, of England, and of human nature," hoping even that "American slavery (the vilest that ever saw the sun)" would vanish in due course.[21]

With the Wesley brothers gone, but the Methodist movement now the fastest growing religious tradition in the transatlantic world, the obvious question is what would happen to the Methodist commitment against slavery. At first sight it seemed that it would be business as usual. The year after Wesley died, one of his closest preachers, Samuel Bradburn, published *An Address to the People Called Methodists; Concerning the Wickedness of Encouraging Slavery*.[22] Bradburn's pamphlet – revealingly published not in London but in Manchester, which was the great early center of artisan antislavery activity – had two principal effects. Urging a sugar boycott helped mobilize Methodist women who were the custodians of domestic supplies, and helped align Methodist antislavery sentiment with the rising tide of artisan radicalism in the industrializing districts of England in the early 1790s. But, this was dangerous territory for the Methodists. Not only was Methodism experiencing bitter internal disputes about how quickly and how completely it should move away from the shelter of the Anglican Established Church now that its founder was dead, but also the itinerant preaching privileges of Methodists could not be guaranteed in a period of life-or-death warfare against not just France, but the very principles of the French Revolution.

As Methodism settled into a lengthy battle to secure its own right to exist in a period of national warfare, culminating in a Methodist-inspired new Toleration Act passed in 1812, the antislavery momentum within the connection that had built up in the years 1787–92 went into apparent decline. But, appearances can be deceptive. Beneath the surface of print,

[21] Wesley, Letter to William Wilberforce (24 Feb. 1791), *Letters* (Telford), 8:264–65.
[22] Samuel Bradburn, *An Address to the People Called Methodists; Concerning the Wickedness of Encouraging Slavery* (Manchester: T. Harper, 1792). This text is reproduced in Irv A. Brendlinger, *Social Justice Through the Eyes of Wesley: John Wesley's Theological Challenge to Slavery* (2006), 201–23.

preaching, and politics were at least five slow-burning fuses that had the capacity to ignite a subsequent Methodist mobilization against slavery: These fuses were the slow politicization of women who had taken a lead in the sugar boycott in the 1790s; the rapid growth of interdenominational and Methodist Sunday Schools which spread literacy among the English working classes; the *de facto* separation of Methodism from the Church of England in 1795, which further eroded Methodism's filial debt to the established order; the continued expansion of Methodist missions, especially in the Caribbean Islands; and, despite official resistance, the participation of Methodists in many of the radical causes of the early nineteenth century. According to recent calculations, during the high water mark of petitioning against slavery in British society in 1832–33 Methodists accounted for about 80 percent of all Nonconformist signatures, with over 95 percent of all Wesleyan Methodists signing petitions against slavery. This proportion was the highest by far of any English religious denomination and pays tribute to the importance of John Wesley's antislavery convictions. Perhaps less nobly, but also a reflection of John Wesley's political theology, English and Irish Methodists were also at the forefront of petitioning against Roman Catholic emancipation in the early nineteenth century. African slaves, it seems, were more the subject of Wesleyan compassions than British and Irish Roman Catholics.

THE HALÉVY THESIS

According to the great French historian Élie Halévy, early industrial England, by comparison with its European neighbors, possessed an unusual and potentially volatile degree of political, economic, and religious freedom that could easily erode the stability of the British state.[23] In Europe's most advanced industrial and capitalist society, structural pressures such as those that occasioned the French Revolution had the capacity to undermine social order and promote anarchy. What saved the day in Britain according to Halévy was a remarkable resurgence of popular Puritanism in the shape of the evangelical and Methodist revivals. Methodism was thus the antidote to the revolutionary Jacobinism that undermined the *ancien régime* in France and "the free organization of the sects was the foundation of social order in England." Social order was secured in two ways. The first was the forging of a rough harmony of values between the moralistic religion of the middle classes and that of the skilled and respectable sections of the English working classes who were

[23] See Élie Halévy, *The Birth of Methodism in England* (1971).

notorious in Europe for their solid virtue and capacity for organization. The second was the way in which the English Established Church "left the sects outside her borders entire liberty of organization, full power to form a host of little states within the state." Hence evangelicalism in general, and Methodism in particular, gave rise to a large number of religious societies and associations that worked for the reformation of society not primarily by revolutionary action, but by the power of voluntary effort and disciplined religious enthusiasm. Moreover, new religious traditions displayed a capacity to separate from the Established Church, and then from one another, in a peaceful and disciplined way. In this way, English freedoms were secured by the proliferation of communities of grace which inculcated discipline, respect, and organizational ability among their members.

There is now an almost general agreement among historians that although Methodism made an important contribution to the stability of the British state in the era of the French Revolution, Halévy probably exaggerated the potential fragility of England's *ancien régime* and the power of Methodism to save it from collapse. Even under the pressures of costly wars with America and France the British state did not experience a debilitating financial crisis (as did the French state), its government did not lose control over the instruments of power, its social structure did not collapse under the pressure of urbanization and industrialization, and its dissidents and radicals either never abandoned reformist strategies or were unable to mobilize violent resistance on a sufficiently threatening scale. There were of course some creaky moments when famine undermined patriotism in the mid-1790s, or when economic crises fueled popular discontent after the end of the war with France in 1815, or when the pace of political reform seemed too slow (as in the Reform Bill crisis of 1831–32), but overall the British state proved surprisingly resilient in ways than cannot be attributed solely to the success of popular evangelicalism.

Even if one can agree that Methodism alone did not save British society from undergoing the kind of revolutionary changes experienced by some of its European neighbors, the Halévy thesis has nevertheless remained influential for historians trying to estimate Methodism's impact on British society in the era of the French and industrial revolutions. In the year of Halévy's death, Robert Wearmouth published his *Methodism and the Working Class Movements of England 1800–1850* (1937) in which he offered support to Halévy's thesis by showing that Methodism trained very large numbers of the working classes in the arts of leadership and also modeled, through its organizational structures, a disciplined movement that was later imitated by radical reformers. In this way both Methodist leaders and Methodist organizational techniques supplied the English working classes with the kind of solid disciplines and respect for the law that Halévy so much admired in them.

Another son of the Methodist tradition whose work bears on the viability of the Halévy thesis is E. P. Thompson, whose *Making of the English Working Class* contains perhaps the most influential chapter on Methodism ever written. Stemming from his Marxist ideas, Thompson stated that Methodism supplied the work discipline for England's industrial revolution, deflected the working classes from their legitimate political objectives, created sexually repressed automatons, and subverted the noble traditions of English religious and political dissent. Such bald statements do not do justice to the poetic brilliance of Thompson's prose or to his talent as a social historian, but they draw attention to the ubiquitous ways in which the Halévy thesis can be constructed.

The most conceptually integrated alternative to Thompson's interpretation, and the one based on the best command of the sources, is offered by W. R. Ward. With all due attention to Methodist theology, organization, and personal motivation, he nevertheless views Methodism's great age of expansion in English society as part of much wider structural changes in the generation overshadowed by the French Revolution.[24] In this period, a complex of social tensions caused by population growth, subsistence crises, and the commercialization of agriculture, and further exacerbated by prolonged warfare, sharpened class conflict and undermined the old denominational order. The rising social status of the Anglican clergy and their unprecedented representation on the bench of magistrates in the English localities cemented the squire and parson alliance at the very time that establishment ideals in British society were most under attack. In such circumstances, the Church of England was in no position to resist a dramatic upsurge in undenominational itinerant preaching and cottage-based religion that even the various Methodist connections struggled hard to keep under control.[25]

From this perspective, Methodism was a form of popular religion peculiarly well adapted to the kind of economic, social, and political transformations that were changing the face of English society and that

---

[24] William R. Ward, *Religion and Society in England 1790–1850* (1972). The main themes are expressed in a shorter and more accessible form in "Revival and Class Conflict in Early Nineteenth-Century Britain," in W. R. Ward, *Faith and Faction* (1993), 285–98.

[25] See Deborah M. Valenze, *Prophetic Sons and Daughters* (1985); Deryck W. Lovegrove, *Established Church, Sectarian People: Itinerancy and the Transformation of English Dissent, 1780–1830* (1988).

were inexorably loosening the control of the Established Church at the end of the eighteenth century. Religious associations eroded the Church of England, therefore, not primarily by political means, which for long had been the fear of the church's most ardent defenders, but through the cottage prayer meetings and itinerant preaching of a vigorously mobilized laity. In that respect, at least, Methodism, in its fundamentally religious challenge to the religious structures of England's confessional state, may be seen more plausibly as a religious expression of social empowerment than as a reinforcement of *ancien régime* control.[26] Its alternative structure of voluntary religious societies, organized into a connectional system, posed the same kind of threat to the Church of England as the radical Corresponding Societies posed to the British state.

There is no question that Halévy was on to something important in his delineation of the legal, reformist, and constitutional aspects of the English radical tradition which Methodism helped reinforce. But, he underestimated the extent to which those characteristics were already deeply embedded in the well-established traditions of the "freeborn Englishman," which predated the evangelical revival, and he overestimated the impact of evangelicalism on the English lower orders, which even in the most generous estimates did not comprise more than 20 percent of the most politicized section of the adult lower orders.[27] Moreover, an overconcentration on the Halévy thesis can militate against a more sophisticated grasp of the religious, social, and political milieu of Methodist communities during the industrial revolution. The issues that aroused the most intense passions were not always to do with class conflict, parliamentary reform, and the extension of the suffrage. The chief priorities of most Methodists were religious and moral, and when they did rouse themselves to political action they were as much concerned with protecting itinerant preaching, abolishing slavery, resisting Catholic emancipation, and reforming public morals as they were about a more conventional radical platform. Within the Methodist chapel communities, conflicts over who controlled the preachers and the buildings, disputes over the collection and allocation of money, rows over the conduct of revivals and styles of worship, and disagreements over

---

[26] For slightly different interpretations of Methodism's contribution or otherwise to England's *ancien régime* see Clark, *English Society 1688–1832*; and Hempton, *Religion of the People*, 77–90.

[27] This figure is taken from one of the best of the recent interpretations of the Halévy thesis: Alan Gilbert, "Religion and Political Stability in Early Industrial England," in P. O'Brien and R. Quinault, eds., *The Industrial Revolution and British Society* (1993), 79–99.

the curriculum of the Sunday schools generated as much heat as the more familiar problems investigated by historians. In that respect, if the Halévy thesis has helped generate interest in the history of Wesleyan Methodism, it has also deflected attention away from the actual religious convictions and political concerns of many of the Methodist faithful.

As the debates surveyed in this chapter indicate, setting Wesley in his context is no easy task, not least because his life intersected with some of the most powerful forces in early modern England, from the rise of consumerism to the emergence of industry, and from the challenges facing established churches to the growth of voluntary associations. Ironically, John Wesley, who was born into an Anglican family that was bitterly divided by the religious and political divisions of the seventeenth century, created a movement within the Church of England that unintentionally helped undermine England's confessional state in the era of the French and industrial revolutions. Partly because of his interstitial roots and unconventional methods there is an elusive quality to Wesley and the movement he founded that defies easy categorization. To place Wesley in context, therefore, it makes more sense to raise complex questions than offer tidy answers. He remains, as in the title of Richard Heitzenrater's book, the *Elusive Mr. Wesley*.

Part III
Wesley's work

4 Wesley as revivalist/renewal leader

CHARLES I. WALLACE JR.

Distinguishing religious *revivalism* from the *cultural revitalization* that often seems to accompany it, the late American religious historian William McLoughlin defined the former as "the Protestant ritual (at first spontaneous, but since 1830 routinized) in which charismatic evangelists convey 'the Word' of God to large masses of people who, under this influence, experience what Protestants call conversion, salvation, regeneration, or spiritual rebirth."[1] McLoughlin was describing the revivals, awakenings, and reform that he saw recurring periodically in American history, but the description fits the English evangelical revival that John Wesley led, with two qualifications. First, Wesley lived long enough to contribute mightily himself to its routinization. Second, that routinization involved not only a quickly developing tradition of preaching, but also the support of nurturing small group structures that were adapted from preexisting models and evolved into a remarkably effective organization. The revival *was* a "Protestant ritual," which Wesley helped cobble together from a number of sources, contributing to its eventual institutionalization as Methodism.

The corporate expression of revived individuals is an "awakening." Awakenings are, according to McLoughlin, "the most vital and yet most mysterious of all folk arts . . . , periods of cultural revitalization that begin in a general crisis of beliefs and values and extend over a period of a generation or so, during which time a profound reorientation in beliefs and values takes place."[2] Whereas individual conversions beg for theological and psychological analysis, a society's newly awakened and renovated worldview calls for scrutiny from historians, sociologists, and anthropologists. We should add one further mode of inquiry here. Wesley's role as a revivalist and renewal leader also opens up the study of ecclesiastical

---

[1] William G. McLoughlin, *Revivals, Awakenings, and Reform* (1978), xiii.
[2] Ibid.

reformation. If, as Wesley put it, God had raised up Methodist preachers "not to form any new sect; but to reform the nation, particularly the Church; and to spread scriptural holiness over the land,"[3] institutional renewal should join personal regeneration and cultural revitalization to enrich the story. Wesley's leadership was working at all three levels: helping individuals "flee the wrath to come," contributing to the renewal of North-Atlantic Christianity, and helping British society modernize (while subjecting it to a premodern ethical critique that continues to have bite in our own era).

Even though Wesley put his stamp on the eighteenth-century English revival, he neither began it nor ever wholly owned it. In one sense the revival exemplified a periodic necessity in all human cultures – thus anthropologist A. F. C. Wallace lists Wesley alongside the Ghost Dance, Ikhnaton's new religion in ancient Egypt, and the Taiping Rebellion as "revitalization movements." But, it can also be seen as a specific manifestation of a peculiarly Christian genre, such as the "revivalism" that Gary Dickson identifies throughout medieval Europe or the periodically recurrent "Methodist element" – revivalist, but not sectarian – that Rupert Davies purported to find in late second-century Montanism, as well as among the Waldensians, the Franciscans, and the German pietists.[4]

Wesley owed an immediate debt to pietism, among other renewal movements of the seventeenth century. Along with Davies, Reginald Ward and Ted Campbell have emphasized that revivalism or "religion of the heart" did not rise spontaneously in Whitefield, the Wesley brothers, and the other Oxford Methodists, but emerged from European beginnings in the two centuries immediately following the Reformation. The same religious and cultural currents found expression in other Protestant settings (for example, Puritanism, especially on Britain's "Celtic fringe" and in North America), in semi-heretical figures like Jakob Boehme, in various Counter-Reformation Catholic communities, and even among the Hasidic movement within eastern European Judaism.[5]

---

[3] "Large Minutes," Q. 3, *Works* (Jackson), 8:299.

[4] Anthony F. C. Wallace, "Revitalization Movements," *American Anthropologist* 58 (1956): 264; Gary Dickson, "Revivalism as a Medieval Religious Genre," *Journal of Ecclesiastical History* 51 (2000): 475, 477–78; and Rupert E. Davies, *Methodism* (1976), 11–21, 35–37.

[5] Wesley is at the center of Ted Campbell's wide-ranging compact narrative, *The Religion of the Heart: A Study of European Religious Life in the Seventeenth and Eighteenth Centuries* (1991). W. Reginald Ward's *The Protestant Evangelical Awakening* (1992) attends primarily to Protestantism in the eighteenth century.

"AS IT WAS IN THE BEGINNING"

Wesley's published *Journal* provides a major window to the historical particularities of his revivalism. In 1742, Wesley brought out the third installment of his *Journal*, recounting events in the early spring of 1739 in and around the bustling West Country port of Bristol. His purpose in publishing this installment, as noted in the preface, was "to declare to all mankind what it is that the Methodists (so called) have done and are doing now – or rather, what it is that God hath done and is still doing in our land."[6] Although Wesley was clearly concerned to frame his own role, and justify his novel behavior, the installment also sheds light on several key features of the broad revivalist tradition he was simultaneously joining and shaping. The extracts quoted below cover what is generally seen as the beginning of the revival.[7] Virtually all elements of the Methodist revival are either on show or clearly implied in these early apologetic accounts.

Revivalist preaching and polity

A dutiful son of the religious and educational establishment, the 35-year-old Wesley depicted here was making, in Albert Outler's words, a "radical shift in his commitment to the revival as his new vocation."[8] Called to a new ministry within and beside his previous identity as an Anglican priest, fellow of an Oxford college, and (failed) missionary, Wesley felt the need several years after the events he described to justify his controversial activity and "new" theology.

The third installment of the *Journal* begins by recounting the radical step that George Whitefield was urging on Wesley. Whitefield, the eighteenth-century revivalist *par excellence* (Wesley's sometime friend, associate, and soon-to-be theological antagonist), had started the evangelistic work in Bristol several months earlier. He was now planning to journey to Wales and then sail for America again, posing the need for an appropriate substitute to carry on the work in Bristol. In their brief overlap before his departure Whitefield urged Wesley to take up field preaching. Wesley was also quickly immersed in other important, although less spectacular, revivalistic activities like itinerating and teaching/ preaching behind closed doors in small fellowship groups.

---

[6] *Works*, 19:3.

[7] In addition to the third *Journal* extract (*Works*, 19:46–65), insight into this early part of the revival can be gained from Wesley's diaries (*Works*, 19:382–93) and letters (*Works* 25:614–59) during this time period.

[8] Albert Outler, Introduction to Sermon 1, *Salvation by Faith*, *Works*, 1:109.

Thursday, March 29 [1739]. I left London and in the evening
expounded to a small company at Basingstoke. Sat. 31. In the
evening I reached Bristol and met Mr. Whitefield there. I could
scarce reconcile myself at first to this strange way of preaching
in the fields, of which he set me an example on Sunday, having
been all my life (till very lately) so tenacious of every point relating to decency and order that I should have thought the saving of
souls almost a sin if it had not been done in a church.

April 1. In the evening (Mr. Whitefield being gone) I begun
expounding our Lord's Sermon on the Mount (one pretty remarkable precedent of field preaching, though I suppose there were
churches at that time also) to a little society which was accustomed to meet once or twice a week in Nicholas Street.

Wesley had been socialized to respect the Church of England's
ancient parish boundaries, crossing them for ecclesiastical purposes only
when invited, and then only in appropriately consecrated churches and
chapels. However, his by-the-book approach had already begun to crack.
As a young don, he had met with small groups of Oxford undergraduates
for a variety of extracurricular academic and devotional purposes, even
venturing beyond the university to perform community service with
prisoners and the poor. Although quite atypical, such activity attracted
little more attention than the derisive names pinned on the groups by
less pious students: the "Holy Club," "Bible Moths," "Methodists," and
the like. In Georgia, where he served briefly as the Church of England
priest in Savannah, Wesley found himself less involved with Chock-
taws and Creeks – and African slaves – than with a hodgepodge of
fellow European colonists. Among them, along with his own English
flock, were Spanish Jews and Italian, French, and German Christians.
In this multicultural context, Wesley attempted to run a tight ecclesiastical ship while he experimented at with gathering "societies" of
serious parishioners outside regular church hours, introducing hymn
singing, and closely observing the practices of some of his neighbors.
These unconventional attempts at converting and nourishing others (and
himself) in the faith were frustrated. His intense adherence to *Book of
Common Prayer* rubrics and his attempts to replicate "primitive Christianity," abetted by a somewhat obsessive and obtuse personality, were
not suited to the Georgia frontier. He finally had to admit defeat and
leave the colony in order to avoid prosecution.

Returning to England as an outward failure and preoccupied with his
own spiritual search, Wesley let his scruples regarding Anglican polity

slip even further. Scholars debate whether his famous warm-hearted experience in a gathering at Aldersgate Street in London, late May 1738, can bear the mythological weight that Methodist tradition has heaped on it.[9] It was surely not the only evangelical turning point in his life. But, there is no denying that it represented his *assurance* of God's pardoning love in Christ, an assurance that many of his friends (most recently, his own brother Charles) had experienced, but that had so far eluded him. This intense moment of personal and vocational clarification put into perspective his recent experiences, good and bad, in North America; indeed, it made sense of his life thus far. The experience paralleled what he had learned from his Moravian friends and from reading Jonathan Edwards's *Faithful Narrative* of the recent "awakening" in New England. Through Whitefield, the Wesley brothers, and others, such experiences would soon begin to resonate as well with dozens, hundreds, then thousands more women and men for whom current models of belief and practice were inadequate or unavailable.

Wesley's experience of assurance at Aldersgate occurred nearly a year before the events in Bristol. It took place on unconsecrated property used jointly by a "society" of Christians with informal ties to the Church of England and by the Moravians – the most influential group of German pietists Wesley had encountered as fellow missionaries in Georgia. It was the Moravians who had pulled him back from an emphasis on the Anglican "holy living" tradition that was implicit in his high church upbringing, in his studies at Oxford, and in his work for the Society for the Propagation of the Gospel in Georgia. They reintroduced him to the Protestant side of his heritage, bringing renewed awareness of "justification by faith." This recessive Puritan gene, inherited from both his parents, together with his equally underappreciated birthright from the Church of England itself, could now recombine in his consciousness. Looking back, he found the "new" doctrine of justification by grace available in such key documents as the *Book of Common Prayer*, including "The Thirty-nine Articles of Religion," and the *Book of Homilies*. As a result of this theological and emotional refocusing of his life and thought, Wesley's preaching of justification by faith became so insistent that many clergy began to bar him from their pulpits.[10]

---

9 For a particularly discerning analysis see Henry E. Rack's chapter, "The Road to Aldersgate Street," in *Reasonable Enthusiast*, 137–57. See also Randy L. Maddox, ed., *Aldersgate Reconsidered*.

10 A signal example was the sermon *Salvation by Faith* that he preached "before the University" in Oxford on June 11, 1738 and elsewhere. See Outler's introductory comment in *Works*, 1:109–11.

In addition to this reclaiming – or recentering – of a key Reformation doctrine, Wesley's spiritual renewal in 1738 was facilitated by participation in some new practices. As his 1739 account reveals, Wesley was involved from the beginning in supervision of *extra-parochial groups of converts*, a key mark of the gathering revival. His experience at Aldersgate, followed by a visit to Moravian headquarters in Germany[11] and continuing leadership in the Moravian-dominated Fetter Lane Society in London, surely contributed to the presence of this feature in the "societies" at Nicholas Street and the Baldwin Street in Bristol (frequently mentioned in this *Journal* installment).

One model for such revival-friendly gatherings was the *ecclesiolae in ecclesia* ("little churches within the Church") or *collegia pietatis* ("colleges of piety") recommended by German pietist leaders such as P. J. Spener and A. H. Francke. Another prototype was the related Anglican religious societies that had met for "the reformation of manners" as well as other spiritual and missionary endeavors in late seventeenth and early eighteenth century England.[12] Although equally pious, the latter societies were less warm-hearted, more moralistic, and more male-dominated than those of the Moravians. The small groups that Wesley had gathered in Oxford and in Georgia fit this earlier English pattern. The "society" meetings that emerged in the early revival period (along with the spin-off "bands" and "classes") were adapted from Moravian roots and characterized by more intense fellowship along with accountability.

The various small groups that Wesley introduced into the early renewal movement were a crucial element in revivalist polity, as they helped ensure the "routinization of charisma" necessary for the renewal movement to persist. This point is often made through specific contrast to George Whitefield. Wesley's erstwhile Calvinist friend possessed unparalleled rhetorical (and public relations) skills, drawing thousands to his outdoor sermons and melting the heart of so notorious a skeptic as Benjamin Franklin. But, Whitefield paid little attention to organizing those who responded, with the result that the fruit of his evangelism faded fairly quickly after his death. Even though Wesley's homiletic skills were less spectacular than those of Whitefield, his attention to organizational elements like the Society and class meetings resulted in a movement that thrived, not only throughout his ministry, but long thereafter and further afield. Of course, these organizational features

---

[11] See Richard P. Heitzenrater, *Wesley and the People Called Methodists*, 82–85.

[12] For perspective on both precedents, see Scott Thomas Kisker, *Foundation for Revival: Anthony Horneck, the Religious Societies, and the Construction of an Anglican Pietism* (2007).

also posed growing questions about revivalism's (and particularly Wesleyanism's) relationship to the established Church.

Another commonplace of the broad eighteenth-century evangelical revival was *itinerancy* (alternatively, itineracy). The third installment of Wesley's *Journal* demonstrates how central this element was to early Methodism as it recounts his movement from London to Bristol and points in between, and then around Bristol, its suburbs, and neighboring territory, meeting with converts in existing societies and adding to their number through his preaching. Rationalizing this (unorthodox) practice by appeal to his status as a fellow of an Oxford college, Wesley famously concluded in a letter to a colleague at the University,

> I look upon all the world as my parish; thus far I mean, that in whatever part of it I am I judge it meet, right, and my bounden duty, to declare unto all that are willing to hear the glad tidings of salvation. This is the work which I know God has called me to. And sure I am that his blessing attends it.[13]

The tension with the Church of England created by this transgressing of previously sacrosanct boundaries for her priests was heightened as Wesley not only invited other Anglican clergy to join him in this irregular itinerant ministry but, eventually, recruited a cadre of lay "helpers" (who lacked both university training and ordination) to share in itinerant supervision of the growing number of local societies – a role that included allowing them to preach but not to preside at sacraments.

The first step in this direction was Wesley's embrace of *field preaching*. He was preceded and invited into this role by George Whitefield, the "Grand Itinerant." Wesley's *Journal* entry for April 2, 1739, suggests his attraction to the practice, which offered a solution both to the decline of pulpit invitations from brother clergy and the increasingly obvious fact that numbers of people were not darkening church doors of their own accord. Still, Wesley felt constrained to call on biblical precedent and numerical success in his description of this new venture.

> At four in the afternoon I submitted to "be more vile," and proclaimed in the highways the glad tidings of salvation, speaking from a little eminence in a ground adjoining to the city to about 3,000 people. The scripture on which I spoke was this (Is it possible anyone should be ignorant that it is fulfilled in every true minister of Christ?): "The Spirit of the Lord is upon me, because he hath anointed me to preach

---

[13] Letter [to Revd. John Clayton?], ([28 Mar. 1739?]), *Works*, 25:616.

the gospel to the poor; he hath sent me to heal the broken-hearted, to preach deliverance to the captives and recovery of sight to the blind, to set at liberty them that are bruised, to proclaim the acceptable year of the Lord."

The "glad tidings of salvation" phrase echoes Wesley's justification of trespassing ecclesiastical boundaries in the letter quoted above. The drama is further heightened by reference to the numbers present (a continuing preoccupation of revivalism) and by taking as his text (Luke 4:18–19) the same passage from Isaiah that Jesus used in *his* first sermon. Like the Hebrew prophet and the Christian savior, Wesley might not expect universal approval, particularly with the implication that the poor, the broken-hearted, the captives, the blind, and the bruised were the focus of ministry and that some kind of Jubilee might be coming to disrupt society's business as usual. In submitting "to be more vile," quoting another of the Lord's anointed, King David (2 Samuel 6:22), Wesley was raising just such a specter. David had just danced before the ark, glorifying God but bringing shame to his wife Michal, and Wesley seemed similarly willing to cross the English establishment in answering God's call.

Field preaching was certainly not something Wesley had prepared to do. Many have pondered the relationship between his fairly dry published sermons and the robust response his field preaching often engendered. Richard Heitzenrater offers evidence that Wesley preached in a more lively and timely way than he published.[14] This lively preaching generated both positive and negative responses, especially early in the revival. Many found it to be "plain truth for plain people," effective in bringing glad tidings to those who had not heard them or understood their relevance. But it evoked fear among others, especially those in power, that such emotional rhetoric might rouse the rabble, as had happened in the civil war of the previous century and among the partisans of the Stuart pretender to the throne in the current one.

Many who were drawn to early field preaching were, in fact, poor and disenfranchised, on the fringes of or uprooted by the changes in eighteenth-century society. To be sure, the middling classes and the rich also participated in the new burst of evangelical energy. George Whitefield, in particular, was able to hobnob with and attract support from the well-off. Some of these more affluent supporters, like Selina Countess of Huntingdon, created their own short-lived denominations. Others, like William Wilberforce M.P. and the "Clapham sect," remained

---

[14] Richard P. Heitzenrater, *Mirror and Memory*, 162–73.

entrenched as evangelicals within the established church. In significant contrast to such examples, Wesley's revivalist concern was characterized by more focus on the poor.[15] In that, as in field preaching, Wesley seems to have been consciously imitating Christ, and thus following the recommendation of Thomas à Kempis, a leading medieval proponent of "holy living."[16]

Wesley's *Journal* entry for April 2, 1739, continues with a quick summary of his activity later that evening and over the next couple of days, adding further texture to his view of the growing revival.

> At seven I began expounding the Acts of the Apostles to a Society meeting in Baldwin Street. And the next day, the Gospel of St. John in the chapel at Newgate, where I also daily read the Morning Service of the Church.
>
> Wed. 4. At Baptist Mills (a sort of suburb or village about half a mile from Bristol) I offered the grace of God to about fifteen hundred persons from these words, "I will heal their backsliding, I will love them freely."
>
> In the evening three women agreed to meet together weekly, with the same intention as those at London, viz., "To confess their faults one to another and pray one for another, that they may be healed." At eight, four young men agreed to meet in pursuance of the same design. How dare any man deny this to be (as to the substance of it) a means of grace, ordained by God? Unless he will affirm (with Luther in the fury of his solifidianism) that St. James's Epistle is "an epistle of straw"?

Wesley highlights his "expounding" (irregularly) in the Baldwin Street Society and the next morning preaching (regularly) at the invitation of the jailer at the chapel in the Newgate prison. The next afternoon, irregularly and publicly to another large outdoor crowd at Baptist Mills, he preached from the prophet Hosea. That evening three women and, separately, four young men committed to meeting weekly, in the Moravian model of single-sex "bands." The James 5:16 reference not only gives scriptural warrant for those meetings (extraordinary in contemporary Anglican practice) but also represents a repudiation – not so much of Luther as of the more radical Moravian quietism that was beginning to

[15] See Richard P. Heitzenrater, ed., *The Poor and the People Called Methodists, 1729–1999* (2002), 15–38 and passim.
[16] Cf. Ted A. Campbell, "The Image of Christ in the Poor: On the Medieval Roots of the Wesleys' Ministry with the Poor," in ibid., 44–49.

irritate Wesley by the time of publication.[17] Meeting together for Christian conversation, he argues, is a means of grace. Although it went beyond the Church's usual sacramental definition, that designation authorized, even required, one's making use of it, no matter the state of one's soul. In short, this entry catches Wesley in the act of balancing both sides of his heritage (holy living and free grace; his ordinary call and his extraordinary call to ministry) as he began his life's work.

This wide variety of activity continued in the Bristol area. A quick survey of the five brief *Journal* entries covering April 5–15 yields the following highlights. There were preaching stops at three religious societies – Castle Street, Gloucester Lane, and the Weavers' Hall, respectively – on Thursday, Friday, and Saturday evenings. On Sunday he preached three sermons in Bristol and Kingswood to a total estimated crowd of 7,500 – in addition to reading prayers at St. Peters, attending the Baldwin Street Society, and meeting with the bands that same day. Tuesday evening and Wednesday morning he preached twice outdoors in nearby Bath (3,000 together) and once back in Baptist Mills near Bristol in the afternoon to a congregation of 2,000. Skipping to Saturday, he mentions a sermon to 300–400 in the Bristol poorhouse and to twice that number outside, preaching (appropriately!) on the forgiving of debtors in Luke 7:42. And Sunday more huge crowds: 5,000–6,000 at 7:00 A.M. and 3,000 in the mid-morning at Kingswood; a "crowded congregation" at Newgate in the afternoon; and 5,000 in the early evening, plus a sermon at the Society in Baldwin Street. This was a dizzying evangelistic pace by any standard.

Revivalist enthusiasm and liturgy

A further characteristic feature of the early Methodist revival appears in the April 17 *Journal* entry: *heart-felt physically expressed emotional behavior*, sometimes disparaged by Wesley's enemies, and occasionally Wesley himself when he felt it got out of hand, as "enthusiasm."

> Tue. 17. . . . Thence I went to Baldwin Street and expounded, as it came in course, the fourth chapter of the Acts. We then called upon God to confirm his word. Immediately one that stood by (to our no small surprise) cried out aloud, with the utmost vehemence, even as in the agonies of death. But we continued in prayer, till "a new song was put in her mouth, a thanksgiving

[17] See the account of the dispute in the Fetter Lane Society in London in late 1739 in Heitzenrater, *Wesley and the People*, 106–7.

unto our God." Soon after two other persons (well known in this place, as labouring to live in all good conscience towards all men) were seized with strong pain and constrained to "roar for the disquietness of their heart." But it was not long before they likewise burst forth into praise to God their saviour. The last who called upon God, as out of the belly of hell, was J[ohn] E[llis], a stranger in Bristol. And in a short space he also was overwhelmed with joy and love, knowing that God had healed his backslidings. So many living witnesses hath God given that "his hand is still stretched out to heal, and that signs and wonders are even now wrought by his holy child Jesus."

Wesley found it necessary to interpret for his readers the deep groanings of the sinful together with the deep peacefulness and ardent praises of the subsequently forgiven. He understood these experiences personally, even if he had not been so demonstrative at Aldersgate. In any case, such expressions became a commonplace of revival, and could be judged both as evidence of the divine power that the Enlightenment did not often prize (although John Newton's lyrical testimony to grace was thoroughly in line with Lockean empiricism: "Was blind, but now I see") and as examples of vile, base, or mad carryings on that polite society ought not countenance. Early on, as we see here and in further accounts from this visit to the Bristol area, such behavior was taken as appropriate evidence of conversion (God's confirmation of his word in individuals) and, in the aggregate, of revival. At the same time, Davies' defense of such experiences concludes with a point well taken: "the vast majority of Wesley's converts, . . . perhaps even in Bristol in the early years, never went through such experiences at all."[18]

Emotional individual conversion was often tied to what we might call *"revival liturgy."* Liturgy – patterned "work of the people" – is dramatic action that often carries a tradition's deepest messages. It should not be equated simply with formal processions and exact repetition of age-old words and gestures. Other prominent forms would include field preaching and hymn-singing, arguably the best known and most important of the Methodist revival's contributions to the wider church.

Wesley's diary records that he "sang" two to four times a day while in the Bristol area, an activity as frequent as preaching, meeting with bands and societies, praying, "religious talk," letter writing, and tea. On Wednesday, April 11, for instance, there is no entry at all in the *Journal*, but Wesley's manuscript diary notes his evening's activity:

18 Davies, *Methodism*, 61.

"8 At Baldwin Street, the male bands. 9 At home; supper, religious talk, sang, prayed"; or, as his letter back to his Fetter Lane friends put it, "the remainder of the evening was spent in singing, conference, and prayer."[19] The *Journal*, usually silent on such details at this juncture, notes singing when Wesley and members of the Baldwin Street Society met for the first time in their unfinished "New Room" on June 3. They sang the Charles Wesley hymn "Arm of the Lord, awake, awake" out of the *Hymns and Sacred Poems* (1739), published in London only a few weeks prior. The *Journal* and diary together give evidence on May 31 of singing as well as preaching on Kings Weston Hill, when local rowdies tried to disrupt an outdoor revival meeting that interestingly had an Ascension Day theme.

Hymn singing was not a Methodist invention, but it was a very limited practice in English-speaking churches prior to the Wesleys. Charles Wesley's hymns (together with John's translations of German hymns), and the growing repertoire that included the Congregationalist divines Isaac Watts and Philip Doddridge and Anglicans such as William Cowper and John Newton, represented a sea change in English Christian worship and spirituality. The Wesley hymns, in particular, not only taught the liturgical year with lyrics for the great Christian feasts, but also gave voice to the evangelical experience and theology of revival. As Hempton notes, the themes are invitational, celebratory, and anticipatory, all stressing the "pleasantness of religion" and the "goodness of God." They concentrate not so much on doctrine as such, but rather "on the Christian life as a pilgrimage, a journey from earthly despair to heavenly blessing." And, they found use in every gathering of the faithful (and the curious), as well as in private devotion, and became a mark of the movement.[20]

From a revival perspective the Wesley hymns are more than two Oxford-trained priests foisting metrical theology on untutored converts in a one-way fashion. According to Oliver Beckerlegge,

> the hymns were "rather the result of the revival experiences
> with the poor and unlettered." "The whole area of the operations
> of the Spirit in the heart is there charted out with firmness and
> precision." As sung by the believer,
> What we have felt and seen
> With confidence we tell
> was nothing more nor less than the literal truth.[21]

---

[19] Letter to James Hutton and the Fetter Lane Society (16 Apr. 1739), *Works*, 25:632.

[20] David Hempton, *Methodism: Empire of the Spirit*, 69–71.

[21] Oliver Beckerlegge, quoting Louis FitzGerald Benson in Introduction to *Collection of Hymns for the Use of the People Called Methodists*, *Works*, 7:62.

From *A Collection of Psalms and Hymns*, issued in Georgia in 1737, to the *Collection of Hymns for the Use of the People Called Methodists*, that "little body of experimental and practical divinity" that appeared in 1780, publication alone signaled the importance of hymns to the Wesleys and their adherents. "Where Shall My Wond'ring Soul Begin," the hymn associated with Charles Wesley's (and John's) conversions and the magnificent "Come, O thou Traveller unknown," which Watts praised as "worth all the verses he himself had written," are just two of dozens of classic revival lyrics.[22]

If, as has been suggested, the corpus of Wesley hymns are to Methodists what the *Book of Common Prayer* is to Anglicans and the canon of the Mass is to Catholics, we may not be surprised to observe the development of other parallel liturgical expressions of the revival. Field preaching or a society, class, or band meeting could easily be mistaken for the primary worship service in a given area – a more lively replacement for Morning Prayer in a parish church, despite Wesley's protestations. And early on another parallel to Church practice appeared, a *revivalist "sacrament"* borrowed like the bands from the Moravians: the Love Feast. John Walsh has characterized the ceremony (in which cakes and a two-handed loving-cup were shared around the group, and each participant was urged to witness to his or her religious experience) as a "kind of domesticated, democratised folk Eucharist."[23] Examples of this fervent ritual of spiritual fellowship abound in the early Methodist literature, and were already present in Bristol – a women's Love Feast held in Bristol, for example, according to Wesley's diary, on April 15, 1739; another, the first at the Baldwin Street Society, on April 29.

Revivalist "clergy"

Whitefield, the Wesley brothers, and a handful of other leaders of the revival were ordained clergy in the Church of England, but their work drew on traditions, both pietist and moralistic, that prized and involved lay people. The mission was aimed at *all*: the clergy, of course, but, especially, the unchurched and under-churched increasingly rootless lay folk of the British Isles. Because fewer of the ordained were willing to sign on to the work of revival, renewal, and revitalization, the very real talents uncovered in the bands, classes, and societies were soon invested, both male and female (but not necessarily in equal proportions or roles) in leadership positions. The employment of laity,

---

[22] See *Works*, 7:116–17, 250–52 and passim.
[23] John Walsh, "John Wesley and the Urban Poor," *Review Francaise de Civilisation Britannique* 6 (1985): 23.

probably Wesley's most effective early improvisation, led to enhanced evangelistic proclamation and continuing nurture to thousands. Some remained within their local communities as leaders of bands and classes, but others became full time itinerant preachers under Wesley's direction. Ultimately, this strategy would result in a *revivalist "clergy,"* not in name but (nearly) in function. As the first conference that Wesley held in 1744 put it, the helpers (later, the assistants) were "in the absence of the minister, to feed and guide the flock."[24]

John Walsh characterized the early Methodist societies as "gathered promiscuously from a motley assortment of those seeking salvation." They were Anglicans, Dissenters, Quakers, and occasionally Catholics; soldiers, immigrants, refugees, and other mobile people; the poor, the middling, and occasionally the well-off. Marginal, but, revived and empowered, these people brought important gifts.[25] In the Bristol area, unchurched colliers listened and responded to Wesley's and Whitefield's outdoor sermons, but there were numerous others as well. Among the first men's band that gathered on April 4 were a surgeon, an upholsterer, a distiller (!), and a carpenter, the last of whom became one of first lay preachers to join with Wesley.[26] Another recruit was a converted Quaker woman who later became a leader of a band.[27] Women turned out and joined up in larger numbers than men, eventually gaining Wesley's support in serving as lay preachers.[28]

Wesley called John Cennick, a layman of Reading, to help supervise the societies in Bristol and Kingswood in his absence later in the summer of 1739. Cennick exhorted with effect in both places (a practice that Wesley distinguished from "preaching" or exposition, which he still reserved for clergy). When Cennick turned Calvinist, Wesley tried to replace him with Joseph Humphreys, a Moravian disciple of Whitefield, who was preaching at Wesley's London headquarters, the Foundery, by late 1740. But, Humphreys too fell afoul of the Calvinist-Arminian split and left Wesley's employ. Thomas Maxfield, whose emotional conversion took place when Wesley preached at the Nicholas Street Society on May 21, 1739, eventually came to the Foundery and helped out there.

Maxfield's story supplies the foundational myth for lay preaching. In late 1739 or early 1740, on an occasion when Wesley was away and

---

[24] "Large Minutes," Q. 25, *Works* (Jackson), 8:25.
[25] John Walsh, "'Methodism' and the Origins of English-Speaking Evangelicalism," in *Evangelicalism*, edited by Mark A. Noll et al. (1994), 28–32.
[26] *Journal* (4 Apr. 1739), *Works* 19:47; see footnote 98.
[27] *Journal* (18 Apr. 1739), *Works*, 19:49–50; see footnote 20.
[28] See Paul Wesley Chilcote, *John Wesley and the Women Preachers of Early Methodism.*

had left him in charge, Maxfield felt led to go beyond "exhorting" and began preaching in the Society. When Wesley expressed irritation about this upon his return, his elderly mother retorted famously, "Take care what you do with respect to that young man, for he is as surely called of God to preach, as you are. Examine what have been the fruits of his preaching, and hear him yourself."[29] John took Susanna Wesley's advice, and Maxfield was soon joined by Thomas Richards and Thomas Westall (one of those early band members from Bristol) in the same full-time itinerant ministry. Although Charles Wesley, ever the more observant Churchman, objected, these preachers were forerunners of a corps of unordained helpers/assistants/preachers who in many ways made the revival (and certainly Methodism) possible.[30]

Revivalist resistance

A measure of the revival's success was the resistance it provoked from individuals, the established Church, and society in general. Anti-revival activity in Bristol foreshadowed what would continue to erupt in coming years and in other parts of the country. That the movement was able to survive the most virulent anti-Methodist activity was due, in part, to Wesley's steady leadership.

Some individuals showed up at meetings to expose the fraud of revivalism, only to be won over. A classic example in this early setting was the Bristol weaver John Haydon, a zealous Churchman who sought evidence of people falling into "strange fits" at society meetings. In the process Haydon underwent his own bout of temporary "madness," culminating in a dramatic conversion.[31] Such conversions became another commonplace of revival mythology, a more dramatic version of the "fools" in Oliver Goldsmith's *The Deserted Village*, who "came to scoff [but] remain'd to pray."[32]

We have already noticed the closing of pulpits to Wesley and others. In addition to this "passive resistance" among ecclesiastical peers, a Bristol rector attacked Wesley in print and Joseph Butler, the philosopher and Bishop of Bristol, summoned Wesley in for interviews in mid-August 1739. In the conversation, Wesley calmly defended himself against the charges of theological irregularity, preaching in others' parishes,

---

[29] Recorded in Henry Moore, *The Life of the Rev. John Wesley* (New York: Bangs & Emory, 1826), 1:293.
[30] See Heitzenrater, *Wesley and the People*, 113–16.
[31] See *Journal* (2 May 1739), *Works* 19:54.
[32] Oliver Goldsmith, *Poems and Plays*, ed., Tom Davis (1975), 185.

administering the sacrament in the societies, and people "falling into fits" in his society meetings.[33]

High society also took offense, and, in early June, rumors circulated. People "threatened terrible things," and "there was great expectation at Bath of what a noted man was to do to me there." This turned out to be Beau Nash, arbiter of Bath's social life, who interrupted Wesley's sermon, charging him with holding an illegal conventicle. "And beside," he went on, "your preaching frightens people out of their wits." Wesley kept his wits and bested Nash verbally, but, one of the congregation stepped forward to deliver the *coup de grace*. "Sir, leave him to me. Let an old woman answer him. 'You, Mr. Nash, take care of your body. We take care of our souls, and for the food of our souls we come here.'"[34]

Later opposition involved death threats and anti-Methodist mobs, which Wesley and his associates often had to "look in the face" in such places as Wednesbury, the Pendle Forest, and Cork (in Ireland). David Hempton listed the issues which drove popular opposition as "sexuality, money, secrecy, hypocrisy, novelty, loyalty, family, and community." He concludes, "a new religious movement outraged the sensibilities of both social elites and popular constituencies."[35] But, the sporadic regional outbreaks of ritualistic violence, which peaked in the 1740s and 1750s, eventually subsided and institutional Methodism survived.

"Is now, and evermore shall be?"

Individual conversions and changed lives among the marginal; a revival that prodded the established Church, inspired other religious bodies, and became itself a denomination (and quickly thereafter an international denominational family); and a culturally revitalizing force that contributed mightily to the making of modern Britain – these are all highly plausible, and highly debatable, outcomes of the English evangelical revival. Other contributors to this volume illuminate areas that this essay can only touch on: psychological, theological, spiritual, and ethical changes in women and men whom the revival reached; ongoing analysis of the historical setting and the continuing trajectories of what David Hempton has called an "Empire of the Spirit"; and deeper consideration of the ways in which an early modern religious revival reoriented the

---

[33] Wesley's transcript of the interview with Bishop Butler is reproduced in *Works* 19:471–74. Butler's most famous accusation was "Sir, the pretending to extraordinary revelations and gifts of the Holy Ghost is a horrid thing, a very horrid thing."

[34] See *Journal* (4–5 June 1739), *Works* 19:63–64.

[35] Hempton, *Methodism*, 87–92.

core values of a nation (or two, or more). If McLoughlin's appropriation of Anthony Wallace's paradigm is at all likely, then there is not only theological and historical meaning to plumb, but important cultural sense to make, in examining the gifts and graces of John Wesley, revivalist and leader of a renewal movement.

5 Wesley as preacher

WILLIAM J. ABRAHAM

INTRODUCTION

On October 3, 1749, Charles Wesley married Grace Murray to John Bennet. It was a devastating moment for John Wesley. Despite a host of earlier reservations about getting married, he had concluded that Grace Murray was indeed the woman for him. So much so, that he had even entered into various legal commitments to her. However, Charles had intervened and stopped any future developments in its tracks by literally carrying her off and marrying her to Bennet, a rival suitor. John worked through his distress in two ways. He wrote a moving poem that vented his suffering on God. More significantly, he returned to his work as a preacher. Such was Wesley's commitment to preaching, that one can well believe that this brought some relief amid of deep personal grief. As he noted in 1757, "About noon I preached at Woodseats, in the evening at Sheffield. I do indeed *live* by preaching."[1] Such is the legacy of preaching in his ministry that much of Methodism even to this day looks upon their ministers first and foremost as preachers. Failure in this arena spells failure overall.

The legendary statistics are well known. Wesley rode up to 20,000 miles a year on horseback. He preached 800 sermons a year to crowds as large as 20,000. In a typical day he was up at 4.00 A.M., he preached at 5.00 A.M., and he was on the road to the next assignment at 6.00 A.M. Consider this neat snapshot of his work taken from Wednesday, July 21, 1779.

> The House was filled at five, and we had another solemn opportunity. About eight, calling at Hinckley, I was desired to preach; also at Forcell, ten or twelve miles further. When I came to Coventry, I had found notice had been given for my preaching in

[1] *Journal* (28 July 1757), *Works*, 21:118.

the park but the heavy rain prevented. I sent to the mayor, desiring the use of the townhall. He refused; but the same day gave the use of it to a dancing-master. I then went to the women's market. Many soon gathered together, and listened with all seriousness. I preached there again in the morning, Thursday, 22, and again in the evening. Then I took the coach to London. I was nobly attended; behind the coach were ten convicted felons, loudly blaspheming and rattling their chains; by my side sat a man with a loaded blunderbuss, and another upon the coach.[2]

Beyond the extraordinary performance of preaching across the length and breadth of England, Wesley made his sermons available in printed form. Along with his *Explanatory Notes on the New Testament*, the published sermons now serve as official standards of doctrine for much of Methodism. Although they clearly reflect the style of the day, they are still read with spiritual profit throughout the world.

THE BREAK WITH CONVENTION

The place of preaching within Anglicanism was secure. Article of Religion XIX makes clear that preaching is critical to the very essence of the church. "The visible Church of Christ is a congregation of faithful men, *in which the pure Word of God is preached*, and the sacraments be duly ministered according to Christ's ordinance in all things that of necessity are requisite to the same." Back of this lay the Pauline observation that "Christ had not sent him to baptize but to preach the gospel" (1 Cor. 1:17). Indeed, God had ordained that it was through the preaching of the cross in the power of the Spirit, rather than through wisdom, that human agents gained salvation. So, Wesley inhabited an ecclesial world where preaching was central.[3] The tacit theology in place was that preaching is a divinely appointed vocation. It was a vocation to which persons were inwardly called by God. The divine call in turn was sustained by the judgment of the church, accompanied by ecclesial authority, and vindicated by the results of ministry. So Wesley was initiated into a world that set great store by the office and practice of preaching.

Initially Wesley operated within the conventional practices of the Church of England. He was not naturally one to depart from tradition.

---

[2] *Journal* (21 July 1779), *Works*, 23:141–42.
[3] For Wesley's place in the history of preaching, see O. C. Edwards, *History of Preaching* (2004), 426–50.

This cost him dearly in his ministry in Georgia, where he tried to impose the ways of the University on the wayward flock he sought to direct. By the time he came back to England in 1739, he was a broken man: a failure in love, a failure as a missionary, and a failure in the life of faith. His Aldersgate experience, once it had been sorted through spiritually and theologically, clearly gave him a confidence and a passion that set him free to explore the full force of the preached Word.[4] It is also clear that the results of his preaching had a loopback effect on his own sense of assurance: he saw ordinary folk enter the spiritual liberty that he himself had experienced, and he saw the gospel confirmed experientially before his eyes. But, there were untoward effects as well, for he found himself over time excluded from the churches. By necessity, rather than by choice, he was driven to preach in the open air.

His description of his first efforts in this arena show just how startling this move into field preaching in Bristol was for him.

> At four in the afternoon I submitted to be more vile, and pro-claimed in the highways the glad tidings of salvation, speaking from a little eminence in a ground adjoining to the city, to about three thousand people. The scripture on which I spoke was this (is it possible any one should be so ignorant that it is fulfilled in every true minister of Christ?), "The Spirit of the Lord is upon me, because He hath anointed Me to preach the gospel to the poor. He hath sent Me to heal the broken-hearted; to preach deliverance to the captives, and recovery of sight to the blind; to set at liberty them that are bruised, to proclaim the acceptable year of the Lord."[5]

The language of submitting "to be more vile" highlights how far Wesley had been a hard line traditionalist. He was a stickler for decency and order; the saving of souls was almost a sin if it did not take place in church. It was his colleague George Whitefield who invited him into the open air. Once he found his voice, the spiritual benefits were so obvious that there was no going back. His vocation was now matched by a whole new venue of communication.

This radical innovation took place on Monday, April 2, 1739. One of the first fruits of this work was the conversion of Thomas Maxfield. Early in 1741, Wesley appointed Maxfield to work with the Society in London, permitting him to pray with the members and to give them appropriate

---

[4] For an illuminating account of the Aldersgate experience see Heitzenrater, *Mirror and Memory*, 106–49.

[5] *Journal* (2 April 1739), *Works*, 19:46.

advice in his absence. Maxfield soon overstepped the allotted assignment and started preaching. When word got back to Wesley, he hastened to London to put a stop to such irregularity. The first complaint was lodged with his mother. She took the measure of his tacit objection head on.

> John, you know what my sentiments have been. You cannot suspect me of favoring readily anything of this kind. But take care what you do with respect to that young man, for he is surely called of God to preach as you are. Examine what have been the fruits of his preaching and hear him yourself.[6]

Wesley took his mother's advice, which was backed up by Lady Huntingdon. Thus began the standard account of the office of lay preacher within Methodism, an office that extended, albeit more in principle than significant practice, even to women in Wesley's own day.[7]

THE HAZARDS AND SATISFACTION OF PREACHING

The political and ecclesiastical problems associated with field preaching and lay preaching were obvious to Wesley's contemporaries. He was flirting with irregularity, schism, and dissent. Yet, even when Wesley set up his societies to cope with the converts who had found faith under Methodist preaching, he held firm in his commitment to work within the established Church of England. At least while Wesley lived, the standard charges against him could be rebutted readily enough. He was hard-pressed, however, to make the case for his innovations. He wielded his characteristic mixture of piety, expediency, and logic to that end. The issue was also far from trivial legally. He was careful to claim that field-preaching was lawful, yet he conceded that he did so as a last resort. He was also well aware of the weakness of the powers that be in the establishment – after all, if bishops came down hard on field preaching, they might also have to come down hard on card-playing and on frequenting taverns.

The driving force beneath Wesley's apologetic was a steely combination of personal call, divine revelation, and providence. This comes out in his response to an Anglican priest who called him to account for preaching outside the boundaries of parish life.

> Suffer me now to tell you my principles in this matter. I look upon all the world as my parish; thus far, I mean, that in whatever part of it I am, I judge it meet, right and my bounden duty

---

[6] Henry Moore, *Life of John Wesley* (1824), 1:506.
[7] See Chilcote, *John Wesley and the Women Preachers of Early Methodism*.

to declare, unto all that are willing to hear the glad tidings of salvation. This is the work which I know God had called me to; and sure I am that His blessing attends it. Great encouragement have I, therefore, to be fulfilling the work He hath given me to do. His servant I am; and, as such, am employed according to the plain direction of His word – "as I have opportunity, doing good unto all men." And his providence clearly concurs with His word, which has disengaged me from all things else, that I might singly attend on this very thing, "and go about doing good."[8]

It would be easy but superficial to see in this a mere messianic complex on Wesley's part. What was at issue for him was the spiritual welfare of those who preferred the ale-house or idle diversion to attendance at church on Sundays. He was determined not just to go to those who needed his ministry but to those who *most* needed his ministry. He was forthright in noting that his critics were not exactly queuing up to take on the hardships involved in this work.

Can you bear the summer heat to beat upon your naked head? Can you suffer the wintry rain or wind, from whatever quarter it blows? Are you able to stand in the open air without any covering or defence when God castest abroad his snow like wool, or scattereth his hoar-frost like ashes? And yet these are some of the smallest inconveniences which accompany field-preaching. Far above all these, are the contradiction of sinners, the scoffs both of the great vulgar and the small; contempt and reproach of every kind; often more than verbal affronts, stupid, brutal violence, sometimes to the hazard of health or limbs or life?[9]

This compact description of the hazards of preaching in the open air was not rhetorical overkill. Wesley's *Journals* are filled with episodes that confirm the dangers to which he and the early Methodist preachers were exposed. In the absence of police, public riots were often just below the surface of society; anti-Methodist riots were therefore not exactly unexpected. The most serious took place in the towns of Walsall and Wednesbury, Staffordshire in late October 1743. The local magistrates declined to help, so Wesley and his companions were left to fend for themselves. In Walsall there were cries of "Drown him!" "Hang him!" and "Crucify him!" Eventually the man who led the mob lifted Wesley

---

[8]   Letter to the Rev. John Clayton (?) (28 March 1739?), *Works*, 25:616.
[9]   Wesley, *Farther Appeal to Men of Reason and Religion*, Pt. III, III.24, *Works*, 11: 307.

on his shoulders and carried him through the river to safety. One rough lout set out to strike Wesley with his fist; suddenly he melted and stroked his head, saying, "What soft hair he has!"[10]

Wesley was a man intoxicated with a sense of special providence, so he took all this in his stride. Yet, he was not a fool when it came to dealing with mobs. He avoided places with a plentiful supply of stones that could be used as artillery; he refused to be discourteous or angry; he knew how to stare down a mob; he could beat a well-executed retreat; he was not put off by the organized opposition of gentry and clergy; and he figured out how to handle an ox, a bull, a herd of cows, and a gentleman who threw money into the crowd to distract their attention. There were moments of humor in all of this. When one opponent showed up with his pockets filled with rotten eggs, a young man slipped up upon him unawares, clapped his hands on each side, and smashed them all at once. "In an instant he was perfume all over, though it was not so sweet as balsam."[11] In time, the mobs subsided, but it took extraordinary courage in the early days to stay the course.

The satisfaction that arose from the effects of preaching more often than not offset the dangers involved. As already noted, preaching was not for Wesley a prosaic, mundane affair; it was a pivotal means of grace ordained by God to bring people salvation. It requires imagination to enter into the spiritual world registered by many of his hearers. Thousands came at times to hear him; within that number a solid minority heard the voice of God and found rest for their souls. Such was the impact that folk would go to great lengths to hear Wesley preach. Dame Summerhill of Bristol, who lived to be 104, met Wesley when she was in her fifties:

> When he first came to Bristol I went to hear him preach; and, having heard him, I said, "This is the truth." I inquired of those around, who and what he was. I was told that he was a man who went about everywhere preaching the Gospel. I further inquired, "Is he to preach here again?" The reply was, "Not at present." "Where is he going to next?" I asked. "To Plymouth" was the answer. "And will he preach there?" "Yes." "Then I will go and hear him. What is the distance?" "One hundred and twenty-five miles." I went, walked it, heard him and walked back again.[12]

[10] See *Journal* (20 October 1743), *Works*, 19:347.
[11] *Journal* (19 September 1769), *Works*, 22:206.
[12] Quoted in William Doughty, *John Wesley, Preacher* (1955), 110.

This is a far cry from the response Wesley got at Oxford when he took his turn to preach in St. Mary's Church in August 1744. Here is how William Blackstone, the distinguished lawyer, heard Wesley.

> We were last Friday entertained at St Mary's by a curious sermon by Wesley the Methodist. Among other equally modest partic-ulars he informed us; first, that there was not one Christian among all the Heads of Houses; secondly, that pride, gluttony, avarice, luxury, sensuality and drunkenness were the character-istics of all Fellows of Colleges, who were useless to a prover-bial uselessness. Lastly, that the younger part of the University were a generation of triflers, all of them perjured, and not one of them of any religion at all. His notes were demanded by the Vice-Chancellor, but on mature deliberation is has been thought proper to punish him by a mortifying neglect.[13]

Not surprisingly, Wesley abandoned Oxford as a site of preaching and gave himself wholeheartedly to the Dame Summerhills of his day. His heart was among the plain people and the poor. As we have seen, this was not an easy choice, for the opposition to Wesley for much of his ministry was broad and deep. No doubt some of the opposition stemmed from Wesley's stubborn judgmentalism. Renewalists and revivalists are rarely lacking in hidden forms of superiority that hearers can pick up instantly in the tone and disposition of the rhetoric used. However, there was also an offense at the very core of the message that was inescapable. Wesley was not content to settle for a dead orthodoxy, he was determined to bring people to the point of repentance and draw them into a whole new world of divine action and grace. Hence, his aim was to deploy plain truth for plain people. He was more than ready to lay aside his technical academic training but not the learning it fostered to reach the masses.

THE CONCERN WITH TECHNIQUE AND THEOLOGICAL CONTENT

This does not mean that Wesley was diffident about technical mat-ters related to style, diction, and rhetorical effect. The New Room in Bristol was constructed in such a way that trainee preachers could pri-vately observe both the actions of the preacher and the congregation. Windows were strategically placed so that observers could see what was

---

[13] Ibid., 108.

going on but not be seen. They could thereby note the skills appropriate for effective preaching.

Wesley was an acute observer of human nature and had a knack of articulating or borrowing from others what was needed for communication. Thus in 1749 he made available a short manual entitled *Directions Concerning Pronunciation and Gesture*. This was an abridgement of a work by Michel Le Faucher (1585–1657). It deals with such topics as: how we may speak as to be heard without difficulty and with pleasure, general rules for the variation of the voice, particular rules for varying the voice, and appropriate gestures. It is a little masterpiece of linguistic economy and good sense. It is also brutally realistic, fitted for the kind of rough tongues Wesley was recruiting for the work of preaching. Thus: "labor to avoid the odious custom of coughing and spitting while you are speaking. And if at some times you cannot wholly avoid it, yet take care you do not stop in the middle of a sentence, but only at such times as will least interrupt the sense of what you are delivering."[14]

Compared to the histrionics of Whitefield, Wesley's demeanor and style as a preacher was remarkably moderate and serene. He overturns the stereotype of the evangelist as an energetic windmill exploiting the emotions of his listener. Professor J. H. Liden, of Uppsala, heard Wesley preach on October 15, 1769, on a visit to England, and provides this neat description.

> The sermon was short but eminently evangelical. He has not great oratorical gifts, no outward appearance, but he speaks clear and pleasant.... He is a small, thin old man, with his long and straight hair, and looks as the worst country curate in Sweden, but has learning as a bishop and zeal for the glory of God which is quite extraordinary. His talk is very agreeable, and his mild face and pious manner secure him the love of all rightminded men. He is the personification of piety, and he seems as a living representative of the loving Apostle John.[15]

Liden's comments are borne out by Wesley's strictures about preaching. In his day, as in ours, some Christians readily pontificate on the nature of real "gospel preaching." A 1751 letter shows how carefully Wesley had thought about this core of his activity as a preacher. He defines gospel preaching as "preaching the love of God to sinners, preaching the life, death, resurrection, and intercession of Christ, with all

---

[14] "Directions Concerning Pronunciation and Gesture," I.5, *Works* (Jackson), 13:521.
[15] Quoted in Doughty, *John Wesley, Preacher*, 113.

the blessings which, in consequence thereof, are freely given to true believers."[16] Controversy swirled around how best to do this. It was cast in terms of a debate between the relative merits of law and gospel that went back to Luther. Some insisted on preaching law as the means of begetting spiritual life, others opted for the gospel only. Wesley argued for an appropriate balance between them. He proposed that the preacher should begin with a promissory note of the good news of the gospel, then focus on the law as a means of awakening conviction of sin, and finally move to the exposition of the gospel. This became an effective model for later evangelists in the Wesleyan tradition. It did so because it shows remarkable spiritual sensitivity to those who are tempted to run at the first sign of judgment in the preaching of the law. Yet, it also undergirds the moral content of the spiritual life after conversion to a living faith. For Wesley, the law was both food and medicine; it initiated the hearer into a robust vision of obedience to God. Once this was in place, the emphasis on the gospel made clear the resources that were available to deal with the guilt and spiritual inadequacy such initiation induced. Wesley's summary at this point is a felicitous synthesis of the insights of Luther and Calvin on the relation between law and gospel. "God loves *you*; therefore, love and obey him. Christ died for *you*; therefore die to sin. Christ is risen; therefore rise in the image of God. Christ liveth evermore; therefore, live to God, till you live with him in glory."[17]

Wesley's homiletical ruminations were engendered both by careful observations of his own ministry and by the mistakes he noted in others. He was especially annoyed by the development associated with the preaching of James Wheatley, whose views spread like a virus among some of the preachers. The latter opted for a soft, sentimental form of preaching that focused exclusively on the promises of the gospel and set aside the demands of the law. Wesley sarcastically notes that the result is

Verses, smooth and soft as cream

In which was neither depth nor stream.[18]

Such preaching was spiritually dangerous.

The gospel preachers, so called, corrupt their hearers; they vitiate their taste, so that they cannot relish sound doctrine; and spoil

---

[16] Wesley, Letter to an Evangelical Layman (20 December 1751), *Works*, 26:482.
[17] Ibid., 488.
[18] Ibid., 486; quoting Ben Jonson, *Explorata*, II:714–15.

their appetite, so that they cannot turn it into nourishment; they as it were, feed them with sweatmeats, till the genuine wine of the kingdom seems quite insipid to them. They give them cordial upon cordial, make them all life and spirit for the present; but meantime, their appetite is destroyed, so that they can neither retain nor digest the pure milk of the word. Hence it is, that... preachers of this kind (though quite the contrary appears at first) spread death, not life, among their hearers.[19]

Given this assessment, it is not surprising that Wesley is ruthless in his rejection of what often passed for "gospel sermons" in his day.

The term has become a mere cant word. I wish none of our Society would use it. It has no determinate meaning. Let but a pert, self-sufficient animal, that has neither sense nor grace, bawl out something about Christ and his blood or justification by faith, and his hearers cry out, "What a fine gospel sermon!"[20]

THE DISTINCTION BETWEEN ORAL AND WRITTEN FORM

There has long been a query about how far Wesley's spoken sermons differed from those that he published. Some of the published sermons, like *Free Grace*, were issued as individual pamphlets. The majority appeared in collected volumes of *Sermons on Several Occasions* (eventually totaling nine volumes) and in the pages of the *Arminian Magazine*. These published sermons are a model of prosaic, closely argued expositions of scripture (even if it is clear that Wesley is reading as much of his theology into scripture as he is reading theology out of scripture). The cerebral nature of these printed sermons makes it hard to see how Wesley should have been such an effective and controversial preacher. On the surface they do not appear to be suitable for popular consumption, despite his claim to present plain truth for plain people. Contemporary students typically find the material archaic. Even when they get past this and learn to read Wesley carefully, they find the analytical and conceptual dimensions to be a serious challenge intellectually and theologically. So the question arises: How much continuity was there between the oral and written versions of the sermons?

We now have a clear answer to this query. Richard Heitzenrater, who had the skill and good fortune to identify at least two verbatim accounts

---

[19] Ibid., 487–88.
[20] Letter to Mary Bishop (18 October 1778), *Letters* (Telford), 6:326–27.

of oral sermons of Wesley taken down in shorthand, has provided a characteristically measured analysis of the evidence.[21] Heitzenrater also cites several brief descriptions of Wesley's oral preaching. For example, John Whitehead noted that Wesley's style was "neat, simple, perspicuous, and admirably adapted to the capacity of his hearers"; and George Burder, having heard Wesley several times, records that "he illustrates almost every particular with an anecdote."[22] The conclusion Heitzenrater draws is that there was clear continuity between the content of Wesley's oral and written sermons, but he added appropriate illustrations in the oral version that do not show up in the written form. This helps explain the success of Wesley as a preacher – he effectively adjusted his mode of presentation to the audience.

The distinction between oral and written presentation raises other interesting queries. Did Wesley practice what he preached with respect to preaching? In another study, Heitzenrater carefully compared Wesley's practice of preaching against his proposals about preaching as set forth in his *Rules of a Helper* and *Rules for Preaching*.[23] The result was a mixed one. Generally speaking, Wesley did keep to his own principles, but there were exceptions. Thus, he preached by far the majority of his sermons – more than ninety percent – indoors to the Methodist Societies rather than in the open field. He also broke his rules on the length of a sermon and on frequency of preaching. Although he generally stuck to the rule of being *homo unius libri* (a person of one book), he drew on a host of other sources tacitly in constructing his sermons. He certainly kept to the strictures already noted with respect to gospel preaching, but at least one critic noted that his sermons "consisted of nothing more than a string of mystical raptures about the new birth."[24]

One of the most interesting issues posed by the written form of Wesley's sermons can be approached initially by noting the following disparity. Only five of Wesley's favorite thirty-five preaching texts in his lifetime are the topic of published sermons. Only sixteen of the forty-three sermons that appear in the first four volumes of *Sermons on Several Occasions* (1746–60) show up in the relevant preaching register. His second and fourth most favorite texts for preaching (2 Cor. 8:9 and Isaiah 55:7) are not available in written or published form. This raises the question of how best to think of the written corpus. Should we see them

---

[21] See Heitzenrater, *Mirror and Memory*, 162–74.

[22] Ibid., 163.

[23] Richard P. Heitzenrater, "John Wesley's Principles and Practice of Preaching," in *Methodist History* 37 (1998–99): 89–106.

[24] See Heitzenrater, *Mirror and Memory*, 163.

as a haphazard collection of miscellaneous items? Or do they represent a measured effort to achieve ends that are central to Wesley's spiritual and ecclesiastical project as a whole?

In 1763, Wesley issued the "Model Deed" to guide decisions about who could preach in Wesleyan Methodist preaching houses. This deed stipulated that preaching must be in keeping with the doctrine contained in his *Explanatory Notes* and the "four volumes of *Sermons*." At that point, there were only four volumes of *Sermons on Several Occasions*, which contained forty-three sermons by John Wesley and one by Charles Wesley. The long practice in British Methodism has been to treat these forty-four sermons (as distinguished from others published later) as the *Standard Sermons* that serve as a doctrinal norm. In minor deviation from this practice, Methodists in North America bestowed the designation of *Standard Sermons* upon the four volumes of sermons in Wesley's first edition of collected *Works* (published in the early 1770s), which added nine more sermons by John Wesley to the collection.[25] However, in recent years there has been a growing contention in North America, especially among United Methodists, for giving preference to the full corpus of Wesley's 151 extant sermons. Two reasons are given for this preference. First, they argue that some of Wesley's best sermons fall outside the narrower range of the *Standard Sermons*. Second, and more importantly, they look to the development of Wesley's views over time as a model for constant rethinking of the Christian faith in new times and situations. This has led to the publication of an alternative collection of sermons – which serves as the de facto textbook for students in this tradition – that spans the whole of Wesley's life and amply illustrates the shifts and changes in Wesley's theological pilgrimage.[26] This collection fits a model of scholarship and study that puts a premium on a historical reading of Wesley, which in turn dovetails with a progressive, revisionist conception of Christian theology.[27]

---

25 See *Wesley's Standard Sermons, consisting of Forty-Four Discourses . . . to which are added Nine Additional Sermons*, edited by Edward Sugden (US ed., 1920; British ed. 1921), which details the divergence in the two lists. The first fifty-three sermons in *Works* (vols. 1–2) correspond to the North American list.

26 Albert C. Outler and Richard P. Heitzenrater, eds., *John Wesley's Sermons, An Anthology* (1991).

27 This is clearly visible in the following comment of Albert C. Outler. "It is . . . misleading to handle Wesley's sermons chiefly as historical curios. He was no antiquarian himself, and he would scorn any proposal that his sermons should ever be turned into puzzlers for pedants. Their real test is their continuing power as witness – the possibility that their essential message may be updated and reformulated, again and again, while generations succeed each other" (in his Introduction to *Works*, 1:98).

There is obvious merit in having access to the internal development of Wesley's thought as seen in his sermons. Wesley was not a static thinker. When accused of innovation and hasty change of mind by hostile critics, he was quick to insist on the continuity of his theology over the years; however, he was a lifelong learner who was flexible in his language and open to intellectual adjustment in the light of new evidence. Moreover, it is vital to read each of his sermons in the context of relevant developments in Wesley's very particular pilgrimage. This elementary hermeneutical principle applies to Wesley as much as it applies to any other historical figure. However, there is another dimension of his work that is equally important. Sermons are a unique form of oratory. Their aim is fundamentally spiritual. Their teleology is that of spiritual instruction and formation. This insight applies equally well to the written form of sermons; their goal is inescapably spiritual in nature. Hence, Wesley's written sermons function as a handbook of spiritual direction. When read from that angle the canonical *Standard Sermons* are a remarkable achievement. Seen synchronically as a whole, they present an important experiment in spirituality that is something new and unique in the history of Protestantism.

This way of approaching the sermons transcends their placement in the context of Wesley's spiritual journey. It also overcomes the worry that the sermons are not good models of biblical exegesis or of homiletical excellence; on this score they fare well in their day, but are clearly limited to their context in the eighteenth century. What is proposed here is that they should be seen as a manual of spiritual direction and judged accordingly. It is this function of the *Standard Sermons* that deserves attention in the future.

It is this function that also explains in part the anomalous presence of a sermon of Charles Wesley in the corpus under review. Charles Wesley's sermon, "Awake Thou that Sleepest," fits snugly into an initial network of fifteen sermons that deal with becoming a Christian as understood from a Methodist perspective. These sermons deal with the fundamental issues of salvation, faith, justification, repentance, the witness of the Holy Spirit, new birth, and victory over evil. They provide the kind of basic conceptual and practical instruction essential to finding one's feet in the faith for the first time. A second batch of sermons – thirteen in number – move from this to describe what it is to be a Christian. Here, Wesley uses the Sermon on the Mount in Matthew as his text. The aim is to spell out what being a Christian looks like once one has properly embarked on the first steps in a life of holiness. A third and final set of sermons, sixteen in number, operate as a form of practical wisdom that addresses the kind of problems a Christian will face if they undergo the kind of Christian initiation Wesley prescribes for his converts. Thus, they deal with a rag bag of relevant issues: antinomianism, false zeal, bigotry, judgmentalism, failure to attain Christian Perfection, distraction, temptation, the depth of sin, spiritual depression, self-denial, getting control of one's tongue, and wealth. The divisions are not perfect, but, the overall development through the corpus as a whole and within the sections just designated is very clear. Taken as a whole, the *Standard Sermons* (or first four volumes of *Sermons on Several Occasions*) constitute a significant experiment in ascetic theology that is unique to Western Christianity.

CONCLUSION

It is becoming increasingly clear that it is important to view the life and career of Wesley from the angle of ascetic theology. Much effort has been expended over the last fifty years in attempting to resist this kind of move and to place Wesley in the canon of great theologians in Western Christianity. One can understand why this has happened. First, Wesley has his own inimitable way of developing a host of theological insights that are worth pondering. Second, in ecumenical circles, Methodists have been keen to match the claims of their dialogue partners by insisting that Wesley can hold his own as a theologian. Thus, he has been claimed as a champion of the "Wesleyan Quadrilateral," the four-fold appeal to scripture, tradition, reason, and experience. Hence, Wesley has been seen as arguing for a unique solution to problems that circle around issues of authority and theological method. However, it is much more accurate and illuminating to see Wesley first and foremost as an evangelist and spiritual director.[28] He belongs in the canon of saints and evangelists more than he does in the canon of theologians. More precisely, he belongs in the canon of the church's preachers. Once this has been grasped, an appropriate deflationary account of his theology falls naturally into place. He can be allowed to stand as he is, that is, as a modest and attractive figure in the history of preaching and spiritual direction. Wesley lived by preaching; he gave himself totally to mastering a practice that has a unique and lasting place in the life of the

---

[28] For more on this see William J. Abraham, "The End of Wesleyan Theology," *Wesleyan Theological Journal* 40 (2005), 7–25.

church. His greatest joy was to see people find God for themselves, not least when he was the agent of the Holy Spirit in the awakening of faith and the fostering of holiness. His whole life is standing testimony to the beauty of a spiritual art that can bring lasting healing to disoriented and hurting souls.

6 Wesley as biblical interpreter

ROBERT W. WALL

INTRODUCTION

John Wesley famously called himself *homo unius libri*, "a man of one book." He was, of course, an Oxford-educated man of many books, who assembled, edited, and then published a well-stocked *Christian Library* for ministers of the Methodist movement. What he meant by this self-appellation is that the Bible was always the one book close at hand, an indispensable auxiliary of the Spirit's formative work throughout his life and gospel ministry.

Yet, Wesley never wrote a treatise or preached a sermon on the doctrine of Scripture. In part, this omission reflects a former day when the Bible's authority was widely assumed and the skepticism that emerged during the nineteenth century had not yet taken hold. The biblical criticism of early modern England was interested in the more modest tasks of discerning genuine from embellished texts, and orthodox from spurious interpretations, according to the standards established by the ancient Church and reaffirmed during the Protestant Reformation.

Jane Shaw has made the case that England's initial reception of the Enlightenment at the beginning of its long eighteenth century was not centered in philosophers' academic discourse, but in discussions among ordinary believers who gathered together in the teahouses and alehouses throughout England to debate whether local testimonies of dramatic conversions or healing miracles were credible according to biblical teaching and the rules of reason.[1] These same rank-and-file believers comprised Wesley's public of interested readers who, even though unschooled, could detect obscure allusions to Scripture in popular literature. Biblical commentaries topped the list of books borrowed from the public libraries and the purchase of inexpensive Bible study aids quadrupled the sales of

---

[1] Jane Shaw, *Miracles in Enlightenment England* (2006).

any other kind of publication.[2] Wesley contributed to this robust market of ordinary readers by publishing his best-selling *Explanatory Notes upon the New Testament* (1st ed., 1755).

This brief profile of England's readers is important for understanding Wesley's work as a biblical interpreter, which was largely shaped by his deep sense of priestly vocation. He reports in the Preface to his New Testament *Notes* of receiving "a loud call from God" to compose the comments on the biblical text.[3] In the Preface to his parallel Old Testament *Notes* he stresses that his intent is to keep the comments "as short . . . and as plain as possible to assist the unlearned reader . . . to keep his eye fixed on the naked Bible."[4] Only then could biblical words become "the language of the Holy Ghost."[5] Wesley's interpretation of Scripture was not only responsive to a widespread cultural interest in Bible study then, it was also engaged with a particular reading audience and what this required of him as their spiritual director. Perhaps for this reason, he rarely mentions contemporary controversies of the educated elites – not because he thought them impious or unimportant, but for fear that to "inflame the hearts of Christians against each other" might distract his readers from hearing "the Master's word, to imbibe his Spirit, and to transcribe his life into our own."[6]

Although Wesley left us without a treatise on the doctrine of Scripture, we have his many sermons, which was his preferred way of doing theology. His conception of Scripture is best deduced from how he preached it. For example, one easily senses the authority he grants the words of Scripture by noting the distinctive phraseology in the sermons. Most include long strings of different Bible verses cobbled together, one glossing the other to express Scripture's sense in Scripture's phrase. As Wesley once explained, "The Bible is my standard of language as well as sentiment. I endeavour not only to think but *to speak* as the oracles of God."[7] Wesley sometimes expressed concern for a preacher's orthodoxy upon hearing a sermon that did not contain much quoted Scripture. His concern was not rhetorical but theologically adduced: quoting Scripture is a matter of trusting Scripture.

[2] Thomas R. Preston, "Biblical Criticism, Literature, and the Eighteenth-Century Reader," in *Books and their Readers in Eighteenth-Century England*, edited by Isabel Rivers (1982), 97–126, 98–102.
[3] *NT Notes*, Preface, §2, *Works* (Jackson), 14:235.
[4] *Explanatory Notes upon the Old Testament* (1765), Preface, §8, §15, *Works* (Jackson), 14:248, 252.
[5] *NT Notes*, Preface, §12, *Works* (Jackson), 14:239.
[6] *NT Notes*, Preface, §9, *Works* (Jackson), 14:237–38.
[7] Letter to John Newton (1 April 1766), *Letters* (Telford), 5:8.

This makes it ironic that many contemporary scholars avoid the topic of Wesley's use of Scripture, either embarrassed by his uncritical biblicism (by contemporary standards) or because the topic seems unimportant when compared to his doctrine of salvation or his heroic ministry as a pioneering evangelical revivalist and leader of the Methodist movement. The goal of this chapter is not to detail Wesley's comments on biblical exegesis; others have done this work.[8] Rather, Wesley is put forward here as an exemplar of theological interpretation of the Bible, whose practices actively participate in a people's ongoing struggle to live holy lives before a God who is light and love.

WESLEY'S SOCIAL LOCATION

Bible scholars are fond of saying that, like politics, "all interpretation is local." Axiomatic in the study of any exemplar in the history of biblical interpretation is social location. No one approaches the Bible in an unbiased bid to retrieve meanings. Beliefs and interests are shaped by the dynamic interpenetration of ideas, cultural traditions, and social practices where people live, work, and worship. Biblical interpretation engages in a kind of circularity, according to which religious beliefs and cultural preferences continue to find their support in interpreted texts – even if self-critically engaged and scrupulously rendered.

Wesley was a leading Anglican churchman at a pivotal moment and in a crucial place in the history of the Christian Bible – in eighteenth-century England, where the study of Scripture collided head-on with an emerging scientific humanism that gave birth to the tools of modern biblical criticism. Whether in the teahouses of London or the classrooms of Oxbridge, England's earliest reception of the Enlightenment focused on questions of epistemology and divine revelation. Central to the hard intellectual battles provoked was the rejection of *mere* religious tradition and the insistence that any claim for revealed truth must be held accountable to human reason and experience. Wesley agreed and worked hard to construct firm supports for his theology. Trained in Aristotelian empiricism at Oxford, and resonating with the empirical emphasis in John Locke, Wesley assumed that any person could and should apply scientific reasoning to what we learn from experience. He considered close observation of life as foundational for understanding human nature and divine revelation.

---

8 See particularly Scott J. Jones, *John Wesley's Concept and Use of Scripture*; and Robert Michael Casto, "Exegetical Method in John Wesley's *Explanatory Notes upon the Old Testament*" (Duke University Ph.D. thesis, 1977).

Wesley's spiritual re-awakening at Aldersgate was also a defining moment of his intellectual journey. His religious experience prompted him to challenge Locke's suspicion of the reliability of the physical senses, and to extend empiricism to include spiritual senses – that is, capacities to experience the spiritual world occupied by a transcendent God and marked out by the work and witness of God's Spirit.[9] In Wesley's mature view, we learn God not only through the outward media of revelation but also by means of our inward and manifest experiences of God, which confirm and are confirmed by the Church's creed and canon.

Wesley received and studied creed and canon with gratitude and scrupulous attention. He was no dissenter or latitudinarian. He embraced the Reformation's emphasis on the individual believer's freedom to interpret the Bible, and he was well-schooled in Renaissance humanism with its keen interest in the Bible's original sources. Wesley was shaped by the Enlightenment projects and embraced the critical methods of his day, including a lifelong interest in textual criticism and the importance of reading sacred texts in their linguistic and historical contexts. Although he firmly rejected the skepticism of David Hume, he famously responded to those who accused him of uncritical "enthusiasm" that "to renounce reason is to renounce religion . . . and that all irrational religion is false religion."[10]

The concerns of the Enlightenment for individual progress also shaped Wesley's interpretive interests. As David Bebbington reminds us, the evangelical revival of the 1730s, in which Wesley played a significant role, carried theological freight keenly influenced by the optimistic tempers of England's Enlightenment.[11] But, this optimism was chastened by the revival's simultaneous emphasis on a person's inability to flourish in the face of persistent sin without a radical intervention of divine grace. Aldersgate taught Wesley that the way forward toward true human well-being is predicated on an "optimism of grace."

WESLEY'S CANON WITHIN THE CANON

A second axiom that guides the study of a biblical interpreter is critical recognition that the social location that shapes interpretation also privileges particular biblical texts – the texts that most clearly affirm what one brings to reading Scripture. Because these texts serve as

---

[9] See Mark T. Mealey, "Tilting at Windmills: John Wesley's Reading of John Locke's Epistemology," *Bulletin of the John Rylands Library* 85.2–3 (2003): 331–46.

[10] *Letter to the Rev. Dr. Rutherforth* (1768), III.4, *Works* 9:382.

[11] David Bebbington, *Evangelicalism in Modern Britain* (1989), 50–66.

the theological criterion for reading the rest of Scripture, scholars refer to them (sometimes negatively) as a "canon within the canon." The word "canon" is a theological metaphor for a religious norm. A faithful believer or a faith community grants canonical status to certain materials that they take as a trusted "ruler" to measure the content of what is believed or embraced as a code of conduct. Although the entire Bible has authority for Wesley, one part of this biblical whole held extra special resonance for him – the first epistle of John. This epistle was his canon within the canon.

Wesley admitted as much in his *Sermons* and *Journal*. In the preface to a fifth volume of his *Sermons*, written at the end of a long and productive life, he writes: "If the preacher would imitate any part of the oracles of God above all the rest, let it be the first epistle of St. John."[12] This exhortation echoes a comment made years earlier in his famous sermon on the witness of the Spirit: "Never were any children of God from the beginning of the world unto this day . . . farther advanced in the grace of God and the knowledge of our Lord Jesus Christ than the apostle John at the time when he wrote these words [from 1 John]."[13] Similar comments are scattered through his *Journal*, identifying 1 John as "the deepest part of Holy Scripture . . . [combining] sublimity and simplicity together, the strongest sense and the plainest language,"[14] and describing it as "that compendium of all the Holy Scriptures."[15]

Wesley's conception of the primacy of 1 John integrates commitment to progressive revelation with a historical reconstruction of apostolic succession. The concluding comment in his sermon *Christian Perfection* makes this point well to underwrite his most distinctive doctrine: "Here the point, which till then might possibly have admitted of some doubt in weak minds, is purposely settled by the *last* of the inspired writers [John], and decided in the *clearest* manner."[16] Whether or not we accept Wesley's doctrine of Christian perfection, this quote nicely expresses a reasonable warrant for his special treatment of 1 John: the apostle John is the "last of the inspired writers" and by implication offers the New Testament's most current and incisive witness, presenting the Gospel's message in its "clearest manner." Whereas Wesley's extensive use of biblical citations and allusions in his sermons instantiate an interest

---

[12] *Sermons on Several Occasions*, Vol. 5, Preface, §6, *Works*, 2:357.
[13] Sermon 10, "The Witness of the Spirit," I.4, *Works*, 1:272.
[14] *Journal* (18 July 1765), *Works*, 22:13.
[15] *Journal* (9 November 1772), *Works*, 22:352.
[16] Sermon 40, *Christian Perfection*, II.20, *Works*, 2:116.

in letting each part of Scripture engage the whole – obscure texts illuminated by more lucid ones – his final court of appeal is 1 John.

Content analysis confirms Wesley's elevated appraisal of this single brief letter. Counting quotations, echoes, and allusions, 1 John is among the biblical books that appear most often in his *Sermons* and *Journal*. Moreover, critical analysis of how he invokes 1 John verifies a canonical concern, not only to illustrate, but to *warrant* key points being made.

WESLEY'S USE OF I JOHN

Wesley's preference for 1 John is somewhat surprising. None of his contemporaries held the epistle in special regard.[17] And, why should they? It is a brief letter whose argument is difficult to follow. Moreover, its theological grammar differs from the Pauline witness – the canon within the canon of most Protestant communions. This helps explain why Wesley's comments on 1 John in his New Testament *Notes* reflect a depth of exegetical engagement much less dependent upon the prior work of others than the rest of the volume. It also casts in sharp relief his normative claims about key texts in the epistle.[18]

Sometimes, an interpreter's intuitive sense can override custom to recognize the practical relevance of some neglected writing when dealing with a particular spiritual crisis. In Wesley's case, 1 John spoke plainly to eighteenth-century England, with its high view of religious truth tested by human experience. The letter also helped Wesley defend his sometimes awkward integration of his core belief about the gospel – salvation from sin by grace through faith – with its most distinctive experience – a life of practiced holiness that marks out who is "not almost but altogether Christian." Although Wesley's post-Aldersgate emphasis on justification by faith alone was well known and mostly admired by his contemporaries, his insistence on a holy life of perfect love as the *expected* yield of a believer's regeneration provoked many Protestant readers. If the Pauline witness underwrites his core belief, then 1 John supplies the biblical warrant of the second claim by setting out the assured results of saving grace: an experience of emancipation from sin's power and spiritual rebirth marked out by a life of perfected love.

Protestant churches have struggled with deeply ambivalent beliefs about the sins of reborn believers, which may help explain their routine

---

[17] Cf. James H. Williams, "'Why Should I strive to Set the Crooked Straight?': Wesley, His Luminaries, Modern Critics, and the "Sinlessness Contradiction" in 1 John 1:8,10 and 3:6, 9" (University of Sheffield Ph.D. thesis, 2001), 141–75.

[18] E.g., *NT Notes*, 1 John 1:5; 2:15; 4:19; 5:6, 20.

neglect of 1 John. The verb for sin (*hamartano*) and noun for darkness (*skotia*), a principal metaphor for evil in Scripture, occur in 1 John far more frequently than in any other biblical book. The epistle addresses the spiritual crisis of neglected sin that remains *in believers* rather than, as for Paul, the sin of those people outside of the body of Christ (and therefore a sin beyond the reach of believers who dwell "in Christ" by the Spirit). Wesley recognized clearly what few have before him or since: 1 John much better than Paul takes to task "that grand pest of Christianity, a faith without works."[19]

The ambivalence about sin among Protestants may be explained by their separation from Rome's sacramental apparatus two centuries earlier. Believers who received the sacrament in the mass or absolution in the confessional were assured by the Roman church that the damage of their sins had been repaired by a gracious God. Now left on their own, the Reformation tended to produce Lutherans who were spiritual fatalists and neglected sin because they could not do anything about it, Calvinists who neglected sin because it cannot count against their divine election, pietists who neglected sin because they thought it unseemly, evangelicals who preoccupied themselves with the sins of others, and Anglicans who concerned themselves with moral virtue more than with vice. And, of course, there were the Methodists who were so troubled by their imperfection that they could not rest assured in God's forgiveness of their sins. The Reformation hatched a batch of believers who did not know what to do with their own sins!

Wesley's appointment with 1 John was prompted by this species of theological crisis. Not only does he find his audience addressed in practical terms by 1 John's pastoral exhortation, the passages that Wesley quotes most frequently follow the letter's internal argument to authorize a roadmap for the *via salutis* and its destination of perfected love. Although the route to that happy end is revised with age and audience, the essential analogy of 1 John and Wesley's grammar of faith do not waver.

Already in the 1741 sermon *Christian Perfection* Wesley appeals to John's epistle in making a series of normative statements about the nature of Christian existence. Whereas believers are hardly perfect in an absolute sense, Wesley claims that spiritual perfection – or holiness – is not only a real possibility for believers, but the expected effect of their regeneration. He points his audience to 1 John 3:9 as the clearest proof-text of this kind of perfection and concludes that "in conformity

---

[19] Sermon 61, "The Mystery of Iniquity," §19, *Works*, 2:459.

therefore both to the doctrine of St. John, and to the whole tenor of the New Testament, we fix this conclusion: 'A Christian is so far perfect as not to commit sin.'"[20]

Taking this text as the plumb-line of regenerated existence, Wesley chides other interpreters who water it down – for example, by adding that only habitual sinning is contrary to one born of God; or by joining Locke in glossing this text by biblical stories of great people (Moses, David, Peter) who sin, but still enjoy full fellowship with God. The plain meaning of 1 John 3:9 is canonical for Wesley and establishes the tenor of Scripture in setting out the essential characteristic of one who is "altogether Christian."

Wesley does recognize with every exegete of 1 John the apparent internal contradiction between 1 John 3:9 and 1:8–10. His solution to this puzzle is illuminating, not for its exegetical skill but for the manner of its resolution. He settles the problem on the principle that the "plain" text (3:9) interprets the "obscure" (1:8–10), but in a manner that coheres with the tenor of Scripture (which itself is established by 3:9). This hermeneutical circularity requires Wesley to interpret the sins falsely denied by the interlocutor in 1:8–10 ("we have no sin...we have not sinned") as referring to past sin, not to present sin. Past sins must be confessed, and when they are the one confessing is cleansed from "all unrighteousness." Such confession claims the truth of Wesley's core theological belief – justification by grace through faith alone. But his keen emphasis remains on its experienced effect – that *all* sin is henceforth removed so that we can "go and sin no more." Hereby Wesley's normative definition of salvation is set out as an emancipation from every unrighteousness, not only "from its guilt and power...but from every kind and every degree of it."[21]

Over time Wesley became more careful in describing the phenomenology of this emancipation from all sin, stressing that it occurred by degree as we respond ever more deeply and faithfully to God's gracious renewing work. The three rubrics used in 1 John 2:12–14 for members of a congregation – children, young men, and fathers – are used by Wesley as metaphors of one's spiritual progress in the Christian life. "Children" are those believers who have entered into life with God through justification by faith and new birth. They experience freedom from the guilt of past sin and power to resist the continuing inclination to sin. "Young men" refer to believers who are finding the growing fruit of the Spirit

---

[20] Sermon 40, *Christian Perfection*, II.20, *Works*, 2:116.
[21] *NT Notes*, 1 John 1:9.

offsetting and weakening this continuing inclination. "Fathers" are those mature spiritual leaders whose lives are now characterized by the full fruit of the Spirit, a constant love for God and neighbor.

Regarding the nature of sin, 1 John 2:15–16 is Wesley's favorite blanket reference to the continuing inclination toward sin that threatens a believer's spiritual progress. Here is a triad of inward appetites by which one may "slide into the love of the world by the same degrees that . . . the love of God will go out of the heart."[22] In his sermon "Spiritual Idolatry" Wesley vividly relates a "desire of flesh" – tasting, smelling, and feeling – to the evils of intemperance and self-indulgence; a "desire of eye" – seeing and hearing – to things that gratify the imagination; and the "pride of life" as the vain preoccupation of seeking happiness in the praise of others rather than God.[23] Significantly, Wesley often contrasts these verses about the character of sin in 1 John with Phil 2:5: "Let the same mind be in you that was in Christ Jesus." The latter passage portrays rejection of these worldly desires as the essential mark of faithful discipleship.

The Reformation occasioned a pervasive concern among England's religious leaders for an assured faith. This concern cut two ways for Wesley. On the one hand, "children" who have confessed their past sins need assurance of God's forgiveness if they surrender anew to their continuing inclination of sin. Wesley points to 1 John 2:1–2 for a third alternative between despair because they continue to sin and a false ease that neglects the need for God's grace. His exhortation, following this text, is that believers need not sin because they can reasonably depend upon an effective advocate – "Jesus Christ the righteous one" – and upon his propitiation to a faithful and just God that extends "as wide as sin."[24]

On the other hand, even mature believers require assurance that emancipation from the act of willful sin is a real possibility. Wesley repeatedly combines 1 John 3:9 ("Those who have been born of God do not sin, because God's seed abides in them") with 5:18 to add the latter's curious phrase, found in the *Textus Receptus*, of one who "keeps himself" (*tārei eauton*) from sin.[25] Although the threat of sin remains, the believer's sense of having already been freed from its power provides the assurance of a holy life that sustains purposeful and self-controlled progress.

[22] Sermon 68, "The Wisdom of God's Counsels," §16, *Works*, 2:561.
[23] Sermon 78, "Spiritual Idolatry," I.5–18, *Works*, 3:105–11.
[24] *NT Notes*, 1 John 2:2.
[25] E.g., Sermon 8, "The First-fruits of the Spirit," II.4, *Works*, 1:238.

A final text from this epistle norms the very nature of life without sin: 1 John 4:19, which Wesley claims is "the sum of all religion, the genuine model of Christianity."[26] Note the role it plays in one of Wesley's pivotal reflections: "We must love God before we can be holy at all; this being the root of all holiness. Now we cannot love God till we know he loves us: 'We love him, because he first loved us.' And, we cannot know his pardoning love to us till his Spirit witnesses it to our spirit."[27] Wesley's theo-logic is unimpeachable: if God is love, then love is a "natural" disposition for those born of God. Moreover, those who are birthed by God to love do so because God who is love is the first to love, thereby establishing the model, providing the motive, and awakening the very possibility of human love. Wesley considers 1 John 4:19 the sum of true religion because it supplies the cipher of the holy life – a life without willful sin – which is the mark of genuine Christianity. By this verse, he is able to complete Paul's incomparable claim that believers know themselves to be children of God – and so emancipated from sin according to 1 John – by the witness of God's Spirit in their spirit. The "Abba" of Romans 8:15 is the God of 1 John "who first loves us."

WESLEY'S INTERPRETIVE PRACTICES

It is time to widen the focus and sketch broadly Wesley's interpretive practices, seeking to show how these practices instantiate a characteristic doctrine of Scripture and a deep concern for the faithful hearing of God's word.

1. The intuited text

The Bible is never free of interpreters. The best of the lot rely upon sanctified intuition to recognize what is true and important in a biblical text. Wesley recognized the truth of God's gospel and the struggles of his own world in 1 John without the prompting of others – his intuition led him to 1 John. Intuition is not the same as personal opinion or common sense; it is an intellectual faculty brought to maturity over time by rigorous study and spiritual discipline.

John Webster notes that most recent discussions of biblical interpretation imply that the human act of reading a sacred text is somehow independent of the church's teaching and the operations of the Holy

---

[26] *NT Notes*, 1 John 4:19.
[27] Sermon 10, "The Witness of the Spirit," I.8, *Works* 1:274.

Spirit.[28] They offer thin accounts of an interpreter's spiritual formation, which they suppose is incidental to the activity of interpretation. But, the formation of the mind to read sacred texts faithfully cannot go unacknowledged. Intuition is a virtue for reading that can only be forged within a worshiping community and by the filling of the Spirit.[29]

In this regard, it is critical to observe how Wesley links Spirit and Scripture. He does so differently than many Protestants, for whom the Spirit guarantees Scripture's authority rather than the interpreter's illumination. Much like we find in the Book of Acts, later in Origen, and then picked up by the Reformers, Wesley understands the Spirit instead as opening and enlightening "the eyes of the soul," enabling the reader to discern the spiritual things of God in Scripture.[30] In a Wesleyan key, then, the Spirit's witness funds the interpreter's sensitivity to read Scripture after the mind of the risen One.

2. The naked text

What Wesley called "the naked Bible," modern criticism calls its "plain sense." Influenced by Newton's science of critical observation, Wesley demands that an interpreter pay close attention to what the text plainly says. He often ridicules "abstract reasoning" when substituted for textual and literary analysis. This is not anti-intellectualism or critical naiveté but a commitment to the meaning of words and phrases rooted in his core belief that those words and phrases are revelatory of God.

Although some accuse Wesley of unsophisticated biblicism, he actually employed the range of interpretive strategies available to him in the eighteenth century. He was alert to the emerging tools of biblical criticism and employed them all, even if with caution and modesty. Not only did he have an appetite for biblical languages, he was especially interested in textual criticism, which was the primary critical method of his day. On occasion he offered corrections to the *Textus Receptus*, used in the King James version (KJV) translation – a dangerous activity in those days, since the transmission of the biblical text was linked to its revelatory role.[31]

---

[28] John Webster, "Reading Scripture Eschatologically," in *Reading Texts, Seeking Wisdom*, edited by D. F. Ford & G. Stanton (2003), 245–70, 245–46.

[29] Stephen E. Fowl & L. Gregory Jones, *Reading in Communion: Scripture and Ethics in Christian Life* (1991), 29–55.

[30] Sermon 43, *The Scripture Way of Salvation*, II.1, *Works*, 2:160–61.

[31] For a full comparison of how Wesley's translation of the New Testament differed from the KJV, see *John Wesley's New Testament Compared with the Authorized Version*, edited by George Croft Cell (1938).

This critical activity equipped him to function in a role that John Barton likens to a tour guide, whose skill in leading travelers is in proportion to an intimate knowledge of every nook and cranny of the place visited.[32] By analogy, students who apprentice themselves to Wesley will learn the tools of biblical criticism to become intimately familiar with every linguistic nook and cranny of the biblical text. One must understand what the text is saying in discerning whether it has anything to contribute to the spiritual formation of its contemporary readers.

3. The canonical text

It is not clear that Wesley knew his Oxford contemporary Jeremiah Jones, or his pioneering book on the formation of the New Testament canon.[33] But, whatever the source, Wesley manifests a nuanced sense for how the Bible's different collections were arranged to perform together as an integral whole. In particular, his use of the Catholic Epistles, 1 John, and James closely coheres to the role assigned to this collection during the formation of the New Testament canon. The canonical function of this second collection of letters was to supply an internal check to the misuse of Paul to approve a pattern of salvation secured by profession of faith alone. Wesley appeals to 1 John not to undermine the Pauline witness, but to make it more plain. Paul's gospel is not that believers should keep on sinning so that God's grace might abound all the more (cf. Rom 6:1–14); his point is rather that God's abounding grace, set loose by Christ's atoning death, makes it possible for believers to sin no more (cf. Rom 6:15–23). The sophistication of Wesley's move in using 1 John to correct that nasty "pest," a faith without works based upon a Protestant re-reading of Paul, suggests a depth of discernment concerning the integral nature of the canon of Scripture.

4. The community's text

The Bible is not for lone rangers; it belongs to the Church and so its interpretative practices are communal, conversational, and participatory. We learn Scripture in the company of saints. Although somewhat autocratic as leader of the Methodist movement, Wesley received and studied Scripture with other interpreters on whom he depended and from

---

[32] John Barton, *The Nature of Biblical Criticism* (2007), 112.

[33] Jeremiah Jones, *A New and Full Method of Settling the Canonical Authority of the New Testament* (London: Clark & Hett, 1726). Cf. Nicholas Keene, "'A two-edged sword': Biblical Criticism and the New Testament Canon in early modern England,' in *Biblical Scholarship in Early Modern England*, edited by A. Hessayon & N. Keene (2006), 94–115.

whom most of his explanatory notes derive.[34] Beginning with his parents and Oxford tutors, these include Johann Bengel, Philip Doddridge, John Guyse, Matthew Henry, John Heylyn, Matthew Poole, and many others who were counted among the leading biblical interpreters of his day and formed with Wesley a diverse community of interpretation. Indeed, he often challenged those whose idiosyncratic commentary transgressed the community's rule of faith. His sermons reflect someone actively engaged *with* biblical texts, but also in conversation with many others *about* biblical texts.

5. The salvific text

Wesley admits to the Bible's difficult, confusing, unsettling texts, whose meaning for believers remains obscure. Although modern biblical criticism is at its best when mining the Bible for its rich but seemingly intractable diversity, Wesley concentrates upon Scripture's simultaneity or unity. Every biblical text is rendered as part of an integral whole. In Bengel's phrase, the Bible forms within itself a "whole connection."

For Wesley, 1 John is that plumb-line that makes plain Scripture's "whole connection" precisely because 1 John makes plain God's way of salvation from sin. In this sense, a right reading of Scripture is not measured by an explanation of its historical background or by proving its scientific accuracy. Rather, a right reading of Scripture attends to the message and experience of salvation.

This practice of reading Scripture for salvation qualifies Wesley's concern for the plain meaning of texts. Interpretation is never a mere matter of linguistic analysis and meaning-making, but of rendering the manner of God's grace in real people in real places. One without the other subverts the practical importance of Scripture.

6. The ruled text

In making a similar point, Albert Outler argued that the most important property of Wesley's interpretation of the Bible is the "analogy of faith" – a non-negotiable core of theological beliefs, which rightly order Scripture's diverse witnesses by stipulating the message of salvation to which every interpretation must cohere.[35] In commenting upon Paul's use of "analogy of faith" in Romans 12:6, Wesley refers to it as "that

---

[34] This point is emphasized in Donald A. Bullen, *A Man of One Book? John Wesley's Interpretation and Use of the Bible* (2007).

[35] Outler, Introduction to *Sermons, Works*, 1:57–59.

grand scheme of doctrine which is delivered therein, touching original sin, justification by faith, and present, inward salvation. . . . Every article therefore concerning which there is any question should be determined by this rule; every doubtful scripture interpreted according to the grand truths which run through the whole."[36] If the meaning retrieved from Scripture does not agree with this grand scheme, then it is the interpretation that is discarded, not the church's rule. Although Wesley's theological conception is insufficiently Trinitarian and concentrates too keenly on an individual's salvation, his interpretive practice of constraining the meaning of a biblical text by a rule of faith is one we should admire and seek to emulate.

The practice of applying a rule to protect the theological shape of the text against its arbitrary interpretation may seem misguided by critical standards. At least since the late nineteenth century, historical criticism has assumed that the real need is to protect the text from the imposition of the church's theology upon the author's "original sense" of its meaning. But, if the nature of the biblical text is revelatory of God, a theological rule is the more appropriate constraint; the imposition of an historical referent upon exegesis is what typically subverts the text's theological meaning.

7. The preached text

Wesley's most important interpretive practice is also the most evident: the Bible is a preached text. A grace-filled sermon invokes and cultivates the faith of those who hear it. Even Wesley's discourses for university audiences were in the form of sermons preached, not academic lectures presented. Significantly, when Wesley was preparing for his ordination in the Anglican communion he read a manual for ministers that defined theology as a "practical science."[37] That is, learning theology should not be equated with mastery of an elaborate system of doctrine, because theology is essentially a formative activity, something enacted and acted upon, especially in the literary form of a sermon that helps ordinary believers track down a living God.

Wesley the biblical interpreter, who preached his theology, would, therefore, be puzzled to find the study of Scripture separated from theological reflection, as it is in most contemporary conceptions of theological education. Nothing could be farther from Wesley's outlook than

---

[36] *NT Notes*, Rom. 12:6.
[37] George Bull, *A Companion for the Candidates of Holy Orders* (London: Richard Smith, 1714), 18.

an act of exegesis executed by historians interested in "what was," who then hand off their reconstructions to theologians who artfully reimagine the past into "what is" for the present. Preaching translates Scripture in immediate ways.

8. The responsive text

A preached Bible claims a congregation's most attentive ear. Bible performances are not spectator sport. Wayne Booth's notion of an "ethics of reading" suggests that readers approach texts for personal improvement and expect that *what* they read will challenge and change them.[38] To read or listen to a text with suspicion or critical detachment subverts the experience of being "taken over" and shaped by what is read.

Booth helps us understand why Wesley concludes his sermons with action points. He invites a congregation to be taken over by the claims the preached text makes on their lives. James calls believers to be doers of the word, not hearers only. The practice of inclining one's ear to hear the sacred text in order to do it is properly motivated by a routine experience of being "taken over" by Scripture time and time again. We know from experience that this Word is living and active, sharper than any two-edged sword. We learn from experience that Scripture is a dangerous book and not for the timid, for it is a word from God that arrives at our heart's door in the company of the Spirit of power, love, and self-discipline.

9. The performed text

Wesley preaches the Bible to the issues of his day. An alert interpreter understands not only the text, but also the contemporary context in which an interpretation must ring true. Wesley's Bible performances are informed by his close observations of the practical needs of ordinary believers to whom he ministered. His chief concerns were their doubts and disputations – issues that threatened their relationship with the Lord. Although Wesley the theologian surely desired that his sermons would also form sound doctrine, his principal interest was a practical divinity, a lived love.

Opponents still sometimes accuse Wesley of abandoning reason for experience. They do so without understanding his epistemology of theology, which is firmly anchored by the hard evidence of transformed hearts and changed lives.

[38] Wayne C. Booth, *The Company We Keep: An Ethics of Fiction* (1988).

10. The sacramental text

Finally, Wesley's practice of stringing quotations of biblical texts together envisages an oracular manner of preaching.[39] The Bible was Wesley's "second language." Not only does his extensive quotation of Scripture envisage a deep reverence for the Bible's sacred words, his firm confidence that those biblical words deliver the word of God without need of human mediation create a prophetic "thus saith the Lord" address. Put differently, Wesley's prolific use of Scripture turned his sermons into sacraments, means for the body of Christ to ingest the sacred words and to experience in them afresh the Holy Spirit's active presence in our hearts.

[39] See Isabel Rivers, *Reason, Grace, and Sentiment* (1991), 1:214–22.

7 John Wesley as diarist and correspondent

TED A. CAMPBELL

The expression "know yourself" served as an epitome of ancient wisdom according to which appropriate self-knowledge is the ground of all other knowledge. This sentiment also came to expression in Christian theology and spirituality. Jesuit founder Ignatius Loyola began his *Spiritual Exercises* with a week of exercises designed to bring a retreatant to consciousness of her or his many sins. The Protestant Reformer John Calvin – whose career at the University of Paris may have overlapped that of Ignatius Loyola by a few weeks in the summer of 1535 – began later editions of his *Institutes of the Christian Religion* with a consideration of "The Knowledge of God and of Ourselves Mutually Connected" and Calvin's point was that there is no proper knowledge of the self except in relationship to God: "The fear of the LORD is the beginning of wisdom" (Prov. 1:7).

Thus, John Wesley wrote to one of his correspondents in 1768, "The knowledge of ourselves is true humility."[1] Wesley's mature understanding of the "way of salvation" involved not only a spiritual "awakening," by which a sinner came to know himself or herself in the eyes of God as desperately needing divine grace, but also the "repentance of believers" according to which the believer has continually to "acknowledge and bewail our manifold sins and wickedness."[2] The careful examination of one's own experience was a critical component of the Christian life as Wesley taught it.

John Wesley's correspondence, his private diaries, and his published *Journal* afford the modern reader not only an intimate view of the inner and personal events of the man's life; they also reveal much of his self-understanding and specifically his self-understanding in the presence of the divine. However, although much of Wesley's correspondence was

[1] Letter to Miss March (March 14, 1768), *Letters* (Telford), 5:82.
[2] Prayer of Confession, *Book of Common Prayer* (1662 version).

private, it is important to understand that a great deal of it was intended to be public. He published some of his letters and others were intended to be read aloud or shared in other ways in groups. Similarly, although John Wesley's diaries were strictly private and personal – and, for the most part, tediously boring – his *Journal* was a published literary work intended for popular readership. Taken together, the letters, diaries, and *Journal* of John Wesley offer us an unusually rich perspective on the private and public life of this eighteenth-century figure. This chapter offers a brief introduction to these three forms of his writing, then considers a day in the life of Wesley – April 2, 1739 – as revealed in these forms considered together.

WESLEY'S CORRESPONDENCE

John Wesley wrote thousands of letters – a reasonable estimate would be almost 18,000 in the period from November 3, 1721 (his first extant letter), up to six days before his death, when on February 24, 1791, he wrote a well-known letter to William Wilberforce, a member of Parliament and abolitionist, encouraging Wilberforce's efforts to end the practice of slavery in British dominions. Wesley's epistolary output is similar in size to that of other Christian leaders of his age.[3]

Only a small percentage of Wesley's letters have been preserved, raising the question of how to estimate the total number he wrote over the course of his life. Frank Baker carefully examined Wesley's diaries through several sample months at different points in his career, noting when Wesley indicated that he had written a particular letter, or when he simply wrote, "writ letters," meaning that he had written two or more letters on that date. This sampling suggested a general average of Wesley writing five times as many letters as have been preserved from those months. But, Baker also recognized that letters from later in Wesley's career, especially from the 1760s forward, were more likely to be preserved than earlier letters, because, by the 1760s, John Wesley had become a celebrated character.[4] Adapting Baker's method more broadly, Kevin M. Watson has estimated the number of letters that Wesley wrote by decade as follows.[5]

---

[3] On the prodigious letter writing of some of Wesley's contemporaries, see W. Reginald Ward, *The Protestant Evangelical Awakening* (1992), 2.

[4] See Baker's introduction to *Works*, 25:28–30.

[5] Watson has been serving as my assistant in the Wesley Letters editorial project, which is completing the volumes of letters for *Works*.

Decade	Number of extant letters written	Estimated frequency of extant letters written	Estimated total number of letters written	Estimated frequency of total letters written
1721–1730	30	about 3 per year	150	15 per year
1731–1740	200	less than 2 per month	1,000	2 per week
1741–1750	200	less than 2 per month	1,000	2 per week
1751–1760	300	less than 3 per month	1,500	3 per week
1761–1770	500	about 4 per month, 1 per week	2,500	5 per week
1771–1780	1,000	about 8 per month, 2 per week	5,000	10 per week
1781–1790	1,300	about 11 per month, 2.5 per week	6,500	12.5 per week
TOTALS:	3,530 extant letters[6]		17,650 estimated letters written	

Over the seventy years of letter-writing activity between 1721 and 1791, this total would average roughly 250 letters per year, or twenty per month.

Almost all of Wesley's letters were written on a single sheet of paper, roughly 12 by 8 inches (about 30 by 20 cm). He used relatively high-quality "laid" paper that has withstood the test of time, and he wrote with quill pens, which he fashioned and sharpened himself, typically from goose feathers. Once written, he sometimes used fine sand to help dry the ink. Grains of sand are still present in some preserved letters! He utilized both sides of a sheet of paper and folded the single sheet in a complex way to form its own "envelope" – separate envelopes were not employed until after Wesley's time. The letter was sealed with wax and stamped with his seal as a guarantee of privacy and authenticity, then posted.[7] For more important letters, Wesley sometimes wrote out a draft. He also often made copies of letters that he had written (usually identifiable by their lack of an address on the reverse side of the page). He occasionally employed an amanuensis or secretary to take down correspondence, though the great majority of letters were written in his own very legible hand.[8]

---

6 This is the count Baker had in the late 1970s. Although more letters have been found, this would not change the data on how many were written.

7 For these and other details see Baker's introduction in *Works*, 25:14–28 and 45–78.

8 Ibid., 25:38–45.

A few of Wesley's letters were published in his lifetime, including the public letters mentioned above and selected private letters, which he published in the *Arminian Magazine*. The first large collection of letters (400) was published by Joseph Benson in his edition of John Wesley's *Works* (1813). Thomas Jackson's edition of John Wesley's *Works* (1829–31) included about 900 letters.

In 1915, George Eayrs published a volume of 300 John Wesley letters, including almost 70 that had never been printed before. Eayrs offered a critical introduction to the 300 letters he included and added some important background, but the first inclusive and critical edition of the letters was that of John Telford, published in eight volumes in 1931, containing 2,670 letters. Telford generally utilized original copies or transcriptions of original copies made by some of his assistants, although some errors crept in through the process of transcription.

The *Bicentennial Edition of the Works of John Wesley* is still in process and will eventually include eight volumes of letters. Two of these were edited by Frank Baker and are already in print, covering letters in the period 1721–55. As editor for the remaining volumes, I am currently at work on the third volume, which will include letters from 1756 through (we estimate) 1766. The *Bicentennial Edition* includes not only John Wesley's own "outgoing" letters but also a number of letters to John Wesley ("incoming" letters), which can greatly assist one's understanding of the correspondence and its contexts. Frank Baker's introduction to this series offers a very comprehensive account of John Wesley's correspondence, including (for example) a great deal of information on the postal service of eighteenth-century Britain.[9]

John Wesley's correspondence includes everything from learned treatises intended for publication to very short missives for which today we would probably employ email. In fact, some of his short letters read very much as email or perhaps even text messages today, offering only a sentence or two giving a direction or expressing a sentiment. In 1773, for example, John Wesley wrote to Francis Wolfe as follows:

Bristol, September 15, 1773

Franky, are you out of your wits? Why are you not at Bristol?[10]

Although this example is unusually short, a great deal of Wesley's correspondence consisted of such brief, to-the-point messages. There are

[9] See *Works*, 25:1–140.
[10] *Letters* (Telford), 6:41; cf. *Works*, 25:51–52 for this and similar brief letters.

longer examples of letters addressed to particular tasks. On May 18, 1774, for example, John Wesley wrote to his wife Mary,

> MY DEAR LOVE, – I am just now come hither from Glasgow, and take this opportunity of writing two or three lines. I desire you would let Mr. Pine have an hundred pounds of that money which is in your hands, provided he gives you his full account first: which I must beg of you to send to London to John Atlay, together with fifty pounds for Mr. Nind, the paper-maker, and fifty pounds for Robert Hawes. There is no use in letting the money lie dead. If I do not administer, I can but pay this again. I am just going to preach, and am in great haste. – My dear Molly,
>
> Your affectionate Husband.[11]

In contrast to such task-oriented examples, some of Wesley's letters were written for public purposes and many of these were published, such as his *Letter to the Reverend Dr. Conyers Middleton* (1749), which was originally issued as a 235-page tract.[12] Similarly, a 1748 letter to the Reverend Vincent Perronet was published as *A Plain Account of the People Called Methodists*.[13]

Many of John Wesley's letters were intended for communities. For example, a letter addressed on April 2, 1739, sent to James Hutton was addressed to "My dear brethren (and sisters too)" because it was intended for a gathering of English Moravians (the text of this letter is given below). W. Reginald Ward has shown that correspondence was often a communal event among Evangelical and Pietistic groups in the eighteenth century.[14] Wesley's letters were often intended to be shared in such gatherings.

Yet, many of Wesley's letters were strictly private, and we can be sure that his intent was for no one except the addressee to see the letter. These letters often concerned particular spiritual issues that correspondents had faced. They are also laced with indications of Wesley's innermost thoughts and affections. The letter to his wife cited above was a private letter and shows his affection for her; it is addressed to "My dear love," and signed, "your affectionate husband." In fact, John Wesley often expressed in private letters his deep affection for both men and women.

---

[11] Letter to Mary Wesley (May 18, 1774), *Letters* (Telford), 6:87.
[12] In *Letters* (Telford), 2:312–w88.
[13] See *Works*, 9:254–80.
[14] Ward, *Protestant Evangelical Awakening*, 1–3.

He carried on an extensive correspondence with younger women, and he enjoyed the expressions of affection he received from them in response to those that he himself expressed. For example, he wrote to Ann Bolton in 1775, when he was 72 years of age and she was 32 years:

> I have narrowly observed you for several years; I have read
> you over with a lover's eye, with all the friendly jealousy I
> could.... And if I have sometimes thought your affection to *me*
> was little cooler than formerly, I could not blame you for this; I
> know something of myself, and therefore laid the blame where it
> was due. And I do not desire you to love me any further than it
> is a scale. Whereby to heavenly love thou may'st ascend.[15]

Wesley concluded this letter with a postscript encouraging her to write back, "Write soon, and write freely." In 1787 after extensive correspondence he would write back to her, "I cannot tell you how much I love you; you are exceeding near and dear to me."[16]

JOHN WESLEY'S DIARIES

The diaries and *Journal* of John Wesley do not offer anything like the level of intimacy found in private letters. The diaries consist almost entirely of routine reporting of events, and the *Journal* was intended for publication. Nevertheless, they fill out the story of Wesley's life in great detail.

Wesley began keeping a diary in the season of Lent, 1725, as a response to a suggestion he read in Jeremy Taylor's *Rules and Exercises of Holy Living*. He kept diaries from that year until a week before his death in 1791. However, not all of these diaries have survived. Most notably, the entire set between 1742 and 1783 is missing. Richard P. Heitzenrater has concluded that the diaries from this period were probably destroyed when a number of materials were burned after Wesley's death.[17] There are also gaps in the extant diaries for 1727–29, 1734, 1737, and 1738, including, for example, the day of Wesley's Aldersgate-Street experience, May 24, 1738. The earliest diaries recorded simply three lines per day, relating what had happened in the morning, afternoon, and evening. By January 1734, the diaries took on a more detailed form,

---

[15] Letter to Ann Bolton (Nov. 26, 1775), *Letters* (Telford), 6:190–91; the fragment of poetry is from Milton, *Paradise Lost*, 8:591–92.

[16] Letter to Ann Bolton (Sept. 18, 1787), *Letters* (Telford), 8:9.

[17] See *Works*, 18:304.

which John and Charles Wesley, Benjamin Ingham, and other Oxford "Methodists" called an "exacter" format, including a line for every hour of the day.[18] This pattern was often embellished by Wesley with notes on readings, hourly ratings of the fervor of his devotion, and other data such as resolutions kept or broken during the day. In 1735, he began to incorporate shorthand into his diaries. He experimented with a number of shorthand systems and eventually settled on the form published by his acquaintance John Byrom as *The Universal English Shorthand* (1767). John Wesley and other members of the Oxford Methodist society also utilized a series of symbols and abbreviations to represent their more intimate thoughts.[19]

For the most part, Wesley's diaries read as a rather dull table of data recounting his daily activities. Little is revealed about his feelings, although occasionally an event he regarded as important is marked with an exclamation point. Although the pattern of a line per hour was the general form, he often included notes of other events on the half hour. As a sample given shortly will show, the diary entries usually record only a word or two describing events, many of these being consistent entries like "writ letters" or "necessary talk (religious)."

John Wesley's diaries were not published in printed form until the twentieth century. Portions appeared first in Nehemiah Curnock's edition of Wesley's *Journal* (1909–16). All of the extant diaries that cover the years of the published *Journal* are now available in the *Bicentennial Edition*, edited by W. Reginald Ward and Richard P. Heitzenrater. The diaries from Wesley's years at Oxford will appear in a future volume in this edition.

JOHN WESLEY'S JOURNAL

Unlike his private diaries, the various fascicles (installments) of *The Journal of the Reverend John Wesley, A.M.* were written for publication, presenting his reflections and commentary on the events of his life. The *Journal* was designed as a narrative to support Wesley's particular wing of the Evangelical Revival. Rather than reading the *Journal* simply as an account of what happened on particular dates in Wesley's life, then, it should be read as apologetic literature published at very

---

[18] Richard P. Heitzenrater, ed., *Diary of an Oxford Methodist: Benjamin Ingham, 1733–34* (1985), 4–5.

[19] Heitzenrater discovered the key to these symbols on the inside covers of one of Benjamin Ingham's diaries. See the previous note.

particular moments in his career. The first fascicle of the *Journal*, for instance, deals with the years between 1735 and 1738 (although the introductory letter whose first sentence is cited below was from 1732 and was appended before the *Journal* proper began on October 24, 1735). But, it was not written and published until the late spring and early summer of 1740, well after Wesley's first field preaching (April 1739) and his organization (or reorganization) of the Bristol and other societies. By the spring of 1740, John Wesley was in direct conflict with a particular group of London Moravians, and the first fascicle of the *Journal* must be seen as an apologetic and polemical document vindicating the impending separation of Wesley's London societies from the London Moravian community.[20]

The *Journal* chronicles fifty-five years of Wesley's life, from October 14, 1735 through October 24, 1790. It is complete for the forty-one-year stretch (1742–83) for which the diaries are missing. Fascicles of the *Journal* were widely distributed through the network of Wesleyan societies, with several thousands of copies printed in the later decades of Wesley's life. The *Journal* was witty and engaging, utilizing Wesley's considerable rhetorical skills. For example, it grabs the reader's attention by beginning with one of Wesley's letters from 1732:

> Sir,
>
> The occasion of my giving you this trouble is of a very extraordinary nature. On Sunday last I was informed (as no doubt you will be e'er long) that my brother and I had killed your son . . . [21]

With this arresting beginning, the *Journal* follows in many respects the format of the popular travel journal of the eighteenth century and so was designed for a broad reading public.

The *Journal* consistently offered its readers not only a charming narrative of travel, witty conversations, attacks by ignorant mobs, and solemn conversions, but, a continuous narrative of divine providence, showing how God had blessed and guided John Wesley and the Methodists associated with him. The *Journal* set a pattern for subsequent Methodist historical narratives that depicted the rise of Methodism as a divinely guided enterprise, raised up by the Almighty to correct the deteriorating state of Christian piety and morals in Wesley's day.[22]

---

[20] Cf. *Works*, 18:81–82.
[21] *Works*, 18:123.
[22] See Russell Richey, "History as a Bearer of Denominational Identity," in J. Carroll and W. C. Roof (eds), *Beyond Establishment* (1993), 270–95.

The *Journal* of John Wesley has been reprinted many times. Wesley himself re-issued earlier fascicles of the *Journal*, sometimes with significant corrections. He included the portions available prior to 1770 in the first published edition of his *Works*, a seriously defective collection published by William Pine in 1771. The complete *Journal* was published in the Benson (1831) and Jackson (1829–31) editions of the *Works*. The first critical edition of *Journal*, with some material from the diaries, was that edited by Nehemiah Curnock published in eight volumes between 1909 and 1916. However, Curnock and those who assisted him made some very serious errors in scholarship, and often included only vague references to other printed editions of Wesley's works. Thus, the only reliable critical edition of Wesley's *Journal* is that recently completed as part of the *Bicentennial Edition*, edited by W. Reginald Ward and Richard P. Heitzenrater.[23]

A DAY IN THE LIFE OF JOHN WESLEY: READING THE LETTERS, DIARY, AND JOURNAL TOGETHER

Let us examine in greater detail the portrait of John Wesley reflected in his letters, diary, and *Journal* by considering all of these sources as they describe one particular day in his life: Monday, April 2, 1739. This was the day when Wesley first preached in the open air at Bristol. The diary, *Journal*, and letters on this date paint a relatively complete picture of what was happening, both in the life of John Wesley and in the early history of the Methodist movement.

Wesley had been in Bristol since Saturday, March 31, having traveled there by horse from London. He was staying in Bristol at the home of a Mrs. Grevil. On Sunday, April 1, he had witnessed George Whitefield preach in the open air for the first time. This had clearly disturbed Wesley, who later wrote in the *Journal* of this experience:

> I could scarce reconcile myself to this *strange way* of preaching in the fields, of which he set me an example on Sunday, having been all my life (till very lately) so tenacious of every point relating to decency and order, that I should have thought the saving of souls *almost a sin* if it had not been done *in a church*.[24]

Wesley noted that on the evening of that day he began expounding the Sermon on the Mount, which he called "one pretty remarkable precedent for field preaching."[25]

[23] See *Works*, vols. 18–24.
[24] *Journal* (March 31, 1739), *Works*, 19:46.
[25] *Journal* (April 1, 1739), *Works*, 19:46.

The diary gives its typically brief account of the events of Monday, April 2, as follows (transcribed here from Wesley's shorthand by Richard P. Heitzenrater):

> Monday [April] 2. 7 Sang, necessary talk (religious). 8:45 at Mrs – -; tea, religious talk, sang, prayed. 10 At home; George Whitefield read letters. 12 Dinner, prayed. 1 George Whitefield went; sang, necessary talk (religious). 2 Meditated; writ diary. 2:30 Writ to the brethren. 4 At the Glasshouse (three or four thousand). 6 At Mrs Norman's, tea, religious talk, sang. 7 At Baldwin Street Society, sang, etc. 9:15 At home; Easy there; supper, religious talk, prayed. 10:45.[26]

The day began at 7:00 A.M. according to the diary. Those accustomed to thinking of Wesley as rising at 5:00 A.M. every day may find this disappointing, but it is worth noting that on the previous evening he had celebrated Holy Communion with thirty persons at the home of a Mr. Deschamps at 11:00 P.M. and had not gone to bed until 1:00 A.M. The day began with singing and "necessary talk (religious)." The latter reference shows Wesley's consistent practice in these early decades of noting whether his personal conversations were "necessary" (and thus not trifling) and "religious." One might presume that this earlier conversation was with his hostess, Mrs. Grevil. At 8:45, he had tea with an unnamed woman, and again notes "religious talk" as well as singing and praying (presumably with her). He was back at "home," that is, at Mrs. Grevil's home, by 10:00 A.M., and there entertained George Whitefield and "read letters."

The diary notes that at 2:00 P.M. John Wesley "meditated" and "writ diary." Diary keeping itself consumed some of Wesley's time each day, and the diary afforded him a first occasion to consider what was happening in his life. As we shall see, not only the *Journal*, but also the writing of letters gave him further occasions to reflect on the events of his life and their meaning for the Methodist movement. But, this initial period of meditation and diary keeping was only thirty minutes, according to the diary itself.

At 2:30 P.M., John Wesley "Writ to the brethren." This activity seems to have occupied an hour and a half, although one could imagine that he spent some of this time preparing emotionally for the new step in field preaching he was to undertake at 4:00 P.M. Wesley's letter "to the

---

[26] Diary (April 2, 1739), *Works*, 19:383. I have removed the reference in square brackets (supplied by the editors) indicating that Whitefield's departure on this date was not actually his leaving for America.

brethren" has survived, and spends a good deal of time recounting, much as the *Journal* would later, Whitefield's outdoor preaching. It may well have been, then, that the writing of this letter served to help steel Wesley for his first attempt at open-air preaching. The letter was addressed to James Hutton and the brethren ("and sisters too") at the Fetter Lane Society in London. The text of the letter is as follows:

Bristol, April 2, 1739.

My dear brethren (and sisters too),

The first person I met with on the road hither was one that was inquiring the road to Basingstoke. We had much conversation together till evening. He was a Somersetshire man, returning home, very angry at the wickedness of London, and particularly of the infidels there. He held out pretty well to Basingstoke, but during the expounding there (at which between twenty and thirty were present) his countenance fell, and I trust he is gone down to his house saying, "God be merciful to me a sinner."

I stayed an hour or two at Dummer in the morning with our brother Hutchings, who is strong in faith, but very weak in body; as most probably he will continue to be so long as he hides his light under a bushel. In the afternoon a poor woman at Newbury and her husband were much amazed at hearing of a salvation so far beyond all they had thought of or heard preached. The woman hopes she shall follow after, till she attains it. My horse tired in the evening, so that I was obliged to walk behind him, till a tradesman who overtook me lent me one of his, on which I came with him to Marlborough, and put up at the same inn. As I was preparing to alight here, my watch fell out of my pocket with the glass downward, which flew out to some distance, but broke not. After supper I preached the gospel to our little company, one of whom (a gentleman) greatly withstood my saying, till I told him he was wise in his own eyes, and had not "a heart right before God". Upon which he silently withdrew, and the rest calmly attended to the things that were spoken.

In the morning, I prayed to Him that "saveth both man and beast," and set out, though my horse was so tired he could scarce go a foot-pace. At Calne (twelve miles from Marlborough), I stopped. Many persons came into the room while I was at breakfast, one of whom I found to be a man of note in the place, who talked in so obscene and profane a manner as I never remember to have heard any one do, no, not in the streets of London. Before I went I plainly set before him the things he had done. They all stood looking at one another, but answered nothing.

At seven, by the blessing of God, I came hither. At eight our dear brother, Whitefield expounded in Weavers' Hall to about a thousand souls. On Sunday morning to six or seven thousand at the Bowling Green; at noon to much the same number at Hanham Mount; and at five to I believe thirty thousand from a little mount on Rose Green. At one today he left Bristol. I am straitened for time. Pray ye, my dear brethren, that some portion of his spirit may be given to your poor, weak brother.

John Wesley

Dear Jemmy,

None of my things are come. I want my gown and cassock every day. Oh how is God manifested in our brother Whitefield! I have seen none like him, no, not in Herrnhut!

We are all got safe to Bristol; praised be God for it![27]

The reader may note that this letter offers essentially an account of Wesley's dealings over the past four days (since leaving London), and in this respect is similar to the way in which he would describe events in his *Journal*. One can readily understand the sequence of events that transpired on this afternoon: at 2:00 P.M. he wrote out his diary for the previous few days; based on this recollection, he then wrote out the letter to the Fetter Lane Society, offering a more lively account of the same period intended for a public readership. Because the letter gave prominence to George Whitefield's preaching, one can also understand how its writing also served to prepare Wesley for his first experiment in open-air preaching, which followed immediately after the letter was completed.

Wesley's account of April 2, 1739 in his published *Journal* focuses exclusively on the open-air preaching. The original fascicle of the *Journal* was published in 1742, and it reads as follows:

Mon. 2. At four in the afternoon I submitted to "be more vile", and proclaimed in the highways the glad tidings of salvation, speaking from a little eminence in a ground adjoining to the city, to about three thousand people. The Scripture on which I spoke was this (is it possible anyone should be ignorant that it is fulfilled in every true minister of Christ?): "The Spirit of the Lord is upon me, because

[27] *Works*, 25:619–20.

he hath anointed me to preach the gospel to the poor. He hath sent
me to heal the broken-hearted, to preach deliverance to the captives
and recovering of sight to the blind, to set at liberty them that are
bruised, to proclaim the acceptable year of the Lord."[28]

This public preaching occurred in central Bristol at a place identified in
the diary as "the Glasshouse." Contemporary interpreters believe this
to have been near a brickyard whose owner Wesley knew; the site is
very near the present rail terminal in Bristol. Wesley's diary estimated
the crowd at "three or four thousand," and the *Journal* says "about
three thousand people." But, the reader should understand that Wesley's
estimates of the sizes of crowds were unscientific and often amounted
to what has been described as "pastoral estimates" of a congregation.
Attempts at measuring how many human bodies could actually fit into
the locations where Wesley preached (such as Gwennap Pit in Cornwall)
have raised serious questions about the reported sizes of the crowds to
whom he spoke. But whatever the size of the crowd, here in Bristol on
April 2, 1739, John Wesley had made a decisive move in his work of
evangelization, a move that was to mark the Wesleyan movement from
this time on.

The remainder of the day was unremarkable, at least to judge from
the diary. He had tea with Mrs. Norman after preaching. He met with
the Baldwin Street Society. He returned to Mrs. Grevil's home, had a
meal, and noted he was "easy there." A relief after the adventurous step
he had taken in the afternoon? He went to bed at 10:45 P.M.

The diary for April 2, 1739, the letter to the Fetter Lane Society
written on that date, and the *Journal* entry for the same reveal a great deal
about John Wesley's inner life in this period. His confidential partners
included three women with whom he had tea: Mrs. Grevil in the early
morning, an unidentified woman in the late morning, and Mrs. Norman
in the late afternoon. His only other conversational partner, so far as we
can tell from these records, was George Whitefield, with whom he spoke
at mid-day. A significant portion of his afternoon was spent alone. It was
in this time that he "meditated," wrote up his diary, wrote the letter to
the Fetter Lane Society, and steeled his courage (perhaps through each of
these private exercises) to preach in the open air.

The confluence of these three sources also reveals something about
the origins of the Methodist movement. At this early point in the life
of the movement, three strands of piety were interwoven, which would

---

[28] *Journal* (April 2, 1739), *Works*, 19:46.

soon unravel: the Moravian strand, which had been the original basis of the Fetter Lane Society; the Calvinistic wing of the Evangelical Revival, led by Howell Harris in Wales and George Whitefield in England (and soon in the American provinces); and the Wesleyan branch of the Revival, to be led by John and at some points Charles Wesley. Each of these three strands of the revival movement figure in the events of April 2, 1739. Whitefield had shown Wesley the practice of open-air preaching, but many in the Calvinist wing of the movement would eventually abandon itinerant preaching in favor of working within the existing structures of Anglican parish churches. The Wesleyan branch of the revival would take up itinerant preaching as a distinct part of its culture, a practice bequeathed to subsequent Methodist churches throughout the world. The Moravians had not (and did not) take up itinerant preaching, but had chosen to work through small groups and societies.

Within four or five years of this event, the Wesley brothers began to separate themselves from the Moravians and from the Calvinist Evangelical preachers. The formal issue with Moravians would be the use of the "means of grace" prior to conversion; the formal issue with the Calvinists would be the doctrine of limited atonement and (later on) the Wesleys' insistence on the need for good works in the way of salvation. But on April 2, 1739, these conflicts lay in the future, allowing us to see a tiny nucleus of the Evangelical movement in Wesley's letter and diary. By 1740, when he wrote the *Journal* account, relationships with the Moravians were already strained. Thus, the *Journal* account of this day minimized any role the Moravians played in his experience at the time.

CONCLUSION

The distinction between John Wesley's public self and his private self appears very clearly in the letters, diaries, and *Journal*. The *Journal* was a public document from start to finish; Wesley's diaries were intended to be private. Wesley's letters can be divided between those that were intended for a public readership and those intended only for one reader. It is worth noting this division because Wesley's spirituality placed a strong emphasis on open accountability to a community of faith. As he reflected upon his life by writing out the diaries, then re-telling the events of his life in public letters, and eventually in the *Journal*, he made his own experience, as he understood it in the light of God's work in his time, available to the public. There was a richness to the public self that

Wesley presented: he could be pious, prescriptive, penitential, witty, and even funny on different occasions.

There was a side of John Wesley that was kept from public view, and his private self was as complex as his public self. His private letters often reveal a character that could be emotionally manipulative or voyeuristic with respect to his most intimate correspondents. Comments like "Write soon, and write freely" appear very frequently in his letters to these confidants and confidantes. The remarkable thing about the resources for studying John Wesley is how much of life that he – like most people – chose to keep private is now available for public consideration.

The confluence of the letters, diaries, and *Journal* offers exceptionally rich insight into the life of John Wesley. For decades of his life we can study events at an hourly level, and sometimes at even finer levels of detail. Add to these resources his *Sermons* and other writings, many of which can be dated and contextualized, and the range of materials for understanding John Wesley's life is very rich indeed.

8 John Wesley as editor and publisher

ISABEL RIVERS

The importance and extent of John Wesley's career as an editor and publisher have long been known to historians of Methodism, although not perhaps to historians of literature. Three key individuals, two in the nineteenth century and one in the mid twentieth, established the main facts. Thomas Jackson edited and published the extended second edition of Wesley's *Christian Library* (1819–27), as well as the third edition of Wesley's *Works* (1829–31). Richard Green compiled the first chronologically ordered bibliography of *The Works of John and Charles Wesley* (1896; 2nd ed., rev., 1906). Building on Green, Frank Baker compiled *A Union Catalogue of the Publications of John and Charles Wesley* (1966), which provisionally – and very ambitiously in the pre-electronic age – listed all known editions and the whereabouts of surviving copies. The second edition of Baker's *Union Catalogue* (1991) added some additional materials that had been located and finalized the numbering system for Wesley's publications being used in *The Bicentennial Edition of the Works of John Wesley*. The two-volume bibliography for this edition will include Baker's extended descriptions of the text history of many of these items.

In the early twenty-first century, thanks to the online English Short Title Catalogue (ESTC), we have a much clearer idea both of the numbers of religious books published in the eighteenth century in relation to the whole field of publications, and of the sheer size of Wesley's output as editor and publisher. What does the ESTC tell us? Michael Suarez, who has done a series of important statistical analyses of eighteenth-century publishing using the ESTC, has established that "religion, philosophy and ethics," one of eleven categories into which he divides all eighteenth-century publications, constituted the most important category at the beginning of the century, but declined as a proportion of the whole by the end. In the mid-1750s, there were about 550 religious publications of about 2,800 total publications a year, and in the mid-1790s, when publishing of all kinds increased dramatically, about 800 religious publications out of about 15,300 total publications a year.

Anyone working regularly with the ESTC knows that there are considerable gaps in the record, which means that we have to proceed with caution. This is especially true with respect to the publication of small religious books. It is difficult to provide an accurate account of the proportion of books published by size and subject matter, because, as Suarez emphasizes, the big expensive books (folios and quartos) are much more likely to have survived than the small cheap ones. Slightly more than half the surviving books published throughout the eighteenth century were octavos (roughly 5 by 8 inches). Duodecimo books (roughly 4 by 7 inches, the favored format for popular religious books) are almost certainly under-represented in the ESTC, as they are the ones most likely to have worn out and been thrown away. According to Suarez's statistics, in the middle of the century, duodecimos constituted about 20 percent of the market, but the true figure must have been much higher than that.[1] Even if we ignore the loss of such material, it is clear that with the possible exception of Daniel Defoe (whose attributions are much disputed), Wesley was editor, author, or publisher of more works (the majority of them short religious pamphlets in duodecimo format) than any other single figure in eighteenth-century Britain.[2]

It is obviously impossible to do justice in a short compass to the range of Wesley's editorial and publishing activities over a period of almost sixty years. This essay will begin by considering how far his methods were original, and whether the critical responses of some readers to the free hand he gave himself in selecting and abridging the works of others as he saw fit are justified. It will then survey his publications in terms of audience, source, author, religious denomination, and format, and sketch the arrangements he made for printing and distributing them. Finally, Wesley's favorite genres and publications will be assessed for the light they throw on his beliefs.

[1]   Michael F. Suarez SJ, "Towards a Bibliometric Analysis of the Surviving Record, 1701–1800," in Michael F. Suarez SJ and Michael Turner (eds.), *The Cambridge History of the Book in Britain*, vol. 5, *1695–1830* (2009), 46–48, 56–59. I am very grateful to Michael Suarez for allowing me to use his unpublished tables.

[2]   The ESTC (accessed February 2009) lists 1536 publications with John Wesley as author, and 2042 publications with John Wesley as "any word." The former figure represents different editions of works written, edited, abridged, or prefaced by Wesley, and the latter includes works addressed to or about Wesley. For comparison, Defoe has 1643 and 2073 in these categories; Isaac Watts 1292 and 1359; Alexander Pope 1119 and 1266; Samuel Johnson 720 and 1427; George Whitefield 707 and 787. Frank Baker estimated that John and Charles Wesley issued about 450 works, in about 2,000 editions, averaging 2,000 copies each; Baker, *John Wesley London Publisher 1733–1791* (1984).

THE CONTEXT OF WESLEY'S ACTIVITIES

Some Methodist historians from the nineteenth century onwards have wrongly assumed that because Wesley's editing and publishing activities were so prominent he was unique in what he was doing, and indeed that his methods antedated later popular publishing practices.[3] Some more or less hostile critics and commentators, such as Richard Hill in the eighteenth century and David Bebbington in the twenty-first century, writing out of loyalty to some of the authors Wesley appropriated, have accused him of changing the meaning of his sources.[4] It is quite right for students of Wesley to emphasize the scale and importance of his editorial work. But, it is inaccurate to see him as a pioneer in the publishing and distributing of popular religious works, or as the sole abridger to alter the doctrinal emphases of the authors whose works he edited. If Wesley's editions are read in the wider context of what was edited, published, and distributed by members of other organizations or denominations, the importance and intrinsic interest of what he was doing remains as strong; but it becomes obvious that to some extent he was following in the footsteps of others, and that even where there was no influence in either direction members of other denominations or groups were engaged in parallel activities. There was an established tradition after the Reformation of Protestants adapting popular Catholic books for their purposes, and eighteenth-century editors felt similarly free to make earlier works fit the requirements of their denominations and theological positions. Protestants reshaped Catholic books; Arminians reshaped books by Calvinists; heterodox Unitarians reshaped books by orthodox Trinitarians.[5]

In *John Wesley and the Church of England*, Baker published his transcription of a document of July 19, 1733, in which Wesley made a

---

3 For example, Tyerman, Curnock, and Baker all assume incorrectly that Wesley was the first to start a tract society: see Luke Tyerman, *The Life and Times of the Rev. John Wesley, M.A.* (3rd ed., London, 1876), 3:369; Nehemiah Curnock (ed.), *The Journal of the Rev. John Wesley, A.M.* (1909–16), 6:343n; and Frank Baker, *A Charge to Keep: An Introduction to the People called Methodists* (1947), 171.

4 [Richard Hill], *A Review of All the Doctrines taught by the Rev. Mr. John Wesley* (2nd ed., 1772), 41, 123, where he draws attention to the doctrines of John Bunyan that Wesley has expunged; D. W. Bebbington, "The Reputation of Edwards Abroad," in Stephen J. Stein (ed.), *The Cambridge Companion to Jonathan Edwards* (2007), 241, where he comments on Wesley's "characteristic disregard for the wishes of an author."

5 See Isabel Rivers, "Writing the History of Early Evangelicalism," *History of European Ideas* 35 (2009): 110. For examples of the reshaping of à Kempis, Scougal, and Bunyan, see Rivers, "Religious Publishing," in *Cambridge History of the Book in Britain*, 5:595–96.

covenant with God. Baker points out that it "reveals the genesis of his amazing publishing career." Wesley's list of ways in which he would devote his life to God includes:

> By Writing – either by Composing (1) Geneses and Letters for my Pupils, Relations, Friends, Acquaintance, (2) Practical Treatises for the P[oo]r and Wicked, (3) Sermons for all:

> Or by Abridging (1) Uncommon treatises for Pupils and Acquaintance, (2) Plain ones (as Christian Monitor) for the Poor and Wicked:

> Or (1) By translating True Divinity for all.[6]

Although Wesley's publishing agenda was amazing, there were several individuals and groups in the seventeenth and eighteenth centuries with similar aims.

An important model was Richard Baxter (1615–91), a Puritan minister of Kidderminster during the Interregnum and nonconformist writer based in London after the Restoration. Baxter had a keen sense of the importance of pitching his writings at different rhetorical levels, depending on the educational standing of the target audience and how far they had advanced on the road to salvation. He understood that his cheaper and easier books would have an impact on the poor only if they in fact reached the poor. He prefaced his *Poor Man's Family Book* (1674) with "A request to the Rich," urging them to give this or similar books away. He gave away large numbers of his books to his Kidderminster parishioners. After the Restoration, he was a member of the Trust established in 1674 by his fellow nonconformist Thomas Gouge to translate English works of practical divinity into Welsh and distribute them in Wales.[7] In addition to Bibles, Testaments, and Psalters, the Trust distributed writings by ministers ejected from the Church of England in 1662, especially Baxter and Gouge, and earlier Puritan favorites, such as William Perkins's catechism, *The Foundation of Christian Religion*, Arthur Dent's *Plain Man's Pathway to Heaven*, and Lewis Bayly's *Practice of Piety*.

Although Wesley was an admirer of Baxter, and published abridged editions of his *Aphorisms of Justification*, *The Saints' Everlasting Rest*,

---

6 Frank Baker, *John Wesley and the Church of England* (2nd ed., 2000), 35–36. Wesley refers to John Rawlet's much reprinted *The Christian Monitor* (first published 1686).

7 See Geoffrey F. Nuttall, "The Emergence of Nonconformity," in Nuttall et al. (eds.), *The Beginnings of Nonconformity* (1964), 26–32; and Richard L. Greaves, "Gouge, Thomas (1605–81)," in *The Oxford Dictionary of National Biography* (2004).

and *A Call to the Unconverted*,[8] a more immediate model for his publishing activities was the Society for Promoting Christian Knowledge (SPCK). The SPCK was founded in 1698 by Dr Thomas Bray and others as a Church of England society with an extremely ambitious program, both at home and in the American colonies: (1) improving the education of clergy through the establishment of libraries, (2) teaching poor children to read and write and to understand the principles of the Christian religion, and (3) distributing Bibles and devotional and didactic works to poor families, servants, prisoners, soldiers, and sailors.[9] John Wesley's father Samuel became a corresponding member in 1700. In 1701, the SPCK's overseas activities were brought under a separate society, the Society for the Propagation of the Gospel in Foreign Parts (SPG), at whose invitation John Wesley went in 1735 as a missionary to Georgia. The SPCK had a considerable impact on the book trade, and was a major educational force, but reacted negatively to the rise of Methodism. Charles Rivington, who published one of Wesley's first books, an edition of Thomas à Kempis, in 1735, quarreled with Wesley in 1740 as Methodism took off; Rivington's son John, who became the official publisher for the SPCK in 1765, regularly brought out anti-Methodist literature.[10] The SPCK became objectionable to Methodists and to dissenting and Church of England evangelicals later in the century because many of the works it distributed ignored what they regarded as the essential doctrines of the gospel. But, its methods were a significant influence in the formation of later tract societies. It perfected the process whereby suitable books – whether practical devotional works, such as *The Whole Duty of Man*; guides to Church of England services, such as Robert Nelson's *Companion for the Festivals and Fasts*; or Josiah Woodward's many "monitors" for soldiers, sailors, and others – were selected by committee, kept in print, and given to corresponding members to distribute. Although Wesley's procedures for choosing and distributing books, and the books he chose to edit and publish, differed in many respects from those of the SPCK, there is no doubt that he learned from their example.

---

[8] See Isabel Rivers, "Dissenting and Methodist Books of Practical Divinity," in Rivers (ed.), *Books and their Readers in Eighteenth-Century England* (1982), 141–42.

[9] See Scott Mandelbrote, "The Publishing and Distribution of Religious Books by Voluntary Associations," in *Cambridge History of the Book in Britain*, 5:613–30.

[10] See Frank Baker, "John Wesley and the 'Imitatio Christi'," *The London Quarterly and Holborn Review* 166 (1941): 82; and Clive Field, "Anti-Methodist Publications of the Eighteenth Century: A Revised Bibliography," *Bulletin of the John Rylands University Library of Manchester* 73 (1991): 159–280.

AUDIENCES

From early in his career as editor, Wesley considered carefully what instructions about reading he should give the audiences for whom his books were designed. His *The Christian's Pattern* (1735), an edition of a 1677 English translation of the *Imitatio Christi* attributed to Thomas à Kempis, contained a lengthy preface drawn from four different sources. The fourth part was an excerpt of the "Praemonitio ad lectorem" [advice to the reader] in the Cologne edition of 1682. In Wesley's version:

> the following advices are proposed, concerning the manner of reading this (or any other religious) treatise.... *First,* Assign some stated time every day for this employment, and observe it, so far as you possibly can, inviolably.... *Secondly,* Prepare yourself for reading by purity of intention, singly aiming at the good of your soul.... *Thirdly,* Be sure to read, not cursorily or hastily; but leisurely, seriously, and with great attention; with proper pauses and intervals, that you may allow time for the enlightenings of the divine grace. To this end, recollect every now and then what you have read, and consider how to reduce it to practice. Further, let your reading be continued and regular, not rambling and desultory.... Whatsoever book you begin, read therefore through in order: not but that it will be of great service, to read those passages over and over, that more nearly concern yourself and more closely affect your inclinations or practice.... *Fourthly,* Labour to work your self up into a temper correspondent with what you read. For that reading is useless, which only enlightens the understanding, without warming the affections.[11]

In Wesley's pocket (24°) version of the same year and some of his later abridgements of *The Christian's Pattern*, this long preface was reduced to a slightly altered statement of these directions, which hence became far more prominent, and came to be identified as Wesley's own. Indeed, a 1740 edition of George Stanhope's earlier paraphrase of à Kempis incorporated a simplified and rather cruder version of the directions, attributing them to Wesley.[12]

The emphasis on the reader's need for time, care, and the appropriate frame of mind was hardly peculiar to Wesley. He took these instructions from a seventeenth-century Latin edition and he shared

---

[11] *The Christian's Pattern* (1735), xxii–iii. The author of the "Praemonitio" (not identified by Wesley) was Jacob Merlo Horstius (1597–1644), a Catholic priest in Cologne.

[12] Thomas à Kempis, *The Christian's Pattern* (Manchester: R. Whitworth, 1740), viii.

the views expressed with many contemporaries. The influential Roman Catholic writer Richard Challoner (1691–1781), who brought out a new and equally popular translation of à Kempis in 1737, gave similar instructions in his much reprinted devotional handbook *The Garden of the Soul*.[13] Wesley was not the first eighteenth-century writer on religion to target a wide range of readers. The Congregationalist educator, theologian, and philosopher Isaac Watts (1674–1748) was famous for addressing different publications to children and students as well as to congregations, fellow ministers, and families.[14] But it would perhaps be fair to say that Wesley was the first such writer systematically to create his own audiences.

Who were the readers of Wesley's editions? He stated many years later that his first publication in 1733, *A Collection of Forms of Prayer*, was for his students at Oxford.[15] His publication of abridgements of two treatises by John Norris in 1734 and of à Kempis in 1735 were designed in part for the same audience.[16] He published his first hymn book, *A Collection of Psalms and Hymns*, at Charleston, South Carolina, in 1737 for his Georgia parishioners, adapting hymns from a number of writers, especially Watts. But, it was on his return to England, in the course of his establishment of his version of Methodism from 1739 to 1744, that he became an editor and distributor of books on a serious scale. In this four-year period, works he edited and abridged, which were to have a very long shelf life included the life of Thomas Haliburton, A. H. Francke's *Nicodemus*, the life of M. de Renty, William Law's *Christian Perfection* and *Serious Call*, and Henry Scougal's *The Life of God in the Soul of Man*. From 1740 onwards, Wesley's designated audiences for the great majority of his publications were members of the Methodist societies and his itinerant lay preachers. But, a few were for children; some were Latin texts for the students of Kingswood School, which inevitably had a restricted circulation, and some (like the publications of the SPCK) were meant to be given away to the poor by the subscribers to his tract society of 1782 (see later).

The people called Methodists were expected to be readers. Wesley reaffirmed this expectation in a letter to George Holder, one of his preachers, towards the end of his life: "It cannot be that the people should grow in grace unless they give themselves to reading. A reading people will

---

[13] Richard Challoner, *The Garden of the Soul* (London, 1755 ed.), 172–73.

[14] See Rivers, *Reason, Grace, and Sentiment*, 1:173–74.

[15] *Journal* (14 May 1765), *Works*, 21:510–11.

[16] Details of these and subsequent publications can be found in the works by Richard Green and Frank Baker mentioned in the opening paragraph of this chapter.

always be a knowing people."[17] But, as he warned in the *General Rules* of 1743, they were to avoid "*reading* those *books*, which do not tend to the knowledge or love of God."[18] In the early Minutes of 1746 and 1747, the preachers were given explicit instructions about what, when and how to read: they were to consider themselves "as young students at the university," they were to read for seven hours a day, and they were to read the books Wesley advised and no others.[19] As the Minutes were revised over the years, and the range and numbers of Wesley's publications increased, so the instructions to preachers about what to read were abbreviated, presumably because catalogues were now available. Thus, the 1746 Minutes list the titles and authors of books of practical divinity Wesley had already published, including Scougal, à Kempis, Bunyan, and Law, and "our other Tracts and Poems," as well as other named works of theology and ecclesiastical history, whereas the *Large Minutes* refer more generally to *The Christian Library*, "the other books we have published in prose and verse," and those recommended in the rules of Kingswood School.[20] (Wesley observed that anyone going through the suggested four-year course of academical learning at Kingswood would "be a better scholar than nine in ten of the graduates at Oxford or Cambridge."[21]) In his *Journal*, he wished all his preachers would follow his example "and frequently read in public and enforce select portions of the *Christian Library*."[22] In addition, the *Large Minutes* specified one of the tasks of assistants (preachers) in each circuit as "To take care that every society be duly supplied with books; particularly with 'Kempis,' 'Instructions for Children,' and the 'Primitive Physic,' which ought to be in every house."[23] These lists and injunctions make clear that Wesley had a high idea of the intellectual level that ordinary Methodist members and their preachers might achieve through reading the books he recommended.

SOURCES AND AUTHORS

How did Wesley come to choose the books he edited and published? We can distinguish four main categories of books that he decided to make more widely available: older and more recent books that formed

[17] 8 November 1790, *Letters* (Telford), 8:247.
[18] *General Rules*, §4, *Works*, 9:71.
[19] "John Bennet's Copy of the Minutes of the Conferences of 1744, 1745, 1747 and 1748," *Publications of the Wesley Historical Society* 1 (1896): 36, 50.
[20] *Minutes of Some Late Conversations*, Q. 29, *Works* (Jackson), 8:314.
[21] *Short Account of the School in Kingswood*, *Works* (Jackson), 13:289.
[22] *Journal* (13 May 1754), *Works*, 20:486.
[23] *Minutes*, Q. 40, *Works* (Jackson), 8:319.

an essential part of his intellectual and religious milieu at Oxford; older books that he was introduced to by individuals or different evangelical groups at various stages of his religious development, for example by the Moravians, or as Methodism began to take off in 1739; newly published books that he encountered throughout his life in the ordinary course of reading; and shorter accounts that he commissioned for publication from his preachers or members of his societies.[24]

It is possible to trace Wesley's choices through a variety of means, including his journals, letters, and prefaces. A few examples will make this clear. We know from an early letter to his mother that he read à Kempis in 1725, and he later drew attention in his *Journal* and in *A Plain Account of Christian Perfection* to the importance of his early reading of à Kempis, Jeremy Taylor, and Law.[25] It appears from his unpublished diary that he did not read Bunyan's *Pilgrim's Progress* until 1739; he published his abridgement of Part 1 four years later.[26] By now, he was actively looking for works to publish. In the Minutes for 1744, we hear Wesley asking "What shall I write next? What abridge?"[27] A new work that influenced him profoundly and that he abridged and published soon after first reading it is Jonathan Edwards's *Faithful Narrative of the Surprising Work of God*: he read this in 1738 and published his abridgement in 1744.[28] This was followed closely by two other works by Edwards, *The Distinguishing Marks of a Work of the Spirit of God*, which Wesley abridged and published in 1744; and *Some Thoughts concerning the Present Revival of Religion in New-England*, which he abridged and published the following year. A much later example of a very different kind of work is Archibald Maclaine's translation of the German historian Mosheim's *Ecclesiastical History*: Wesley drew the reader's attention to the translation in his *Journal* entry for August 1771 ("a very sensible translator of a very sensible writer"), and published his abridgement ten years later, explaining in the preface his rather more critical attitudes to the author and his translator, his motives for undertaking the project, and his improvements.[29] For the last twelve years of his life, he was much occupied with collecting and editing materials for publication in

---

[24] For a sense of the range of books read by the Oxford Methodists see the "Bibliography of Ingham's Reading," in Richard P. Heitzenrater (ed.), *Diary of an Oxford Methodist: Benjamin Ingham, 1733–1734* (1985).

[25] See Letter to Susanna Wesley (28 May 1725), *Works*, 25:162–63; *Journal* (24 May 1738), *Works*, 18:243–44; *Plain Account*, §§2–4, *Works* (Jackson), 11:366–67.

[26] Diary (8 October, 2 November 1739), *Works*, 18:410, 414.

[27] "John Bennet's Copy of the Minutes," 18.

[28] *Journal* (9 October 1738), *Works*, 19:16.

[29] *Journal* (12 August 1771), *Works* 22:287. The preface can be found in *Works* (Jackson), 14:297–99.

the *Arminian Magazine*; his insistent letters from 1780 to 1783 to the reluctant John Valton, one of his preachers, culminated in the appearance of Valton's account of his life in the *Arminian Magazine* in 1783–84.[30]

Wesley's chosen authors came from an extraordinary range of nationalities and denominations, and included his contemporaries as well as historical figures, lay people as well as ministers, and women as well as men. Analysts and interpreters of Wesley's reading and editing have rightly emphasized his eclectic affinities with a range of earlier churches, denominations, and groupings.[31] The non-English authors he edited included early Christians, such as Macarius; pre-Reformation and post-Reformation Roman Catholics, such as à Kempis, Pascal, Molinos, Fénelon, Fleury, and Mme Guyon; continental Lutherans and pietists, such as Arndt and Francke; and New England protestants, such as Edwards and Brainerd. His English authors from the late sixteenth to the mid-eighteenth centuries included Puritans, nonconformists, and dissenters, such as Bolton, Preston, John Owen, Joseph and Richard Alleine (or Allein), Baxter, Howe, Bunyan, and Watts; members of the Church of England of different leanings, such as Taylor, John Smith, Cudworth, More, Barrow, Tillotson, and Norris; and the nonjurors Ken and Law. The Scots included the episcopalians Scougal and Leighton, and the Presbyterian Halyburton (or Haliburton). In among these male theologians and ministers of different churches and traditions in Wesley's collections and catalog, all well known to modern historians, are many members of his Methodist societies, male and female – for example Mary Gilbert, Elizabeth Harper, Jane Cooper, Mrs. Lefevre, John Nelson, and John Haime. Some of these assumed some celebrity through nineteenth-century reprints, but most are now scarcely known, despite the fame that Wesley's editions gave them at the time.

FORMATS

Wesley published the works of these writers in a range of formats and prices, all designed to meet the needs of his different audiences, and all stamped in different ways with his authority. He was not concerned by questions of authorship that bother modern readers. He sometimes

---

[30] See *Letters* (Telford), 7:17, 35, 43–4, 100–1. On the preachers' lives see Isabel Rivers, "'Strangers and Pilgrims': Sources and Patterns of Methodist Narrative," in *Augustan Worlds*, ed. J. C. Hilson et al. (1978), 189–203.

[31] See, among others, Jean Orcibal, "The Theological Originality of John Wesley and Continental Spirituality," in Rupert Davies and Gordon Rupp (eds.), *A History of the Methodist Church in Great Britain*, vol. 1 (1965); and Robert C. Monk, *John Wesley: His Puritan Heritage* (1966).

left the author's name off the title page, and usually added his own, in the form "an extract of [the title of the work] by John Wesley." He thus drew to the attention of his readers the fact that these works were his because they were chosen, shaped, and published by him, and that through this process he had given them a specific meaning. This meant that he was open to the accusation of inconsistency when works that formed part of a larger collection did not appear to cohere theologically, an accusation made by Richard Hill in relation to *A Christian Library* that Wesley had difficulty in rebutting.[32] It also meant, as we shall see, that book-sellers (publishers in modern parlance) might intervene to protect their property.

Wesley published these works *either* individually (a few in octavo, but the majority in duodecimo; very occasionally complete, but usually in various stages of abridgement) *or* as part of multi volume collections. The three main collections are: *A Christian Library*, fifty volumes duodecimo (1749–55); *The Works of the Rev. John Wesley*, thirty-two volumes duodecimo (1771–74); and *The Arminian Magazine*, octavo (monthly from 1778, continuing after his death in 1791 with material prepared by him). Richard Heitzenrater has recently pointed out that Wesley first offered his works as a fifteen-volume collection in 1746 with "Wesley's Tracts" on the spine (of the 65 items, 25 were extracts of other authors), and that this should be considered as the first of four collections.[33]

The title of the *Christian Library* continues: *Consisting of Extracts from and Abridgments of the Choicest Pieces of Practical Divinity, which have been Publish'd in the English Tongue.* Wesley explained his principles of selection and abridgement in the preface to the first volume.[34] The collection contains a good deal of fascinating material that he never published elsewhere. Although Wesley designed it as a virtually self-contained library for his preachers' use, it should not be regarded as representing his most important editorial work and it should not be studied in isolation. His misnamed (to the modern eye) collection of *Works of John Wesley* contains not only his own sermons, journals, and treatises but also several of his favorite authors, such as Law and Brainerd, whose works he had already published individually, and popular short pieces by and about Methodists. This mixture is even more evident in the *Arminian Magazine*, which was published in monthly parts and sold as a bound annual. Wesley founded it to counteract the

---

[32] See Rivers, *Reason, Grace, and Sentiment*, 1:219.

[33] Richard P. Heitzenrater, "John Wesley's *A Christian Library*, then and now," *American Theological Library Association Summary of Proceedings* 55 (2007): 133–45, at 139.

[34] See *Works* (Jackson), 14:220–23.

Calvinist doctrine of the *Spiritual* and *Gospel Magazines*, and its title page advertises that it consists of *Extracts and Original Treatises on Universal Redemption*. What made the *Arminian Magazine* such an attractive work was that, in addition to defences of universal salvation, the lives of holy men of various denominations, and poetry, it included "Accounts and Letters, containing the experience of pious persons, the greatest part of whom are still alive."[35]

Wesley's most important single-volume collection was *A Collection of Hymns for the Use of the People called Methodists* (1780). The fruit of his experience of editing over twenty hymn books for a period of over forty years, the *Collection* went through multiple editions right through the nineteenth century.[36] Consisting largely of hymns by Charles Wesley, it also contained several by English authors (notably Watts) and translations of German hymns. Wesley's three-volume anthology, *A Collection of Moral and Sacred Poems from the Most Celebrated English Authors* (1744), was an ambitious, but unsuccessful, compilation of shorter and longer poems by seventeenth-century poets such as Milton, Herbert, and Cowley and more recent ones such as Prior, Watts, Elizabeth Rowe, Pope, Samuel Wesley Jr., and Young. Wesley was obliged to pay £50 in compensation to the bookseller Robert Dodsley for publishing poems by Rowe and Young that were Dodsley's property, and to promise not to do so again.[37]

Wesley also edited substantial multi volume works of general scientific and historical knowledge: *A Survey of the Wisdom of God in the Creation* (discussed in Chapter 9), which eventually reached five volumes; *A Concise History of England* based on Goldsmith, Smollett, and Rapin, in four volumes (1776); and *A Concise Ecclesiastical History* abridged from Mosheim, in four volumes (1781). More surprisingly, he produced a two-volume abridgement of Henry Brooke's novel *The Fool of Quality* as *The History of Henry Earl of Moreland* (1781). The effort that went into producing these collections and multi volume works was substantial, but they do not represent the heart of Wesley's editorial and publishing endeavors. For this, we must turn to his individually published items.

Most of Wesley's editions were of single works, usually abridged by half or more. They were not necessarily short. Judging from the number of new editions, in Wesley's lifetime and after, some of the most successful and influential were (in chronological order with the date of

---

[35] "To the Reader," §7, *Arminian Magazine* 1 (1778): v–vi; *Works* (Jackson), 14:280.
[36] See *Works*, 7:22–34, Appendix B.
[37] Letter to Robert Dodsley (21 Dec. 1744), *Works*, 26:119.

Wesley's first editions): John Norris's *A Treatise on Christian Prudence*
and *Reflections upon the Conduct of Human Life* (1734); *The Christian's Pattern* (1735); *An Extract of the Life and Death of Mr. Thomas
Haliburton* (1739); *The Nature and Design of Christianity* (1740),
extracted from Law's *Christian Perfection*; *An Extract of the Life of
Monsieur de Renty* (1741); *The Pilgrim's Progress* (1743); Law's *Seri-
ous Call* (1744); Edwards's *The Distinguishing Marks of a Work of the
Spirit of God* (1744); Scougal's *Life of God in the Soul of Man* (1744);
Instructions for Children, from Abbé Fleury and Pierre Poiret (1745);
An Extract of the Life and Death of Mr. John Janeway (1749); *An
Extract of the Life of the Late Rev. Mr. David Brainerd*, from Edwards's
Account and Brainerd's own *Journal* (1768); *Directions for Renewing our
Covenant with God*, from Richard Allein's *Vindiciae Pietatis* (1780);
Joseph Allein's *An Alarm to Unconverted Sinners* (1782); and Baxter's
A Call to the Unconverted (1782). Alongside this much-reprinted group
we can place several works by Methodists: two by preachers, *An Extract
from John Nelson's Journal* (1782) and *A Short Account of God's Dealings with Mr. John Haime* (1785); and three by or about women, *Letters
wrote by Jane Cooper* (1764), *An Extract of Miss Mary Gilbert's Journal* (1768), and *A Short Account of the Death of Elizabeth Hindmarsh*
(1777).

The prices for these editions varied enormously, from 1d for short
single works to 10s or more for multi volume collections. Thus in 1746
The Nature and Design of Christianity was advertised at 1d (pence),
Christian Prudence at 3d, *Instructions for Children* at 3d, *The Pilgrim's
Progress* at 4d, *Life of de Renty* at 4d, *Life of Haliburton* at 6d, *A Christian's Pattern* at 8d, and *A Serious Call* at 1s 6d.[38] The *Works* cost 6d per
weekly number, and the *Arminian Magazine* 6d per monthly part. Wesley's tract society, founded in 1782, offered thirty titles for subscribing
members to give away, the first four being *A Serious Call* at 8d, Allein's
Alarm at 3½d, Baxter's *Call* at 2½d, and *The Nature and Design of Christianity* at 3s (shilling) per hundred.[39] At the higher end, in 1790, *Henry
Earl of Moreland* was advertised at 6s and *Moral and Sacred Poems* at
7s 6d, and, in 1807, *A Concise Ecclesiastical History* was advertised

[38] Prices are taken from the list at the end of Wesley, *A Farther Appeal to Men of Reason
and Religion* (3rd ed., 1746). 1 shilling (s) = 12 pence (d).

[39] "A Plan of the Society instituted in January, 1782, to distribute Religious Tracts among
the Poor," *Arminian Magazine* 8 (1784): facing p. 620 (in Bodleian Library copy). The
names of the subscribers and amounts subscribed are listed in *A State of the Society
for Distributing Religious Tracts among the Poor, for the Year 1782* (1783).

at 10s sewed, 13s sheep, and 15s calf.[40] From their formats and prices, we can see that Wesley's editions were aimed at those members of the Methodist societies who could afford short cheap books (the vast majority), the assistants who would keep the societies stocked, and the better off who could buy more expensive books for themselves and give cheap ones to the poor.

PUBLISHING AND DISTRIBUTION

Wesley's complex entrepreneurial activities as commissioner, publisher, printer, and distributor can only be summarized briefly here.[41] From 1738 until 1779, he employed a number of different printers and booksellers in the main Methodist centers: London, Bristol, Newcastle, and Dublin. The printers at different periods included John Bowyer, William Strahan, Henry Cock, Robert Hawes, and Joseph Fry in London; John Gooding in Newcastle; Felix Farley and William Pine in Bristol; and Samuel Powell in Dublin. The booksellers included Thomas Trye in London and R. Akenhead in Newcastle. The title pages of Wesley's publications usually designate the name of the printer, followed by the bookseller and his location. They usually also state that they are sold at the Foundery in Moorfields, Wesley's London headquarters, and sometimes at the New School (or the New Room) in the Horsefair, Bristol; later they specify that they are sold "at the Rev. Mr. Wesley's preaching-houses in town and country" or "at the Methodist preaching-houses in town and country," and after 1778 "at the New Chapel, City Road." Until 1778, the Foundery was the center (among many other activities) of Wesley's bookselling and distribution business; after the building of the City Road Chapel, he moved the business there and installed a printing press in the Foundery where he employed his own printer, John Paramore, to be succeeded by his brother George Paramore. Two examples of printing details from title pages, early and late, show this development very clearly: *A Serious Call to a Holy Life* (Newcastle upon Tyne, 1744): "printed by John Gooding, on the Side: sold by R. Akenhead, on Tyne Bridge, Newcastle; by T. Trye, at Gray's Inn Gate, Holbourn, at the Foundery, near Upper-Moorfields, London; and at the New-School in the Horse-Fair, Bristol"; *An Extract from John Nelson's Journal*

---

40 *Catalogue of Books published by the Rev. Mr. Wesley* (?1790); *A Catalogue of Books, for the Year 1807, Originally Published by the late Rev. Mr. Wesley.*

41 The main sources are Baker, *A Charge to Keep*, chapter 5; Baker, *John Wesley London Publisher 1733–1791* (1984); and Frank Cumbers, *The Book Room: The Story of the Methodist Publishing House and Epworth Press* (1956).

(London, 1782): "printed by J. Paramore, at the Foundery, Upper Moor-fields. And sold at the Rev. Mr. Wesley's New Chapel, in the City Road, and at all his preaching-houses in town and country."

Book stewards in London and assistants in the provinces were responsible for running the business, and the travelling preachers carried the books for sale at the preaching houses around the country. The scale of the business is indicated by the inventory taken after Wesley's death in 1791 by John Parsons and James Barker: Wesley owned 254,512 copies of 351 titles valued at £3930.[42]

WESLEY'S FAVORITE GENRES AND BOOKS

What light do Wesley's editions throw on his own activity as a writer? How much attention should students of Wesley's thought give to them? As suggested earlier, Wesley evidently regarded them as part of his own *oeuvre*, and it seems a mistake not to take his valuation seriously. Wesley's publications fall into a number of distinct genres, which tell us a good deal about what he perceived the function of religious books to be. The 1790 catalog divides the books (those he wrote and those he edited) into six categories: poetical, practical, historical, controversial, political, and miscellaneous. His most popular works fall into the practical and historical categories. The practical category includes such items as *The Christian's Pattern*, *The Life of God in the Soul of Man*, and *The Pilgrim's Progress*; the historical includes Wesley's own journals, and the journals and lives of a multitude of Methodist and other exemplary figures, such as Nelson, Brainerd, Miss Gilbert, Haliburton, de Renty, Haime, and Janeway. We can further subdivide what Wesley called historical works into a number of other categories: biography, autobiography, journals, letters, and accounts of holy deaths.[43] Two points are worth stressing. The first is that these dominant genres – the practical guide to the holy life, and the historical exemplification of those who lived it – embody the essence of Wesley's thought. The second is that his favorite books were by writers of very different Christian traditions – Roman Catholic, episcopalian, mystic, Presbyterian – whose opinions he sometimes disliked and explicitly dissociated himself from.

---

[42] Vicki Tolar Burton, "'Something for the people to read': John Wesley's Book Inventory (1791)," *Bulletin of the John Rylands University Library* 85.2–3 (2003): 227–49, at 230.

[43] For the importance of the biographical genre to Wesley see Isabel Rivers, "John Wesley and Religious Biography," *Bulletin of the John Rylands University Library* 85.2–3 (2003): 209–26.

Thus, he quarreled ferociously with William Law, but, he did everything he could to make Law's books central to his publishing enterprise and to the reading experience of Methodists.[44] To understand Wesley, we have to make sense of this paradox and try to read with his eyes.

[44] See Isabel Rivers, "William Law and Religious Revival: The Reception of *A Serious Call*," *Huntington Library Quarterly* 71:4 (2008): 633–49.

9 Wesley's engagement with the natural sciences

RANDY L. MADDOX

Among the many topics that could be included in a *Companion* to John Wesley, readers might be surprised to find a chapter devoted to Wesley's engagement with the natural sciences.[1] Or, based on some influential precedents, they may anticipate an exposé of Wesley's opposition to scientific theories and reasoning. Over a century ago, in his *History of English Thought in the Eighteenth Century* (1876), Sir Leslie Stephen contended that "we already find in Wesley the aversion to scientific reasoning which has become characteristic of orthodox theologians" (2:412). Andrew Dickson White echoed this evaluation twenty years later in his (in)famous *History of the Warfare of Science with Theology in Christendom* (1896).

One shortcoming of these critiques of Wesley is that they relied mainly on secondary sources and passing comments in his *Sermons* and *Journal*. As a result, they provide little sense of the scope of Wesley's interest in and publications about the natural world. In 1763, Wesley issued for the benefit of his Methodist people *A Survey of the Wisdom of God in Creation; or, A Compendium of Natural Philosophy*, a two-volume work distilling his reading of several book-length works as well as extracts from the *Philosophical Transactions* of the Royal Society for the Improvement of Natural Knowledge and other journals. By its third edition in 1777 this *Survey* had grown into a five-volume collection. To increase its availability to his followers, Wesley serialized excerpts from the *Survey* in his monthly *Arminian Magazine* beginning in 1781. In addition to this broad ranging work, he also published *The Desideratum; or, Electricity Made Plain and Useful* (1760) and included a number of short pieces about unusual natural phenomena in the *Arminian Magazine*.

[1] For more discussion and documentation of points in this chapter, see Randy L. Maddox, "John Wesley's Precedent for Theological Engagement with the Natural Sciences," *Wesleyan Theological Journal* 44.1 (Spring 2009).

These broader works have been central to a lesser-known series of *positive* appeals to Wesley's precedent for theological engagement with the natural sciences, which paralleled the negative evaluations. For example, in 1893, William Mills gave a lecture on "John Wesley an Evolutionist" at the Chit-Chat Club in San Francisco. The lecture was circulated as a booklet and a summary was published in *Popular Science Monthly* the following year.[2] Sparked by Mills, James Lee enlightened readers of the *Southern Magazine* the same year that "the founder of Methodism wrote out the whole theory of evolution and the origin of species . . . eighty-four years before Mr. Darwin published his celebrated work upon the same subject."[3] This astonishing claim was echoed by several voices in the 1920s, championing Wesley as a forerunner for accepting evolution in the midst of the controversy that peaked in the Scopes trial. Some of these advocates broadened the argument, presenting Wesley as a pioneer of scientific empiricism in general (in the mode of Francis Bacon and John Locke) and of empirical theology in particular.[4]

The suggestion that Wesley advocated the evolution of species was based on a misreading of his affirmation of the biological model of the "chain of being."[5] This was just one of many examples where *both* the sneering dismissal and the sweeping praise of Wesley's engagement with the natural sciences betray their anachronistic nature – casting Wesley within the scientific models and debates of their time, instead of evaluating his publications on science topics within their original context.

PLACING WESLEY'S ENGAGEMENT IN HISTORICAL CONTEXT

The goal of this essay is to help readers avoid such anachronism, by providing sufficient background to understand and appreciate Wesley's interactions with study of the natural world within their socio-historical

---

[2] William Harrison Mills, *John Wesley an Evolutionist* (1893); summarized in *Popular Science Monthly* 46 (1894–95): 284–85.

[3] James W. Lee, "A Methodist Evolutionist," *Southern Magazine* (Louisville) 4 (1894): 348.

[4] See in particular Frank Wilbur Collier, *John Wesley Among the Scientists* (1928).

[5] They typically quote a passage about nature "raising herself to man" from the ape in Wesley, *Survey of the Wisdom of God in the Creation* (4th ed., 1784), 4:102. But, they fail to appreciate that this is a climb in quality of "being," not in time; as one emphasis of the "chain of being" model was that there is neither new creation nor extinction of species.

context. It builds on scattered similar efforts over the last half century, but emphasizes insights from the recent flourishing in study of the history of science and of Christian interactions with science.

Even the best treatments of Wesley to date have tended to share a set of assumptions about the nature of the "science" he engaged. This is understandable, because these assumptions were championed by standard historical surveys – such as Herbert Butterfield's *The Origins of Modern Science* (1949) – through most of the twentieth century. These surveys contended that "science" was understood in England by the outset of the eighteenth century among leading practitioners like Isaac Newton as a mode of inquiry that was:

1) focused on elucidating how the processes of nature work, so that these processes could be used for human betterment;
2) grounded in a hypothetico-deductive methodology, wedding the certainty of mathematics with the objectivity of rigorous empirical verification of hypotheses; and
3) independent from religious constraints, thus at home in all cultures and times.

If this model was firmly in place by Wesley's day, then divergence in his writings from these emphases could be read as resistance to science. Thus, among characteristics that Stephen, White, and others have identified as "anti-scientific" in Wesley are his demure from providing causal models for natural phenomena, his criticism of relying on hypotheses in developing such models, his hesitance to endorse Isaac Newton's cosmology, his openness to providential accounts of events like earthquakes, and his ascription to the Genesis account of an idyllic creation (which conflicts with the Darwinian model of evolution).

But, recent scholarship on the history of science has demonstrated that the emphases just listed for the "modern" understanding of science remained *contested* among leading practitioners through most of the eighteenth century, particularly in England.[6] Three points that these scholars highlight are crucial for understanding and evaluating Wesley's writings in this genre.

---

[6]   See Andrew Cunningham & Perry Williams, "De-centering the 'Big Picture': *The Origins of Modern Science* and the Modern Origins of Science," *British Journal for the History of Science* 26 (1993): 407–32; and, more generally, Peter J. Bowler & Iwan Rhys Morus, *Making Modern Science: A Historical Survey* (2005).

Transitional character of "science" in eighteenth-century England

First, this recent scholarship encourages us to take seriously that folk like Isaac Newton labeled their studies of nature not "science," but "natural philosophy" (e.g., *Philosophiae Naturalis Principia Mathematica*, 1697). This latter name reflects important continuities with earlier academic study of nature.

Medieval education stressed the difference between pursuing *understanding* of reality (*scientia*; science) and acquiring *practical knowledge* or know-how (*ars*; art). The base of university education was the seven liberal *arts*: grammar, rhetoric, dialectic, arithmetic, geometry, astronomy, and music. These sets of practical knowledge provided the foundation for students to approach the capstone study of the nature of reality itself (*scientia*) – in philosophy and theology. By the eighteenth century, philosophy was subdivided into logic, metaphysics, moral philosophy, and natural philosophy. The latter was focused on *understanding* the natural world.

What then were the assumptions of natural philosophy about its task and methods as it entered the eighteenth century?[7] Consider the case of studying the heavens. As a *scientia*, natural philosophy focused on questions like what the heavens are made of; what moves the sun, moon, and planets; and whether the universe is finite or infinite. By contrast, astronomy – as an *art* (integrally connected to mathematics) – was devoted to tracking lights in the sky, developing formalized descriptions and predictions of their movements, offering reliable calendars, and other practical tasks. It had been rare for astronomers to ask what the heavenly bodies were made of or why they moved, whereas natural philosophers had devoted little attention to mathematics or the practical use of their explanations of reality.

Challenges to these disciplinary distinctions began to emerge in the late seventeenth century. On one front, Francis Bacon injected the suggestion, which gained increasing hold, that the value of *any* study of nature was proportionate to the technological benefits it provided for human betterment. On another front, Newton's *Principia Mathematica* began to elevate the centrality of mathematics to accounts of the nature of the universe. By the beginning of the nineteenth century, these and other threads had woven together the distinct agendas of *scientia* and

---

[7] This summary draws on several sources; one of the most recent is Peter Dear, *The Intelligibility of Nature* (2006), 1–14.

ars in the study of nature. This reality was signaled by the fading of the label "natural philosophy," with "science" in its modern sense taking its place. But this transition stretched *through* the eighteenth century in England, resulting in numerous works with mixtures of the relevant emphases. Few works in this period embody consistently the assumptions of "modern science" outlined earlier, including Wesley's *Survey*. The fact that Wesley discounted mathematics in this "compendium of natural philosophy," for example, is evidence less of his resistance to "science" than of his location in this transitional period.

Preference for "experimental" over "speculative" natural philosophy

Recent scholarship has also demonstrated that the field of natural philosophy witnessed prolonged debate among competing models of physics and cosmology in eighteenth-century England, with particular focus on Newton.[8] Everyone recognized that, with its mathematical advances (particularly calculus), Newton's *Principia* provided more accurate description of the movements of planets, comets, and tides. But this was a task traditionally assigned to the *art* of astronomy, not the *explanatory* goal of natural philosophy, which Newton claimed in the title of his work. Thus Newton's *Principia* was often greeted by his professional peers with puzzlement.

Some background will aid in understanding this reaction. Through most of the medieval period the reigning physics was that of Aristotle, which accounted for all natural motion by "final causes," which were integral to every type of being. Thus, planets moved in their orbits because they were realizing their *entelechy* (the "innate desire to fulfill one's nature"). As the medieval period waned, dissatisfaction with the anthropomorphic nature of this explanation grew, spawning alternative *mechanical* accounts of motion in the heavens. The starting premise of these accounts was that entelechy was limited to living beings; physical matter was inert, and was moved solely by the application of external force.

But how was this force applied? Here a divergence emerged within mechanical accounts of cosmic motion, framed by the question of whether space was a void. Accepting that space was a void made it difficult to account for application of force at a distance, such as the influence of the moon on the earth's ocean tides. So, most insisted that space was

---

[8] Good surveys of these debates are available in *The Cambridge History of Science; Vol. IV: The Eighteenth Century*, ed. Roy Porter (2003), 23–43; 285–304.

entirely filled by matter of varying size, including sizes not visible to empirical observation. René Descartes developed the most sophisticated mechanical account in this vein, ascribing planetary motion to the carrying force of vortices in this cosmic "stew." If one instead accepted that space *was* a void, they typically either attributed motion to direct causation by God or echoed suggestions of earlier mystical thinkers about "resonance" across distance between certain elements.

Newton stepped into the middle of these ongoing debates. Aligning with the mechanists, he rejected entelechy, agreeing that matter was inert. Yet, he eventually spurned the suggestion of forms of matter too small for empirical detection. This left space as a void. Although Newton was willing to speak about God intervening occasionally to adjust the motion of planets and other cosmic bodies, he believed that the regularity and interdependence of this motion indicated instead the presence of an abiding natural law. He named this law of mutual influence of bodies upon one another "gravity." But, he immediately conceded that he could not explain how gravity conveyed its impact across the void of space. To many of his peers, Newton's "gravity" seemed like an appeal to discredited "mystical" influences. Most others simply concluded that he had failed to do what natural philosophers were supposed to do – provide an account of *how* the movements of bodies take place.

In hindsight, Newton ventured a promising suggestion about how gravity worked in the "General Scholium" he added to the second edition (1713) of *Principia*. At the end of this short piece, he referred to an "electric and elastic spirit" that appears to pervade all gross bodies, noting that there was not yet sufficient experimental input to provide an account of its impact.[9] It would take a century of further experimentation to detail electromagnetic fields, and correlate these with gravitational fields. Only at this point was Newton's "natural philosophy" fully achieved. It is anachronistic to condemn many of his professional peers, and more general readers like Wesley, for hesitating to endorse Newton's revision of cosmology and physics early in this process.[10]

But, the key point to note in this episode is how Newton *agreed* with his peers. His reason for rejecting Descartes' cosmology was its reliance on the "hypothesis" of imperceptible matter. Here, Newton embodied the dominant tendency in England by the late seventeenth century to reject "speculative" natural philosophy, in favor of an

---

[9] English translation, *The Mathematical Principles of Natural Philosophy* (1729), 2:393.

[10] This general point is made well in relation to cases like Galileo in David C. Lindberg & Ronald L. Numbers, eds., *When Science and Christianity Meet* (2003).

"experimental" approach.[11] He specifically defended his demure from offering an *explanatory* account of gravity on the grounds that one should not turn to "hypotheses" as a substitute for experimental evidence.[12]

Theological dimension of eighteenth-century natural philosophy

Many of the emphases of "modern science" that earlier scholars suggested were firmly in place by the outset of the eighteenth century in England have been called into question already. The suggestion which recent scholarship has most contested is the separation of "scientific" investigation from religious or theological considerations. In keeping with its medieval roots, natural philosophy at the outset of the eighteenth century retained an overarching theological perspective.[13] Its subject matter was nature, but it typically approached nature as the "book of God's works." Moreover, it assumed that part of its task was to elucidate the attributes of God that could be demonstrated from God's works.

Newton can again serve as our example. The "General Scholium" that he added as the capstone to *Principia* was devoted mainly to insisting that "this most beautiful system of the sun, planets, and comets could only proceed from the counsel and dominion of an intelligent and powerful being," and then elucidating the attributes of this being which we can deduce from "his most wise and excellent contrivances of things." He concluded these reflections with an explicit affirmation that such discourse about God, drawn from consideration of nature, "does certainly belong to natural philosophy."[14]

There were occasional figures like Thomas Hobbes who adopted purely materialistic accounts of nature, but these remained rare in England into the last quarter of the eighteenth century.[15] Thus, Wesley was echoing the methodological assumption of most of his sources when

---

[11] See Peter R. Anstey, "Experimental versus Speculative Natural Philosophy," in P. Anstey & J. Schuster (eds.), *The Science of Nature in the Seventeenth Century* (2005), 215–42.

[12] Newton, *Mathematical Principles* (1729), 2:205 and 2:392.

[13] This point was pressed initially by Andrew Cunningham. Most have come to agree; cf. Peter Dear, "Religion, Science and Natural Philosophy: Thoughts on Cunningham's Thesis," *Studies in the History and Philosophy of Science* 32 (2001): 377–86; and Peter Harrison, "'Science' and 'Religion': Constructing the Boundaries," *Journal of Religion* 86 (2006): 81–106.

[14] Newton, *Mathematical Principles of Natural Philosophy*, 2:388–92.

[15] See Jeremy Gregory, "Christianity and Culture: Religion, the Arts, and the Sciences in England, 1660–1800," in Jeremy Black (ed.), *Culture and Society in Britain* (1997), 102–23.

he described the goal of his compendium of natural philosophy as "not barely to entertain an idle barren curiosity, but to display *the invisible things of God*, his power, wisdom, and goodness."[16] If Wesley went beyond his sources, it was in his characteristic hope that the collection would also "warm our hearts, and fill our mouths with wonder, love, and praise!"[17]

CHARACTERISTICS OF WESLEY'S ENGAGEMENT WITH THE NATURAL "SCIENCES"

By this point, it should be clear that it would be anachronistic to speak of Wesley bringing "science" and "religion" into dialogue. He was not engaging "science" as a discipline separated carefully from theological considerations. Nor was he interested in "religion" in general. His main goal in publishing *Survey* (and related items) was to enable his readers to benefit from "book of God's works" as well as the "book of God's Word," by distilling and presenting – in accessible format – current studies of the natural world. In the judgment of some historians of science, the result was the best single survey treatment of natural philosophy in the eighteenth century for general readers.[18]

Focused on descriptive natural philosophy

Wesley's concern to speak to general readers surely contributed to a central characteristic of his writings in this area – the dominant focus on *describing* the natural world. He articulated this focus directly in the preface to *Survey*:

It will be easily observed that I endeavor throughout not to *account for* things, but only to *describe* them. I undertake barely to set down what appears in nature, not the cause of those appearances. The facts lie within the reach of our senses and understanding, the causes are more remote. That things are so, we know with certainty; but why they are so, we know not.[19]

Although this restricted goal falls short of the full agenda of natural philosophy, it is not hard to catch echoes of Newton in Wesley's

---

[16] Wesley, *Survey*, Preface, §1, *Works* (Jackson), 14:300.
[17] Ibid., §7, *Works* (Jackson), 14:302.
[18] Robert Schofield, "John Wesley and Science in 18th Century England," *Isis* 44 (1953): 337–38.
[19] Wesley, *Survey*, Preface, §5, *Works* (Jackson), 14:301.

delimitation. Besides, Wesley's "compendium of natural philosophy" was not intended to *advance* the discipline, but to survey the most interesting and instructive aspects of nature highlighted in recent work in the discipline.

As with his publications in biblical studies, English history, and church history, Wesley worked more as an editor than an author in the area of natural philosophy. To frame and provide the largest portion of text for the first edition of *Survey* he chose a Latin text by Johann Franz Buddeus.[20] The bulk of Buddeus's text was devoted to surveying the natural world – beginning with the human body; moving to other animals; then to plants, fossils, and the physical elements of earth, fire, and water; before turning toward the heavens, considering air, meteors, and cosmology. Wesley retained each of these sections in *Survey*, although he omits a subsequent section devoted to debates in physics (in keeping with his limitation to "describing," not "accounting for"). His abridgements within the various sections are infrequent, and sometimes amusing – such as deleting descriptions of human reproductive organs.

More striking are Wesley's additions to Buddeus. He incorporated into the first edition of *Survey* entire new chapters describing birds, fish, and reptiles, as well as numerous scattered additional examples of natural species and phenomena. Apparently judging that Buddeus's text did not provide *enough* description of the wonders of God's creation, Wesley scoured a number of books and journals to supplement. This gathering of additional information continued after the first edition of *Survey* was issued, being incorporated into later editions to swell the original two-volume work to five volumes. Wesley also laced his *Journal* and the *Arminian Magazine* with his own observations on natural phenomena and excerpts from his reading on the topic.

Inclined to a modest natural theology

To be sure, Wesley pauses periodically in *Survey* to offer theological reflections upon the wonders of the natural world being described. These reflections lead some to describe the *Survey* as a "natural theology." Although understandable, this could be misleading.

"Natural theology" was a sub discipline in medieval education devoted to knowledge about God that could be demonstrated by rational reflection on (1) the human soul; (2) human moral insight, or "natural law"; and (3) the natural world. Thus, natural theology drew the occasional theological reflections of natural philosophy into a larger

[20] J. F. Buddeus, *Elementa Philosophiae Theoretica* (Halle: Glauche-Hallensis, 1706).

systematic conversation about what could *theoretically* be known about God apart from special revelation.

I stress the theoretical nature of this knowledge, because natural theology was part of the Christian curriculum and its wisest medieval practitioners were aware that they were reflecting on the "book of nature" through lenses shaped to some degree by the "book of scripture." Their concern was less to elicit faith from nonbelievers than to confirm and enrich nascent faith. But, not all voices were so wise. Thus, there was plenty of fodder to fuel the suspicion of Protestant reformers about the triumph of unregenerate reason over revelation in the enterprise of natural theology. Although they did not set the enterprise aside entirely, the Reformers' emphasis on the sufficiency of God's revelation in Scripture rendered theological appeal to the "book of nature" clearly subordinate and surely not essential for Christian life.

This is a point where Anglican theological reflection diverged from more staunchly Protestant approaches. The roots of this difference go back to Richard Hooker, who argued that, although scripture is sufficient for the knowledge of salvation, all Christians should be encouraged to seek the fullness of understanding and felicity, which is derived from *conjoined* study of scripture and nature. This emphasis underlies the significant interest in natural theology that emerged in England in the middle of the seventeenth century and carried through Wesley's life into the nineteenth century.[21] Wesley drew upon several of these works in natural theology for the theological reflections interspersed through *Survey*.

Given the use of these sources, why did Wesley designate the *Survey* a work in "natural philosophy" instead of "natural theology"? Part of the answer was the difference in amount of attention given to nature itself in each genre. Works in natural philosophy devoted the majority of their time to describing the natural world, usually gathering their explicit theological reflections in a short section at the end. By contrast, efforts in natural theology – like William Derham's *Physico-Theology* (1713) and *Astro-Theology* (1715) – were organized around and dominated by theological reflection, interspersing brief appeals to the natural world as spring boards for or evidence backing their theological claims. On this spectrum, Wesley's *Survey* lines up much closer to the "natural philosophy" pole.

Another reason for Wesley's choice, I would suggest, was difference in tone. Prominent works of natural theology in his day were sliding

---

[21] See Richard G. Olson, *Science and Religion, 1450–1900* (2004), 84–91; and David M. Knight, *Natural Science Books in English 1600–1900* (1972), 47–62.

from the more modest classical stance of seeking to *confirm belief*, into the more ambitious Enlightenment *evidentialist apologetics*.[22] The latter is a stance that assumes that the path to reliable knowledge requires first setting aside all belief, then accepting as truth only those claims for which there is undeniable evidence. On this model, the prime task of natural theology becomes demonstrating God's *existence*, not merely reflecting upon evidence of God's wisdom and character; and the standard to be attained becomes *certainty*. This model could also encourage more strident rhetoric. John Ray's *Wisdom of God Manifested in the Works of Creation* can serve as an example. Peppered through this work are comments that anyone who does not recognize that the world was produced by divine reason and art must be "stupid as the basest beasts," "stupid as the dirt one walks on," "forsaken of reason," and "sottish."[23]

Wesley recognized this shift in some of his sources, and he was *not* ready to follow. But, it is easy to miss this point. One must pay attention to Wesley's *selective* appropriation of his sources. For example, although he incorporated at least four extracts from Ray's *Wisdom of God* into *Survey*, Wesley chose none with the type of strident apologetic agenda just cited. Although we still await a critical edition of *Survey* that highlights such editorial decisions, initial comparative study shows that Wesley typically edits his sources to remove evidentialist apologetics.[24] Thereby the theological reflections incorporated into *Survey* portray on balance a modest tone and agenda. They value consideration of the "book of nature" not as the *foundation* for belief in God or God's various attributes, but as a means of *strengthening* the faith, reverence, and love awakened by scripture, a means of building nascent convictions into demonstrative convictions. John Hedley Brooke, recent Professor of Science and Religion at Oxford University, has argued that Wesley's *Survey* remains of theological interest today precisely because its modest claims are less prone to the dangers in more evidentialist natural theologies.[25]

---

[22] See Nicholas Wolterstorff, "The Migration of the Theistic Arguments: From Natural Theology to Evidentialist Apologetics," in R. Audi & W. Wainwright (eds.), *Rationality, Religious Belief, and Moral Commitment* (1986), 38–81.

[23] Ray, *The Wisdom of God Manifested in the Works of Creation* (4th ed., enlarged; 1704), 39, 47, 122–23, 249, 389.

[24] See details in Maddox, "John Wesley's Precedent." The Center for Studies in the Wesleyan tradition, Duke University, is at work on a critical edition of the *Survey*.

[25] John Hedley Brooke, "Science and Dissent: Some Historiographical Issues," in Paul Wood (ed.), *Science and Dissent in England, 1688–1945* (2004), 21.

Convinced of God's care for the whole creation

Wesley's engagement with natural philosophy is also of continuing interest because of how it led him to revise a received theological viewpoint, moving to a stance that could do better justice to scripture! Although scripture speaks of God's ultimate salvific goal as the "new heavens and earth" (i.e., transformation of everything in the universe), a variety of influences led Christians through the first millennium to assume increasingly that our final state is "heaven above." The latter was seen as a realm where human spirits, dwelling in ethereal bodies, join eternally with all other spiritual beings – a category that did not include animals! – in continuous worship of the ultimate spiritual being, God. By contrast, they assumed that the physical universe, which we abandon at death, would eventually be annihilated. Wesley imbibed this understanding of our final state in his upbringing, and through much of his ministry it was presented as obvious and unproblematic.

In the last decade of his life, however, Wesley reclaimed the biblical imagery of God's cosmic renewal, shifting his focus from "heaven above" to the future new creation.[26] After a tentative defense of animals having "souls" in 1775, he issued a bold affirmation of salvation for animals in the 1781 sermon "The General Deliverance." Although not without precedent, this sermon was unusual for its time and is often cited as a pioneer effort in reaffirming the doctrine of animal salvation in the Western church. Broadening the scope even further, Wesley's 1785 sermon on "The New Creation" refused to limit God's redemptive purposes to sentient beings, insisting that the very elements of our current universe will be present in the new creation, though they will be dramatically improved over current conditions.

What contributed to Wesley's reclaiming of the biblical theme of the cosmic scope of redemption? A central factor was his engagement with works in natural philosophy that utilized the model of the "chain of beings." This model conceived of nature as a hierarchy of beings organized by relative excellence of abilities. Fish were higher in the chain than plants, dogs higher than fish, humans higher than dogs, and celestial beings higher than humans. A central assumption of the model was that the only type of cosmos fitting for a Perfect Being to produce was one in which every conceivable niche was occupied by its appropriate type of being. The task of natural philosophers was to place each creature

---

[26] See Randy L. Maddox, "Nurturing the New Creation," in M. D. Meeks (ed.), *Wesleyan Perspectives on the New Creation* (2004), 21–52.

in its appropriate niche – a task kept lively in the eighteenth century by accounts of species in the new world from European explorers.

Although it was eventually replaced, Clarence Glacken argues that the model of the chain of beings was a crucial source for the modern ecological ideas of the unity of nature and the balance and harmony of nature.[27] Glacken particularly highlights the role of John Ray and Charles Bonnet in adapting the model to frame surveys of the burgeoning knowledge of the natural world in the eighteenth century. Wesley was familiar with Ray's *Wisdom of God* from the early 1730s. He encountered the writings of Charles Bonnet, a prominent Swiss naturalist, in the early 1770s. It was through Bonnet that Wesley gained deeper appreciation for the implications of the chain of beings. Indeed, he came to value the model so highly that he incorporated an abridgement of Bonnet's two-volume overview of the chain of beings into *Survey* in 1777.[28]

One significant emphasis that Bonnet reinforced for Wesley was our human connection with the rest of the chain. He retained in his abridgment of Bonnet a response to the suggestion that it would be better if humans were angels, which counsels:

> Confess your error and acknowledge that every being is endued with a perfection suited to the ends of its creation. It would cease to answer that end the very moment it ceased to be what it is. By changing its nature it would change its place and that which it occupied in the universal hierarchy ought still to be the residence of a being resembling it, otherwise harmony would be destroyed. In the assemblage of all the orders of *relative* perfections consists the *absolute* perfection of this whole, concerning which God said "that it was good."[29]

If this is taken seriously, there can be no eschatological ideal that limits salvation to humanity (even in the subtle form of stressing that humans are "microcosms" of the whole cosmos). It would be a thwarting of God's creative will and a deprivation of all concerned!

Wesley's pondering of this point as he read and abridged Bonnet in the mid-1770s surely played a role in his reclaiming of cosmic redemption shortly thereafter. As an Anglican, raised with deep appreciation for the *conjoined* witness of the book of scripture and the book of nature, Wesley welcomed an insight from the study of nature in his day that

---

[27] Clarence J. Glacken, *Traces on the Rhodian Shore* (1967), esp. p. 379.
[28] Charles Bonnet, *The Contemplation of Nature* (1766); cf. *Survey* (3rd ed., 1777), 4:60–333.
[29] Wesley, *Survey* (3rd ed., 1777), 4:62.

brought back into focus a biblical (and early Christian) theme that had been obscured.

Dedicated to placing knowledge in service to all

One other characteristic of Wesley's engagement with the study of nature in his day deserves attention. It concerns the *purpose* of this study. Rejecting earlier notions of natural philosophers as individual seekers after the arcane mysteries of the natural world, Francis Bacon helped make standard by Wesley's day a self-understanding of natural philosophers as public figures in service of the public good.[30]

Wesley's embrace of this basic emphasis is evident in *The Desideratum; or, Electricity Made Plain and Useful* (1760). Like *Survey*, this volume contains extended extracts from recent works on electricity by Benjamin Franklin, Richard Lovett, and others. But, Wesley makes clear in the preface that he is much less interested in the "philosophical" parts of these treatises that posit explanations of how electricity works than he is in the scattered accounts of medical benefits of electrical shock.[31] Whereas some viewed these accounts with scorn, Wesley collected them and added accounts from his own experiments in public clinics with "electrifying machines." He then published them inexpensively, for the public benefit of the poor in particular. (For more on Wesley's medical interests, see the Chapter 10.)

But, there was a specific current in Bacon's writings on natural philosophy which Wesley resisted – the tendency to emphasize human control and exploitation of the natural world.[32] Wesley was familiar with champions of this anthropocentric, exploitive emphasis in scientific investigation. He had to look no further than William Derham, who insisted "We can, if need be, ransack the whole globe, . . . penetrate into the bowels of the earth, descend to the bottom of the deep, travel to the farthest regions of this world, to acquire wealth, to increase our knowledge, or even only to please our eye or fancy."[33]

This is one of the passages from Derham that was *not* selected by Wesley for inclusion in *Survey*. Nor does anything in its vein from other sources appear there. Part of the reason is that Wesley imbibed more deeply than Derham the convictions of the chain of beings model of nature. Although this model highlights (as ecologists would today) a

---

[30] See Stephen Gaukroger, "The *persona* of the Natural Philosopher," in C. Condren et al. (eds.), *The Philosopher in Early Modern Europe* (2006), 17–34.

[31] See *Desideratum*, Preface, §§2–3, *Works* (Jackson), 14:242.

[32] See Carolyn Merchant, *The Death of Nature* (1980), 164–90.

[33] Derham, *Physico-Theology* (1713), 112.

range of ways that any particular species might contribute to the well-being of others above or below it in the chain, it also insists that every species has intrinsic value and a right to exist for its own purposes. John Ray, who was deeply shaped by this model, emphasized the relevant implication: "It is a generally received opinion that all this visible world was created for man, that man is the end of creation, as if there were no other end of any creature but some way or other to be serviceable to man.... Yet wise men nowadays think otherwise."[34] Although Ray went on to insist that, in this interdependent chain, all species are in some sense serviceable to humanity and we would frustrate the purposes of their creation if we did not make appropriate use of them, he offered Wesley a model of *modest* anthropocentrism.

Wesley appropriated this model in a way that moved beyond Ray through his distinctive emphasis regarding our role as "stewards." This emphasis is seen most clearly in his instructions on the use of money, where he criticizes any suggestion that resources put at our disposal are for us to use however we see fit. Wesley insists instead that everything belongs ultimately to God; that it is placed in our care to use as God directs; and that God directs us to use it for the benefit of others once our basic needs are met.[35] Extending this principle to the rest of creation, the focus of Wesley's environmental ethic is better characterized as *theocentric* than anthropocentric. He portrayed the ideal relationship of humanity with creation (modeled by Adam in the Garden of Eden) as one of *modest stewardship*, where we devote our distinctive gifts to upholding God's intentions for the balance and flourishing of all creation.[36]

Most in Wesley's day shared his assumption of the idyllic nature of the original creation, with peace abounding between all creatures and humans possessing the knowledge to promote the thriving of the whole. They also shared the recognition that this was very unlike the world in which we live now, with "nature red in tooth and claw" (Tennyson) and humans largely at the mercy of the forces of nature. Differences emerged around the implications drawn from the present condition for human interaction with the rest of nature. Many resigned themselves to the situation, as long as we are in the present world. Among the ones who believed that change was possible, the most significant distinction

---

[34] Ray, *Wisdom of God* (4th ed., enlarged; 1704), 127–28.

[35] See Sermon 28, "Sermon on the Mount VIII," §§11, 25–26, *Works*, 1:618–19, 628–29; Sermon 50, "The Use of Money," *Works*, 2:266–80; and Sermon 51, "The Good Steward," §I.1, *Works*, 2:283.

[36] See Sermon 60, "The General Deliverance," §I.6, *Works*, 2:444.

emerged between those (like Francis Bacon) who championed the mandate to *reclaim the mastery* over creation that was lost in the fall, and those (like Wesley) who pleaded for *resuming the loving stewardship* of creation that we inverted in the fall.[37] Although the first two alternatives could acquiesce to (or even justify) the aggressive domination of other creatures by humans, Wesley is representative of the third alternative in his portrayal of such domination as the epitome of the fallen practices that must be set aside.[38] Deeply aware of how much damage we have done, the stewardship that Wesley called for us to resume is not only modest but *chastened*.[39]

This ideal, alongside Wesley naming his compendium of natural philosophy a *Survey of the Wisdom of God in Creation*, suggests a significant revision of Bacon's rationale for the study of nature. We should seek this knowledge not to increase our ability to exploit nature, but to increase our awareness of the wondrous range of creation and deepen our sensitivity to our integral connection with it all – so that we might more effectively imitate God in showing mercy to *all* of creation.

[37] See Peter Harrison, "Subduing the Earth: Genesis 1, Early Modern Science, and the Exploitation of Nature," *Journal of Religion* 79 (1999): 86–109; esp. 102–3.

[38] See esp. his description of the negative impact of humanity upon creation in Sermon 60, "The General Deliverance," II, *Works*, 2:442–45.

[39] See Randy L. Maddox, "Anticipating the New Creation: Wesleyan Foundations for Holistic Mission," *Asbury Journal* 62 (2007): 49–66.

10 Wesley as advisor on health and healing

DEBORAH MADDEN

I

John Wesley's theological and literary productions are, by any standards, prodigious. Even within his lifetime, Wesley's output ran to thousands of pages, hundreds of volumes, which included sermons, journals, tracts, edited abridgements, and numerous other commentaries. Readers today, however, might be surprised to discover that a slender medical manual, written first in 1747 to "prepare and give" physic to the poor, ran to more editions and stayed in print longer than any of Wesley's other publications – twenty-three editions went to press although the Methodist leader was alive, with the last and thirty-seventh edition being published in 1859. Wesley's medical manual had broad reach geographically and was republished in Europe and the United States. Such sustained demand firmly established within eighteenth-century medicine the popular and controversial status of *Primitive Physic: or, An Easy and Natural Method of Curing Most Diseases* (1747).[1] However, this has not been adequately reflected in historical scholarship of the period, which has tended to treat Wesley's text as idiosyncratic or backward-looking. This attitude has meant that scholars have failed to examine the theological, intellectual, and cultural resonances of Wesley's enormously successful medical work, which he believed helped to heal sickness, remove pain, and save lives.

Early twentieth-century scholarship investigating Wesley's interest in health, medicine, and the sciences seems mainly to have been published either in the journals of professional medical and scientific societies, or religious, Methodist, and Wesleyan organizations. This, in itself, has created some interesting methodological problems. Scholarly

[1] [John Wesley] *Primitive Physick: or, An Easy and Natural Method of Curing Most Diseases* (London, 1747). The title was spelled *Physick* in the earlier editions, being changed to *Physic* with the twentieth edition in 1781; the final spelling is used consistently in this essay.

176

attention in these early years was largely cleft along medical and theological lines with each, until very recently, following its own distinctive trajectory. Traditionally, the history of medicine was concerned to distinguish medical "quackery" from its own orthodox canon. In so doing, the rise of "professional" medicine has been too easily charted. By contrast, exponents writing on behalf of religious, Methodist, or Wesleyan organizations sought to downplay Wesley's medical practice by treating it as another form of Georgian "folk" medicine.[2]

Twentieth-century historical scholarship has also ignored, overlooked, or expressed skepticism about the important place of medicine and science in Wesley's thought. As a theologian and leader of an ardent evangelical movement, historians have placed John Wesley in opposition to other Enlightenment medics, scientists, and philosophers. Thinking on this stemmed primarily from nineteenth-century intellectual suppositions, which saw a "conflict" between science, medicine, and Christianity. These Victorian anxieties framed much twentieth-century historiography, seen best in J.H. Plumb's dismissal of Wesley's *Primitive Physic* as an "absurd, fantastic compilation of uncritical folklore."[3] Plumb regarded Wesley as an oddity – an unthinking religious enthusiast, responsible for a movement that was reacting violently to Enlightenment rationalism, particularly Newtonian science.

The tenacity of these claims has proved difficult to dislodge. New interpretative frameworks and approaches developed during the late 1960s meant that social and cultural historians sought to unpack or examine further the perceived conflict between medical science and religion. These historians also questioned the supposed professional status of medicine during the eighteenth century.[4] Yet, even exponents of this historiography were reluctant to give full weight to Wesley's contribution by regarding *Primitive Physic* as being nothing more than a populist medical manual to be dismissed on this basis. Roy Porter's early work followed a similar path to that of his mentor and old supervisor, J.H. Plumb, although Porter's views on Wesley did modify and change over time.[5] Echoing Plumb's criticism, Akihito Suzuki argued that

²   See the bibliography and analysis in Randy L. Maddox, "Reclaiming the Eccentric Parent: Methodist Reception of John Wesley's Interest in Medicine," in *"Inward and Outward Health": John Wesley's Holistic Concept of Medical Science, the Environment, and Holy Living*, edited by Deborah Madden (2008).
³   J.H. Plumb, *England in the Eighteenth Century* (1950), 95–96.
⁴   Roy Porter (ed.), *Patients and Practitioners* (1985).
⁵   Cf. Roy Porter, *Mind-Forg'd Manacles: A History of Madness in England from the Restoration to the Regency* (1987); and Porter, *Health For Sale: Quackery in England 1660–1850* (1989).

Primitive Physic was an "aggressively anti-intellectual, anti-theoretical, and populist medical advice manual intended explicitly for the poor."[6] The works of L.S. King and G.S. Rousseau, on the other hand, stand out as notable exceptions that bucked this trend. Both briefly summarized Wesley's contribution in its wider eighteenth-century setting, although observing that Wesley represented the best of the empirical tradition in medicine.[7] Following on from where these works left off, there has been a concerted effort in very recent years to see Wesley as a critical admirer of Enlightenment principles, as a deeply pious individual who could minister to the physical and spiritual welfare of the poor, applying remedies for the body or prayer for the soul when appropriate.[8]

II

In 1748, Wesley, responding to a request from his good friend and confidant, the Rev. Vincent Perronet, vicar of Shoreham in Kent, wrote and published *A Plain Account of the People Called Methodists*, outlining their practice, the principles upon which it was grounded, "the occasion of every step they have taken, and the advantages reaped thereby."[9] In this account, Wesley sought, among other points, to give precise and cogent reasons for his decision to practice physic (i.e., medicine). His Methodist stewards, those instructed to manage the temporal affairs of the Society, were struggling to attend the vast numbers of sick within their district. To mitigate this Wesley instituted an office of "visitors of

6   Akihito Suzuki, "Anti-Lockean Enlightenment? Mind and Body in Early Eighteenth-Century English Medicine," in *Medicine in the Enlightenment*, edited by Roy Porter (1995), 336–59, 349.

7   L.S. King, *The Medical World of the Eighteenth Century* (1958); and G.S. Rousseau, "John Wesley's 'Primitive Physic' (1747)," *Harvard Library Bulletin* 16 (1968): 242–56.

8   J. Cule, "The Rev. John Wesley, M.A. (Oxon.), 1703–1791: 'The Naked Empiricist' and Orthodox Medicine," *The Journal of the History of Medicine* 45 (1990): 41–63; H.D. Rack, "Doctors, Demons and Early Methodist Healing,'" in *The Church and Healing*, edited by W.J. Sheils (1982); Rack, *Reasonable Enthusiast*; J.W. Haas, "John Wesley's Views on Science and Christianity: An Examination of the Charge of Anti-Science," *Church History* 63 (1994): 378–92; P.W. Ott, "'John Wesley on Health and Wholeness," *Journal of Religion and Health* 30 (1991): 43–57; James G. Donat, "Empirical Medicine in the 18th Century: The Rev. John Wesley's Search for Remedies that Work," *Methodist History* 44 (2006): 216–26; Randy L. Maddox, "John Wesley on Holistic Health and Healing," *Methodist History* 46 (2007): 4–33; and Deborah Madden, *"A Cheap, Safe and Natural Medicine": Religion, Medicine, and Culture in John Wesley's Primitive Physic* (2007). Maddox and Donat are co-editing a critical edition of the entire corpus of Wesley's medical work as part of the *Bicentennial Edition of the Works of John Wesley*, due for publication in the United States in 2010.

9   Wesley, *Plain Account of the Methodists*, §1, *Works* 9:254.

the sick," whose responsibility it was to "see every sick person within his or her district thrice a week." Visitors needed to enquire after both bodily and spiritual health, procuring advice and offering pain relief. To aid this process, Wesley prepared and published for the visitors a pamphlet, *Collection of Receipts for the Use of the Poor* (1745), based on his own medical reading and experience. Reflecting in 1748 to Perronet on these early initiatives, Wesley derived obvious pleasure from the fact that Methodist charitable endeavors closely corresponded to ancient examples set down in the primitive Church: "what was Phebe the deaconess," he asks, "but such a visitor of the sick" (Rom. 16:1).[10]

Wesley soon discovered that the scale of the problem was much bigger than he had originally anticipated – so many of the poor became sick, whereas the cost and accessibility of medicines were far removed from their reach. After looking into whether hospital treatment might resolve some of these problems, Wesley asked the advice of several physicians who seemed unable to help. In the meantime, he was forced to watch "poor people pining away and several families ruined" because they were without basic medicines for their ills. Finally, out of a "desperate expedient," Wesley resolved to prepare and give physic to the poor himself. This was in 1746, and that same year Wesley opened dispensaries in London and Bristol to treat greater numbers at little or no expense to the patient. Taking into his assistance an apothecary and experienced surgeon, Wesley resolved never to go out of his depth, leaving all complex cases to trained physicians, treating only chronic (as opposed to "acute") distempers. At the dispensaries Wesley promised to offer the best advice he could, and the best medicines he had.[11] Society members and non-Methodists alike were treated in droves, instructed to follow Wesley's prescribed regimen and medicine, which he insisted alleviated distempers generally thought incurable.

Spurred by this initial response, Wesley corrected and expanded the *Collection of Receipts*, issuing it under the new title *Primitive Physic* in 1747. The collection now spanned 119 pages, which included a 24-page Preface. The diseases and illnesses treated, arranged in alphabetical order, increased from 93 to 243, whereas Wesley's suggested remedies swelled from 227 to 725. By the twenty-third edition, the scope had expanded to 288 diseases, matched with 824 remedies. *Primitive Physic* was published anonymously until the ninth edition in 1761. All editions between that of the first in 1747 and twenty-third in 1791 were edited,

---

[10] *Plain Account of the Methodists*, XI.4, Works, 9:274.
[11] Ibid., XII.1–3, Works, 9:275.

corrected, and enlarged by Wesley himself. In 1755 (fifth edition) he added footnotes and marked "tried and tested remedies."[12] He also omitted or reduced the use of what he regarded as the "extremely dangerous," but commonly used "Herculean" medicines, which included opium, Peruvian bark, steel, and quicksilver (mercury). In 1761, electrical therapy was added. The twentieth edition in 1781 was carefully revised and contained a postscript to readers that explained how criticism of previous editions resulted in the omission and alteration of particular remedies. Absence of proper medical help for the poor created an urgent need for this type of popular medical manual, which became part of everyday life in the Georgian period. The assurance that Wesley's remedies could reach a much bigger audience, plus a strong commitment to Christian charity and individual enlightenment, influenced his decision to publish *Primitive Physic*.

In the account to Perronet Wesley, Wesley highlighted three themes that lay at the heart of his theological mission and which characterized the Methodist movement as a whole. These themes are also central to his medical text: primitive Christianity, the important role of empirical experience, and the giving of alms or practical piety. These values mirrored Wesley's mode of Biblical interpretation, which involved first and foremost Scripture, interpreted by Christian tradition, reviewed by reason, but confirmed by practical experience. Wesley's theology, and its practical outworking, was concerned to revive features of the apostolic era and its immediate aftermath with the emergence of the primitive Church. Wesley believed that this golden age was blessed with exceptional purity and hoped Methodism would follow in its example. So, he specifically reminded his friend Perronet about the parallel between early Church almsgiving and latter-day charitable efforts undertaken by Methodists.

These primitivist ideals had been stitched into the fabric of Methodism from the outset when John and Charles Wesley, while undergraduates at Oxford, gathered a group of students for a more serious pursuit of spiritual life (1720–35). Intended at first to form a fellowship for the study of Scripture and classical literature, this Holy Club[13] soon

---

[12] See E.B. Bardell, "Primitive Physick: John Wesley's Receipts," *Pharmacy in History* 21 (1979): 111–21, 116; Deborah Madden, "Experience and the Common Interest of Mankind: The Enlightened Empiricism of John Wesley's *Primitive Physic*," *British Journal for Eighteenth-Century Studies* 26 (2003): 41–53, 44, 52; and Maddox, "Reclaiming the Eccentric Parent."

[13] There was no consistent name used for these small group gatherings at Oxford, either by the Wesley brothers or by their detractors. The name most commonly adopted in later accounts is the "Holy Club."

identified primitive Christianity and the cultivation of practical piety as being preeminent amongst its key principles. The Holy Club regarded itself as an experiment in early Christianity and, reminiscing late in life, Wesley claimed that its members sought to practice the "community of goods" modeled in the book of Acts. In reference to early Methodist activities involving medical treatment Wesley added the warrant of empirically grounded experience – telling Perronet that physic, as well as anatomy, had long been the diversion of his leisure hours.

Wesley had in fact nourished this interest since his student days, when George Cheyne's *Essay of Health and Long Life* (1724), with its prescribed regimen, dietary habits, and health strictures, first caught his imagination, ostensibly because it complemented the moral temperance and spiritual virtues espoused by Holy Club members. Wesley's passion for medicine is evident from his concerns and preoccupations as a young man, long before *Primitive Physic* was compiled and published. Further evidence of this can be seen in repeated instances of medical advice or observations given by Wesley in letters to family, friends, lay-preachers, and followers. Wesley's *Journal* also reflects a strong desire to keep up with the latest developments and discoveries that were taking place within the medical sciences.

Primitive Physic, although designed to empower patients to heal themselves, was premised on a desire to carefully mediate Wesley's medical knowledge to the laboring poor. Wesley's interest in their physical and spiritual health was shaped by his training as an ordained minister in the Church of England. Through most of the eighteenth century this training included study of medicine, and the Church dispensed medical licenses for priests to practice physic – valuing highly this dimension of their overall ministry, particularly in remote areas where access to treatment was scarce. Thus, whereas Wesley's charitable initiatives in health and welfare were informed by the theological and spiritual ideals of primitive Christianity, his casuist concern for practical medical works flowed out of a bigger program of Anglican duties to God, neighbor, and oneself. In his account to Perronet Wesley makes mention of a number of other charitable works in which Methodists were taking an active role, such as providing education to poor or orphaned children. This social care echoed earlier Anglican philanthropic movements typical of the late seventeenth and early eighteenth centuries, like the Society for the Reformation of Manners (SRM) founded in 1677, and the Society for Promoting Christian Knowledge (SPCK) instituted in 1698. Wesley's father and his eldest brother were prominent in both of these groups, which had established schools and hospitals in Westminster, London, as part of a broader campaign to reform manners and morality. The compulsion to save lives as well as souls ran deep within Wesley's family background and its influence can be clearly felt in the pages of *Primitive Physic*.

III

Primitive Physic was underpinned by a belief in the vocation of Anglican practical piety, which developed out of Wesley's holistic view of nature and healing inspired by primitive Christianity. Wesley believed that human nature and health were inextricably linked; that we are a unity of body, mind, and soul. He did not suggest that health of the body, mind, and soul were one and the same. Nor did Wesley seek to cure physical illness and disease in *Primitive Physic* via spiritual means – though his *Journal* accounts indicate that he fully endorsed and believed in faith-healing. For Wesley, as an Anglican churchman, the most pressing theological and intellectual challenge involved reconciling rationalism and faith, science and religion, head and heart. Thus, although he evoked Christ as the divine physician in the Preface to *Primitive Physic*, he does not proffer providential medicine in the main body of the text. Similarly, though Wesley echoes St. Augustine's view of Original Sin, he does not portray sickness of the flesh as divine punishment, to be accepted in resignation. A merciful God had provided the antidotes to nature's poisons, wrought by humanity's disobedience and subsequent Fall as recorded in Genesis.[14]

Wesley's stated motivation for writing *Primitive Physic* was to "set down cheap, safe, and easy medicines; easy to be known, easy to be procured, and easy to be applied by plain, unlettered men."[15] His deployment of "plain speech" in *Primitive Physic* was orientated towards the readership of Methodist followers, most of whom were the laboring poor. For this reason, Wesley's medical manual sold for one shilling, as compared to William Buchan's *Domestic Medicine* (1769), which sold for six shillings. Complex medical knowledge was simplified and mediated through *Primitive Physic*, which Wesley charged the Methodist lay preachers to disseminate widely.

Wesley's empirical, experimental approach to medicine sought to free itself from speculative, abstruse medical theory and jargon. Here, Wesley was influenced by exponents of seventeenth-century British empirical philosophy, such as Robert Boyle, John Locke, and Thomas

---

[14] Wesley, *Primitive Physic*, Preface, §§1–6, *Works* (Jackson), 14:307–10.

[15] Wesley, *Primitive Physic*, Postscript, §2, *Works* (Jackson), 14:316. The Postscript was added starting with the 5th ed. (Bristol: J. Palmer, 1755).

Sydenham, whose medical works were underwritten by an empiricist method. Wesley called this empiricist method an "ancient standard" in medicine, which he believed had been lost in an age of modernity.

The word "primitive" in the title of Wesley's manual refers, not to primitive medicines or remedies, but to this ancient standard in medical practice, which was based on the empirical principles of observation and experience. In the same way that he looked to the primitive Church for divine inspiration, Wesley wanted to revive an ancient standard in medicine, which he thought could produce much better healing results. Wesley thought that very few doctors in the modern era understood the true dignity of medicine, which rested on this empirical standard. As examples of those who did utilize it, Wesley cites approvingly in the Preface to *Primitive Physic* George Cheyne, "the great and good Dr. [Thomas] Sydenham," and Thomas Dover (a student of Sydenham, who became a leading physician in his own right during the Georgian period). Wesley esteemed these physicians over and above current members of the medical faculty. His high estimation resultes in part from the strong element of piety that informed their medical practice. Wesley praised Sydenham, Cheyne, and Dover for following in good faith their God-given calling or vocation by putting their skills to the service or benefit of humankind.

Wesley charged that this contrasted markedly with so-called "faculty" physicians in the eighteenth century. Faculty physicians, belonging to the Royal College, liked to protect their status by drawing on systematic or mechanical philosophy in their theoretical works, which were usually written in Latin. Faculty physicians distinguished themselves from other "professional" physicians who had not received their medical degrees from Oxford or Cambridge, as well as from unqualified or lay medical practitioners. In the Preface to *Primitive Physic* Wesley specifically condemned faculty physicians for keeping medicine out of the reach of ordinary men.

Both faculty and other "professional" physicians defended their status and prestige by branding lay medics like Wesley "empirics" or "quacks." This was despite the fact that eighteenth-century practitioners – faculty or otherwise – were forced to rely on empirical methods when practicing physic and treating patients. The most celebrated "professional" attack upon Wesley's *Primitive Physic* came in 1776, from Dr. William Hawes, founder of the Royal Humane Society, apothecary, and noted physician to the London Dispensary. Hawes published an *Examination of the Rev. Mr John Wesley's Primitive Physic*, which worked systematically through Wesley's prescriptions with a critical eye. The dispute between Hawes and Wesley produced a flurry of acrimonious correspondence in broadsheets and the popular press.[16]

Despite the caricatures presented by both sides of this dispute, the reality of Georgian medical practice was a good deal more fluid than either Wesley or Hawes were prepared to admit. Both "professional" and "lay" medics shared clinical knowledge in a market that was becoming increasingly commercial and patient-led. Professional physicians relied on empirical methods and preventative measures like regimen because they were popular with patients. An example of this can be seen in the fact that empirical principles set down by Thomas Sydenham continued to wield enormous influence. Indeed, Sydenham was commonly referred to as the "English Hippocrates." Furthermore, many faculty and professional physicians – such as Richard Blackmore, Richard Mead, George Cheyne, and William Buchan – published medical volumes that were written in the vernacular and aimed at popular readership. Even faculty physicians, who made a show of disdaining popular vernacular works, understood that medical volumes dealing with particular issues like sexually transmitted diseases were commercially successful and therefore extremely lucrative.

Wesley's critical stance toward faculty physicians in his Preface is suggestive of someone opposed to orthodox medicine and its practitioners. Yet, most of the remedies listed in *Primitive Physic* can be traced back to authoritative sources and judged against the best medical standards of his day. Although not a professionally trained medic, Wesley possessed detailed knowledge of methods and compound medications used by leading physicians. His particular admiration for "the learned and ingenious" Cheyne is evidenced by his citing many of the remedies that this physician had prescribed in *Essay of Health and Long Life*. Use was also made of Cheyne's *Natural Method of Curing Most Diseases* (1742).[17] Wesley's dependence on Cheyne is such that contemporary critics and modern scholars have castigated him for simply lifting whole sections of Cheyne's work and adapting them for his own use.

Although Cheyne provided a framework for *Primitive Physic*, a plethora of contemporary medical and scientific developments were also hugely influential and woven into the text. There are numerous

---

[16] See Maddox, "Reclaiming the Eccentric Parent"; and Deborah Madden, "Contemporary Reaction to John Wesley's *Primitive Physic*: or, The Case of William Hawes Examined," *Social History of Medicine* 17 (2004): 365–78.

[17] George Cheyne, *The Natural Method of Curing Most Diseases of the Body, and the Disorders of the Mind Depending on the Body* (London, 1742).

references to other well-known physicians like Richard Mead, John Huxham, the Dutch physician and botanist Hermann Boerhaave, and the famous Swiss professor of medicine Samuel Tissot. Wesley's medical thinking and writings were profoundly colored by Tissot's *L'Avis au Peuple sur sa Sante* (1765).[18] Tissot lived in Lausanne, but his text went to nine editions throughout Europe. Wesley did not obtain any of the remedies for the first edition of *Primitive Physic* from Tissot, but, he integrated the doctor's findings into later editions. He also (anonymously) produced an abridged version of *L'Avis* in 1769, which was entitled *Advices with Respect to Health*. In the introduction, Wesley praised Tissot for his plain language, use of regimen, and empirical approach to medicine. He was not, however, completely uncritical, taking Tissot to task for recommending the use of clysters (enemas), and his "violent fondness for bleeding," which Wesley thought was recommended "on the most trifling occasions." Wesley remained unconvinced about the medical efficacy of over-purging or over-bleeding patients. He also severely criticized Tissot for recommending internal medicine for the external skin complaint, scabies.[19] All of this demonstrates that Wesley did not simply cull from leading authoritative medical texts to source his remedies. He responded critically to other physicians, using his experience to make cautious changes to subsequent editions of *Primitive Physic*.[20]

The empirical methodology for maintaining wellness found in *Primitive Physic* adopts the common structure of seeking to regulate the six "non-naturals": diet, sleep, exercise, air quality, evacuations (bowel movements), and the passions. In the Preface, Wesley outlines his "plain and easy" rules for a healthy regimen, which he notes have been taken chiefly from Cheyne. Echoing Cheyne and other pietistic physicians, Wesley's rules emphasize *preventative* strategies for good health – as contrasted to the tendency of most Georgian physicians to rely heavily on medical interventions in treating patients. It is clear that part of Wesley's interest in preventative care is its potential to foster personal accountability and reduce costs.

---

[18] Samuel August Andre Tissot, *L'Avis au Peuple sur sa Sante* (1762), 2nd ed., trans. J. Kirkpatrick (London, 1765). This was the version Wesley used and abridged. Wesley was also familiar with Tissot's other works, *Onanism* (1760) *Treatise On Epilepsy* (1770), *Nervous Diseases* (1782) and *Diseases of the Men of the World* (1770).

[19] [Wesley (ed.)], *Advices with Respect to Health; extracted from a late author* (Bristol 1769), "Introduction," 3–5 in *Works* (Jackson), 14:255–59.

[20] Madden, "Experience and the Common Interest of Mankind," 47.

Central elements of Wesley's recommended regimen include a sparing or light diet (avoiding too much red meat and rich food), drinking copious amounts of water, and getting as much exercise as possible, preferably in the clean country air. Horseback riding was specifically prescribed by Wesley in letters to family, friends, or followers, and here he followed both Sydenham and Locke in their enthusiasm for this exercise. It was essential to go to bed early, but also to rise early – Wesley condemned oversleeping, which he believed relaxed the body's fibers, thereby inducing nervous disorders. *Cold* bathing was also frequently commended, to brace or toughen one's constitution. Of course, it contributed as well toward Wesley's recommendation that individuals be "clean and sweet" in their houses, clothes, and furniture. Cleanliness was associated with health, whereas dirt denoted disease, even death. Georgian medics and philanthropists made this connection well before the discovery of bacteria and germ theory. Wesley was obsessed with cleanliness and its virtues were frequently extolled in letters to lay ministers who were asked to spread his message. However, he did not invent the phrase, "cleanliness is next to Godliness," as some have suggested. This moral injunction predates the Methodist leader, who used it on scattered occasions.[21]

Avoidance of excess in the non-naturals increased longevity and Wesley preached the importance of avoiding all extremes in food, drink, and the passions. This might mean total avoidance of certain items. At times, he placed tea and coffee in this category, noting their high cost and how they could produce unwanted symptoms, such as trembling, shaking, or nervous complaints. By contrast, he did not advocate a complete ban on alcohol, allowing consumption of clear beer and wine in moderation. The danger of excess in this area was focused on "drams" or spirits (distilled liquor), especially gin, which Wesley judged thoroughly poisonous and the cause of many nervous disorders. Drams increased the passions and avoiding it would help one control violent emotions, which was key to staving off acute disease. Long-lasting grief or despair, on the other hand, produced chronic conditions. It was commonly believed that the application of medicines to diseases caused by the passions, whether they were violent or those of a more languid emotional state, was useless until the root cause had been cured first. Like Cheyne, Wesley believed

---

[21] See especially "Large Minutes," Q. 44, *Works* (Jackson) 8:320; Sermon 88, "On Dress," §5, *Works* 3:249; and Sermon 98, "On Visiting the Sick," §II.6, *Works* 3:392.

that prayer and the love of God was a useful balm for soothing the passions.

Although *Primitive Physic* was by far the most circulated, Wesley wrote and abridged other works of medical science and natural philosophy. His fascination for the new scientific advances recorded by Joseph Priestley, Richard Lovett, and Benjamin Franklin led him to champion the use of electricity as a means of healing.[22] Wesley's passion for electricity resulted from the fact that it was cheap and effective; it perfectly complemented the sensible regimen and natural remedies advocated in *Primitive Physic*. In 1756, he set up locations in London and Bristol where electric treatment was given using a frictional machine. Wesley incorporated these findings into subsequent editions of *Primitive Physic*, but also published anonymously in 1759 a separate tract on the issue, *The Desideratum: or, Electricity Made Plain and Useful*.[23]

In 1763, Wesley published *A Survey of the Wisdom of God in the Creation: or, A Compendium of Natural Philosophy* in 1763. This two-volume work would grow to five volumes by its third edition in 1777. The backbone of the original *Compendium* was a Latin work, *Elementa Philosophiae Practicae et Theoreticae* (1703), written by John Francis Buddaeus. To the structure taken from Buddaeus Wesley added a wealth of extracts from sources like the *Philosophical Transactions* of the Royal Society, John Ray's *The Wisdom of God Manifested in the Works of the Creation* (1691), William Derham's *Physico-Theology* (1713) and *Astro-Theology* (1715), and Oliver Goldsmith's *History of the Earth and Animated Nature* (1774). Scattered through the volumes is both advice for preserving health and identification of the medical benefits of various species.

As noted earlier, in 1769 Wesley published anonymously *Advice with Respect to Health*, a translation of Tissot. In 1774, he abridged and amended William Cadogan's *Dissertation on the Gout, and All Chronic Diseases* (1771), including it as a tract on gout in his collected *Works*. The central theme running through all of these original and edited works was consistent. They all encouraged the use of preventative strategies

---

[22] Benjamin Franklin, *Experiments and Observations on Electricity* (London, 1751); Richard Lovett, *The Subtil Medium Prov'd* (Part 1, London, 1756; Part 2, London, 1759); Lovett, *An Appendix on Electricity rendered Useful in Medical Intentions* (London, 1760); Lovett, *The Electrical Philosopher* (Worcester, 1774); and Joseph Priestley, *History and Present State of Electricity* (London, 1767).

[23] See Linda S. Schwab, "'This Curious and Important Subject': John Wesley and *The Desideratum*," in *Inward and Outward Health.*"

in the form of regimen, combined with cheap, safe, and common or accessible medicines, and supplemented with prayer to achieve health and long life.

IV

Throughout his life, Wesley kept abreast of medical and scientific advances. He drew on leading practitioners of medicine when compiling and re-editing subsequent editions of *Primitive Physic*. These physicians were cited after the sixteenth edition of 1774, following Hawes's criticism in 1776. Wesley's view of disease was theologically informed and he believed that alleviation if not cure could be found in the natural world provided by God. Yet, his methodological approach to medical practice was empirically based and informed by reason. In terms of remedy and explanation, Wesley never mixed medicine and religion. Even his recommendation of prayer in *Primitive Physic*, although not rationalist, contained a logical rationale. When contemporaries (and subsequent scholars) accused Wesley of spiritualizing medicine in a Puritan fashion, this criticism was based on ignorance of his medical work or a sectarian and political desire to discredit Methodism and its leader. Wesley himself recognized that any attempt to assert faith as a curative power was too often countered by the natural suffering of sickness, pain, and even death. In his journals and *Arminian Magazine*, which were meant to aid spiritual inspiration and enlightenment, Wesley retained a place for faith-healing and supernatural or miraculous instances of recovery and cure. These spiritual episodes were not included in *Primitive Physic*, which offered practical advice to those needing urgent medical attention.

Unlike many of his Calvinist contemporaries, Wesley insisted that the medical sciences should be utilized to improve the human condition in a fallen, corrupt world. He refused to separate reason from faith and, in everything, whether it was preaching a sermon on the Fall or compiling efficacious remedies for the ague or fever, Wesley appealed to both head and heart simultaneously. In *Primitive Physic* Wesley brought together the rational and emotional, idealist and pragmatist, scholarly and populist. Here, he also combined faith and good works, Scripture and tradition, God's sovereignty and human freedom, Christian liberty and ordered polity, Original Sin and Christian Perfection. All of these powerful elements were blended into a holistic practical piety that sought to cleanse and heal. If Original Sin meant that human nature was burdened with disease and death, God had given humans the ability to mitigate our suffering. Nature had a remedy for every disease and salvation was the remedy for Original Sin. *Primitive Physic* not only reveals Wesley's unique holistic theological approach to healing the *dis-ease* of our fallen state, but underscores the typicality of his empirical medical practice in Georgian England. Wesley's unified conception of humanity and nature in *Primitive Physic* reconciled all contradictory forces to find a median point. It was this median point that would ensure health, happiness, holiness, and ultimately Christian Perfection.

11 Wesley's theological emphases
JASON E. VICKERS

To understand and appreciate John Wesley, it is imperative to locate his life and work within the intellectual, social, and political context of England's long eighteenth century.[1] Other essays in this volume deal at length with Wesley's social and political context. This essay will focus primarily on the ways in which Wesley inhabited and deeply enriched a particular theological tradition, namely, English Arminianism. To that end, it is important to begin with a few background considerations.

BACKGROUND DEVELOPMENTS

One of the most intractable disputes within Wesleyan studies has to do with where to locate John Wesley within the wider Christian theological tradition. For example, whereas some scholars insist that Wesley belongs to the magisterial Protestant tradition, others maintain that he was deeply indebted to Roman Catholicism or Eastern Orthodoxy. Among those who associate Wesley primarily with Protestantism, there is a lively debate concerning which of the Protestant traditions he inhabited most deeply. For example, some argue that he was essentially Lutheran in outlook, whereas others suggest that he is best understood within the Reformed tradition. Nor does the debate end there. Thus, some scholars insist that Wesley belongs specifically to the German-Pietist tradition, whereas others contend that he was ultimately a Puritan in outlook.[2]

The most obvious explanation for the scholarly disagreement about where to locate Wesley on the theological map has to do with the dynamic and diverse character of Anglicanism in the long eighteenth century. Throughout this period, Anglican theologians were engaged in

---

[1] For an account of Wesley's life and work in its intellectual, social, and political context, see Jason E. Vickers, *Wesley: A Guide for the Perplexed* (2009).
[2] For a helpful review of this debate, see Randy L. Maddox, "Reading Wesley as Theologian," *Wesleyan Theological Journal* 30.1 (1995): 7–54.

the scholarly study of Eastern Patristic, medieval Catholic, and Magisterial Protestant texts. Like so many others, Wesley encountered and embraced insights from the full spectrum of Christian traditions. Consequently, it is understandable that scholars disagree concerning which of these traditions influenced him most deeply.

Although Anglican theologians in the long eighteenth century engaged this broad range of sources, they also spoke a common theological language – namely, the language of covenant. To be sure, it is common to associate covenantal theology primarily with Puritanism, but the language and logic of covenant was hardly exclusive to the Puritans. It was native to the wider Reformed tradition shared by Puritans and Anglicans alike. As Gordon Rupp once put it, "not only Susanna Wesley, but Hoadly and Clarke as well as William Law could talk about the 'covenanted terms of salvation.'"[3] Indeed, one way to understand Anglican theology in the long eighteenth century is to see it as an extended argument over the meaning and implications of the covenant of grace. On the one hand, there were those who maintained the standard interpretation of the covenant of grace within the Reformed theological tradition. On the other hand, a growing number of theologians shaped by that tradition were now critiquing the standard Reformed interpretation of the covenant of grace.

At this stage, some terminological clarification is in order. Although it is both natural and common to depict the argument over the meaning and implications of the covenant of grace as an argument between "Calvinists" and "Arminians," both of these identifiers are problematic. To begin with, it is misleading to term one pole of the argument "Calvinist," as though all English theologians, including "Arminians," were not deeply influenced by the Reformed tradition. Terming the other pole "Arminian" can be equally misleading, if this is taken to mean that the voices on this side of the argument drew their emphases primarily from contact with the continental Arminian tradition.[4] Although they had clear interpretative similarities with continental Arminians, eighteenth-century English theologians critical of the standard Reformed interpretation appear to have derived their "Arminian" reading of the covenant of grace primarily from engagement with Patristic (Greek and Latin) and medieval Catholic sources. Thus, in what follows, I will refer to classical Calvinists or classical Calvinism to identify a particular interpretive tradition within eighteenth-century English theology,

---

[3] Gordon Rupp, *Religion in England, 1688–1791* (1986), 343.
[4] Continental Arminianism refers to the early seventeenth century Dutch Reformed Remonstrant movement associated with Jacob Arminius.

and I will refer to English Arminians or to English Arminianism to denote an interpretive tradition that, although similar to continental Arminianism, appears to have originated independently.

What, then, were the specific areas of disagreement between classical Calvinists and English Arminians? From the standpoint of English Arminians, there were at least two major problems with the classical Calvinist or standard Reformed interpretation of the covenant of grace. First and foremost, classical Calvinists maintained that the covenant of grace had to be interpreted within the framework of a doctrine of *election*, according to which God's absolute freedom and sovereignty were expressed in the issuing of eternal divine decrees. Through these eternal divine decrees, some persons were eternally predestined for salvation, while everyone else was eternally predestined for damnation. For early English Arminians like William Laud and the Caroline Divines, the doctrines of divine inscrutability and unconditional double predestination turned a merciful God into the fiercest of tyrants. Over against these doctrines, they argued that God's absolute freedom included the freedom to make God's will known with such clarity that a common plowman could understand it. Moreover, it included the freedom on God's part providentially to enter into a covenant with human persons that made salvation dependent upon human cooperation with the divine will. Grace, as they would say, was not irresistible; it had to be freely received and embraced.

Second, English Arminians like Jeremy Taylor and the so-called "holy living divines" suspected that the classical Calvinist understanding of the covenant of grace encouraged antinomianism. More specifically, they maintained that the doctrine of unconditional double predestination and a one-sided focus on justification by faith led to apathy and indifference concerning the call to a holy life readily discernible in the Scriptures. By contrast, Taylor and others insisted on the importance of holiness or holy living as the proper goal of the Christian life.

With the dissolution of the Puritan Commonwealth in 1660, the English Arminian tradition began to flourish in unprecedented ways. As we have just seen, the tradition was already present in nascent form in the works of a number of gifted theologians and church leaders. However, it had not yet found its most eloquent and influential spokesman.

More than anyone in the history of English Protestantism, John Wesley brought to full expression the two-fold Arminian emphasis on free grace and holiness. To be sure, the bringing of English Arminianism to full expression involved the hard work of teaching the central tenets of Arminianism to a wide and diverse audience in a manner that was both intellectually and spiritually satisfying. Yet, it would be a mistake to think that Wesley merely popularized what others before him had said concerning the covenant of grace. Rather, he brought the English Arminian tradition to full expression by identifying and responding to questions that the tradition was generating. In doing so, he deeply enriched the English Arminian tradition from within. To see how he did this, we need to consider the basic framework of Wesley's theology.

THE BASIC FRAMEWORK: CREATION, FALL, AND REDEMPTION

We should acknowledge from the start that, viewed against the classical Calvinist doctrine of a limited atonement, the doctrine of universal or unlimited atonement was the linchpin in Wesley's Arminianism. Remove this from the equation, and Wesley's whole theology collapses like a house of cards. Wesley acknowledged as much when he said, "Nothing in the Christian system is of greater consequence than the doctrine of Atonement."[5] However, Wesley viewed the atonement within the wider framework of Arminian theology. Thus, the best place to begin is not with the atonement, but with Wesley's account of creation.

When Wesley spoke of creation, he routinely resorted to the language and logic of covenant, referring to creation as "the covenant of works." He did not use "the covenant of works" to refer to the Mosaic covenant, as though the distinction between the covenant of works and the covenant of grace paralleled a distinction between law and gospel. Rather, he insisted that the covenant of works applied to "none but Adam before the fall."[6]

It is important to notice that the language and logic of the covenant of works imply a divine will or purpose. For Wesley, the divine will or purpose in creation was expressed most clearly in the moral law, which was nothing less than "an incorruptible picture of the high and holy One that inhabiteth eternity." The moral law was "he whom in his essence no man hath seen or can see, made visible to men and angels." Moreover, he says that the moral law given at creation was "the face of God unveiled; God manifested to his creatures as they are able to bear it; manifested to give and not to destroy life; that they may see God and live." Wesley continues, "[The moral law] is the heart of God disclosed to man. Yea, in some sense we may apply to this law what the Apostle

---

5 Letter to Mary Bishop (7 February 1778), *Letters*, Telford, 6:297.
6 Sermon 35, "The Law Established Through Faith, Discourse I," §II.3, *Works*, 2:27.

says of his Son – it is 'the streaming forth' or outbeaming 'of his glory, the express image of his person.'"[7]

A little later in this sermon, Wesley equates the moral law of God with the mind and nature of God, saying, "The law of God . . . is a copy of the eternal mind, a transcript of the divine nature; yea, it is the fairest offspring of the everlasting Father, the brightest efflux of his eternal wisdom, the visible beauty of the Most High." He then hastens to add that the moral law has three noteworthy properties: "It is 'holy, just, and good'."[8]

Having maintained that the moral law mirrors the "heart of God," the "divine nature," and the "eternal mind," Wesley insisted that God created humankind in God's own image and likeness so that the moral law was "coeval" with their nature. Indeed, says Wesley, God wrote the moral law not upon "tables of stone, or any corruptible substance," but upon the human heart so that "it might never be far off, never hard to be understood; but always at hand, and always shining with clear light, even as the sun in the midst of heaven."[9] Thus, Adam was not simply "capable of God, capable of knowing, loving, and obeying his Creator," but he actually "did know God, did unfeignedly love and uniformly obey him," so that from this original state and the "right use of all his faculties, his happiness naturally flowed."[10] Wesley referred to this aspect of human nature at creation as the "moral image" of God.[11]

Although Wesley believed that humans were created in the moral image of God, so that holiness, justice, and goodness reigned in their hearts, he also taught that humans were made in the natural image of God. By this he meant that God created individuals with a liberty to choose whether they would go on obeying the moral law within or whether they would reject it. Thus, he says,

> Now "man was made in the image of God." . . . He was, after the
> likeness of his Creator, endued with *understanding*, a capacity
> of apprehending whatever objects were brought before it, and of
> judging concerning them. He was endued with a *will*, exerting
> itself in various affections and passions; and lastly, with *liberty*,
> or freedom of choice, without which all the rest would have
> been in vain, and he would have been no more capable of serving

[7] Sermon 34, "The Original, Nature, Properties, and Use of the Law," §II.3, *Works*, 2:9.
[8] Ibid., §III.1, *Works*, 2:10.
[9] Ibid., §§I.3–4, *Works*, 2:7.
[10] Sermon 60, "The General Deliverance," §I.2, *Works*, 2:439.
[11] Sermon 45, "The New Birth," §I.1, *Works*, 2:188.

his Creator than a piece of earth or marble. He would have been as incapable of vice or virtue as any part of the inanimate creation. In these [things]... the natural image of God consisted.[12]

Elsewhere, Wesley describes God's gift of freedom to humankind at creation in a way that is thoroughly Arminian, denying that there is any causal relation between eternal divine decrees and the decision of Adam and Eve to reject the moral law. For example, in a sermon on the image of God, he asserts,

> What made his image yet plainer in his human offspring was... the liberty he originally enjoyed; the perfect freedom implanted in his nature, and interwoven with all its parts. Man was made with an entire indifference, either to keep or change his first estate: it was left to himself what he would do; his own choice was to determine him in all things. The balance did not incline to one side or the other unless by his own deed. His Creator would not, and no creature besides himself could, weigh down either scale. So that, in this sense, he was the sole lord and sovereign judge of his own actions.[13]

At this stage, Wesley follows the well-worn path in Christian theology of creation, fall, and redemption, taking up the fall from the covenant of works into sin. In his account of Adam's decision to reject the moral law, Wesley is consistent in his equation of the moral law with the presence of God. Adam did not simply reject an impersonal moral code that was enforced by an indifferent judge. Rather, he rejected the tie that bound him to God, namely, a heart characterized by love and holiness. Thus Wesley says, "it was not long before man rebelled against God, and by breaking this glorious law well nigh effaced it out of his heart; 'the eyes of his understanding' being *darkened* in the same measure as his soul was 'alienated from the life of God.'"[14]

The inability to apprehend the presence of God within had one additional consequence: people lost their freedom to know, to obey, and to love God. In other words, they were now in bondage to sin. Contrary to popular perceptions of Arminianism as implying free will, this consequence of the fall into sin was not lost on Wesley. Indeed, Wesley could describe human bondage to sin as vividly as Augustine or Luther. For example, he writes, "[Our sins]... are chains of iron and fetters of

---

[12] Sermon 60, "The General Deliverance," §I.1, *Works*, 2:438–39.
[13] Sermon 141, "The Image of God," §I.3, *Works*, 4:295.
[14] Sermon 34, "The Original, Nature, Properties, and Use of the Law," §I.4, *Works*, 2:7.

brass. They are wounds wherewith the world, the flesh, and the devil, have gashed and mangled us all over. They are diseases that drink up our blood and spirits, [and] that bring us down to the chambers of the grave."[15]

After noting the devastating consequences of sin, Wesley was quick to observe that God "did not despise the work of his own hands." Rather, he says, God once again revealed God's true nature to humankind, "being reconciled to man through the Son of his love," and thereby "[re-inscribing] the law on the heart of his dark, sinful creature."[16] In other words, after Adam rejected the covenant of works in creation, God made available a covenant of grace – initially through the Mosaic Law and ultimately through the life, death, and resurrection of Jesus Christ.

In turning to the covenant of grace, Wesley stressed four things. First, he insisted that the covenant of grace made available in Christ was not to be contrasted with the covenant made available through Moses, but with the covenant of works in creation. For example, in a sermon on Romans 10:5–8, he declares,

> The Apostle does not here oppose the covenant given by Moses to the covenant given by Christ. If we ever imagined this it was for want of observing that the latter as well as the former part of these words were spoken by Moses himself to the people of Israel, and that concerning the covenant which then was. But it is the covenant of *grace* which God through Christ hath established with men in all ages ... which St. Paul here opposes to the covenant of *works*, made with Adam while in paradise, but commonly supposed to be the only covenant which God had made with man, particularly by those Jews of whom the Apostle writes.[17]

Second, although Wesley stressed the continuity of the covenant of grace "given by Moses" with the covenant "given by Christ," he was also clear about what made the latter covenant distinct, namely, its universal scope. The atonement for sin undertaken by Christ on the cross was not for a particular group of individuals, but for all. In making this move, Wesley was clearly siding with the English Arminians over against the classical Calvinist interpretation of the covenant of grace. That he was

---

[15] Sermon 26, "Upon our Lord's Sermon on the Mount, Discourse the Sixth," §III.13, *Works*, 1:586.
[16] Sermon 34, "The Original, Nature, Properties, and Use of the Law," §I.4, *Works*, 2:7.
[17] Sermon 6, "The Righteousness of Faith," §1, *Works*, 1:202–3.

very aware of both interpretive positions is evident in the following passage from his sermon on free grace:

> And, "The same Lord over all is rich in mercy to all that call upon him." But you say, "No: he is such only to those for whom Christ died. And those are not all, but only a few, 'whom God hath chosen out of the world'; for he died not for all, but only for those who were 'chosen in him before the foundation of the world.'" Flatly contrary to your interpretation of these Scriptures also is the whole tenor of the New Testament; as are in particular those texts: "Destroy not him with thy meat for whom Christ died" – a clear proof that Christ died, not only for those that are saved, but also for them that perish. He is "the Saviour of the world." He is "the Lamb of God, that taketh away the sins of the world." "He is the propitiation, not for our sins only, but also for the sins of the whole world." "He (the living God) is the Saviour of all men." "He gave himself a ransom for all." "He tasted death for every man."[18]

Third, in good Arminian fashion, Wesley denied that the universal or unlimited scope of the atonement meant that all people would be saved. To be sure, it was God's *intention* to save all. Yet, just as Adam was free to reject the covenant of works in creation, so now people were free to accept or reject the covenant of grace. The good news was that they had only to repent of their sins and to put their faith in the atoning sacrifice of Christ. In other words, Wesley strongly affirmed the doctrine of justification by faith.

But what, precisely, did Wesley mean by faith? What was the act of faith that justified? The best way to answer this question is to distinguish between faith as intellectual assent (*assensus*) and faith as personal trust in the atoning sacrifice of Christ for one's sins (*fiducia*). While Wesley did not deny the importance of a careful consideration of the cognitive contents of Christianity, he believed that the faith that justified and therefore saved was of the latter kind, namely, faith as *fiducia* or personal trust. Thus in his sermon "Salvation by Faith," he says,

> What faith is it then through which we are saved? It may be answered: first, in general, it is a faith in Christ – Christ, and God through Christ, are the proper object of it. Herein therefore it is sufficiently, absolutely, distinguished from the faith either of ancient or modern heathens. And from the faith of a devil it is

[18] Sermon 110, "Free Grace," §21, *Works*, 3:553.

fully distinguished by this – it is not barely a speculative, ratio-nal thing, a cold, lifeless assent, a train of ideas in the head; but also a disposition of the heart....

Christian faith is then not only an assent to the whole gospel of Christ, but also a full reliance on the blood of Christ, a trust in the merits of his life, death, and resurrection; a recumbency upon him as our atonement and our life, as *given for us*, and *living in us*. It is a sure confidence which a man hath in God, that through the merits of Christ *his* sins are forgiven, and *he* reconciled to the favour of God; and in consequence hereof a closing with him and cleaving to him as our "wisdom, righ-teousness, sanctification, and redemption" or, in one word, our salvation.[19]

By defining faith primarily in terms of personal trust rather than mere intellectual assent, Wesley set the stage for a fourth and final point of emphasis. Although it is only the act of putting one's trust in the aton-ing sacrifice of Christ that justifies or saves, obedience or works follow immediately from such an act. From Wesley's perspective, works were not antecedent to justification, but they were an immediate consequence of it. Thus, after denying that anyone other than Adam was ever under the covenant of works, Wesley comments, "All [God's] sons were and are under the covenant of grace. The manner of their acceptance is this: the free grace of God, through the merits of Christ, gives pardon to them that believe, that believe with such a faith as, working by love, produces all obedience and holiness." He continues,

The case is not therefore, as you suppose, that men were *once* more obliged to obey God, or to work the works of his law, than they are *now*. This is a supposition you cannot make good. But we should have been obliged, if we had been under the covenant of works, to have done those works antecedent to our accep-tance. Whereas now all good works, though as necessary as ever, are not antecedent to our acceptance, but consequent upon it. Therefore the nature of the covenant of grace gives you no ground, no encouragement at all, to set aside any instance or degree of obedience, and part or measure of holiness.[20]

We can now see that, in the basic framework of his theology, Wesley gave eloquent expression to the English Arminian tradition, affirming

---

[19] Sermon 1, "Salvation by Faith," §§I.4–5, *Works*, 1:120–21 (emphasis original).
[20] Sermon 35, "The Law Established Through Faith, Discourse I," §§II.3–4, *Works*, 2:27 (emphasis original).

the covenant of works at creation, the gift of liberty or freedom to accept or reject that covenant, the fall into sin and the resulting situation of total depravity, the covenant of grace made available to all through the atonement, the doctrine of justification by faith, and the insistence that obedience or works was the evidence of true faith. On Wesley's analysis, salvation was for everyone, but it was conditioned on repentance, trusting faith, and obedience. Without obedience, there was no real faith, and without faith the universal scope of salvation went unrealized.

If Wesley was committed to the basic tenets of English Arminian theology, then he also knew that the Arminian tradition was not without its problems! Indeed, Wesley found himself constantly responding to three questions related to the doctrine of the Christian life. In answering these questions, he developed a robust account of the work of the Holy Spirit, deeply enriching Arminianism from within. It is to this aspect of his work that we now turn.

AN EMPHASIS ON THE HOLY SPIRIT: AWAKENING, ASSURANCE, AND SANCTIFICATION

The first big question that arose within Wesley's basic Arminian framework was triggered by the doctrine of total depravity. On Wesley's own analysis, total depravity meant that people were incapable of discerning, much less accepting and entering into, the covenant of grace on their own accord. According to Wesley, entering into the covenant of grace required being born all over again. Thus he writes,

> Before a child is born into the world he has eyes, but sees not; he has ears, but does not hear. He has a very imperfect use of any other sense. He has no knowledge of any of the things of the world, nor any natural understanding.... How exactly does the parallel hold in all these instances! While a man is in a mere natural state, before he is born of God, he has, in a spiritual sense, eyes and sees not; a thick impenetrable veil lies upon them. He has ears, but hears not; he is utterly deaf to what he is most of all concerned to hear. His other spiritual senses are all locked up; he is in the same condition as if he had them not. Hence he has no knowledge of God, no intercourse with him; he is not at all acquainted with him. He has no true knowledge of the things of God, either of spiritual or eternal things. Therefore, though he is a living man, he is a dead Christian.[21]

---

[21] Sermon 45, "The New Birth," §II.4, *Works*, 2:192.

Here, Wesley portrays the consequences of the fall into sin in terms of a complete impairment of the spiritual senses. Thus he says that one's spiritual senses are so "locked up" that they are "in the same condition as if [one] had them not." If this was the case, then how could one possibly come to apprehend the covenant of grace and begin to live therein?

In response to this question, Wesley turned to the person and work of the Holy Spirit. Being born again, he informed his readers, required nothing less than "the mighty working of the Spirit of God" within the human heart. According to Wesley, the Holy Spirit restores the spiritual senses, enabling one to see "the light of the glory of God . . . in the face of Jesus Christ" and to hear "the inward voice of God, saying, 'Be of good cheer, thy sins are forgiven thee: Go and sin no more.'" When this happens, says Wesley, people become conscious of "a peace which passeth all understanding," and they feel "a joy in God," as well as "the love of God shed abroad" in their hearts "by the Holy Ghost which is given unto [them]." Moreover, through the Spirit's rehabilitation of the spiritual senses, they begin "to discern spiritual 'good and evil'" and daily to increase "in the knowledge of God, of Jesus Christ whom he hath sent, and of all the things pertaining to his inward kingdom." Only then can they "properly be said *to live*: God having quickened [them] by his Spirit, [they are] alive to God through Jesus Christ." Finally, Wesley insisted that the Spirit does not depart after awakening the spiritual senses. Thus he developed and deployed a doctrine of spiritual respiration to describe a person's life after the new birth as follows:

> God is continually breathing, as it were, upon his soul, and his soul is breathing unto God. Grace is descending into his heart, and prayer and praise ascending to heaven. And by this intercourse between God and man, this fellowship with the Father and the Son, as by a kind of spiritual respiration, the life of God in the soul is sustained: and the child of God grows up, till he comes to "the full measure of the stature of Christ."[22]

Before we move on to the second question that arose within Wesley's basic Arminian framework, two observations are in order. On the one hand, it is important to note that Wesley believed that people were incapable of discerning, much less entering into the covenant of grace on their own accord. Because of the devastating effects of the fall, the Holy Spirit must restore the spiritual senses, enabling them to discern the covenant of grace and assisting them to respond favorably to it.

[22] Ibid., §II.4, *Works*, 2:192–93.

Although the technical term for this was *prevenient grace*, it should be noted that, at the level of the restoration of the spiritual senses, it was also *irresistible grace*. People could reject the covenant of grace that they were able to discern with their newly restored faculties, but they could not reject the Spirit's initial restoration of the faculties.

On the other hand, we should note that Wesley did not simply invent the appeal to the work of the Holy Spirit within the human heart. Rather, he was retrieving the riches of the Anglican theological tradition. Thus when he introduces the appeal to the person and work of the Holy Spirit, he tells his readers that he is using "the language of our Church."[23] This in itself was no mean feat, as the doctrine of the Holy Spirit had been idling for more than a century in many quarters within Anglicanism.

The second big question to emerge within Wesley's basic Arminian framework had to do with the doctrine of assurance. Seventeenth- and eighteenth-century Anglican theologians on all sides were wrestling with the question, how could people be assured that they were saved? The prevalence of this question resulted in large part from the classical Calvinist doctrine of divine inscrutability. For many people, the inscrutability of the divine will led to an anguishing uncertainty concerning whether they were among the elect. In some cases, this uncertainty even led to suicide.

Arminianism originally took hold in England because it offered an alternative solution for the problem of assurance. Thus, early English Arminians like William Laud insisted that, if people simply put their faith in Christ, then they could be assured of their salvation. However, Laud and other seventeenth-century Arminians defined faith primarily as intellectual assent. They argued that this was especially fitting because the covenant of grace was available to all. If all people were endowed with reason, then all people were capable of giving intellectual assent to the clear and intelligible propositions contained in scripture.

As we have seen, Wesley did not conceive of faith primarily as assent. Although faith involved assent, it also had a deeper, more demanding dimension – personal trust in God. Thus, despite his insistence on the importance of belief in the Trinity, Wesley was clear that belief was not enough. For example, in a sermon called "The Way to the Kingdom," he says,

> For neither does religion consist in *orthodoxy* or *right opinions*; which, although they are not properly outward things, are not in the heart, but the understanding. A man may be orthodox

[23] Ibid., §II.4, *Works*, 2:193.

in every point; he many not only espouse right opinions, but
zealously defend them against all opposers; he may think justly
concerning the incarnation of our Lord, concerning the ever
blessed Trinity, and every other doctrine contained in the oracles
of God. He may assent to all the three creeds – that called the
Apostles', the Nicene, and the Athanasian – and yet 'tis possible he may have no religion at all, no more than a Jew, Turk, or
pagan. He may be almost as orthodox as the devil ... and may
all the while be as great a stranger as he to the religion of the
heart.[24]

If assent to orthodox Christian doctrine was not the criterion of
assurance, then what was? For Wesley, the solution to the problem of
assurance lay in the doctrine of the inner witness of the Holy Spirit.
To see this, he reasoned, one had only to recognize that "the testimony
of the Spirit must, in the very nature of things, be antecedent to 'the
testimony of our own spirit.'" He continues,

We must be holy in heart and life before we can be conscious
that we are so. But we must love God before we can be holy at
all, this being the root of all holiness. Now we cannot love God
till we know he loves us.... And we cannot know his love to us
till his Spirit witnesses it to our spirit.[25]

Wesley then brings a rather lengthy argument to its conclusion, saying,
"The sum of all is this: the testimony of the Spirit is an inward impression on the souls of believers, whereby the Spirit of God directly testifies
to their spirit that they are children of God."[26]

The problem with the appeal to the inner witness was that it invited
charges of enthusiasm. Of course, from Wesley's point of view, half of
the point of the appeal to the inner witness was to counter charges
of enthusiasm. Nonetheless, Wesley provided further safeguards from
charges of enthusiasm by insisting that the inner witness of the Spirit
had to be accompanied by the fruits of the Spirit. Thus, he cautioned,

Let none ever presume to rest in any supposed testimony of
the Spirit which is separate from the fruit of it. If the Spirit of
God does really testify that we are children of God, the immediate consequence will be the fruit of the Spirit, even "love, joy,

---

[24] Sermon 7, "The Way to the Kingdom," §§I.5–6, *Works*, 1:220–21 (emphasis original).
[25] Sermon 11, "The Witness of the Spirit, II," §III.5, *Works*, 1:290.
[26] Ibid., §V.1, *Works*, 1:296.

peace, long-suffering, gentleness, goodness, fidelity, meekness, temperance."[27]

The third and final big question that arose within Wesley's Arminian theological framework was triggered in part by his insistence that the fruits of the Spirit would be evident in the lives of believers. In truth, the question that Wesley faced was two-fold. On the one hand, there was the question of how believers were to acquire the fruits of the Spirit. On the other hand, there was the question of the degree to which believers could expect the fruits of the Spirit to be manifest in their lives. After all, Wesley himself knew only too well that the fruits of the Spirit could wax and wane. Thus, he admits, "Neither joy nor peace are always at one stay; no, nor love; as neither is the testimony itself always equally strong and clear."[28] In attempting to answer this two-part question, Wesley formulated the most controversial aspect of his theology, namely, the doctrine of entire sanctification.

In keeping with his Arminian theological framework, Wesley insisted that people had a role to play in their sanctification. Thus he taught that believers were actively to participate in the outward means that Christ had ordained "for conveying his grace into the souls of men."[29] These "means of grace," he says, are "outward signs, words, or actions ordained of God, and appointed for this end – to be the *ordinary* channels whereby he might convey to men preventing, justifying, or sanctifying grace."[30]

Whereas there is some debate about what Wesley regarded as means of grace, it is clear that he regarded public and private prayers, Scripture, baptism, and the Lord's Supper as such. Whether or not we expand this list to include other things, the most important thing to note about the means of grace is Wesley's insistence that the "end" for which they were given is what ultimately mattered. Indeed, Wesley was worried about the possibility that people might mistake the means of grace for the essence of religion. Thus he writes,

> But we allow that the whole value of the means depends on
> their actual subservience to the end of religion; that conse-
> quently all these means, when separate from the end, are less
> than nothing, and vanity; that if they do not actually conduce
> to the knowledge and love of God they are not acceptable in his

[27] Ibid., §V.3, *Works*, 1:297.
[28] Ibid, §II.7, *Works*, 1:288.
[29] Sermon 16, "The Means of Grace," §I.1, *Works*, 1:378.
[30] Ibid., §II.1, *Works*, 1:381 (emphasis original).

sight; yea, rather, they are an abomination before him; a stink in his nostrils; he is weary to bear them – above all if they are used as a kind of "commutation" for the religion they were designed to subserve.[31]

Despite this worry, there is abundant evidence that Wesley highly valued the means of grace. For example, Wesley left the Fetter Lane Society precisely because they discontinued the use of the means of grace. And, although Wesley's departure from Fetter Lane suggests that he valued the means of grace for justification, he clearly emphasized their role in entire sanctification and Christian perfection as well.

As Wesley's warning about the means of grace demonstrates, he believed that the essence and goal of religion was the knowledge and love of God, not outward obedience per se. Indeed, Wesley repeatedly said that what really mattered in religion was love for God and love for neighbor. Moreover, he was convinced that obedience followed a change of heart. It was the consequence of a right ordering of one's affections. Yet, there is a real sense in which obedience and love are in a dialectical relationship in Wesley's theology. Thus, on the one hand, he insists that participation in the means of grace was most beneficial when it was done out of love. On the other hand, however, he believes that the Spirit works through the means of grace to bring about an ever-deepening love for God and neighbor in the human heart.

If Wesley believed that the essence and goal of religion was the filling of the human heart with love for God and neighbor and that the Spirit worked in and through the means of grace toward that end, then he also insisted that sanctification did not happen automatically. Participating in the means of grace did not automatically result in the transformation of the heart. Although Christians were responsible for obeying the commands of Christ to participate in the means of grace, it was the Spirit who brought about change in their hearts. Thus, we do not have to do here with sanctification by works. On the contrary, Wesley taught that sanctification was as much a matter of grace as justification. For this reason, he stressed the relative unpredictability of sanctification, saying,

> There is likewise great variety in the manner and time of God's
> bestowing his *sanctifying grace*, whereby he enables his children
> to give him their whole heart, which we can in no wise account
> for. We know not why he bestows this on some even before
> they ask for it (some unquestionable instances of which we have

---

[31] Ibid., §II.2, *Works*, 1:381.

seen); on some after they have sought it but a few days; and yet permits other believers to wait for it perhaps twenty, thirty, or forty years; nay, and others till a few hours or even minutes before their spirits return to him.[32]

Finally, what exactly did Wesley have in mind when he spoke of entire sanctification or Christian perfection? We have been hinting at this all along. For example, his understanding of entire sanctification shows up in his comment about the knowledge and love of God being "the end of religion," and in his remark about the varying lengths of time it takes for people to give God their whole hearts. To be sure, Wesley sometimes spoke of entire sanctification in terms of freedom from sinful thoughts. Yet, he regarded entire sanctification or Christian perfection as having above all to do with the filling of the human heart with love for God and neighbor and the governing of all subsequent thoughts, words, and deeds, by that love. Indeed, Wesley himself sums it up best when he says, "By perfection, I mean the humble, gentle, patient love of God and man ruling all the tempers, words, and actions, the whole heart and the whole life."[33]

A FITTING END: THE TRINITY AND THE NEW CREATION

By turning to the work of the Holy Spirit to answer theological questions that arose naturally within the Arminian framework of his theology, Wesley enriched the English Arminian tradition in creative and powerful ways. In his appeal to the Spirit's work in restoring the spiritual senses, Wesley recognized both the devastating effects of sin and the sheer gratuity of salvation. In his retrieval of the doctrine of the inner witness, he offered a solution to a long-standing and widespread problem within Protestantism that was spiritually disabling for many people. And, in his emphasis on the doctrine of entire sanctification, Wesley infused the English Arminian tradition with an optimism that, with the help of the Holy Spirit, people really could live lives governed by love for God and neighbor.

Having said all of this, it would be a mistake to think that Wesley's contribution to the Arminian stream of English Protestant theology was limited to filling in the gaps and answering a few difficult questions. On the contrary, in his persistent appeals to the person and work of the Holy Spirit, Wesley provided English Arminianism with another language and

[32] Sermon 69, "The Imperfection of Human Knowledge," §III.5, *Works*, 2:584.
[33] Letter to Charles Wesley (September 1762), *Letters* (Telford), 4:187.

logic besides that of covenant – namely, the language and logic of Trinitarian theology. To be sure, this Trinitarian language and logic remained implicit in the early and middle years of Wesley's life. Yet, as he aged, Wesley came to see most clearly the Trinitarian implications of what was by then a very robust doctrine of the Holy Spirit. For example, in a sermon on the Trinity written and published in 1775, Wesley made explicit the Trinitarian direction and logic of the work of the Holy Spirit in assuring believers of their salvation, saying,

> But I know not how anyone can be a Christian believer till "he hath" (as St. John speaks) "the witness in himself"; till "the Spirit of God witnesses with his spirit that he is a child of God" – that is, in effect, till God the Holy Ghost witnesses that God the Father has accepted him through the merits of God the Son – and having this witness he honours the Son and the blessed Spirit "even as he honours the Father."[34]

In coming to emphasize the doctrine of the Trinity, Wesley took strides toward overcoming one of the great dangers of the Arminian theological tradition. From the beginning, Arminianism had anthropocentric tendencies. By insisting that humans had a role to play in their salvation, Arminians ran the risk of worrying too much about the precise nature of that role and the criteria for determining when it had been performed successfully. Indeed, Wesley himself had spent a good portion of his life in this theological cul-de-sac. However, years of reflection on the person and work of the Holy Spirit enabled a mature Wesley to see the Trinitarian direction and shape of Christian theology. Even more importantly, it enabled him to see the Trinitarian shape and direction of the Christian life. Thus, in a fitting conclusion both to his sermon on the new creation and to a lifetime's worth of theological reflection, Wesley insisted that there was something even more to be desired than a deliverance from sickness, pain and death, namely, "an intimate, an uninterrupted union with God; a constant communion with the Father and his Son Jesus Christ, through the Spirit; a continual enjoyment of the Three-One God, and of all the creatures in him!"[35]

---

[34] Sermon 55, "On the Trinity," §17, *Works*, 2:385.
[35] Sermon 64, "The New Creation," *Works* §18, 2:510.

12 Happiness, holiness, and the moral life in John Wesley

REBEKAH L. MILES

The elderly John Wesley, just a few months shy of his eighty-sixth birthday, asked a crowd of Irish Methodists gathered in Dublin a classic question from an unlikely source – the Calvinist Westminster Confession: "For what end did God create man?" One simple answer, Wesley insisted, should be "inculcated upon every human creature: 'You are made to be happy in God.'" Wesley then tendered advice to parents. Even when a child first begins to speak or to run alone, a good parent follows behind saying, many times each day, "He made *you*; and he made you to be happy in him; and nothing else can make you happy."[1]

What is the happiness for which humans were made? Wesley insisted that just "as there is one God, so there is one religion and one happiness."[2] This one human happiness and true religion is the love of God and the love of neighbor. It is, "in two words, gratitude and benevolence; gratitude to our Creator and supreme Benefactor, and benevolence to our fellow creatures."[3]

The active benevolence toward others that is born of our gratitude to God is for Christians the wellspring of the moral life and of human happiness. Happiness is impossible without this grateful love of God and benevolent, active love toward others. And the moral life is one with this happiness. Wesley preached,

> The love of Christ constrains us, not only to be harmless, to do no ill to our neighbour, but to be useful . . . to do good unto all men;" and to be patterns to all of true, genuine morality; of justice, mercy, and truth. *This is religion, and this is happiness; the happiness for which we were made.*[4]

[1] Sermon 120, "The Unity of the Divine Being," §10, *Works*, 4:64.
[2] Ibid., §22, *Works*, 4:70.
[3] Ibid., §16, *Works*, 4:66–67.
[4] Ibid., §17, *Works* 4:67 (emphasis added).

Religion and happiness, then, are always one; their two parts or branches – love of God and love of neighbor – are indivisible. To choose half of this one religion and one happiness, *either* the love of God *or* love of neighbor, is to lose the whole. This one happiness is the heart of Wesley's ethic.

What are some implications of these claims for the moral life? First, in this sermon and throughout Wesley's writings, his vision of the moral life, and the Christian life as a whole, is teleological. It is shaped by the goal or telos for which humans were made and to which they are to be moving – holiness. Humans move toward that end (and help others journey toward that end) as they grow in love of God and neighbor.[5]

Second, in this sermon and through his writings, the moral life of right action, virtue, and right tempers is inextricably linked to the love of God. The whole thing hangs together in one piece. The moral life cannot be separated out from the whole Christian life as if it were a divisible thing. A religion (or a piety) that is not centered on the active love of both God and neighbor is, for Wesley, a false religion. The active love of neighbor is not just an important part of the Christian life; it, along with the love of God, is the unifying *core* of the Christian life.

This leads to a third, and closely linked, implication for *reflections* on Wesley's teaching on ethics. Because he insists that religion and happiness are one, and that true religion incorporates active love of both God and neighbor, it is impossible to sever – or even to distinguish sharply – a study of Wesley's ethics from consideration of his theology or his vision of a holy life. Sondra Wheeler goes so far as to argue that Wesley did not even have a "social ethic."[6] The distinction that has often been made over the last century or so between theology and ethics, as well as the distinction between the personal and the social, were alien to Wesley (as they were to most earlier Christians).

Finally, Wesley's insistence on the link between the love of God and the active love of neighbor points to a question at the heart of Wesley's vision of the moral life: What is the causal connection between the love of God and the love of neighbor? In the sermon cited above, the elderly Wesley focused on two causal links. Human love for God naturally

---

[5]　For conflicting perspectives on how to classify John Wesley's moral theology, see H. Ray Dunning, *Reflecting the Divine Image: Christian Ethics in Wesleyan Perspective* (1998), 33–37; Albert Outler, *Evangelism and Theology in the Wesleyan Spirit* (2000), 127; Ron Stone, *John Wesley's Life and Ethics* (2001), 215; and D. Stephen Long, *John Wesley's Moral Theology* (2005).

[6]　Sondra Wheeler, "John Wesley and Social Ethics" (paper delivered to the Wesley Institute, Washington DC), p.1. Available at http://livedtheology.org/pdfs/Wesleyt.pdf.

fosters gratitude to God, which in turn nourishes active benevolence toward others. But this is not the whole story.

An insistence that human moral life is made possible by our participation in the Holy Trinity runs throughout Wesley's writings. Thus, at the crux of this sermon capping his ministry, in which Wesley is emphasizing the necessity of good works and the transformation of Christian lives into "patterns to all of true, genuine morality; of justice, mercy, and truth," he is careful to highlight the workings of the Trinity as the source of this possibility. Transformation into patterns of genuine morality begins, Wesley wrote,

> when we begin to know God, by the teaching of his own Spirit.
> As soon as the Father of spirits reveals his Son in our hearts,
> and the Son reveals his Father, the love of God is shed abroad in
> our hearts; then, and not till then, we are happy. We are happy,
> first, in the consciousness of his favour, which indeed is bet-
> ter than life itself; next, in the constant communion with the
> Father, and with his Son Jesus Christ; then, in all the heavenly
> tempers which he hath wrought in us by his Spirit; again, in the
> testimony of his Spirit, that all our works please him; and, lastly,
> in the testimony of our own spirit.... And [our] happiness still
> increases as [we] "grow up into the measure of the stature of the
> fullness of Christ."[7]

The happiness and holiness (including moral holiness) expected in a Christian's life are possible only as the believer is engaged and transformed by this divine love into the divine image.

HOLINESS ORGANIZED

John Wesley was a master of small details – founding and overseeing schools, relief agencies, and orphanages; organizing accountability groups and subgroups that provided structure to foster Christian holiness; and devising rules and mechanisms to encourage members of these groups to maintain their disciplines. Wesley left little to chance. He did not just recommend that his people go about doing good, he set about organizing goodness.

It is easy to get caught up in all the details and the many things that were expected of eighteenth-century Methodists and to lose sight of the central story line. For Wesley, this central story was the "way of

---

[7] Sermon 120, "The Unity of the Divine Being," §17, *Works*, 4:67.

salvation" (*via salutis*), a journey into holiness and true righteousness. He could talk about the ultimate goal in many ways – perfection in love, sanctification, or the restoration of the image of God. But, he was relentless in his insistence that all of the many expectations of Methodist life and details of Methodist order were oriented to this goal.

It is important to recognize that Wesley understood this way of salvation, this journey into holiness and happiness, in a holistic manner. It included and had an impact on all aspects of people's lives. For example, Wesley studied and contributed through his writings to the field of medicine precisely because holiness did not stop with a concern for people's souls, but also included love for their bodies as well. Helping people grow in the image of God meant a ministry of restoration involving all parts of their lives – including their physical bodies.[8]

Wesley and the early Methodists were passionate about caring for the physical needs of others. They provided clothing to widows and orphans, food to the hungry, housing for the homeless, and medicine for the sick. They did this not only because it was a scriptural command to care for the poor, but because it was also inextricably linked to the "one religion" and the unity of God. One could no more be a Christian and refuse to love and care for a neighbor than one could be a Christian and refuse to love God. Indeed, in the end, both loves amounted to one thing – the one happiness and one religion.

Holiness organized: groups

Wesley wanted his Methodist people to care for others and to do the right thing. In theory, he could simply have exhorted them: "Be good! Do good! Advise others to do the same!" But, Wesley liked to organize things. He and his early followers were called "Methodists" for good reason; they developed methods and structures for the many aspects of Christian life. Early Methodists had a *program* for growth in holiness and love, and they expected each other to get and keep with the program.

Wesley became convinced early in his ministry that the best way to help nurture growth in holiness and love was to join those seeking salvation together in groups – the Methodist societies and smaller sub-groups within the societies. In *The Nature, Design, and General Rules of the United Societies*, a foundational document for the Methodist movement, Wesley described the societies as "a company of [people] having the form and seeking the power of godliness, united to

---

[8] See Chapter 9, by Deborah Madden; and Randy L. Maddox, "John Wesley on Holistic Health and Healing," *Methodist History* 46 (2007): 4–33.

pray together, to receive the word of exhortation, and to watch over one another in love, that they may help each other to work out their salvation."⁹

The bar for joining a Methodist society was fairly low. These groups were not conclaves for a Christian elite, but infirmaries and nurseries for those *on the way* of salvation. The initial requirement for membership was simply "a desire to flee from the wrath to come, and to be saved from their sins."¹⁰ However, as with any regimen or corporate support group, there were expectations for *continuing* to participate and benefit. Members were expected to evidence their continuing desire to "be saved from their sins" by their daily practices.

Holiness organized: the general rules

As one would expect, early Methodists were not left to their own devices in discerning appropriate practices. Wesley formulated a specific set of guidelines. These General Rules were the most broadly shared and normative feature of early Methodist life. They traveled with the expansion of the Methodist family of churches throughout the world, and remain among the foundational documents of many churches in this family. For example, clergy candidates in the United Methodist Church are still asked whether they know the General Rules and if they will keep them.

Wesley structured the General Rules around three general guidelines: (1) doing no harm, (2) doing good, and (3) attending upon all the ordinances of God. Under each of these broad guidelines he gathered several specific instances.

Before turning to consider these specifics, it is important to note that Wesley did not consider faithful practice of the General Rules to be, in itself, the essence or the dynamic of the holy life. As he discovered in his own journey, this dynamic is fellowship with the Triune God, a fellowship that God initiates and empowers. Apart from this dynamic, Wesley warned that the General Rules become nothing more than the "religion of the world."

> The religion of the world implies three things: 1) the doing no harm...2) the doing good...[and] 3) the using the means of grace....He in whom these three marks are found is termed by the world a religious man. But will this satisfy him who hungers after God? No. It is not food for his soul. He wants a religion

---

⁹ *General Rules*, §2, *Works*, 9:69.
¹⁰ Ibid., §4, *Works*, 9:70.

of a nobler kind, a religion higher and deeper than this, ... the having "fellowship with the Father and the Son"; the "walking in the light as God is in the light"; the being "purified even as He is pure" – this is the religion, the righteousness, he thirsts after.[11]

The General Rules, then, were not commended by Wesley simply as a way to "mark" early Methodists as different from other people. Nor were these practices to be pursued as a self-help strategy for moral improvement. Wesley had come to value them instead as important practices in which we can encounter and through which we nurture fellowship with the Triune God. They were Wesley's seasoned regimen or prescribed therapy for those who "desire of salvation," who long for and are committed to the journey of ongoing growth in Christ.

Do no harm / avoid evil

Under the first heading of the General Rules, Methodists are to "evidence their desire for salvation ... by doing no harm, by avoiding evil of every kind."[12] This broad rule is open ended and could include thousands of possible acts, but Wesley offered some specific things to avoid, "especially that which is most generally practiced" during his time.

Members of the Methodist societies were told to avoid the buying, selling, or holding of slaves. They were advised not to break the Sabbath, "either by doing ordinary work" on the Sabbath "or by buying or selling." They were to avoid wearing "gold and costly apparel," in part because it might lead the wearer toward pride of appearance and, even more important, it was a waste to spend money for luxuries that might have been spent providing necessities for the poor.

More was required of Methodists than avoiding a bit of shopping on Sundays and the wearing of golden rings. They were enjoined in the General Rules as well against: taking the Lord's name in vain; "brawling"; getting drunk; "borrowing without a probability of paying"; speaking evil of government officials; and "singing those songs, or reading those books, which do not tend to the knowledge or love of God."

Do good

Under the second heading, Methodists are enjoined to give evidence of their desire for salvation "by doing good ... of every possible sort, and,

[11] Sermon 22, "Sermon on the Mount, II," §§II.4–5, *Works*, 496–97.
[12] *General Rules*, §4, *Works*, 9:70–71.

as far as possible, to all [people]."[13] Like the first, this rule is extremely broad and could include limitless numbers of things. Once again Wesley offered specifics. Methodists were instructed to help the physical bodies of others "by giving food to the hungry, by clothing the naked, by visiting or helping them that are sick or in prison." They were also exhorted to help the souls of others by instructing and reproving them.

Wesley's conjoining of "avoiding evil" with "doing good" is significant. Here, he avoids any suggestion that the holy life is defined solely by one's relationship to God or simply in terms of staying pure. For Wesley, true holiness is bound up as much in what one *does* as in what one *avoids*. It should also pervade the whole of one's life and all of one's relationships. Thus, whereas he appreciated the potential benefit of select times of spiritual retreat or withdrawal from society, he placed loving engagement with others – at the point of their need – central to his depiction of the Methodist ideal.[14]

Attend upon all the ordinances of God

The third way in which Wesley counseled Methodists to show evidence of their desire of salvation was "by attending upon all the ordinances of God."[15] In his sermon "The Means of Grace" Wesley defined ordinances as the "means ordained of God as the usual channels of his grace."[16] He went on to highlight prayer, study of Scripture, and the Lord's Supper as among these ordained means. The list given in the General Rules is a bit broader, including public worship of God, the ministry of the Word, the Supper of the Lord, family and private prayer, searching the Scriptures, and fasting.

Reflecting on the General Rules

This sketch of the detailed advice gathered under the three General Rules reinforces the holistic nature of the holiness Wesley was hoping to foster among his Methodist followers. It involved one's soul, mind, body, immediate personal relationships, and larger social relationships – as well as the souls, minds, and bodies of others.

It is also apparent that, whereas the three rules are general in nature, many of the specific guidelines reflect particular situations and cultural settings. Indeed, Wesley stressed his concern to address what was "most

---

[13] Ibid., §5, *Works*, 9:72.
[14] See particularly, *The Character of a Methodist*, *Works*, 9:32–42; and Sermon 24, "Sermon on the Mount, IV," I.1–7, *Works*, 1:533–37.
[15] *General Rules*, §6, *Works*, 9:73.
[16] Sermon 16, "The Means of Grace," I.1, *Works*, 1:378.

generally practiced," the most common temptations and needs of the time.[17] This means that any serious attempt to honor Wesley's General Rules today will need to consider revising some of the guidelines, precisely to honor the broader rule. For example, it is not clear in modern democratic political settings that a key way to "do no harm" is never to speak ill of government officials. Many would argue instead the application of holding elected officials accountable for their acts. At the same time, many of the specific guidelines address broadly shared human and cultural traits, such as the tendency to quarrel or to overindulge.

Finally, it is important to recognize that, although the General Rules did not make up the whole or the heart of religion, they were considered essential among early Methodists. They were not just friendly advice for the optional consideration of members; they were requirements for continuation in the society. The last paragraph of the General Rules is very clear about the consequences of serious, ongoing infractions:

> If there be any among us who observe them not, who habitually break any of them, let it be known unto them who watch over that soul as they who must give an account. We will admonish him of the error of his ways. We will bear with him for a season. But then, if he repent not, he hath no more place among us.[18]

This was not an empty warning among early Methodists. Members of societies were often expelled, on occasion many of them at one time. The causes of the expulsions could be as diverse as Sabbath-breaking, quarrelling, and carelessness. Although the notion of expulsions from a religious group might seem harsh today, there were several mitigating factors. First, in early Methodism almost all society members were also baptized members of a church, most often an Anglican church. Those expelled from Methodist societies could still attend worship and receive Holy Communion in their churches. Moreover, those expelled were not cut off permanently. They were given opportunities to return. The early Methodists even set up special groups – penitential bands – for people who had fallen away and now desired to come back into the society.

The practice of expelling members from the society must ultimately be seen in light of the perceived consequences. The General Rules were valued not as rules for rules' sake, but as rules for the sake of a greater goal – the nurturing of holiness in oneself and in others. Early Methodists were convinced that when societies did not require the strict following

---

[17] *General Rules*, §4, *Works*, 9:70.
[18] Ibid., §7, *Works*, 9:73.

of the General Rules, over time the society and its members would diminish in holiness. An early preacher wrote, "I always find where the reins of discipline are slackened, it sinks the state of vital religion much. I found it so here; and the mischief is, there is in people an unwillingness to be brought into order when they have been accustomed to live without it."[19] The General Rules and the threat of expulsion were a reflection of how important it was to live well.

HOLINESS EXEMPLIFIED: STANDS ON PARTICULAR ISSUES

The injunctions to do good and avoid evil were taken to heart by early Methodists. Wesley, his lay leaders, and the people as a whole not only cared for the poor, they also set up institutions, worked for social reform, and organized benevolence.[20] They not only cared for individuals who were sick, they started clinics for the urban poor that provided medical care without cost. They not only visited prisoners, they sought prison reform. They not only cared for children in poverty, they worked for the passage of child-labor laws and set up orphanages. They were also keen to support education, starting the Sunday School movement, setting up schools for poor children, and starting adult literacy programs. Holiness was not simply about transforming one's own life, or even the lives of other individuals. Wesley and early Wesleyans sought the transformation of the whole society.

There is not space to explore in depth Wesley's teaching and concerns about each of these issues. I have chosen three as representative – slavery, suicide, and parenting.

Slavery
John Wesley was an outspoken critic of slavery and the brutality of the slave trade. In the 1770s, he published a tract on slavery in which he wrote, "I strike at the root of this complicated villany; I absolutely deny all slave-holding to be consistent with any degree of natural justice. . . . That slave-holding is utterly inconsistent with mercy, is almost too plain to need a proof."[21] To those who pointed to the law throughout many lands that allowed slavery, Wesley countered, "Notwithstanding ten thousand laws, right is right, and wrong is wrong still."[22]

---

[19] John Telford, *Wesley's Veterans* (1914), 7:75–76.
[20] A helpful survey of these ministries can be found in Manfred Marquardt, *John Wesley's Social Ethics*.
[21] John Wesley, *Thoughts Upon Slavery*, IV.3–4, *Works* (Jackson), 11:70–71.
[22] Ibid., IV.2, *Works* (Jackson), 11:70.

Wesley did not build his case against slavery solely by appeal to natural rights and Scripture, as one might expect. He emphasized as well the impact of slavery on holiness and righteousness. Wesley contended that slavery had been horrible for both the bodies and the souls of the slaves and for the cultures from which the slaves were taken. He went to great lengths to offer evidence that the West African societies from which slaves were taken had been, previous to the rise in the slave trade, characterized by fairness, justice, courtesy, industry, and benevolence. Before slavery, the peoples of the west coast of Africa were, Wesley insisted,

> far more mild, friendly, and kind to strangers, than any of our forefathers were. *Our forefathers!* Where shall we find at this day, among the fair-faced natives of Europe, a nation generally practising the justice, mercy, and truth, which are found among these poor Africans?[23]

The brutality inflicted by the slave-traders had not only hurt the bodies and souls of the slaves, but also, by engaging West Africans in the capture of their neighbors, the virtue and character of the individuals left behind and the health of their larger societies.

Wesley was not worried only about the slaves and the peoples of West Africa. In the last pages of his pamphlet, he addressed three groups concerning the wretched state of their souls: slave-traders, slave-merchants, and slave-holders. He was desperate to convince those connected with slavery to quit their involvement at once – not only for the sake of those who have been enslaved and the cultures from which they had come, but for the sake of their own souls. Wesley believed that souls of those connected to slave-trading were in immanent peril and that the only way to move toward God and avoid spending eternity in hell was to quit any dealings with slavery. The wealth gained through slavery comes at a horrible cost. To the slave-holder, Wesley wrote, "O, whatever it costs, put a stop to its cry before it be too late. . . . Thy hands, thy bed, thy furniture, thy house, thy lands, are at present stained with blood."[24] And, likewise, to the slave-trader: "Today resolve, God being your helper, to escape for your life. Regard not money! . . . Whatever you lose, lose not your soul: Nothing can countervail that loss. Immediately quit the horrid trade."[25]

---

[23] Ibid., II.11, *Works* (Jackson), 11:64–65.
[24] Ibid., V.5, *Works* (Jackson), 78.
[25] Ibid., V.3, *Works* (Jackson), 77.

Evident throughout Wesley's essay on slavery, then, are not simply arguments based on natural rights or economic and political consequences. Wesley was also and perhaps chiefly concerned with the impact of slavery on holiness in its larger sense – concerning the bodies and souls of individuals and the state of the larger societies in which they live.

The significance of the slavery issue for Wesley and early Methodists can be seen in another document. Wesley's last letter, written less than a week before his death, offered a word of encouragement to William Wilberforce, a member of Parliament and a dogged opponent of slavery. Wesley wrote, "Go on, in the name of God and in the power of his might, till even American slavery (the vilest that ever saw the sun) shall vanish away before it."[26] Opposing slavery was important enough to Wesley that he insisted on writing a letter about it in the very last days of his life.

This letter is also important for Methodist identity. A well-known Methodist engraving shows Wesley on his deathbed penning this letter to Wilberforce. Though likely not accurate in historical detail, the engraving reflects with keen accuracy the importance of this letter to the self-identity of many Methodists. As faithful Christians approached death, they were not only to pray and sing hymns on their death-beds, but also, following the model of John Wesley, to continue to speak and work on behalf of those who possess nothing – not even their own bodies.

The laws of countries around the world now prohibit slavery, and many may consider it a thing of the past. Sadly, enslavement is not only still thriving; it is more widespread than it was in the nineteenth century or any other age. Conservative estimates put the number of slaves at approximately 27 million. Wesley's precedent would challenge his heirs today not only to work against the slave trade by lobbying for appropriate government action, but, also, to consider how their ordinary decisions about where to shop and what to buy may help to support or discourage slavery.[27] Might a desire to purchase the cheapest goods available tempt many Christians to turn a blind eye to the source of those goods and the suffering of those who made them? One can hear the echo of Wesley's warning to the slave-holder: "Thy hands, thy bed, thy furniture, thy

---

[26] Letter to William Wilberforce (February 26, 1791), *Letters* (Telford), 8:265.

[27] See Susan Llewelyn Leach, "Slavery is Not Dead, Just Less Recognizable," *Christian Science Monitor* (September 1, 2004), found at http://www.csmonitor.com/2004/0901/p16s01-wogi.html; "Contemporary Forms of Slavery," Fact Sheet No.14, United Nations, Office of the High Commissioner for Human Rights (1991), http://www.unhchr.ch/html/menu6/2/fs14.htm; and Bob Herbert, "Today's Hidden Slave Trade," *New York Times* (October 27, 2007), found http://www.nytimes.com/2007/10/27/opinion/27herbert.html.

[clothing]...are at present stained with blood." His arguments about slavery suggest that a person with any conscious involvement in or support of slavery necessarily diminishes in holiness and imperils their present and future life with God.

Suicide

More than two centuries following Wesley's criticisms of slavery, it is a rare person who would openly disagree. By contrast, from the perspective of our time, some other moral claims by John Wesley seem wrong-headed and even morally offensive. If Wesley's unwavering opposition to slavery was his moral high-water mark, his reflections on suicide may be his nadir.[28]

Wesley's concern about the high rates of suicide among the English in the eighteenth century was understandable, but, his analysis of the problem and recommended solution are next to unfathomable today. Suggesting that the rates might be especially high in England, because the English are, as he put it, "more ungodly and impatient than other nations," Wesley went on to offer a remedy to discourage suicide. What was the remedy? "That the body of every self-murderer, lord or peasant, shall be hanged in chains" in public view.[29]

In a 1784 letter offering advice to British Prime Minister William Pitt, Wesley recommended this "remedy" for lowering suicide rates and also made positive reference to the even more troubling practice of the ancient Spartans who sought to discourage suicide among Spartan women "by ordering that the body of every woman that killed herself should be dragged naked through the streets of the city." Wesley went on to suggest that if Pitt followed his advice to hang in chains the corpses of any who committed suicide, he "would do more service to [his] country than any Prime Minister has done these hundred years."[30]

Given the understanding of suicide and mental illness in our time, Wesley's "Thoughts on Suicide" and his letter to Pitt are so wide of the mark as to be morally abhorrent. But, whereas these two statements about suicide are far out of step with Christian moral reflection today, his underlying concern about the moral seriousness of suicide is not.

Why is Wesley so concerned about suicide? A careful look at Wesley's secondary comments and stories about suicide suggests that his primary

---

[28] See James Clemons, "Wesley's View of Suicide in Cultural Context," *Quarterly Review* 16.2 (Summer 1996): 135–50.

[29] "Thoughts on Suicide," *Arminian Magazine* (April 8, 1790), *Works* (Jackson), 13:481.

[30] Letter to William Pitt (September 6, 1784), *Letters* (Telford), 7:234–36; quotations from 236.

concern was not that suicide was a violation of God's law or civil law, but that it cut short any possible growth in God's love and holiness for the people who commit suicide as well as those with whom they might have been in ministry should they have lived and been brought to fullness in Christ.

Although Wesley wrote few formal statements about suicide, he tells stories about people who had attempted suicide, stories that illuminate his underlying concerns. For example, he told of a woman who had gone out late one night on New Year's Eve planning to drown herself in the river. On her way, she happened to pass by the Foundery where the Methodist society was meeting and she heard the Methodists singing hymns. "She stopped, and went in: She listened awhile, and God spoke to her heart. She had no more desire to put an end to her life; but to die to sin, and live to God."[31]

Wesley translated and recommended a longer story with a similar plot line and lesson by the early church father Ephraim Syrus. A young woman had left a life of holiness and run away with an evil man who used and then abandoned her. Seeing no hope, she considered killing herself. Her uncle and guardian, a holy man, found her and convinced her that God would forgive her. To her uncle's joy, the young woman repented and returned to a life of holiness. Living for forty-five years after her repentance, she was "ceaseless[ly] calling upon God." Through her prayers many were healed of their illnesses. She called "upon God night and day; in so much that all who passed by glorified God, who saveth them that were gone astray."[32]

Wesley published in the *Arminian Magazine* many similar stories about people who had considered or attempted suicide, but who, through the assistance of other Christians and the grace of God, were transformed and then went on to grow in love and to help others grow as well. Many of these stories were autobiographical accounts, written by those who had attempted suicide years before, been transformed by God's grace, and then, in some cases, gone on to become Methodist preachers.[33] These stories, like the two from Wesley's *Journal* mentioned above, were crafted and told to persuade the living, not condemn the dead.

Although these stories do nothing to mitigate Wesley's harsh comments about suicide, they do illuminate what was at stake for him. Wesley's hope was clearly to persuade the living not to cut short the

[31] *Journal* (November 20, 1747), *Works*, 20:196–97.
[32] *Journal* (May 21, 1761), *Works*, 21:322–25; quotation from 322.
[33] See Michael MacDonald and Terence R. Murphy, *Sleepless Souls: Suicide in Early Modern England* (1990), 208–209. See especially note 127.

work that God desired to do both in their lives and through them in the lives of others. He once made this point by warning that suicide (or self-murder as he called it) caused "a poor wretch, by a sin he cannot repent of, to rush straight through death into hell."[34] This claim is jarring for the ear of most people today; so much so, that some traditions descended from the Methodist revival specifically reject it. For example, a statement in the *Book of Resolutions of the United Methodist Church* criticizes those in the church throughout much of its history who have taught that suicide is an unforgivable sin, as well as those who believe that people who commit suicide go to hell.[35] The statement appeals to Romans 8:38–39 for warrant, as does a parallel portion of the "Social Principles" of the United Methodist Church, which states: "A Christian perspective on suicide begins with an affirmation of faith that nothing, including suicide, separates us from the love of God."[36]

Although emphasis on the love of God was central to Wesley's theological stance, he would be troubled by this specific appeal to Romans 8:38–39 because it seems to reject the possibility that a person's *choices* could separate him or her from proper *relationship* to God. Wesley (and other Arminians) insisted on the radical nature of human freedom and responsibility. Wesley's position on suicide – and just about anything else for that matter – is shaped by the fundamental assumption that human choices, whether good or bad, have serious consequences for the fullness of that person's life (and other people's lives) both in time and eternity. He was adamant that God does not save humans without their free consent and cooperation. Our growth in Christ, though made possible by God's grace, could only continue as we freely participate in that growth. From Wesley's point of view, those who choose not only to turn away from God, but also, through suicide, to cut short any possibility of turning back, were cutting themselves off from God. He was not arguing that God would punish those who committed suicide because they disobeyed a law or that God's love for that person would diminish. But he was convinced that God would not overrule a person's freely made unfortunate decision.

Of course, given what we know today, it is difficult to talk about suicide as if a person were making a rational, free decision. Wesley's reflections on suicide, like those of many others who wrote before the

---

[34] Wesley, *Answer to Mr. Church's "Remarks"*, II.14, *Works*, 9:107.
[35] "Suicide: A Challenge to Ministry," §157, *Book of Resolutions of the United Methodist Church* 2004, 406–10.
[36] "Social Principles," II.N, "Suicide," *The Book of Discipline of the United Methodist Church* 2004, 104.

twentieth century, are shockingly inconsistent with our current under-standings of human psychology and depression. At the same time, con-temporary Wesleyans should take care that in their well-meaning and constructive efforts to remove the stigma from suicide they do not under-mine a core Wesleyan claim about the Christian life – that is, that human decisions matter and that over time humans can make decisions that effectively separate them from relationship to God. It is best simply to affirm that people who commit suicide, because of mental illness, are not actually capable of making free and responsible decisions, and to trust in God's mercy.

One additional aspect of Wesley's reflections on suicide should be noted. In *Explanatory Notes upon the Old Testament*, Wesley took a biblical proscription against killing (of self or others) and shifted it to a much broader proscription. Commenting on Exodus 20:13, he extended the commandment "Thou shalt not kill," to include doing anything that is known to be "hurtful to the health or life of your own body or any other's." He filled this out in his commentary on Deuteronomy 5:17, where he asked his readers, "Are you guilty of no degree of self-murder? Do you never eat or drink any thing because you like it, although you have reason to believe, it is prejudicial to your health? Have you con-stantly done whatever you had reason to believe was conducive to it?"

This is classic Wesley; a straightforward moral commandment not to kill is broadened, by way of his holistic model of holiness, into a command to avoid anything that would harm the health of one's own or another's body and an exhortation to do constantly that which is good for the body. This interpretation is a bit of a stretch, but Wesley was aware of the pastoral challenges and temptations of those to whom he was speaking or writing. The chances are good that the average person who happened to read Wesley's *Notes* in the eighteenth century would be in more immediate need of a word of admonishment about eating well than a reminder not to kill. It is likely that the same could be said today.

Parenting

In both his *Journal* and in the *Arminian Magazine*, Wesley published advice about raising children that his mother had written at his request. Later Methodists, such as Adam Clarke, continued to distribute her recommendations. Wesley's mother Susanna Wesley was, at least by the standards of many today, a strict disciplinarian. She wrote, "In order to form the minds of children, the first thing to be done is to conquer their will and bring them to an obedient temper." This breaking of the will included moderate corporal punishment and strict rules about obedience and order. Children as young as one-year-old were expected, for example, to cry softly.[37]

It is important to remember several things about these recommendations on parenting. First, they were consistent with their eighteenth-century context, where the use of corporal punishment and references to breaking a child's will were not the exception, but the norm. Moreover, Susanna Wesley drew on some of the best theories of education of her time, particularly those of John Locke. Indeed, one commentator refers to her advice as an "influential blend of evangelical and Lockean ideas."[38] Some of the Wesley's recommendations were progressive for their time. For example, both Susanna and John Wesley insisted that girls be educated.[39]

Finally, the comments about childrearing need to be placed in the context of an overriding concern for holiness. Susanna Wesley was at her most passionate when she reflected on *why* disciplined parenting was essential. The breaking of the child's will was the foundation for his or her growth in the Christian life. She wrote,

> Religion is nothing else than the doing the will of God, and not our own; that the one grand impediment to our temporal and eternal happiness being self-will, no indulgences of it can be trivial, no denial unprofitable. Heaven or hell depends on this alone. So that the parent who studies to subdue it in his child works together with God in the renewing and saving a soul.[40]

John Wesley's overriding preoccupation with holiness is equally evident in some of his parenting advice. Parents were advised to regard children as "immortal spirits whom God hath, for a time, entrusted to your care, that you may train them up in all holiness, and fit them for the enjoyment of God in eternity."[41] Reflecting on the role of parents helping their child to choose a profession or a spouse, Wesley encouraged them to have a "single eye" in these deliberations; the primary consideration

---

[37] See Letter from Susanna Wesley to John Wesley (July 24, 1732), abridged in *Works*, 25:330–31. Wesley included the full letter in the fifth installment of his *Journal*, published in 1749 (see *Works* 19:286–91); and in *Arminian Magazine* 6 (1784): 462–64.

[38] Charles Wallace, ed., *Susanna Wesley: The Complete Writings* (1997), 368.

[39] Letter from Susanna Wesley to John Wesley (July 24, 1732), *Works*, 19:291.

[40] Ibid., *Works*, 19:288.

[41] Sermon 94, "On Family Religion," II.2, *Works*, 3:337.

should be not wealth or status but holiness. Any parent who, in choosing a spouse for a child, would put wealth and honor above godliness, is like a monster "who devoured the flesh of his own offspring! . . . Man, woman, think what you are about! . . . O take warning in time! Beware of the gilded bait! Death and hell are hid beneath. Prefer grace before gold and precious stones; glory in heaven, to riches on earth!"[42] Wise parents considering marriage partners for their children should not seek wealth, but, instead, "aim simply at the glory of God, and the real happiness of [their] children, both in time and eternity."[43]

Likewise, as a father weighs various professions for his son, he should ask what calling is likely to secure him the highest place in heaven. Wesley had harsh words for a parent who would prefer that a child enter a profession that brought riches and honor over one that increased holiness: "What a fool, what a dolt, what a madman is he, how stupid beyond all expression."[44] Parents should not be concerned if their son "get less money, provided he get more holiness."[45]

Although some of Wesley's eighteenth-century parenting advice may seem archaic, his words here are right on the mark for middle-class and upper-income parents today who are hyper-concerned that their children get the right kind of education and training so that they can get professions with high salaries and status. It is difficult for Christian parents to keep their eyes focused not on their children's long-term success in a competitive economy and social hierarchy, but on their children's ultimate happiness in God and contribution to the good of others. They would do well to remember the advice given by an elderly Wesley to parents of young children: Even when a child first begins to speak or run alone, a good parent follows behind saying, many times each day, "He made *you*; and he made you to be happy in him; and nothing else can make you happy."[46]

ONE RELIGION, ONE HAPPINESS, ONE HOLINESS

In his reflections on the General Rules, slavery, suicide, and parenting (as well as many other issues not addressed here), Wesley began writing about very different topics but ended with an old familiar sermon.

---

[42] Sermon 125, "On a Single Eye," III.3–4, *Works*, 4:127–28.
[43] Sermon 94, "On Family Religion," III.17, *Works*, 3:345.
[44] Sermon 125, "On a Single Eye," III.2, *Works*, 4:126–27.
[45] Sermon 94, "On Family Religion," III.16, *Works*, 3:344.
[46] Sermon 120, "The Unity of the Divine Being," §10, *Works*, 4:64.

Humans were made for happiness, happiness that comes only in God as they love God and one another. This "one religion and one happiness," as Wesley called it, is nothing other than holiness, holiness of body and soul – ours and everyone else's. Throughout all of these writings, it is as if Wesley is following behind the reader, saying many times in many circumstances, "He made *you and everyone else;* and he made you all to be happy in him; and nothing else can make you happy."

13 Wesley's emphases on worship and the means of grace

KAREN B. WESTERFIELD TUCKER

In his *Journal* under the date of April 12, 1789, the elderly John Wesley clarified and defended the intention of the Methodist movement and the course it had taken:

> Being Easter Day, we had a solemn assembly indeed, many hundred communicants in the morning and in the afternoon, far more hearers than our room would contain, though it is now considerably enlarged. Afterwards, I met the society and explained to them at large the original design of the Methodists, viz., not to be a distinct party, but to stir up all parties, Christians or heathens, to worship God in spirit and in truth, but the Church of England in particular to which they belonged from the beginning. With this view I have uniformly gone on for fifty years, never varying of choice – but of necessity – from the doctrine of the church at all nor from her discipline.[1]

In this retrospective, Wesley gave central place to the revitalization of worship in the Methodist project. To worship God "in spirit and in truth" (cf. John 4:23–24) meant to "love him, to delight in him, to desire him, with all our heart and mind and soul and strength; to imitate him we love by purifying ourselves, even as he is pure; and to obey him whom we love, and in whom we believe, both in thought and word and work."[2] From the beginnings of Methodism – when private and public worship were emphasized components of the "method" espoused by the Holy Club at Oxford – to the close of Wesley's life – when Methodists hungered to receive the Lord's Supper regularly (and in their own chapels from Methodist hands) – the worship of God contributed significantly to Methodist life, identity, and mission.

[1] *Works*, 24:128.
[2] Sermon 24, "Sermon on the Mount, IV," *Works*, 1:544.

Wesley also asserted in his *Journal* entry of Easter 1789 that Methodists were not to be a "distinct party" but to "stir up all parties" in the common liturgical task. Almost fifty years earlier in a tract exposing *The Character of a Methodist* (1742), Wesley declared that Methodists were not to be distinguishable from other "real Christians of whatsoever denomination they be" as long as they upheld the "common, fundamental principles of Christianity." Among those fundamental principles Wesley included the triune God, the source and goal of creation; Christ's redemptive work and its ongoing application by the Holy Spirit's power; human sin and the resultant God-given gifts of repentance, forgiveness, and grace; and the fruits of faith, demonstrated by works of piety and mercy in accordance with God's commandments. These principles could be articulated by a variety of opinions and expressions; to that extent persons could thus "think and let think." Therefore despite certain differences, "the unity of the Spirit in the bond of peace" could exist among the various factions of the Church of England and more broadly across Protestant Christianity. Methodists were thus not a distinct party; they were simply a manifestation of "plain, old Christianity" renewing the Church of England from within.[3]

Wesley's perspective of "think and let think" carried over into liturgical matters, for he observed that "as long as there are various opinions there will be various ways of worshipping God; seeing a variety of opinion necessarily implies a variety of practice."[4] A variety of opinions was inevitable, for even though Scripture constituted the "supreme rule" of Christian worship, there could be many rules subordinate to Scripture that did not violate it.[5] Critical of the Church of England's enforcement of modes of worship contrary to the consciences of some, Wesley posited that mutual respect, not separation or division, should be the response in the face of differing liturgical forms and expressions as long as they adhered to Christianity's fundamental principles. Yet, such benevolence was not meant to suggest either a practical latitudinarianism of apathy toward outward expressions of public worship or a speculative latitudinarianism of indifference to all opinions.[6] To Wesley's mind, a "catholic spirit" was to be characterized by a wide generosity, but also by accountability to the norms and precepts of both scripture and primitive Christianity.

---

[3] *Works*, 9:32–42.
[4] Sermon 39, "Catholic Spirit," I.8, *Works*, 2:85.
[5] "Ought we to Separate from the Church of England?" II.4, *Works*, 9:570.
[6] Sermon 39, "Catholic Spirit," III.1–2, *Works* 2:92–93.

Despite Wesley's insistence that the Methodists did not constitute a "distinct party," his claim of "never varying of choice – but of necessity – from the doctrine of the church at all nor from her discipline" and his (and the Methodists') use of liturgical innovations convinced Methodism's detractors that the movement was in fact separating from the Church of England. Methodist practices and their rationales also came under the scrutiny of non-Anglican Christian groups in England and abroad. Thus any examination of Wesley on the topic of worship requires attention to constructive contributions as well as to controversy. Wesley's ideals for Methodist – and more broadly Christian – worship may be classified under three headings that are not mutually exclusive but that permit attention to both the constructive and the controversial: *ressourcement*, simplicity, and personal appropriation.

RESSOURCEMENT

A survey of the history of Christian liturgy shows that movements to revitalize worship are typically accompanied by an examination – and sometimes a retrieval – of what is deemed exemplary and vital from previous periods. Such an approach was taken up, for example, in the mid-twentieth century by theologians and liturgical scholars who advocated for a "return to the sources" (*retour aux sources*) or what they termed *ressourcement*. Seventeenth and eighteenth century England can be characterized as a time of *ressourcement* as various factions related to the national church mined historic documents (especially those of Christian antiquity) not only to invigorate the worship of their day by introducing (or reintroducing) older practices, but also to find a possible liturgical middle ground in which all might in good conscience participate. Such liturgical "comprehension" did not occur, and the *Book of Common Prayer* as formulated in 1661/1662 maintained its legally authorized status.

An avid reader, John Wesley took advantage of the renaissance in patristic studies brought about by this interest in *ressourcement* by studying recently reprinted early Christian documents and secondary historical surveys (e.g., William Cave's *Primitive Christianity*). He was also familiar with much of the literature of previous generations as well as his own that argued for liturgical revision to the Prayer Book and proposed specific textual alternatives. Among the authors he read were Richard Baxter (*The Reformation of the Liturgy*, 1661); William Whiston (*The Liturgy of the Church of England, Reduc'd nearer to the Primitive Standard*, 1713); the Non-Jurors, especially Robert Nelson

(*A Companion for the Festivals and Fasts of the Church of England*, 1704) and Thomas Deacon (*A Compleat Collection of Devotions*, 1734); and John Jones (*Free and Candid Disquisitions relating to the Church of England*, 1749). Wesley's reading of and contact with Thomas Deacon and other Non-Jurors early in his ministry strengthened his interest in the text and practices of the first *Book of Common Prayer* (1549) and of the church of the first three centuries – as well as his conviction that the so-called *Apostolic Constitutions* and *Canons* contained the most ancient liturgy extant (he later revised this latter opinion).

Wesley's own willingness to engage in *ressourcement* is evident by his writing of "An Essay upon the Stationary Fasts" in 1733, in which he argued for the antiquity and obligation of fasting by drawing upon ancient writers (e.g., Augustine) and studies of history (e.g., Peter Gunning's *The Paschal, or Lent Fast, Apostolical and Perpetual*, 1662). Deacon found Wesley's essay so appropriate to his own agenda that part of it appears in his *Compleat Collection of Devotions*. A few years after the "Essay," Wesley recorded personal notes on the *Apostolic Canons* with statements about his own preference for certain older practices which, in addition to fasting, included baptism by immersion, the commixture of water and wine at the eucharist, and the use of a *prothesis* (borrowing from the Eastern church) for the preparation of the communion elements.[7] Wesley's interest in *ressourcement* continued throughout his life, for he believed the doctrine and practice of the church of the first 300 years to exemplify true, uncorrupted, and scriptural Christianity.

The importance the discipline of fasting held for Wesley is evident by his inclusion of it among the "instituted means of grace" in the Minutes of the first Methodist conference in 1744. The phrase "means of grace" was not original to Wesley, a point he makes in his sermon of that title.[8] Wesley understood the means of grace to be "outward signs, words, or actions" that are "ordinary channels" by which God conveys to individuals the type of grace that is needed: preventing or prevenient grace, which elicits a first longing for God; justifying or pardoning grace, by which God brings an individual into a saving relationship; and sanctifying or sustaining grace, which enables continued growth in faith and production of faith's fruits. The means are "instituted" because Christ, as demonstrated in Scripture, ordained them to be used, and the church from the early period onward had practiced them.

---

[7]   See the "Notes" and a commentary on them in John C. Bowmer, *The Sacrament of the Lord's Supper in Early Methodism* (1951), 233–37.

[8]   Sermon 16, "The Means of Grace," *Works*, 1:378–97.

Among the means of grace that Wesley identifies are private, family, and public prayer (utilizing deprecation, petition, intercession, and thanksgiving in each); searching the Scriptures (by reading, hearing, and meditating); spiritual conversation with other Christians (termed "Christian conferencing"); attendance at public worship; and attentive reception of the Lord's Supper. Wesley and the early Methodists expected these instituted means to be diligently observed and set up systems of accountability to ensure that such discipline was kept. To the instituted means they also added "prudential means of grace" – practices that the church had initiated for particular needs in various times and places, such as participation in accountability groups (e.g., the Methodist Society, classes, and bands), visitation of the sick, and attendance at special services of worship. Both the instituted and prudential means were never to be regarded as ends or "works" in themselves but as conduits of God's gifts of love. True Christians were not to be content in the mere "form of godliness" without the power (cf. 2 Timothy 3:5).

The motivation for Wesley's sermon on "The Means of Grace" did not come principally from his desire to promote their use based upon scriptural and apostolic precedent. Rather, the sermon was produced in response to a controversy that arose among the Methodists and Moravians at London's Fetter Lane Society in the late 1730s. The Moravian Philip Henry Molther contended that until persons had full assurance of faith (also understood as "conversion" or the reception of the Holy Spirit) they ought to abstain from any means of grace and be "quiet" or wait upon the Lord until such assurance was perceived. Wesley argued instead that persons with some degree of repentance and faith could participate in the means of grace even if they did not have full assurance, for the means could supply the grace that was needed to realize full assurance. The disagreement between Molther and Wesley in the end precipitated a split, with those who agreed with Wesley forming their own society in 1740.

The situation at Fetter Lane caused Wesley to identify the Lord's Supper – what he regarded to be chief among the means of grace – as a "converting ordinance," for to those baptized yet lacking full assurance, participation in the sacrament could produce the requisite assurance and supply needed grace:

Is not the eating of that bread, and the drinking of that cup, the outward, visible means whereby God conveys into our souls all that spiritual grace, that righteousness, and peace, and joy in the Holy Ghost, which were purchased by the body of Christ once

broken and the blood of Christ once shed for us? Let all, therefore, who truly desire the grace of God, eat of that bread and
drink of that cup.[9]

For this reason, Wesley advised frequent, especially "constant," communion in imitation of what he viewed as scriptural (cf. Matthew 6:11;
Acts 2:46) and apostolic practice, and he himself communicated at least
weekly. In keeping with ancient custom, he sometimes also received the
sacrament each day during the eight days (octave) after Easter and the
twelve days after Christmas.

Wesley expected the Methodists to be at the Lord's table every week
(just as he expected Methodists to attend public worship in the Anglican
parish church or a Dissenting congregation each week), though such was
difficult to accomplish given that many Anglican parishes only administered the sacrament thrice annually as per canonical requirement. To
enable the Methodists to receive the "office of love" more frequently,
they were invited to receive when communion was administered to the
sick (a provision allowed by canon law). Eventually, Wesley permitted
the sacrament to be observed at Methodist assemblies when the cel-
ebrant was an Anglican priest. These gatherings could be attended by
hundreds of hungry souls, who would pass time during the distribution
by singing hymns, among them specially composed hymns on the Lord's
Supper.

In 1745, John Wesley and his brother Charles published *Hymns on
the Lord's Supper*, which drew upon the structure and content of *Christian Sacrament and Sacrifice* (1673) written by the Anglican divine
Daniel Brevint. The 166 hymns are divided into six sections, which
expose theological themes related to the sacrament, including a dynamic
remembrance (anamnesis) of Christ's saving work, the real presence of
Christ (not understood as transubstantiation), the efficacy of the means
of grace, eschatological (future) anticipation, and sacrificial aspects. The
Wesleyan interest in *ressourcement* finds a place here, for some of
the hymns were inspired by the eucharistic liturgy in Book Eight of
Apostolic Constitutions. The presence of an epiclesis (invocation of the
Holy Spirit) there is the likely source for two epicletic hymns in the
collection, though John Wesley was familiar with Non-Juror Jeremy Collier's *Reasons for restoring some Prayers and Directions* (1717), which
argued for the recovery of the eucharistic epiclesis that had been lost
with the revision of the 1549 *Book of Common Prayer*. Hymn 16 draws

---

[9] Sermon, "The Means of Grace," *Works*, 1:389–390.

directly upon *Apostolic Constitutions* VIII.12.39 and its identification of the Spirit as the witness of Christ's sufferings:

> Come, thou everlasting Spirit,
> Bring to every thankful mind
> All the Saviour's dying merit,
> All his sufferings for mankind:
> True Recorder of his passion,
> Now the living faith impart,
> Now reveal his great salvation,
> Preach his gospel to our heart.
> Come, thou witness of his dying,
> Come, Remembrancer Divine,
> Let us feel thy power applying
> Christ to every soul and mine;
> Let us groan thine inward groaning,
> Look on him we pierced and grieve,
> All receive the grace atoning,
> All the sprinkled blood receive.

The singing of hymns in conjunction with the Lord's Supper was an innovation, for hymns were not permitted in the Church of England's liturgy, though they might be sung before or after the service. Through the influences of the Congregationalist Isaac Watts and the Moravians, and with the assurance that hymn singing was practiced by Jesus (cf. Mark 14:26; Matthew 26:30) and urged by St. Paul (cf. Ephesians 5:19; Colossians 3:16), Methodists sang hymns in all their services of worship. The Wesley brothers, with Charles the primary poet and John principally in the role of editor, nourished the desire for singing by the publication of hymn books and hymn pamphlets for a variety of circumstances and occasions, such as the liturgical year, funerals, persons seeking redemption, and the aftermath of the earthquakes of 1750.[10] The first book, *Collection of Psalms and Hymns* (the "Charlestown" hymnal), was published by John in 1737 while in the American colonies. The largest book, *A Collection of Hymns for the Use of the People Called Methodist* (1780), contained representatives from many of the earlier publications that together provided, according to the Preface, a full account of "scriptural Christianity," and that was organized "according to the experience of real Christians." Each compilation was a "little body of experimental

---

[10] These collections are available online at http://www.divinity.duke.edu/wesleyan/texts/.

[experiential] and practical divinity,"[11] for the theology of the Methodist movement was essentially encapsulated in hymnic form.

The catechetical and evangelical functions of the hymn texts were aided by familiar tunes or new tunes in current styles. The Wesleys issued books of tunes for Methodist use that contained suitable melodies in a variety of meters. The melodies in the *Foundery Collection* of 1742 came mostly from English psalm tunes and German (principally Moravian) hymn tunes already in use. The tunebook *Sacred Melody*, first published in 1761, likewise contained established psalm and hymn tunes, but also melodies drawn from other sources: popular instrumental and solo music, tunes in the musical style of the theater (especially Handelian opera and oratorio), and folk and ballad tunes. Many of these tunes were highly ornamented and florid according to the popular preferences of the day, such as those by the Methodist John Frederick Lampe, who collaborated with Charles Wesley to produce *Hymns on the Great Festivals, and Other Occasions* (1746). To help the Methodists to sing at private and family prayer and in public worship, John Wesley issued guides to music theory so that persons might teach themselves to read musical notation. He also, in the tradition of Augustine's *De Musica*, wrote a study of music entitled "Thoughts on the Power of Music" (1779).

Because of the intimate connection between theology and doxology, John Wesley was insistent that singing in worship was to be done by the entire congregation. Wesley vehemently rejected for Methodist worship the use of choirs and choral anthems – what was then the common practice in the Church of England. From his research on the early church, he knew that congregational singing was the most primitive practice, and he wished to recover its simplicity and unifying power in his day. In addition, the singing of choirs, he believed, took away from the people what was appropriately theirs – namely, an opportunity to offer their praises, lamentations, and petitions to God and to share their faith with one another. In his *Journal* for August 9, 1768, Wesley noted his disgust when he preached at the parish church in the town of Neath because a dozen or so persons "kept the singing to themselves" and thereby "quite shut out the congregation."[12] The next day, he was much relieved to hear an entire congregation "sing with the spirit and with the understanding also" (cf. 1 Corinthians 14:15). This Pauline ideal was best achieved, to Wesley's mind, by plain, unharmonized singing. Like

[11] Preface, §4, *Collection of Hymns, Works*, 7:73–74.
[12] *Works*, 22:151–52.

the ancient Christian communities he strove to emulate, Wesley preferred the unison singing of a melody in corporate worship so that the text could be understood and the people edified; counterpoint or "fuging tunes" where different words were sung by various singers at the same time were little more than "vain repetitions" (cf. Matthew 6:7) to be avoided. Nothing was to compromise the clear expression and hearing of the text, and for this reason, Wesley insisted upon unaccompanied, a cappella singing – yet again making a link with Christian antiquity.

The singing of hymns (written for the specific occasion) was a principal component of two special services of early Methodist worship. These services developed out of Wesley's interest in imitating early Christian praxis and meeting the needs of the growing Methodist societies and missions. From his reading of Cave's *Primitive Christianity* and other histories, Wesley knew of the ancient agape or love feast during which Christians of all social classes ate and prayed together, affirmed their unity in Christ, and testified to their love of God. His familiarity with Moravian love feasts only intensified his interest in them, and so he encouraged their practice in the Moravian-Methodist society at Fetter Lane. The Methodists kept the love feast after their break with the Moravians, and it was regularly practiced by the most earnest members of the societies. In his *Plain Account of the Methodists* (1749), Wesley spoke of the nature of these gatherings:

> In order to increase in them a grateful sense of all his mercies,
> I desired that one evening in a quarter all the men in band, on
> a second, all the women, would meet; and on a third, both men
> and women together; that we might together "eat bread" (as the
> ancient Christians did) "with gladness and singleness of heart."
> At these *love-feasts* (so we termed them, retaining the name,
> as well as the thing, which was in use from the beginning) our
> food is only a little plain cake and water. But we seldom return
> from them without being fed, not only with "the meat which
> perisheth," but with "that which endureth to everlasting life."[13]

Prayer, preaching and exhortation, and almsgiving also characterized the occasion, but it was personal and heartfelt testimony that was its centerpiece. Because these events were wrongly criticized as promoting orgiastic behavior, Wesley limited their oversight to those persons directly accountable to him.

[13] *Plain Account*, VI.5, *Works*, 9:267–68.

Wesley at first was hesitant to accept the second type of service, a late-night gathering that developed in Kingswood around 1740 as an alternative for newly spiritually awakened coal miners who had previously been accustomed to spending their evenings in the local pub. Recognizing the event's affinities with the vigils practiced in the early church and allowed by the Prayer Book (a comparison pointed out to critics), Wesley then embraced and promoted these "watchnights":

> We commonly choose for this solemn service the Friday night nearest the full moon, either before or after, that those of the congregation who live at a distance may have light to their several homes. The service begins at half an hour past eight and continues till a little after midnight. We have often found a peculiar blessing at these seasons. There is generally a deep awe upon the congregation, perhaps in some measure owing to the silence of the night; particularly in singing the hymn with which we commonly conclude:
>
> > Hearken to the solemn voice!
> > The awful midnight cry!
> > Waiting souls, rejoice, rejoice
> > And feel the Bridegroom nigh.[14]

Wesley's commitment to *ressourcement* also may have had some bearing on his engagement in a formal revision of the *Book of Common Prayer* and on the choices he took. As early as 1736, Wesley showed a predisposition toward making alterations, as indicated by a brief entry in his diary for March 5 that he "revised Common Prayer book." His dissatisfaction with certain parts of the Prayer Book was stated publicly in his 1755 essay, "Ought we to Separate from the Church of England," and it is possible that his unwillingness to defend the Athanasian Creed and the Office of Confirmation as stated in that essay may stem in part from their post-Constantinian origins. In his version of the Prayer Book entitled *The Sunday Service of the Methodists in North America* (1784), Wesley engaged more in excision than addition, removing entire sections, deleting problematic sentences, eliminating redundancies, substituting words. Many of these changes were sympathetic to the complaints made by Dissenting groups against the Prayer Book from the sixteenth century onward. Surprisingly, given his idealization of early Christian practices, Wesley (unlike some of the Non-Jurors and other Prayer Book

[14] *Journal* (April 9, 1742), *Works*, 19:258–59.

revisers) did not insert new material taken from the apostolic period, such as an epiclesis in the communion rite. Yet, he regarded the final product – considerably reduced from the original – to be consistent with the norms of scripture and primitive practice. In a letter to the American Methodists dated September 9, 1784, Wesley declared that no liturgy in the world "breathed" more of a "solid, scriptural, rational piety" than the Prayer Book, thereby providing the rationale for remaining with that liturgical source in the face of other options. He additionally advised the American Methodists, in a letter dated the following day, that should they find his revision wanting they were at liberty to use the standards he himself had employed – scripture and the primitive church – to create some other.

The publication of Wesley's Prayer Book revision, which was taken to America by three individuals whom Wesley had set apart as a result of being convinced (based upon investigations of the early church by Peter King and Edward Stillingfleet) that presbyters were of the same ministerial order as bishops, scandalized many (including his brother Charles) who saw this as an act of separation from the Church of England. Yet, Wesley insisted otherwise, claiming that he altered nothing just for the sake of alteration, and that much he changed was not essential. Indeed, he argued until his death that Methodists in England should not separate – and had not separated – themselves from the national church.

SIMPLICITY

The simplicity, sincerity, and decorum that characterized Methodist gatherings for worship, in Wesley's view, stood in stark contrast to what was typically found in the Anglican parish church:

> The longer I am absent from London, and the more I attend the service of the Church in other places, the more I am convinced of the unspeakable advantage which the people called Methodists enjoy: I mean even with regard to public worship, particularly on the Lord's Day. The church where they assemble is not gay or splendid, which might be an hindrance on the one hand; nor sordid or dirty, which might give distaste on the other; but plain as well as clean. The persons who assemble there are not a gay, giddy crowd, who come chiefly to see and be seen; nor a company of goodly, formal, outside Christians, whose religion lies in a dull round of duties; but a people most of whom do, and

the rest earnestly seek to, worship God in spirit and in truth. Accordingly they do not spend their time there bowing and courtesying, or in staring about them, but in looking upward and looking inward, in hearkening to the voice of God, and pouring out their hearts before Him.

It is also no small advantage that the person who reads prayers, though not always the same, yet is always one who may be supposed to speak from his heart, one whose life is no reproach to his profession, and one who performs that solemn part of divine service, not in a careless, hurrying, slovenly manner, but seriously and slowly, as becomes him who is transacting so high an affair between God and man.

Nor are their solemn addresses to God interrupted either by the formal drawl of a parish clerk, the screaming of [choir] boys who bawl out what they neither feel nor understand, or the unseasonable and unmeaning impertinence of a voluntary on the organ. When it is seasonable to sing praise to God, they do it with the spirit and with the understanding also; not in the miserable, scandalous doggerel of Hopkins and Sternhold, but in psalms and hymns which are both sense and poetry, such as would sooner provoke a critic to turn Christian than a Christian to turn critic. What they sing is therefore a proper continuation of the spiritual and reasonable service... all standing before God, and praising Him lustily and with a good courage.

Nor is it a little advantage as to the next part of the service to hear a preacher whom you know to live as he speaks, speaking the genuine gospel of present salvation through faith, wrought in the heart by the Holy Ghost, declaring present, free, full justification, and enforcing every branch of inward and outward holiness. And this you hear done in the most clear plain, simple, unaffected language, yet with an earnestness becoming the importance of the subject and with the demonstration of the Spirit.[15]

Yet, Wesley was equally disapproving of too much simplicity, and took issue, for example, with the Scottish (Presbyterian) burial custom of interring the body without speaking a word.[16] Even persons related to

---

[15] Letter "To a Friend" (September 20, 1757), *Letters* (Telford), 3:226–28.
[16] See *Journal* (May 20, 1774), *Works*, 22:408–409.

the Methodist movement were not immune from his criticism when they departed from his standards of decorum and simplicity in worship. Thomas Maxfield was scolded for, among other things, using improper expressions in prayer, "praying to the Son of God only or more than to the Father," and permitting the praying of several at once.[17] The lay preachers and assistants were reminded to correct congregations that stood for prayer and sat for singing (the reverse was "proper") and to squelch the casual conversation that erupted as soon as worship concluded.

As he signaled in his critique of Anglican parish worship, Wesley valued the modest worship spaces that contained simple Methodist worship. Methodist buildings constructed during the eighteenth century were designed principally to house the preaching services consisting of prayer, scripture reading, exhortation and/or sermon, and hymn singing (a pattern not unlike that described in the First Apology of Justin Martyr in the second century), but the Methodist special services, the preaching of funeral sermons, and Christian catechesis found a place there as well. Gatherings in these "preaching houses" or "chapels" were expected to supplement attendance at the Sunday liturgy in the parish church, so services were held at times outside of regular "church hours," typically 5:00 A.M. Buildings adjacent to the preaching houses were constructed in some places to lodge the traveling preachers, an arrangement that Wesley may have borrowed from fourth century models.

Methodist worship spaces were expected to be "plain and decent" inside and out, with minimal decoration and ornamentation. Because the focus was on the proclamation of God's word, the pulpit or reading desk, occasionally in a multi tiered configuration, was centrally located. The congregation sat on benches or stools (pews and chairs with backs were discouraged) on the main floor and, where present, in galleries on an upper level. A wooden rail might extend down the middle of the main floor from front to back, its purpose to divide the seating for men and women as the early Christians had done, although Wesley found this plan difficult to enforce. Attention was given to good acoustics, suitable lighting, and proper ventilation; for the latter, Wesley advised that windows be large and open downward lest the congregation be affected by a draft.

From 1761 to 1776, Wesley encouraged the construction of fourteen octagonal buildings in both England and Scotland,[18] because he believed

---

[17] See *Journal* (November 2, 1762), *Works*, 21:397.

[18] In England, Rotherham (1761), Whitby (1762), Yarm (1764), Heptonstall (1764), Snowfields (1764), Chester (1765), Nottingham (1766), Thirsk (1766), Bradford (1766), Gwennap (Carharrack) (1770), and Taunton (1776). In Scotland, Aberdeen (1764, the first Methodist chapel in Scotland), Edinburgh (1765), and Arbroath (1772).

the design to be the best for public speaking and the most commodious for seating. Octagons were ideal for daytime services because windows could be installed in each wall and for winter use because they could be heated efficiently and economically. Wesley's interest in octagons may have arisen in part because of the ancient church's association of the number eight with resurrection and the new creation: worship in the preaching house was an encounter with the resurrected Lord who offered the gift of new life. Despite Wesley's appreciation of the eight-sided form, difficulties in building stable roofs may in the end have contributed to the limited use of the design.

The style of language used for prayer and preaching was to equal the simplicity and decorum of the place in which worship was held. The printed prayers of the Prayer Book with their strong and dignified language were to be valued equally with heartfelt extemporaneous prayer in the ordinary language of the people. Wesley himself confessed that he added extemporary prayer to his saying of the Prayer Book's rites long before he included an instruction for such in the Lord's Supper liturgy contained in his *Sunday Service*. Preachers were to speak the plain truth for plain people in their language, avoiding words and constructions not easy for them to understand. The method for preaching was itself formulated simply: to invite, to convince, to offer Christ, and to build up.

Those who gathered in the simple building to hear and offer simple words of praise, petition, and thanksgiving were themselves advised to live simply by eating a plain diet and by wearing plain clothes. The money saved by refraining from the purchase of expensive apparel, jewelry, and decoration was expected to be put to the service of the poor; such may be part of the rationale for Wesley's removal of the wedding ring in his revision of the Prayer Book's marriage liturgy. That the matter of unnecessary dress and accoutrements was taken seriously is evident by legislation in the Methodist Minutes, which denied access to the love feast to those who wore "superfluous ornaments" or "calashes, high-heads, or enormous bonnets." Such simplicity of lifestyle and concern for the needy honored the one who emptied himself to become a servant, for as Wesley noted, echoing Augustine's *De civitate Dei*, "it is the best worship or service of God, to imitate him you worship."[19]

PERSONAL APPROPRIATION

From early in the Methodist movement, Wesley expressed grave concern about those who practiced the outward forms of religion, but

---

[19] Sermon 29, "Sermon on the Mount, IX," §6, *Works*, 1:635.

lacked inward religion, the "religion of the heart." "External worship," he argued, "is lost labour without a heart devoted to God." Conversely, "the outward ordinances of God profit much when they advance inward holiness."[20] Forms themselves were not the problem. Rather, focus solely on the outward works and their performance was, and Wesley and the Methodists introduced rules to guard against such in public worship. One remedy was to remind the singing congregation of the purpose of their action by stopping mid-song and asking, "Now! Do you know what you said last? Did you speak no more than you felt?" The experiential, "enthusiastic" aspect of Methodist worship – intentionally cultivated – attracted many to their gatherings, but drew critics from within the Church of England and from without as well.

Wesley's insistence that Christians be known by a lively faith had an impact on his theology of baptism. By observation, he knew that those who had been baptized in infancy, which was the majority of persons in England, did not always live as if they were children of God and instead appeared more as children of the devil. To rely upon baptism in order to identify oneself as a child of God even while engaged intentionally in sin was to ignore the demands of that baptism – its covenant relationship with God and the expectation that a life full of the love of God would issue forth in works of piety and mercy – and to give oneself over to damnation.

Consistent with Anglican baptismal theology, Wesley understood infants at their baptism to be regenerated, that is, born again, for baptism bestowed saving grace. Yet, because the infant as it matured might lose that grace through actual sin, or not find the inward assurance of the Spirit, or lack the expected fruits of faith, another new birth was required, not by water, but by the "circumcision of the heart." A conscious experience of saving grace was necessary to restore what had been distorted, suppressed, or lost. For those who truly repented, God's grace and mercy provided assurance of one's adoption as a child of God. Thus, for most persons baptized in infancy there would be two new births: one sacramental and objective, the other experiential and subjective. Wesley never developed the connection between the two in a systematic way – a fact that had a great impact on later Methodist thinking about baptismal regeneration and the profession of personal assurance. Given Wesley's insistence on the need for a post-baptismal profession of faith, it might seem surprising that he did not include a confirmation rite in his *Sunday Service*. This omission is reasonably explained by the fact that Wesley

---

[20] Sermon 16, "The Means of Grace," I.4, *Works*, 1:379.

did not expect the American Methodists to have bishops – who, in the Church of England, were the only proper administrators of confirmation.

In the case of adults, Wesley believed regeneration in conjunction with the baptismal act to be possible if the candidate sincerely repented and professed faith, and provided no obstacle (known and unknown) to the reception of baptismal grace. But, even though baptism and new birth are inseparable, they are not identical; a person could profess faith and receive baptism, but, perhaps because of lack of true repentance, might not receive the new birth until some time later. Wesley also conceded – on the basis of observation – that it was possible for the new birth to precede the imposition of water. In each of these cases, baptism still could be understood as initiation into the church and a testimony to God's work in the life of the individual.

The deletion of some of the references to regeneration in the baptismal services for infants and those of "riper years" found in the *Sunday Service* signal some of the tensions within Wesley on the subject. Also, in the *Sunday Service*, Wesley deleted all mention of godparents in both rites, even though he had acknowledged in *Serious Thoughts Concerning Godfathers and Godmothers* (1752) the apostolic, although non-scriptural, practice of selecting baptismal sponsors of exemplary faith to instruct and advise the newly baptized. Wesley's elimination of godparents likely stemmed from his sensitivity to those who objected to the practice.

Although it is not overtly stated to be such, one of the special services that Wesley devised for the Methodists functioned as an opportunity for persons to renew the covenant made at their baptism and thereby remain accountable to living the Christian life. Wesley's service included directions for covenanting borrowed from Richard Alleine's *Vindiciae Pietatis: Or, A Vindication of Godliness* (1663) along with prayer, exhortation, and hymns, and typically concluded with the Lord's Supper. Covenant services were in use by the late 1740s, although it was 1780 before Wesley published *Directions for Renewing Our Covenant with God*, and the occasion was limited to those persons in good standing with the Methodist society. A text by Charles Wesley often used at the event soon became known as the "covenant hymn":

> Come, let us use the grace divine,
> And all with one accord
> In a perpetual covenant join
> Ourselves to Christ the Lord,
> Give ourselves up through Jesu's power

His name to glorify,
And promise in this sacred hour
For God to live, and die.
The covenant we this moment make
Be ever kept in mind!
We will no more our God forsake,
Or cast His words behind;
We never will throw off His fear,
Who hears our solemn vow:
And if Thou art well-pleased to hear,
Come down, and meet us now!
Thee, Father, Son, and Holy Ghost,
Let all our hearts receive,
Present with Thy celestial host
The peaceful answer give;
To each the covenant-blood apply
Which takes our sins away,
And register our names on high,
And keep us to that day![21]

Covenant renewal services took place in different seasons (including Good Friday) before eventually being associated principally with New Year's Eve and Day.

CONCLUSION

By recovering early Christian liturgical practices and theological reflection, by encouraging simplicity in worship and all of life, and by urging persons toward a heart-felt, vital religion, Wesley and the Methodists strove to "stir up" and enliven the worship of God in their time. The achievement of their efforts can be measured in the numbers of persons who attended the Methodist worship services and the services in the parish church, purchased hymn books and sang or prayed with them, and found their hearts "strangely warmed." Their success may also be seen in the controversies they raised that met their intention of "stirring up" a renewed interest in the worship of God. Wesley knew that worship was central to Christian life; thus Wesley's emphases on worship and the means of grace are critical to a full understanding of early Methodism.

[21] Charles Wesley, *Short Hymns on Select Passages of Holy Scriptures* (1762), 2:36–37.

Part IV

Wesley's legacy

14 The spread of Wesleyan Methodism

KENNETH CRACKNELL

John Wesley stands alone among the originators of the major protestant denominations in his concern for the world lying beyond the boundaries of the old Christendom. Unlike the sixteenth-century reformers, he had been an overseas missionary. Serving with the Society for the Propagation of the Gospel in Foreign Parts, John Wesley arrived in Georgia in February 1736.[1] In addition to his pastoral duties, he recorded in his *Journal* his intention "to teach the Georgian Indians the nature of Christianity."[2] This particular episode may be deemed a failure. The indigenous people of Georgia were not the docile innocents of eighteenth-century imagination and Wesley was hardly equipped with an adequate missiology for dealing with non-European cultures. But the sense of a world beyond Europe remained with him to the end of his life, and he consistently looked upon all the world as his parish.[3]

Furthermore Wesley expected that a new age was about to break in, when the kingdoms of this world should become "the kingdoms of our God and of his Christ" as George Frederick Handel's Hallelujah Chorus had proclaimed in 1742.[4] Wesley's own expression of this "dawn of the latter-day glory'" is found in his 1783 sermon "The General Spread of the Gospel." These are the times, he declared, when the God of love will "prepare his messengers and make a way into the polar regions, into

---

[1] For the SPG, founded in 1710, and its older sister the Society for the Promotion of Christian Knowledge (1698), see Jeffrey Cox, *The British Missionary Enterprise since 1700* (2008), 8. Cox offers a valuable background against which to set the British Wesleyan missionary enterprises.

[2] *Journal* (1 February 1738), *Works*, 18:214.

[3] Wesley wrote in 1739: "I look upon all the world as my parish; thus far I mean, that, in whatever part of it I am, I judge it meet, right, and my bounden duty to declare unto all that are willing to hear, the glad tidings of salvation." Letter to [John Clayton?], *Works*, 25:616. In its original context this was his justification for preaching in other clergymen's parishes.

[4] This optimistic millennialism characterized the beginning of all the missionary societies of this period. See Kenneth Cracknell, *Justice, Courtesy, and Love: Theologians and Missionaries Encountering World Religions, 1846–1914* (1995), 6ff.

the deepest recesses of America; yea, into the heart of China and Japan, with countries adjoining to them. And 'their sound will go forth into all lands and their voice to the end of the earth.'"[5]

THE SPREAD TO NORTH AMERICA

Wesley's argument in this sermon traced the spread of Methodism into north Britain and Ireland and a few years after into New York, Pennsylvania, and many other provinces in America, even as high as Newfoundland and Nova Scotia. The Methodist community in America had grown from the 1760s onward in response to the preaching of lay people, especially Irish émigrés like Philip Embury and Barbara Heck in New York and Robert Strawbridge in Maryland. Another layman, Thomas Webb a British military captain, had helped organize the first Methodists in both New York and Philadelphia. In 1769 the British Conference appointed two preachers specifically for work in the American colonies. Other British preachers followed, among them Francis Asbury, destined to become the first bishop of the Methodist Episcopal Church. The scattered Methodist groups were gathered into the first Methodist Conference in the American colonies in 1773. But the Revolutionary War severely disrupted the growth of Methodism. Many of the appointed preachers returned to Britain, as did loyalist laypeople like Webb.

Wesley's 1783 sermon referred also to the growth of Methodist work in Canada. This had begun as early as 1760, when the Irish Methodist preacher Lawrence Coughlan (an Anglican clergyman working for the Society for the Promotion of Christian Knowledge) had formed Methodist classes in Newfoundland. The loyalist migrations to Canada after 1776 led an English local preacher, William Black, to travel throughout Nova Scotia organizing Methodist classes. All of this Wesley took as evidence of God's providential leading in spreading the gospel. But circumstances prevented his becoming the true instigator and founder of further world missionary activity. This honor, as we shall see, belongs to the Welshman Dr. Thomas Coke (1747–1814).

Even before the Declaration of Independence, the most significant religious difficulty for these New World Methodists was the uncertainty of their participation in sacramental life. Those who were members of the Church of England could usually still attend parish churches, but those who had been newly converted as Methodists, with no other religious affiliation, most often were never communicants. This pastoral situation was exacerbated with the British military defeat when most

---

[5] Sermon 63, "The General Spread of the Gospel," §23, *Works*, 2:497.

Anglican clergy either returned to England or moved across the border into Canada. This crisis led John Wesley to become more forceful in asking the bishops of the Church of England to ordain men for the pastoral oversight of Methodists in America.

It soon became clear that there was no help forthcoming from the Anglican bishops, and Wesley evolved his own plan of action. He conferred upon Thomas Coke, a young Anglican priest whom Wesley regarded as his chief assistant, the power of ordaining and consecrating, naming him a "superintendent" (Wesley's translation of the Greek word *episcopos*, overseer). Coke was given authority to set apart Francis Asbury as the other superintendent for America. Wesley also ordained two English lay volunteers, Thomas Vasey and Richard Whatcoat, as "elders." In early September 1784, they sailed with Coke to America, bearing a letter from Wesley acknowledging that the American Methodists were now disentangled from the state and the English hierarchy. They were now, Wesley wrote, "at full liberty to follow the Scriptures and the primitive Church."[6]

An urgent pastoral need for ordained clergy had precipitated Wesley's radical step of ordaining Vasey and Whatcoat. In America, the question of authority would remain a vital issue. Francis Asbury saw the dilemma that faced him. In the new democratic nation, any authority he might exercise over the American Methodists had to come from below rather than from above. It would not help him to be seen as having been given his right to exercise authority in American Methodism by John Wesley, who was by then an unpopular figure in America for his views on the American Revolution. Asbury therefore was dismayed when he met the English party at Barratt's Chapel, Delaware, on November 14, 1784, and they told him of Mr. Wesley's plan to commission him as superintendent. He wrote in his *Journal* that he was "shocked," but allowed that "it may be of God." Astutely, he insisted that he had to be elected to the role of superintendent by the American preachers, commenting "I shall not act in the capacity I have hitherto done by Mr. Wesley's appointment." Asbury made his point, and the group of American preachers with him in Delaware put forward the possibility of an independent church overseen by superintendents or "bishops": a Methodist Episcopal Church (MEC).

December 24, 1784, in Baltimore, was set for a conference of all American itinerant preachers. Always referred to as the "Christmas Conference," the nearly sixty preachers who assembled agreed to form themselves, in Asbury's words, "into an episcopal church, and to have superintendents, elders, and deacons." "When the conference was

---

[6] Letter to Our Brethren in America (10 September 1784), *Letters* (Telford), 7:238–39.

seated," Asbury recorded in his *Journal*, "Dr. Coke and myself were unanimously elected to the superintendency of the Church, and my ordination followed, after being previously ordained deacon and elder." By 1788, Asbury had dropped the title "superintendent" in favor of "bishop." He was afterwards always referred to as Bishop Asbury.

Under Asbury's leadership, the Wesleyan movement in the United States grew exponentially for many reasons. It was able to identify closely with the aspirations of the new republic. It was structurally highly mobile; Asbury himself traveled thousands of miles each year and saw it as his first task to create a network of traveling preachers able to follow the new settlers as they spread across the continent. It was able to use to enormous effect the new evangelistic tool known as the "camp meeting." It was able to move into the religious space vacated by the Anglican church, left bereft of bishops and clergy by the revolution and utterly dismayed by the loss of established status.[7] And, it offered a profound and communicable theological revolution in its repudiation of Calvinism and its tireless proclamation of the inexhaustibility of transforming grace.[8]

Before we leave North America we may quickly trace the Wesleyan expansion into Canada. William Black, who as a layman organized Wesleyanism in Nova Scotia, traveled to Baltimore for the Christmas Conference, where he pleaded for more preachers for Canada. The new MEC appointed two to go to Nova Scotia. Black himself was also ordained by Coke and Asbury in 1789. But the link between the Canadian Methodists and the MEC was severed in 1800. Black then turned to Britain for help. The British Wesleyan Conference responded by assigning four preachers to the Canadian mission. The War of 1812 increased tension between the two branches of Methodism in North America, leaving Canadian Methodism to make progress its own way. It had 418,352 members in 1925, when it joined with Congregationalists and Presbyterians to make up the United Church of Canada.[9]

THOMAS COKE, THE CARIBBEAN, AND BEYOND

There is another link between the early work in Canada and the beginnings of British Wesleyan overseas missions. Although Wesley intended Thomas Coke to serve jointly with Asbury as superintendents

---

[7] David Hempton has stressed how early Methodism was a "subspecies of Anglicanism" in *Methodism: Empire of the Spirit*, 18–19.

[8] Wade Crawford Barclay, *History of Methodist Missions*, 6 vols. (1949), tells this story in great detail.

[9] See Neil Semple, *The Lord's Dominion: the History of Canadian Methodism* (1996).

of American Methodism, Coke rarely functioned in this role, being marginalized by his continuing British citizenship and very long absences (between 1784 and 1805 he paid just nine visits to North America, each two years apart).[10] On the second of these trips, a voyage that began on September 24, 1786, Coke intended to stop first in Nova Scotia and then proceed south. He had with him two new preachers for Newfoundland, partly as a result of his lobbying to gain widespread support in British Methodism for overseas missions. This had been set out in January 1786 in his *An Address to the Pious and Benevolent, proposing an annual subscription for Missionaries in the Highlands and adjacent Islands of Scotland, the Isles of Jersey, Guernsey, and Newfoundland, the West Indies and the provinces of Nova Scotia and Quebec.* Although John Wesley had resisted Coke's earlier efforts in this cause, he found this proposal persuasive.[11] "It is," Wesley wrote, "not easy to conceive the extreme want there is in all these places of men that will not count their lives dear unto themselves, so that they may testify the gospel of the grace of God."[12]

But, Coke's ship never reached Nova Scotia. Violent storms in the Atlantic forced the captain to turn south towards the Caribbean islands. On Christmas morning in 1786, Coke and his party landed in Antigua. To their surprise, they found that there were Methodists already there. A West Indian planter, Nathaniel Gilbert had heard Wesley preach in London. Upon his return to Antigua, he had preached what he had heard to his own slaves and established a Methodist Society. After Gilbert's death in 1774, his work had been continued by two women of this group, Mary Alley and Sophia Campbell (reminding us of the role often played by women of humble origin in the spread of Wesleyan Methodism). Later, Nathaniel Gilbert's sister-in-law Mary Gilbert and John Baxter, a government shipwright who had arrived in Antigua in 1778, shared in the leadership. By the time Coke arrived on the island in 1786, there were already 1,500 Methodists. To this congregation, Coke (at Baxter's invitation) preached a now famous Christmas sermon. As the new year began, Coke and his colleagues visited the neighboring West Indian islands. Coke's plans immediately changed. "It is impossible to have any doubt concerning the will of God," he wrote, "all is as clear as it was written by a sunbeam." The preachers intended for the missionary work in Canada

---

[10] The standard work on Coke remains John A. Vickers, *Thomas Coke, Apostle of Methodism* (1969).

[11] In 1783 Coke had published *A Plan of the Society for the Establishment of Missions amongst the Heathen, particularly for the East Indies.* Wesley discounted this suggestion.

[12] Wesley, Letter to Dr. Coke (12 March 1786), *Letters* (Telford), 7:322.

were stationed in St. Vincent and St. Kitts. Upon his return to London Coke worked to ensure that more British missionaries should be stationed in Dominica, Barbados, Nevis, Tortola, and Jamaica. In 1803, the Methodist mission in the Caribbean was extended to the Bahamas and, in 1809, to Trinidad. Although Methodist preaching aroused strong opposition from plantation owners, by 1814, there were twelve Caribbean circuits with 17,000 members.

Noting these developments in the Caribbean some historians have counted 1786, the date of Thomas Coke's *Address*, the year in which British Methodist missionary work began, thus anticipating the foundation of the Baptist Missionary Society by six years. But, the General Wesleyan Methodist Missionary Society was not created until 1818. Unintentionally, Coke contributed to this delay in forming a central missionary body. Impelled by his unbounded enthusiasm for the cause ("I would," he wrote in 1804, "sacrifice everything and myself to the missions"), Coke virtually single-handedly initiated, maintained, and supervised overseas missions for more than twenty years after John Wesley's death. By using his own private income as well as raising funds from non-Methodist sources, he ensured a succession of preachers for the Caribbean and for Canada, as well as opening up new activity in Gibraltar, Sierra Leone, and the Cape of Good Hope. Coke's last great plan was for a mission to India and Ceylon (Sri Lanka) in which he was to take part himself. At the very end of 1813, Coke sailed on his "Asian mission" with a group of seven other preachers. It was to be his last voyage. On May 3, 1814, he was found dead in his cabin. His companions did, however, reach Bombay (Mumbai) and from there went on to Ceylon.

In the last years of Coke's life the British Wesleyan Conference had become increasingly enthusiastic for overseas missions.[13] This new zeal culminated in 1813, with the first Conference-wide missionary meeting in Leeds. All possible steps were then taken to establish the Wesleyan Methodist Missionary Society (WMMS). On the other side of the Atlantic similar forces led to the formation of the Missionary Society of the Methodist Episcopal Church, whose constitution was formally adopted by the General Conference in 1820. The smaller Methodist churches on both sides of the Atlantic followed in due course with their own agencies and thus the structures for home support were in place for the worldwide spread of Wesleyan Methodism We can now trace the story continent by continent.

---

[13] A fully documented account of Coke's relationship with the Wesleyan Conference can be found in Vickers, *Thomas Coke*, 261–86.

AFRICA

The first missionary appointed by the British Conference for work in West Africa was George Warren in 1811. But, as one historian of the Church in Africa has noted "the first was never the first."[14] Methodist laypeople were already active in Sierra Leone when Warren arrived. Within eight months he was dead, but a ready succession of volunteers for West Africa followed. These early missionaries were the equivalents in Africa of the circuit riders in pioneering America and their average life expectancy in West Africa was approximately two years. Such early deaths and necessary early retirements made it difficult to implement consistent missionary policies in West Africa. Despite this, the (British) Methodist Church grew in Sierra Leone and throughout the neighboring countries of West Africa. In 1838, Thomas Birch Freeman (1806–90) arrived from England and served in Cape Coast as a Wesleyan missionary. The son of an African father (a freed slave, hence the surname Freeman) and an English mother, Freeman was quite at home in West African society and he is counted as the founder of Methodism in Ghana, Benin, Dahomey, Togo, and Western Nigeria. In southeastern Nigeria, the Primitive Methodist Church began a very successful enterprise in 1893. Much of this work was brought together by the foundation of the Methodist Church of Nigeria in 1962. Since then the Methodist Church of Nigeria has grown exponentially, with a total of 3,500,000 adherents. Nigeria also has Methodist communities arising from the work of the Evangelical United Brethren in Bauchi province, and there are now nearly 3,000 members related to the United Methodist Church.

The oldest republic in Africa is Liberia, established in 1822 as a homeland for freed slaves. In its first year, a Methodist Episcopal Church missionary arrived, and missionaries from the African Methodist Episcopal Church and the African Methodist Episcopal Church Zion came in 1876 and 1891 respectively. Until 1897, the Liberia Conference of the MEC had oversight of all the MEC work in Africa. William Taylor (1821–1902) was appointed bishop in 1884, having had previous experience in southern Africa as well as in India and South America. Taylor was perhaps the greatest missionary thinker produced by American Methodism. Working to a theory that he called "Pauline missions," he conceived new churches as being independent, self-directing, and entrepreneurial in spirit, therefore generally beyond the control of the home church. Moreover, his south African experiences in the 1860s led him to believe

[14] Bengt Sundkler and Christopher Steed, *A History of Christianity in Africa* (2000).

that African culture was comparable to any western forms. Thus he made no effort to impose the latter, trusting Africans to be able in due course to express the Christian faith in their own ways. In Taylor's view the missionary had nothing to do but plant "the pure gospel seed," and he vehemently objected to the notion that mission boards could make decisions from 10,000 miles away. He also experimented with these methods in India and South America. Taylor set the patterns for Wesleyan expansion between 1884–96, initiating work in Angola, the Congo, and what were then called the Zambezi Districts. But as bishop in Liberia he was most concerned with the neighboring countries of West Africa, particularly Sierra Leone. Today, nearly all West African countries have a Methodist presence. The most recently established among these is in Senegal, where in 2003 there were reported to be eleven new churches founded by Senegalese men and women returning to their homeland.

Further south, the story of the planting of Methodism in present South Africa begins with the arrival of Methodist soldiers in the early-nineteenth century. It was not until 1816, however, that the first English Methodist missionaries in Southern Africa, Barnabas and Jane Shaw, laid the foundation for many other missionaries to move northwards. Barnabas Shaw trained the first indigenous pastor, Jacob Links, whose name was recorded as an 'assistant missionary' in 1822. The second Methodist missionary in South Africa was William Shaw (no relation to Barnabas), who joined a large party of ex-soldiers from Britain intending to settle in the Eastern Cape in 1824. William Shaw found an already existing small Methodist community led by two Methodist military men. From his base in Grahamstown, Shaw moved further inland intending to establish a series of mission stations among the Xhosas. Even now, the main strength of South African Methodism lies along the route of the chain of stations that Shaw helped to found. From these beginnings, Methodism spread through Botswana, Lesotho, Namibia, and Swaziland. By 1883, there were enough Methodists in the region to set up a South African Conference. Today, Methodists in these countries belong to the Methodist Church of Southern Africa. Reaction to white domination led to the formation of Wesleyan-inspired African independent churches like the Ethiopian Church of Mangena Mogone (ECMM). Although American Methodism is not widely present in South Africa, the ECMM was formally adopted by the African Methodist Episcopal Church after a visit from AME bishop Henry M. Turner in 1898. In the Republic of South Africa, so dominated by the ideology of apartheid, the Methodist Conference took a principled stand in 1958, when it declared that the Methodist Church was "one and undivided." Yet, the leadership of Methodism in South Africa remained almost wholly in the hands of the white minority. Although the Methodist Church in Southern Africa elected its first Black president in 1963, the balance of power in Methodism was not to change until the 1980s, when Mmutlanyane Stanley Mogoba was appointed the first black Secretary of the Conference. Today the Methodist community in South Africa numbers just over two million and includes such people as Nelson Mandela.

The spread of Wesleyan Methodism in east and central Africa took place later than in either the west or the south. The British United Methodist Free Church was the first Wesleyan body to engage in work in Kenya, eventually joined by other Methodist groups. Today, the autonomous Kenyan Methodist Church counts a community of 1,200,000. The Primitive Methodists began work in south central Africa in 1889, expanding into northwestern Rhodesia (Zimbabwe) where it was served by, among others, a great anthropologist-missionary, Edwin W. Smith (1876–1957).[15] Smith said of African missionary work: "our aim must be to make of the Africans not European Christians but Christians...and allow them to organize their faith in a manner suited to their traditions and environment."[16] WMMS missionaries joined the Primitive Methodists in central Africa in 1891. MEC interest in east and central Africa grew and in 1896 a new Congo Mission Conference was authorized by the General Conference. This elected Joseph Crane Hartzell (1842–1928) as bishop. Hartzell arrived in what is now Zimbabwe the following year and oversaw the establishment of a chain of Mission Conferences in Central Africa. He also directed the beginning of work in Algeria and Tunisia.

ASIA

Thomas Coke was buried at sea on May 3, 1814, just three weeks' sailing time from Bombay (Mumbai). By the end of the year, some of his party made it to Colombo where they were welcomed by Andrew Armour, a Methodist layman who had arrived in Ceylon a few years before from Madras (Chennai). In a predominately Buddhist country with Hindus in the north, Methodism pinned its hopes for missionary advance on education, establishing primary schools, high schools, and other forms of training. The Methodist Church in Sri Lanka, which

---

[15] Adrian Hastings, *The Church in Africa 1450–1994* (1994), 553, called Smith's 1926 book *The Golden Stool* "the most authoritative text for African missiology in the inter-war years."

[16] Edwin W. Smith, *The Golden Stool* (1926), 263.

became autonomous in 1964, has produced notable world church leaders like D. T. Niles and S. Wesley Ariarajah.

In mainland India, little missionary activity took place until the renewal of the charter of the East India Company in 1813. Its chaplains were to minister solely to the Company's employees. However, there was no law forbidding those employees from offering their Christian witness. Andrew Armour, whom we have just encountered in Sri Lanka, had previously been in the British army in Madras, where he had formed a Methodist Society that was still meeting in 1816. Hearing of the arrival of Coke's team of missionaries in Ceylon, members of this Society asked that one of them might be spared to come to India, and, in 1817, they welcomed the first British Methodist missionary in India, the Irish preacher James Lynch. American Methodists arrived in the mid-nineteenth century, and saw that their mission could most fruitfully be directed to the Dalit community (then called "outcastes") where there were significant mass-movements. Indeed, by 1908 there were 200,000 Indian Methodists associated with the MEC; this figure rose to more than half a million by 1939. British Methodist efforts also saw times of rapid expansion with large numbers of conversions to Christianity in the 1880s among the Telegu-speaking peoples, and later in Hyderabad in the early 1900s. These mass movements continued through the next forty years.

The difference of approach between British and American forms of Methodism in matters of church organization can be seen very clearly in India. The British-related Methodist community was still growing in 1947 when its Southern Province entered into a union with Congregationalists, Presbyterians, and Anglicans to form the Church of South India. British Methodists were participants in another ecumenical breakthrough when the Church of North India was formed in 1970. Methodists of the American traditions have generally kept themselves apart from such schemes, placing a higher value on their links with the United States and the General Conference than on local ecumenical unity. In Pakistan, the small Methodist community became part of the United Church of Pakistan in 1970.

The linguistic, religious, and socio political complexity of South Asia has made the story of Methodist missionary progress an uneven one. Methodist mission began in Burma (Myanmar), for example, in the late-nineteenth century when Burma had been annexed to the British Empire. In the south, Rangoon (Yangon) became the center for American activity from 1873, and, in 1887, British missionaries in Mandalay began work among the tribes people in the north, but, neither British nor American missionaries made significant progress in this predominantly Buddhist culture. The Methodists in both north and south Myanmar became self-governing in 1965. From Burma, Methodism in its American form spread southward to Malaysia and Singapore, then to Indonesia. Malaysia also received Methodist missionaries from Australia and the British Isles. Methodist Christians in both Malaysia and Singapore come chiefly from the Chinese and Tamil communities. In Singapore, these demographics are embodied in three Methodist Annual Conferences. Indonesia has had Methodist work since 1904 and today has two Annual Conferences.

When Methodism began its worldwide expansion China was impregnably closed to foreigners, especially to those perceived to be ruthless European imperialists. The two "opium wars" of 1839–44 and 1856–60 led to the forcible cession of Hong Kong and the opening of the five Treaty Ports. The unequal treaties upon which these acts were based caused deep resentment among Chinese people and greatly hindered the British missionaries. The reputation of Americans was less negative, allowing missionaries of both the MEC and the recently separated MECS (South) to begin work in China in 1847 and 1848, respectively. The MECS started work in Foochow and Shanghai, whereas the MEC moved into the interior. In 1851, the British Wesleyan Methodists arrived in Hong Kong, followed by other British groups. The Methodist New Connexion, the Bible Christians, the United Methodist Free Churches, and the Primitive Methodists all had missions in China by the end of the nineteenth-century. Mass movements occurred in Southwest China. In the twentieth century, there were two disruptions of missionary activity in China: the Sino-Japanese War (1937–1945) and then the Chinese civil war from 1946. The victory of the Communists in 1949 resulted in the severing of Western missionary links, but the seeds of Methodism had taken root. In 1950, there were 21,000 Methodist members (and a wider community of 57,000) in the China districts of the British Methodist Church, with another 190,000 in American-based Methodism. At the behest of the Communist government the Methodists in China had to break all ties with the West in 1951. They became part of the Protestant Three-Self (self-governing, self-supporting, and self-propagating) Patriotic Movement. Between 1950 and 1978, Christians in China had few contacts with the West, yet, they survived the Cultural Revolution and added very considerably to their numbers. Today, Chinese churches are growing rapidly both in China itself and throughout the Chinese diaspora.[17] No mission work by foreigners is permitted in China

---

[17] Some thirty-five million Chinese live in Europe, North and South America, Australia, India, and Africa. See Lamin Sanneh, *Disciples of All Nations* (2008) for a vivid description of contemporary Chinese Christianity.

at present, but Methodist churches around the world have close relations with the Christian churches there.

In Korea, both the MEC and MECS began work in 1884. By the end of World War I, there were 25,000 members of the Methodist Church in Korea. In 1930 the Korean Methodist Church became self-governing. All Christian churches in Korea grew during the period of Japanese hegemony and today there are nearly one and a half million Korean Methodists, with strong leadership and larger congregations. In 2006, the Korean Methodist Church hosted the World Methodist Council.

In the Philippines, there are a variety of Methodist churches, having their origin in missionary work that began after the Spanish-American War in 1898. Today, the Methodist community numbers approximately one million.

All the Asian Methodist churches we have described participate in the Asian Methodist Council, which was set up in Seoul in 2001.

AUSTRALASIA AND OCEANIA

When Samuel Leigh, the first English Wesleyan missionary, arrived in Sydney in 1815 he found the ground prepared for him by Methodist laypeople. The work expanded from Sydney into Tasmania in 1820, to Melbourne in 1836, into Adelaide in 1837, and reached Perth in 1840. All of these places were frontier townships and Methodism grew with them. By 1855 it was possible to form the Australasian Methodist Conference, which immediately assumed responsibility for mission work in the South Pacific. Because of the vastness of Australia, it followed the American pattern of Conferences with a General Conference meeting every three years. Annual Conferences were set up in New South Wales, Victoria, Queensland, South Australia, Western Australia, and Tasmania, as well as one in New Zealand. In 1881 the Australian census recorded that 241,968 persons called themselves Methodists. In early 1900 all the Methodist groups in Australia, including the United Methodist Free Church, the Primitive Methodists, and the Bible Christians, united to form the Methodist Church of Australasia. In 1977, Australian Methodists united with Congregationalists and Presbyterians to make up the Uniting Church in Australia, which retains membership in the World Methodist Council. At the beginning of the twenty-first century the Uniting Church has a community of over one million.

In 1818, Samuel Leigh visited New Zealand, accompanied by an Anglican missionary. When he returned to England on leave, Leigh launched a special appeal for work in those islands and in 1821 he himself was appointed to oversee the missionary work in New Zealand. Missionary history in New Zealand follows two paths. Along New Zealand's east coast Christianity spread through the efforts of Anglicans, and along the west coast it grew as a result of Methodist activity. These years in which the Methodist missions were established coincided with the beginning of the colonization of New Zealand. Both the Church Missionary Society and the Wesleyan Methodist Missionary Society protested colonial expansion. As part of this protest, British Methodists and Anglicans were involved in the negotiations that led to the Treaty of Waitangi in 1840, ensuring some measure of protection of the rights of the Maori people. In terms of organization, New Zealand Methodism began as part of the Australian Methodist Church, becoming an autonomous Methodist church in 1913. Today the Methodist Church in New Zealand is known by the Maori name *Te Haahi Weterianas O Aotearoa* (The Methodist Church of New Zealand).

Methodist missionaries from Britain were present in the islands of the Pacific Ocean from 1822, but faced much hostility from the inhabitants. The turning point for Methodist work in the islands took place in 1830 with the baptism of Taufa'ahau of Ha'apai. He became a Methodist local preacher and in 1845 was enthroned King George Typo I, the first Methodist king anywhere in the world. Today Tonga is a Methodist stronghold. The Free Wesleyan Church ("free" that is from the Australian Methodist Church) reports a membership of more than 30,000 and an extended community of 70,000. Following the lead of local Christians from both the other islands, British Methodist missionaries William Cross and David and Margaret Cargill crossed to Fiji in 1835. Fiji came under British rule in 1874 and then experienced an influx of indentured laborers from India. British Methodists launched an Indian Mission on Fiji in 1892. The autonomous Methodist Conference of Fiji and Rotuma came into being in 1964. Of its 215,000 membership, nearly 3,000 are Indo-Fijian. In 1857, the newly constituted Australian Conference entered Samoa; although not large, the resulting Methodist Church became autonomous in 1964. There are just over 35,000 Samoan Methodist members with another 40,000 in its community.

CENTRAL AND SOUTH AMERICA

In Latin America, the advance of Methodism faced two great obstacles: the long hegemony of the Roman Catholic Church, together with extraordinary diversity of political systems operating on the subcontinent. Wesleyan missionary activity in southern America has mostly been in the hands of the American Methodist churches. Methodists from both the MEC and MECS were in Mexico by 1872, followed by large numbers of missionaries in the next decades. The work of the two missions, MEC and MECS, was combined in 1930 when a self-governing church was organized. The Methodist Church of Mexico had 10,000 members at its founding. By the end of the twentieth century this count had reached nearly half a million. The Methodist Church of Brazil dates from 1835, and grew rapidly when a large influx of Methodists from the southern United States settled in Brazil after the end of the Civil War. In 1867 the MECS formally established a mission. Today the Methodist Church of Brazil is self-governing, with membership of half a million. Brazilian Methodists are largely Pentecostal in their style of worship and practice, though they cherish wider Methodist and ecumenical connections. The Methodist Church of Brazil was the first church in Latin America to become a member of the World Council of Churches, and hosted the World Methodist Council in Rio de Janeiro in 1995.

Three successive waves of American Methodist activity reached into other parts of Central and South America in the nineteenth century. The first wave of missionaries had arrived in Haiti in 1823 and in the Dominican Republic in 1834, pressing southward into Uruguay and Argentina, with MEC work beginning in both places in 1835–36. The second wave is always associated with the outstanding missionary thinker William Taylor, whose work in Africa we have already noticed. Under his inspiration, Methodist churches were planted in Cuba in 1873, in Panama in 1877, in Peru and Paraguay in 1886, in Bolivia and Venezuela in 1890, and in Puerto Rico and Costa Rica in 1900. Contributing to this second wave were Wesleyan Methodists, Free Methodists, the Church of the Nazarene, and the Pilgrim Holiness Church. After 1906, many missionaries, local pastors, and lay people became Pentecostal rather than Methodist. The third wave of Methodist evangelistic work in Latin America has been an internal missionary movement, very much more oriented in the directions of Pentecostalism and only loosely connected with the main traditions of Methodism. Thus, for example, some 75 percent of Chilean Protestants are members of the Iglesia Metodista Pentecostal. In other Latin American countries contemporary Methodism often has forms of worship, preaching, and prayer that are essentially Pentecostal. Yet, powerful testimonies from across Latin America show Methodists with Pentecostal tendencies working for a this-worldly salvation. There is considerable awareness of liberation theology with its concern to transform harmful political and social structures.

EUROPE

Europe became a significant mission field for Methodists when large numbers of European immigrants in America came under the influence of the Methodist Episcopal Church and the German-speaking churches that were closely associated with the MEC – the Evangelical Association and the United Brethren in Christ. Many of these new Methodists had a deep concern for their own people and deliberately returned to their places of birth to share their new-found Wesleyanism. These included influential figures like Wilhelm Nast, Ludwig S. Jacoby, and Ludwig Nipert. The United Brethren formally established a mission to Germany in 1869. The next year the first MEC preachers arrived in Austria. Today there is a Methodist community of more than 100,000 in Germany and of nearly 2,000 in Austria. British Methodists (originating with Thomas Coke) also maintained an interest in establishing missions on the Continent. They initiated work in France as early as 1791, in Italy in 1860 and in Portugal in 1871. In 1853, Ole Peter Person was assigned by the MEC to Norway. The first MEC Society gathered in Denmark in 1899. The Evangelical Association undertook a mission to Switzerland in 1865. The work of the MECS in Belgium, in the former Czechoslovakia, and in Poland grew out of its war relief ministries after 1918. The present United Methodist Northern Europe Conference embraces churches in Sweden, Denmark, Norway, and Finland.

Methodist work in Poland, Russia, and the Baltic States can be traced to the last years of the nineteenth century, as a result of Swedish, Finnish, German, and American evangelistic activity. Methodism was surprisingly successful in the Baltic states at first, but suffered under the terrible violence that marked the region in the twentieth century. In Latvia, Lithuania, and the Western Ukraine, Methodism was actually banned. The beginnings of Methodist missionary work in Russia were extinguished in 1927, not to be renewed until after 1989. The United Methodist Church has engaged in many initiatives to help restore the Methodist presence in the former Soviet Union. There are 4,000 Methodists linked with other Protestant churches in predominantly Roman Catholic Poland. Methodist churches now operate with freedom and are growing in Estonia, Latvia, and Lithuania. Other significant Methodist initiatives are being worked out in Hungary, Bulgaria, the

Federal Republic of Yugoslavia, and the Republic of Macedonia. There is also a growing Methodist presence in Albania, Croatia, and Kosovo. All these countries and many others are linked in the World Methodist Council, a fellowship of over 100 Methodist/Wesleyan denominations in 132 counties, touching in ministry some 75 million people.[18]

CONCLUSION

This all-too-brief account of the spread of Wesleyanism around the world raises many important issues. Some are missiological (concerned with the theory and practice of missionary work), others concern the nature of World Christianity in the twenty-first century.

There are several striking factors in Methodism's missionary outreach. First, we would note the robust and indispensable role of lay people who felt both enabled and equipped to establish Methodist communities wherever they went. In its earliest period, Methodism followed almost exactly the growth of the British Empire, becoming, in David Hempton's phrase, an "empire of the Spirit." The earliest Methodists to occupy new spiritual territory were usually military personnel and pioneering settlers, with itinerant preachers following where they had already gone.

Second, it should be recognized how Methodist women felt especially empowered to engage in missionary outreach, as in the early case of the two slave-women Mary Alley and Sophia Campbell who held together the Methodist Society in Antigua after 1774. A major cause of the demise of mission activity in Methodist history has always been excessive clericalization, which particularly sidelined women.

Third, we should stress that running through all Methodist missionary activity is a sense that the locus where salvation was to be worked out was in this world – that being saved was not, in Wesley's words, "a blessing which lies on the other side of death."[19] Salvation meant not only the transformation of individuals, but actively changing the conditions in which people live. In Wesleyan thinking, God's mission includes a "new creation" in which the kingdoms of this world become the kingdoms of our God and of his Christ (Rev. 11:15). Accordingly, Wesleyan-based missiologies have usually focused on social issues: from the early attempts to abolish the slave trade, through concern for justice for the Maori people of New Zealand; from the provision of clinics

---

[18] For updated information on the World Methodist Council, see its website: http://www .worldmethodistcouncil.org/.

[19] Sermon 43, "The Scripture Way of Salvation," §I.1, Works, 2:156.

and hospitals in Africa and China, all the way to black and feminist theology in North America and liberation theology in Latin America. Methodists have normally embraced "the option for the poor." But not always. Speaking at the World Methodist Conference in Rio de Janeiro in 1996, Bishop Peter Storey of South Africa spoke of a "prosperous Methodism in the developed world and a Methodism with the poor in the rest of the world." He challenged prosperous Methodism to "find ways of engaging with the poor: your souls depend upon it."[20] Similar challenges have echoed through the Wesleyan movement from its beginning.

One other theme in Wesleyan missiology offers great hope for Methodism's ability to respond to the nearly overwhelming challenges that face the whole Christian community in the twenty-first century. This theme begins with Wesley's own conviction that the American part of his movement would do just fine after 1784, being at "at full liberty to follow the Scriptures and the primitive Church." We have also seen two very different Methodist missionaries in Africa echo and develop these words. The American William Taylor believed new churches well capable of directing their own life and the Englishman Edwin Smith declared that African Christians must be allowed to frame their own faith in African ways. Such ideas represent a deep underlying commitment to pluralism and diversity, the very issues that challenge the world Christian community today.

[20] Peter Storey, "Good News to the Poor," in *Proceedings of the Seventeenth World Methodist Conference*, edited by Joe Hale (1997), 159–160.

15 The holiness/pentecostal/charismatic extension of the Wesleyan tradition

RANDALL J. STEPHENS

The twentieth-century explosion of holiness, pentecostal, and charismatic movements may be the most significant recent development in world Christianity. By some estimates, pentecostalism in particular, which recently marked the centenary of its birth in a boisterous revival in Los Angeles in 1906, now comprises nearly one-fourth of Christians worldwide. This amounts to about half a billion people. The only larger Christian group is Roman Catholicism.

The phenomenal growth rate of these movements is only part of the story. They are changing the face of global religion. Scholars have begun to study the "pentecostalization" of world Christianity. Describing the rapid spread of pentecostal and charismatic groups in the southern hemisphere, the historian of religion Philip Jenkins notes: "these newer churches preach deep personal faith and communal orthodoxy, mysticism and puritanism, all founded on clear spiritual authority." For such initiates, "prophecy is an everyday reality, while faith-healing, exorcism, and dream-visions are all basic components of religious sensibility."[1] This chapter traces these characteristic emphases on the Holy Spirit's activity in believers' lives from their roots in early Methodism, through the nineteenth-century holiness movement, and into the emergence of pentecostalism and charismatic renewal.

CHARACTERIZING THE HOLINESS, PENTECOSTAL, AND CHARISMATIC MOVEMENTS

It will help to begin with brief characterizations of the connections and distinctions between the three movements. The holiness movement

---

[1] Philip Jenkins, *The Next Christendom: The Coming of Global Christianity* (2002), 8. More broadly, see Lamin Sanneh, *Disciples of All Nations: Pillars of World Christianity* (2008).

took root in the United States during the second great awakening (mid-1800s). Northern Methodists and various pietist evangelicals, following John Wesley and later Methodist divines, held that Christians could live above willful sin in this life. After an initial conversion, believers might experience "sanctification," "full salvation," the "double cure," or "Christian perfection" – various names for the complete removal of sin. In the nineteenth and early twentieth centuries, new denominations formed around this emphasis. The Church of the Nazarene, the Wesleyan Methodist Church, the Free Methodist Church, the Church of God (Anderson, Indiana), the Church of Christ (Holiness), and – to a lesser extent – the Salvation Army carry the imprint of such perfectionism.[2]

In the early twentieth century, a number of American holiness folk sought further signs of the "baptism of the Spirit," which they associated with sanctification. Alternatively, some considered this baptism to be a third work of grace (beyond justification and sanctification). In both cases their desire was for a *full* Christian experience, like that of the early disciples at Pentecost. Speaking in tongues and other manifestations of Holy Ghost empowerment were essential to this experience, and marked the birth of pentecostalism. Even more than their holiness predecessors, early pentecostals were religious dissidents, scornful of fancy clothes, ornate churches, staid worship, and "worldly ideals." Lively services, apocalyptic fervor, and missionary zeal set off pentecostals from the earliest days. Classic pentecostal denominations – including the Assemblies of God, the Church of God in Christ, and the International Pentecostal Holiness Church – adhere to literal interpretation of scripture and emphasize apostolic gifts and ecstatic worship.[3]

The charismatic movement is more amorphous than the holiness movement and pentecostalism. By the 1960s, some pentecostals were shedding some of the peculiar beliefs and practices that characterized them earlier. Simultaneously healing, speaking in tongues, and millennial beliefs were now shaping the religious lives of those outside of holiness and pentecostal denominations. Many members of mainstream churches began adopting these features, fusing new theologies with their changing ecclesial identity. The term "charismatic" emerged to identify such believers who experience the "in-filling" of the Holy Spirit, commend ecstatic "prayer language," and prefer "free" worship styles, but are not members of pentecostal churches. Most charismatics continue

---

[2] Melvin Easterday Dieter, *The Holiness Revival of the Nineteenth Century* (1996).
[3] Grant Wacker, *Heaven Below: Early Pentecostals and American Culture* (2001).

to identify with mainstream Protestant, Catholic, and Orthodox denominations.[4]

SANCTIFICATION AND EARLY AMERICAN METHODISM

With these brief characterizations in mind, we can trace the historical saga of the three movements in more detail.[5] The story begins
with the heritage passed by the Wesley brothers and early Methodism
in Britain to their North American kin. As other chapters in this volume elaborate, affirmation of the possibility of entire sanctification or
"Christian Perfection" was central to this heritage. But, some characteristic tensions concerning this core doctrine were also critical. There were
disagreements (even between John and Charles Wesley) about relative
emphasis on the gradual or instantaneous nature of attaining Christian
Perfection, and whether to expect it early in one's Christian life or only
near death. Related to these disagreements was debate over the proposal
of John Fletcher that the "baptism of the Holy Spirit," as experienced at
the initial Pentecost, was what brought one to Christian Perfection.

The emergent Methodist community in North America clearly
embraced the emphasis on entire sanctification. First generation leaders like Francis Asbury, Thomas Coke, and Jesse Lee enlisted new
Methodists in the perfectionist crusade. As Methodism fanned out across
the country, itinerants preached regularly on holiness.

The success of these early itinerants, however, began to change the
shape of American Methodism. Initially, the denomination was strongest
in the South. Eighty-seven percent of the members resided below the
Mason Dixon line when the Methodist Episcopal Church was organized
in 1784. That changed rapidly in the early nineteenth century as the
religion of the heart took root in the North as well.[6] Along with demo-
graphic shifts came other changes. The roughhewn camp meeting milieu
faded in the coming decades. Members grew in wealth, church discipline

---

4   P. D. Hocken, "Charismatic Movement," *The New International Dictionary of Pente-
    costal and Charismatic Movements*, eds. S. M. Burgess and E. M. Van Der Maas (2002),
    477–519.
5   Much additional documentation and details for the account that follows can be found
    in Edith Blumhofer, *Restoring the Faith: The Assemblies of God, Pentecostalism,
    and American Culture* (1993); Donald W. Dayton, *Theological Roots of Pentecostal-
    ism* (1987); Randall J. Stephens, *The Fire Spreads: Holiness and Pentecostalism in
    the American South* (2008); and Vinson Synan, *The Holiness-Pentecostal Tradition:
    Charismatic Movements in the Twentieth Century* (1997).
6   John H. Wigger, *Taking Heaven by Storm: Methodism and the Rise of Popular Chris-
    tianity in America* (1998), 5, 7.

declined somewhat, and respectable, urban congregants came to despise the wild revivals of the previous generation. By the 1830s, evangelical-ism was well established in the North and the South. Once on the radical margins of society, Baptist and Methodist sects rose to ascendancy and began claiming the same social status that once belonged solely to their religious betters.

In the South, church members made their piece with slavery, and, for the first time, high-ranking officials even owned slaves. In the North, Methodist leaders like Nathan Bangs and Wilbur Fisk started their careers well outside the religious mainstream. They later embod-ied refinement and the genteel Protestant values of education and mid-dle class respectability. From 1840 to 1860, Methodists founded at least thirty-five higher educational institutions. In these years, the denomina-tion claimed congressmen, governors, and senators among its members. Indeed, Methodism fostered social mobility, argues historian Nathan Hatch. By the 1840s Methodists "had undertaken their own pilgrimage to respectability."[7] Outsiders could no longer accuse the devout of being poor, marginal, religious reactionaries.

A shift in theological emphasis followed suit. By the early 1800s, Methodist ministers were preaching less on sanctification than they once had. Some patriarchs of the movement lamented that neglect. Bishop T. J. Peck warned that the biblical doctrine of holiness was in danger of becoming a novelty among the saints. Georgia Methodist lumi-nary Lovick Pierce castigated rich Methodists who had lost touch with their roots.[8] For him, the church fell away as soon as its members ceased to seek and profess the second work of grace. Indeed, in 1870 and 1878 the General Conference of the Methodist Episcopal Church, South con-firmed Pierce and others' suspicions. "We fear," declared church offi-cials, "that the doctrine of perfect love . . . is too much overlooked and neglected."[9]

Whether holiness preaching actually declined or remained steady in these years, many believed that old precepts had been abandoned. This perception of declension gave new energy to perfectionism's dissemina-tors. The holiness movement developed in the American North under

[7] Nathan O. Hatch, "The Puzzle of American Methodism," *Church History* 63 (1994): 180–81; Nathan O. Hatch, *The Democratization of American Christianity* (1989), 93, 194, 195.

[8] Peck & Pierce are quoted and discussed respectively in Wigger, *Taking Heaven by Storm*, 20; and John Leland Peters, *Christian Perfection*, 101.

[9] *Journal of the General Conference of the Methodist Episcopal Church, South, 1870*, 164–65; *Journal of the General Conference of the Methodist Episcopal Church, South, 1878*, 33.

the leadership of dozens of reforming preachers, authors, and teachers. The heady atmosphere of the Second Great Awakening, and the revival work of Charles Grandison Finney spurred evangelicals on to higher spiritual attainments. Ministers like Asa Mahan, Theodore Dwight Weld, and Timothy Merritt looked to the founders of Methodism for guidance on perfection.

PHOEBE PALMER AND REVIVALISTIC PERFECTIONISM

Phoebe Palmer was the most successful and influential nineteenth-century holiness interpreter of Wesley. The tremendous growth of the American holiness movement owes much to her. A devout Methodist from New York, Palmer struggled with the idea of perfect love throughout the 1830s. After the death of her three infant children, she sought comfort in religious purity. She experienced sanctification in 1837. In her 1866 book *Economy of Salvation*, Palmer implored readers to "listen to important truths from him who, under God, was the founder of Methodism." "You cannot," she insisted, "fail to feel a deep interest in relation to the Bible doctrine of Christian holiness." Without a doubt, it was the "cardinal doctrine of Methodism."[10]

Yet, many scholars charge Palmer with departing from the teachings of John Wesley (and scripture) on this cardinal doctrine – particularly in her motto of "believe that you have it and you have it."[11] Palmer did indeed rework Wesleyan theology in several ways. She was the product of the optimistic, utilitarian environment of the post-Puritan North. Her popular doctrine of perfection exuded Yankee pragmatism. For Palmer, any believer could secure the double cure through an act of faith. Wesley's notion of a long, fraught struggle vanished.

Palmer's practical "shorter way" to sanctification, as it was called, involved a total devotion of self and possessions to God. She turned to Jesus, who proclaimed in Matthew 23:19 that the altar "sanctifieth the gift." Saints who placed all on the altar would be freed from sin. It was as plain an account as one could imagine. "There is no duty set forth more clearly in the Bible than that of *entire consecration*," Palmer told an anxious young woman. And she assured her: "You do not *need* any more light in order to ascertain the duty of an immediate and entire surrender

---

[10] Phoebe Palmer, *Incidental Illustrations of the Economy of Salvation: Its Doctrine and Duties* (New York, 1866), 37.

[11] E.g., Charles Edward White, *The Beauty of Holiness: Phoebe Palmer as Theologian, Revivalist, Feminist, and Humanitarian* (1986), 120–22. More broadly, see Harold E. Raser, *Phoebe Palmer: Her Life and Thought* (1987), 149–226.

of your whole being to God."[12] Thus equipped, the saints preached with "tongues of fire" and underwent "spirit baptism." Commenting on an 1858 revival, Palmer rhapsodized: "the scene we witnessed could not have been greatly unlike that witnessed on the day of Pentecost."[13] Like the early Methodist John Fletcher, Palmer used the language of Pentecost that stressed the urgency of the age and pressed men as well as women to religious activism. Holiness made God's people into useful servants.

Other pragmatic perfectionists expressed similar views. Most antebellum holiness people believed that Christ would return after a millennium inaugurated by social and personal perfection. That postmillennialism revealed northern evangelicals' hopeful beliefs about the world.[14] As William Lloyd Garrison and other abolitionists called for the immediate end of slavery, holiness divines claimed that Christians could be rid of sin in an instant. Methodist leader Timothy Merritt began publishing the *Guide to Christian Perfection*, a paper devoted to the instantaneous attainment of the second blessing, in 1839. Oberlin College became a hotbed of Reformed holiness. Charles Finney, professor and then president of the school, focused on the law of the gospel and the believer's duty of full consecration. Similarly, Presbyterian minister William E. Boardman published his highly influential *The Higher Christian Life* at the peak of the northern revival in 1858. Boardman's book, more than any other publication, spread holiness doctrines broadly among non-Methodist evangelicals in the North and in England.[15]

Few traveled as widely or influenced as many evangelicals in America and England as did Phoebe Palmer. Her 1859 preaching tour in England had a powerful impact on Catherine and William Booth, founders of the Salvation Army. Their decision to enlist women preachers owed much to Palmer's example. Beginning in 1840, and until her death in 1874, Palmer led a prayer and fellowship gathering in her New York City home called the Tuesday Meeting for the Promotion of Holiness. She advocated her shorter way doctrine at the meetings and won high-placed church leaders to the cause. Public testimony was critical to obtaining entire sanctification, Palmer argued. Palmer's practical way to perfect love won over scores of northern and English reformers,

---

[12] Palmer, *Economy of Salvation*, 52.
[13] Richard Wheatley, *The Life and Letters of Mrs. Phoebe Palmer* (New York, 1876), 341–42.
[14] James H. Moorhead, "The Erosion of Postmillennialism in American Thought, 1865–1925," *Church History* 53 (1984): 62.
[15] Timothy L. Smith, *Called unto Holiness: The Story of the Nazarenes, the Formative Years* (1962), 11.

including Harriet Beecher-Stowe and Thomas C. Upham. Methodists and non-Methodists alike absorbed her message.

THE POST CIVIL WAR HOLINESS REVIVAL

Not long after the disruptions of the Civil War, a group of young northern Methodist churchmen, influenced by Phoebe Palmer and other holiness lights, hoped to rekindle perfectionism. Ministers from New York, eastern Pennsylvania, and Boston – John S. Inskip, J. A. Wood, and Alfred Cookman among them – championed a return to primitive, unadorned Methodism. They believed that the war damaged the holiness cause and led to national moral decline. Even before the great conflagration some Methodists left their mother church over slavery (the Wesleyan Methodists in 1843) and others broke off over issues of wealth and perceived degeneracy (the Free Methodist Church in 1860). Postwar jeremiads from the pulpit and press catalogued a variety of sins: novel reading, titillating urban amusements, card playing, declining church discipline, and strong drink. A revival of old time Wesleyan holiness might heal the church and society, so they thought. In mid-July 1867, a group of holiness evangelists organized a large gathering in Vineland, New Jersey. For more than ten days thousands of faithful from the North and West thronged to the teetotaller village to hear about and experience the double cure. John Inskip addressed the crowd, as did a number of other prominent Methodists. A minister from the New York East Conference summed up the feelings of many, evoking Wesley and asking congregants "*when* shall the blood of Christ cleanse from all sin, and *how* does the blood of Christ cleanse from all sin?"[16]

At the close of the meeting participants formed the National Camp Meeting Association for the Promotion of Holiness (NCMAPH). It drew together lay people and clergy to spread holiness doctrine and host other mass meetings from the East to the West coast. The task seemed clear to Inskip. Those who had the "teachings of Wesley, Fletcher, Watson, Clarke, etc., and have used a hymn-book so full of the doctrine as is ours," he announced, "surely need no argument to assure them that it is the will of God they should be 'sanctified wholly,' and 'preserved blameless unto the day of his coming.'"[17]

---

[16] "The Vineland Camp," *Daily State Gazette* (Trenton, NJ), July 22, 1867, 4. Cf. George Hughes, *Days of Power in the Forest Temple: A Review of the Wonderful Work of God at Fourteen National Camp-Meetings from 1867 to 1872* (Boston, 1873), 10–17.

[17] John W. Eaton and Alexander McLean, eds., *Penuel: Or, Face to Face with God* (New York, 1869), 7–8.

THE EUROPEAN REVIVAL AND THE KESWICK CONVENTION

The revival reached far beyond the United States. Enthusiasts in England and on the continent, influenced by American advocates and Methodist founders, elevated holiness to new levels in their churches and in large-scale revivals and conferences. The work of Finney, Palmer, Upham, and William E. Boardman had circulated broadly even before the American Civil War. Like the Palmers, Finney had made highly publicized visits to England. James Caughey, American Methodist itinerant, mounted four successful visits to England. His emotional style and colorful sermons won him large crowds and bitter high-church critics. Robert Pearsall Smith was one of the chief Yankee apostles of sanctification who ventured to England. Smith, along with his wife Hannah Whitall, were raised as Quakers but turned to the holiness movement after experiencing evangelical conversion and entire sanctification. They influenced thousands of English, French, Dutch, and German faithful. The Smiths' transatlantic evangelism reached an apex when they led the 1875 pan-European Brighton revival, which drew between 8 and 10 thousand participants.

That same year, Canon Harford-Battersby organized an outdoor holiness conference in rural Keswick, where he was vicar. The annual Keswick conferences became the center of English holiness activity. Participants highlighted the "higher Christian life" and the need for spiritual power. Like Charles Finney and Asa Mahan, they combined Wesleyan views of sanctification with a Reformed emphasis on duty and law. One Keswick leader, G. Campbell Morgan, pastored Westminster Chapel in London. In a sermon delivered at the conference, Morgan turned to Ephesians 3:16: "That He would grant you, according to the riches of His glory, to be strengthened with might by His Spirit in the inner man."[18]

The emphasis on spiritual empowerment gave the English movement a practical, reformist component, which reflected Wesley's social holiness emphasis. Followers could point to Wesley's famous exposition of the Sermon on the Mount that prodded believers on to "every work of charity included, every thing which we give, or speak, or do, whereby our neighbour may be profited; whereby another man may receive any advantage, either in his body or soul."[19] Outreach to the poor, the establishment of orphanages, and homes for wayward women all pointed in that

---

[18] Herbert F. Stevenson, ed., *Keswick's Authentic Voice* (1959), 470.
[19] Wesley, Sermon 26, "Sermon on the Mount, VI," I.1, *Works*, 1:573.

direction. Women, as animated by the Spirit as men were, became vital leaders in social holiness organizations like the Salvation Army. The precedent set by Hannah Whitall Smith, Phoebe Palmer, and Amanda Berry Smith guided others into the pulpit. Palmer confidently proclaimed that the Bible and John Wesley called women to serve.[20]

GROWING DIVISIONS, HEALING, AND PREMILLENNIALISM

Adherents faced their greatest challenge in the late nineteenth century as church officials rooted out those who rode the so-called doctrinal hobbyhorse of perfection. Methodist Bishop Edward R. Ames, like a growing number of holiness opponents, thought the movement attracted extremists, "who preach entire sanctification year in and year out."[21] Ames considered it a dangerous theological myopia. By the late nineteenth century, even former holiness supporters lashed out at followers. The famous southern preacher Sam Jones remarked wryly: "There are a lot of these holiness folks who must have been preserved in vinegar, they are so sour."[22]

Despite the legalistic fervor of certain advocates, the movement grew precipitously. In the early part of the twentieth century there were as many as 250,000 holiness folk in the United States alone. Baptist, Methodist, and Presbyterian authorities viewed that growth with astonishment and horror. Second-blessing fellowships looked too much like churches within a church. Moreover, by the late nineteenth century adherents across the country and in England began to lay more emphasis on healing and the imminent return of Jesus, a doctrine called premillennialism. That development helped radicalize holiness, distancing it from mainline Protestantism, and leading to the pentecostal explosion of the early twentieth century.

Following the American Civil War, British premillennial theologians, a number affiliated with the Keswick movement, shaped the way American evangelicals understood history and destiny. Late in the century apocalyptic literature flooded the religious marketplace and Bible conferences held in the Northeast spread apocalyptic doctrine. They taught that onslaughts of modernism, industrialism, and immigration threatened the core of Christian civilization. As such, the revivalist

---

[20] See Wheatley, *Life and Letters of Phoebe Palmer*, 611–19.

[21] "Religious Items," the *Inter Ocean* (Chicago), 3 July 1875, 2.

[22] Kathleen Minnix, *Laughter in the Amen Corner: The Life of Evangelist Sam Jones* (1993), 145.

Dwight Moody described the role of the spirit-filled evangelist: "God has given me a life-boat, and said to me, 'Moody, save all you can.'"[23]

Divine healing captured the holiness imagination like premillennialism had.[24] Northern faith healers, including the medical doctor Charles Cullis, A. B. Simpson, R. Kelso Carter, and the "Elijah of Chicago," John Alexander Dowie, won an eager audience among holiness people. Cullis convinced John Inskip of the importance of praying for healing. After Inskip received relief from a debilitating headache through Cullis's ministry, the prominent holiness divine lent his support to what some called the faith cure. Cullis won over other well-known Methodists, Daniele Steele among them, and found favor with William Boardman and Asa Mahan, whose association with the Keswick convention and European holiness gave healing an international dimension. Seekers hoped for both physical relief and spiritual guidance. Christ's sanctifying work might break the chains of sickness as well as sin. The body, so thought many, was perfectible like the soul was. Writing in a holiness paper one devotee declared that "sickness and sins are both represented as being nailed to the cross" in scripture. Southern perfectionist apostle Mattie Perry asked "What makes man sick?" "It must be sin," she concluded, "for we have no account of Adam and Eve ever being sick before they sinned."[25]

Premillennialism and the faith cure looked shockingly novel to mainline critics. Methodist critics of the former branded them a Wesleyan heresy. John Wesley, they claimed, held an optimistic view of grace at odds with the more Calvinistic premillennialism. Opponents of faith healing claimed that miracles belonged to the New Testament era. Regardless, by the 1890s more and more holiness folk saw premillennialism and healing as essential components of Christianity. The doctrines gained a wide following in the American South and the Midwest. Moreover, these popular theologies were firmly linked in the minds of countless stalwarts. Southern preacher W. B. Godbey described that connection succinctly: "greater miracles will attend the second coming of Christ (for which we are constantly on the lookout) than bygone generations have ever witnessed."[26]

[23] Dwight L. Moody, *New Sermons* (New York, 1880), 535. See also Timothy P. Weber, *Living in the Shadow of the Second Coming: American Premillennialism, 1875–1925* (1987).
[24] See Heather D. Curtis, *Faith in the Great Physician: Suffering and Divine Healing in American Culture, 1860–1900* (2007).
[25] R. C. Oliver, "Sin and Sickness," *The Christian Witness and Advocate of Bible Holiness* (20 March 1884), 2; and Mattie Perry, "Divine Healing," *The Way of Faith* (25 December 1895), 3.
[26] W. B. Godbey, *Spiritual Gifts and Graces* (Cincinnati, 1895), 10.

BREAKING AWAY

From roughly 1896 to 1906, black and white holiness folk bat-
tled with church officials over doctrine, authority, and power. Hence,
Methodist perfectionists rankled at being placed in low-profile churches
or forced out of their denomination. Disgruntled sanctificationists who
chose to leave won the label "come outters." For the jaded faithful, one
of the most telling signs of the end was the apostate church. Holiness
people often cited their contempt for mainline religion and their disgust with the fallen church as a clear example of the world's demise.
Early splinter groups, like Daniel S. Warner's Church of God (Anderson), founded in 1880, and the Texas Holiness Association, organized in
1878, were deeply sectarian, intent on restoring the pure New Testament
church. In the 1890s black Baptist officials in Mississippi admonished
holiness leaders like C. P. Jones and C. H. Mason. Authorities rebuked
them for violating Baptist ordinances and espousing the double cure.
Jones and Mason incorporated the Church of God in Christ in 1897. A
variety of similar new denominations and fellowships cropped up around
the United States. The Pilgrim Holiness Church, which traced its roots
to an 1897 holiness union, and the Church of the Nazarene, founded
in 1908, drew together holiness associations and bands from across the
nation.[27]

As Timothy Smith observed, followers formed such unions, in part,
because of "recurrent outbursts of fanaticism among persons who were
members of associations but not of churches."[28] Most upsetting to many
was the "third blessing" heresy. It pointed to spiritual possibilities that
would inspire later pentecostals.

THE THIRD BLESSING

B. H. Irwin, an ex-Baptist itinerant preacher from the Midwest, added
new zeal to John Wesley's message of purity and power. Not satisfied
with his sanctification, Irwin looked for new light in the Wesleyan-
holiness canon. He poured over G. D. Watson's books, Thomas Upham's
biography of the mystic Madame Guyon, and the works of John Fletcher.
Each had written about a baptism by fire, or a purging work of the Spirit
as described by John the Baptist in Matthew 3:11: "I indeed baptize you

---

[27] See David Douglas Daniels, "The Cultural Renewal of Slave Religion: Charles Price
Jones and the Emergence of the Holiness Movement in Mississippi" (Ph.D. diss., Union
Theological Seminary, 1992); and Dieter, *Holiness Revival*, 200–32.

[28] Smith, *Called unto Holiness*, 27.

with water unto repentance: but he that cometh after me is mightier than I, whose shoes I am not worthy to bear: he shall baptize you with the Holy Ghost, and with fire." This third work of grace, Irwin thought, would take place subsequent to sanctification. He claimed to have undergone a "baptism of fire" at Enid, Oklahoma Territory in October 1895. Irwin subsequently reported on the experience in holiness papers. "The whole room seemed to be all luminous," he exclaimed. He was in the "midst of a fiery presence."[29] Irwin's new Fire-Baptized Holiness Church attracted religious adventurers, steeped in the popular theology of the Wesleyan-holiness tradition. Irwin later announced additional works of the Spirit. Using Godbey's translation of the New Testament Greek word for "power" as "dynamite," Irwin preached a "baptism of dynamite" in 1898. It would blast the devil.[30]

Irwin's hyperbolic religious imagination roiled the holiness movement. Moderates lined up to denounce the Iowa firebrand and distance themselves from his church. Yet his small but devoted band spread across the American South and Midwest. When fire-baptized enthusiasts reached Abilene, Kansas a local reporter attended a meeting to hear a long-haired revivalist shout "Fire! Fire! Fire! Bless you brother." "Beware," said the prophet, "Abilene will be destroyed in ninety days."[31] Initiates preached the possibilities of mystical religion and the perils of doomsday. Most importantly, Irwin's novel theology suggested that other works of the Holy Ghost awaited. Even the minister's fall from grace, widely publicized in holiness papers, could not dampen converts' fervor.

RESTLESS VISIONARIES AND THE ROOTS OF PENTECOSTALISM

Around the turn of the century, a number of holiness-affiliated mavericks were searching for new answers. Their practical theology was ad hoc and unsystematic, much as John Wesley's had been. The lives of A. J. Tomlinson, subsequent founder of the Church of God (Cleveland); Charles Fox Parham, a one-time Methodist minister and future pentecostal pioneer; and W. J. Seymour, African American itinerant and pentecostal leader, well illustrate the religious eclecticism of the day. All crisscrossed the nation in the late nineteenth and early twentieth

[29] G. D. Watson, "Rejoicing," *The Way of Faith* (6 November 1895), 2.
[30] Synan, *Holiness-Pentecostal Tradition*, 57.
[31] "A Queer Sect that Lives in Kansas," *Forth Worth Morning Register* (9 September 1900), 6.

centuries, seeking new religious knowledge and Holy Ghost empowerment.

Born an Indiana Quaker, Tomlinson dabbled in Populist politics
before channeling his energies into holiness-style populism.[32] By the
late 1890s he turned to the radical holiness movement. Holiness
Quaker evangelist Seth Cook Rees, the Hoosier "Earthquaker," inspired
Tomlinson as did the radical perfectionist Martin Wells Knapp. The latter's vivid imagery – of revival tornadoes and lightning bolts from pentecostal skies – drew him in. Tomlinson ventured across the United States
for religious direction, leaving behind his wife and children. He jour-
neyed to Frank Sandford's holiness camp called Shiloh, near Durham,
Maine. There, he found solace in Sandford's radical restorationist message and commitment to divine healing. Tomlinson set up a holiness
mission in Appalachia, modeled on Sanford's original. On other travels
Tomlinson learned of the work of Wesleyan visionary G. D. Watson,
higher life evangelist Dwight Moody, end-time healing prophet A. B.
Simpson, the fire-baptizer B. H. Irwin, and Methodist holiness publisher
and preacher H. C. Morrison.

Wesleyan-holiness and Higher Life luminaries shepherded countless
other seekers. Charles Fox Parham took the messages of his predecessors
in very new directions.[33] He looked to holiness and faith healing after
a severe bout with rheumatic fever while in college in Kansas. The
doctrinal and ministerial discipline of the Methodist Church, in which
he was ordained, ill-suited him. He left it in the mid-1890s and set off on
a freewheeling career as a healing preacher and radical holiness disciple.
Like Tomlinson, Parham also embraced Irwin's "third work" doctrine.
He set up a healing home in Topeka, Kansas, and published a bimonthly
journal, *The Apostolic Faith*. Yet, he was unsatisfied with Wesleyan and
Keswick theology; they lacked solid evidence of Holy Ghost anointing,
he worried. In 1900, he trekked across the country in search of tangible
evidence. He also traveled north to Sandford's holiness commune. As he
made his way there from Topeka, he stopped off at Zion City, Illinois,
to examine the work of John Alexander Dowie. He then moved on to A.
B. Simpson's Christian and Missionary Alliance school in Nyack, New
York. But, it was Sandford, in particular, who captivated the restless

---

[32] See R. G. Robins, *A. J. Tomlinson: Plainfolk Modernist* (2004); and H. D. Hunter,
"Tomlinson, Ambrose Jessup," in *The New International Dictionary of Pentecostal
and Charismatic Movements*, eds. S. M. Burgess and E. M. Van Der Maas (2002),
1143–45.

[33] See James R. Goff, Jr. *Fields White Unto Harvest: Charles F. Parham and the Missionary Origins of Pentecostalism* (1988).

Kansas preacher. Most importantly, Parham heard that Sandford's flock spoke in foreign tongues (xenoglossy) after they experienced Holy Spirit baptism.

Back in Topeka, Parham established a radical holiness Bible school. Acts chapter 2 inspired him and his new pupils: "And they were all filled with the Holy Ghost, and began to speak with other tongues, as the Spirit gave them utterance" (Acts 2:4, KJV). Hence, Parham claimed he and his students concluded that tongues-speaking was the sign they had anxiously awaited. By early January 1901 the Spirit had come, so they thought, and they were speaking in what they believed to be dozens of foreign languages. Agnes Ozman, a former Methodist at Parham's school, was the first to receive the gift. Local reporters who descended on the scene tried to make sense of it all. Parham was a disciple of Frank Sandford, wrote one newspaperman, who imparted his strange beliefs to Parham. "I never saw anything like it," one witness exclaimed. "They were racing about the room talking and gesticulating and using this strange and senseless language which they claim is the work from the Most High."[34]

Parham relocated his school to Houston, Texas in 1905, hoping to spread his message further and wider. It was there that he came into contact with another wayfaring seeker, William J. Seymour.[35] An African-American preacher from Louisiana, Seymour enrolled in Parham's school, after crisscrossing the country on a religious quest. Faced with poverty and debilitating Jim Crow laws in his home state, he set out for Indianapolis in 1895. Once there, he was converted at a Colored Methodist Episcopal church, where he took in the teachings of Wesley. Disappointed by Methodist views on end times and revelation, he soon began attending services of the Evening Light Saints, an integrated perfectionist group that would later be known as the Church of God (Anderson). From Indianapolis, Seymour made his way to Cincinnati, where, according to oral tradition, he visited God's Bible School, founded by Martin Wells Knapp. Knapp's premillennialism and radical holiness theories seem to have had an impact on him. Before Seymour ventured to Houston, he made one last stop in Jackson, Mississippi. There, he sought out C. P. Jones, the most prominent African-American holiness figure in the South. Jones' Wesleyan perfectionism and his

---

34 "A Queer Faith," *Topeka Daily Capital* (6 January 1901), 2.
35 See Douglas J. Nelson, "For Such a Time as This: The Story of William J. Seymour and the Azusa Street Revival" (Ph.D. diss., University of Birmingham, 1981); and Douglas Jacobsen, *Thinking in the Spirit: Theologies of the Early Pentecostal Movement* (2003), 59–65.

abilities as a leader impressed Seymour greatly. As a result of his many encounters, Seymour's theology fused Wesleyan perfectionism and Holy Ghost empowerment.

Parham upheld Jim Crow laws in his school in Houston. Seymour was only allowed to participate in classes by sitting in an adjacent hallway. He would also not be allowed to minister to whites. Still, the budding preacher imbibed the pentecostal theology of Parham's Apostolic Faith. Seymour first heard the "Bible evidence" of speaking in tongues from Lucy Farrow, a native of Norfolk, Virginia, niece of the renowned abolitionist Frederick Douglass, and a worker at Parham's school. Seymour's short stay at the school – a total of five weeks – was enough time for him to accept the premillennial view of tongues as a preparation for world missions. Both Seymour and Parham held a Wesleyan view of sanctification as a second work of grace. So, too, did most other early pentecostals. Many added pentecostal baptism, and subsequent tongues speech, to that theological formula.

THE AZUSA STREET REVIVAL

News of Seymour's preaching skills made its way west to a black holiness church in Los Angeles. That congregation invited him to take its pulpit. The church was not prepared for his tongues-as-evidence doctrine, so Seymour and other seekers of Spirit baptism secured a building at 312 Azusa Street in an industrial part of town. The interracial revival that erupted there in April 1906 created a stir in the city and well beyond.[36] Journalists ridiculed the "holy rollers" who crammed into the meetinghouse, and moderate holiness folk shunned "tonguers" as devilish pretenders. But, that did not keep away the curious. Under Seymour's leadership congregants spoke in tongues, performed healings, and prophesied about the end of history. News of the West Coast "Pentecost" swept across the country. Stalwarts viewed themselves as standing at the end of a tradition and the end of the world. Theological predecessors had led the way, but had not arrived. God lifted up Martin Luther to emphasize the doctrine of justification, announced the *Apostolic Faith*, the Azusa mission's monthly. "He raised up another reformer in John Wesley to establish Bible holiness in the church. Then he raised up Dr. Cullis who brought back to the world the wonderful doctrine of divine healing."[37] Still, all of those, according to initiates, lacked the baptism of the Holy Ghost.

---

[36] Cecil M. Robeck, *The Azusa Street Mission and Revival* (2006).
[37] "The Pentecostal Baptism Restored," *The Apostolic Faith* (October 1906), 1; *The Apostolic Faith* (February-March 1907), 7.

Participants who traveled from around the nation and across the Atlantic returned to their churches in America and England and reenacted the Azusa baptism. Holiness and Higher Life newspapers, tracts, and books spread the new message broadly. A. A. Boddy, a British minister and newspaper editor, recounted the remarkable mixing of the races he saw at Azusa. Even "preachers of the Southern States were willing and eager to go over to those negro people at Los Angeles and have fellowship with them," he announced.[38] The miracles and equality of the Spirit at Azusa, thought many, heralded the revival of true religion. Holiness leaders from the Church of God in Christ (Memphis, Tennessee), the Church of God (Cleveland, Tennessee), and the Pentecostal Holiness Church (Georgia and the Carolinas) took pilgrimages to Azusa Street. Later denominations like the Assemblies of God traced their church back to Parham and Seymour. Diversity marked the new movement: pentecostals ranged from Wesleyan-holiness, to Reformed, to Unitarian.

The end-time revival that burst from Azusa Street spread far in the first decades of the century. T. B. Barratt, a Methodist minister from Norway, brought the Azusa message back to his country in 1906. And, the *Apostolic Faith* reported tongues-speaking at revivals in China, Hawaii, Canada, Africa, Australia, and New Zealand. The 1936 religious census registered 350,000 followers in the United States alone. Believers were united in their opposition to modernism and loose living. Yet, their pragmatic impulse led them to adopt the latest technology – printed matter and then radio and television – to spread their message. In the late-twentieth century, pentecostal televangelists – Jimmy Swaggart, Oral Roberts, and Jim Bakker – broadcast the faith to the nation and the world. Musical innovators such as Elvis Presley, Tammy Wynette, B. B. King, Jerry Lee Lewis, Johnny Cash, and Sister Rosetta Tharpe had roots in the tradition. One of the most successful media pioneers of the faith was Sister Aimee Semple McPherson, a Canadian-born evangelist who made her way to California and became a Christian celebrity.

THE CHARISMATIC MOVEMENT

The charismatic revival that boomed in mid-century America harnessed new ideas and technologies as well. Also called neo-pentecostalism, it reflected John Wesley's theology of perfectionist aspiration and the possibility of physical and religious fulfillment in this life. Charismatics are largely white, often attend mainline churches, emphasize the gifts of the Spirit (*charismata* in Greek) – healing, tongues

---

[38] A. A. Boddy, "The Southern States," *Confidence* (September 1912), 209.

speech, and prophecy – and some adhere to a gospel of wealth, known as "word of faith" theology. The movement originated within traditional pentecostalism, but quickly moved beyond it.

Oral Roberts, a Pentecostal Holiness Church evangelist from Oklahoma, led a nationwide healing ministry for decades beginning in the late 1940s. He joined Jack Coe and William Branham as a new kind of pentecostal superstar. Roberts's powerful stage presence and media savvy won him a massive audience. In 1954, Roberts began broadcasting his meetings over nine television stations. Roughly a year later, his weekly program was running on ninety-one domestic and two foreign stations. He went on to found Oral Roberts University and thrust his ministry onto the world stage.

The pentecostal icon appealed not only to pentecostals, but also to Baptists, holiness people, Presbyterians, Catholics, and Methodists. Television watchers eagerly listened as Roberts told them that gifts to his ministry would be returned sevenfold by God. He shocked traditional pentecostals in 1968, when he decided to leave the Pentecostal Holiness Church and become a United Methodist. A Methodist as a youth, he made the change because he thought the United Methodist church "had the widest framework and freest pulpit."[39] Methodism also lent his ministry a respectability that pentecostalism could not. And his acceptance by the United Methodists revealed a change in mainline perceptions of pentecostals.

Roberts's life signaled larger trends in the ever-changing holiness-pentecostal world. He, and many other charismatics, moved slowly toward the religious and social mainstream. Like Methodists in the previous century, pentecostals adopted some of the lifestyles and tastes of the middle class. The eye-popping religious services and jut-jawed stridency of earlier years faded.[40]

Demos Shakarian, an Armenian pentecostal, formed the Full Gospel Businessmen's Fellowship International in 1952. A California dairy entrepreneur, Shakarian organized the group to spread pentecostal experience to those outside the movement. It promoted a gospel of wealth that well suited budding evangelical capitalists. Others crossed the pentecostal/mainline divide. Assemblies of God minister David du Plessis reached out to the ecumenical community from the 1950s forward. However, his denomination excommunicated him in 1962 for doing so. But, many other efforts at rapprochement succeeded. In 1960, the National

---

[39] David Edwin Harrell, Jr., *Oral Roberts: An American Life* (1985), 295.
[40] "The Third Force in Christendom," *Life* (6 June 1958), 113, 116.

Association of Evangelicals made general superintendent of the Assemblies of God church Thomas Zimmerman its head. Once rejected by such organizations, white pentecostals now entered the conservative Protestant camp.

By the 1970s and 1980s, critics questioned the concessions the faithful had made to the culture around them. Speaking of television preacher Jim Bakker, one white pentecostal minister lashed out: "Rhetorically denying that it wanted in any way to be part of this world, the church showed an amazing ability to adapt to prevailing currents."[41] Television has exhibited the tradition's financial and numerical success while bridging the pentecostal/nonpentecostal divide. The nation's most watched religious network, the pentecostal, charismatic Trinity Broadcasting Network, glorifies wealth and success as it transcends classical pentecostalism. John Hagee, T. D. Jakes, and scandal-prone televangelist Robert Tilton preach a gospel of wealth, word of faith, theology to a cross-denominational audience. The network boasts more than 12,500 network and cable television affiliates around the globe.

As black and white pentecostals made their peace with the mainstream, non-pentecostal Protestants looked to the sanctified tradition for guidance. Already by the 1920s, Aimee Semple McPherson was drawing mainline Protestants into her Angelus Temple. Yet, in those years, Methodists, Baptist, and Presbyterian ministers who experienced Spirit baptism faced ostracism or excommunication. In the 1950s and 1960s, as the profile and reputation of pentecostalism rose, denominational officials were less likely to punish charismatics in their midst. In 1960, the Reverend Dennis Bennett announced to his St. Mark's Episcopal congregation that he had received the gift of tongues. That news set off a firestorm of protests, though Bennett gained some support. Removed from his California pulpit, he took a failing Episcopal church in Seattle, which soon boasted 2,000 members. In these years the charismatic Jesus People won a following among dispossessed baby boomers. Neo-pentecostalism also gained converts among Catholic students and faculty at Notre Dame University and Duquesne University. Kevin Ranaghan, a theology professor at the former, acted as a chief apologist for the movement among Catholics.

In the coming decades, charismatic churches and associations spread around the globe, much like holiness groups and pentecostalism had before. Anglican Renewal Ministries and Headway provide resources

---

41 John A. Sims quoted in David Edwin Harrell, Jr., *Pat Robertson: A Personal, Political and Religious Portrait* (1987), 132–33.

and religious guidance for thousands of Christians across the United Kingdom. In Africa and Latin America, independent house churches gather likeminded neo-pentecostals for worship and prayer. Africa contains some of the largest charismatic fellowships in the world. Nigeria, the Ivory Coast, Ghana, and Zimbabwe are home to thriving congregations, small house churches, and mainline renewalist groups. Religious scholar P. D. Hocken observes that Latin America's Protestant churches have undergone a "pentecostalization" in recent years.[42]

Indeed, the movement has flourished in traditional churches.[43] Neo-pentecostalism has made much progress among Baptists, Presbyterians, and Methodists. Methodist charismatics have looked to their denomination's roots for direction. Observers have called them third-wave Methodists. Charismatics within the tradition, borrowing from the language of the culture wars, have referred to themselves as Methodism's silent majority. *Good News* magazine, first published in 1967, from Wilmore, Kentucky, caters to these individuals and others within the Wesleyan tradition. And Aldersgate Renewal Ministries has taken the lead in bringing together renewalists.

In 1976, the United Methodist Church dealt directly with the influence of neo-pentecostalism. Denominational officials counseled patience and understanding. A church-adopted position paper noted that as many as 18 percent of United Methodists identified with the movement. "John Wesley's theology of grace, properly understood," leaders instructed, "can ground charismatic United Methodists in a tradition that can give direction to their enthusiasm.... Let us, therefore, reexamine Wesley's theology of grace in light of the charismatic gifts and experiences."[44]

Non-United Methodist organizations like the Wesleyan Holiness Charismatic Fellowship has gathered former Nazarenes, Free Methodists, and Wesleyans, who embrace tongues speech while still holding to their Wesleyan heritage. Methodists and non-Methodists alike are claiming John Wesley as their exemplar. Methodist churches that participated in the 2007 Worldwide Day of Healing reveal as much. "We have healing prayer at both services," the pastor of Will Rogers United Methodist Church told a Tulsa, Oklahoma reporter. That fit well within

---

[42] P. D. Hocken, "Charismatic Movement," 513.

[43] For material on pentecostal and charismatic trends in mainline denominations, see various chapters in Edith Blumhofer, Russell P. Splitter, and Grant A. Wacker, eds., *Pentecostal Currents in American Protestantism* (1999); and Vinson Synan, ed., *Aspects of Pentecostal Charismatic Origins* (1975).

[44] "Guidelines," *Daily Christian Advocate* (27 April 1976), 55–56.

his tradition, he argued. "The Methodist Church has a long history of praying for healing, going back to John Wesley, its founder."[45]

CONCLUSION

At a fundamental level, the holiness, pentecostal, and charismatic movements bear the imprint of John Wesley. Certainly some denominations and associations – like the Church of the Nazarene, the International Pentecostal Holiness Church, and the Wesleyan Holiness Charismatic Fellowship – are more indebted to Wesley than Unitarian or Reformed wings of the movement (the former represented by the Pentecostal Assemblies of the World and the latter by the Assemblies of God). Still, Wesley's focus on the pursuit of greater works of the Spirit remains evident among all. Furthermore, as Richard P. Heitzenrater indicates, the "Wesleyan heritage takes its vital energy from the dynamic imagery of the spiritual pilgrimage."[46] An openness to innovative worship styles and theological exploration has been critical to holiness, pentecostal, and charismatic experience. The largest of these three movements, pentecostalism, was arguably foremost the product of just such an open Methodist tradition. The religious sociologist David Martin states the point clearly. "In almost every respect," he observes, "Pentecostalism replicated Methodism: in its entrepreneurship and adaptability, lay participation and enthusiasm, and in its splintering and fractiousness."[47] That remark applies as well to holiness and charismatic groups. Unhindered by the same constraints that bind traditional Protestants, their churches continue to outpace more mainline denominations and to test the limits of John Wesley's theology of the Spirit.

[45] "Worldwide Day of Healing Set," Knight-Ridder/Tribune Business News (22 September 2007), eLibrary, Proquest CSA, BOSTON PUBLIC LIBRARY (accessed 5/29/2008) http://elibrary.bigchalk.com.ezproxy.bpl.org/curriculum.

[46] Heitzenrater, *Wesley and the People Called Methodists*, 321.

[47] David Martin, *Pentecostalism: The World Their Parish* (2002), 8.

16 The African American wing of the Wesleyan tradition

DENNIS C. DICKERSON

Blacks embraced Methodism when the first Wesleyan preachers arrived, in 1766, from England to colonial America. The conversion of Betty, a slave in New York City, that same year demonstrates that blacks were among the first Americans to affiliate with the Methodist movement. Moreover, Captain Thomas Webb initiated revivals in Brooklyn in 1766 that laid foundations for a biracial congregation that eventually emerged as the African Wesleyan Methodist Episcopal Church.[1] Through developments like this, African Americans quickly moved beyond being introduced to Methodism by third parties. They were exposed to Wesleyan hymnody, sermons, doctrine, and discipline first hand in innumerable camp meetings, revivals, and chapel services.

As early Methodist members, blacks drew emancipationist themes from Wesleyan beliefs and embedded black spirituality in Wesleyan worship and devotional practices. These interpretations, blacks believed, showed that their understanding of Methodism was the linear embodiment of what John Wesley intended for his religious movement. Piety, deep and expressive spirituality, and social holiness became for African Americans the distinctive marks of Methodism and a basis to judge the authenticity of Methodist professions and practices from both white institutions and white individuals. Black Methodists, whether they remained in organic affiliation with Wesleyan whites or as ministers and members in independent African American religious bodies, participated in various interracial and interdenominational congregations and conferences. Beyond these affiliations, they agreed that black self-determination allowed them an effective witness for the liberationist thrust that lay within Methodist doctrine and beliefs.

Joining Captain Thomas Webb as one of numerous white Wesleyan preachers who evangelized biracial audiences were Francis Asbury, Freeborn Garrettson, James O'Kelly, and several others. African Americans

---

[1] This is the present day Bridge Street AME church in Brooklyn, New York.

welcomed their salvific messages and responded to Methodist stands against slavery. Although statistics are sketchy, the census of blacks in various venues showed their broad embrace of Methodism. In 1784, for example, 1,500 blacks comprised 10 percent of the country's 15,000 Methodists. In 1786, there were 1,890 Wesleyan blacks and, in 1797, they numbered 12,215. James O'Kelly reported that the number of his black Methodist parishioners in Virginia stood at 1,990 in 1790; 2,328 in 1791; and 1,117 in 1796.

EARLY AFRICAN AMERICAN METHODIST LEADERS

Winthrop S. Hudson, in explaining why the Baptists and Methodists enjoyed wide success among African Americans in the eighteenth century, credited both sects for their openness in authorizing blacks to preach.[2] Black Methodist clergy, sometimes in cooperation with white colleagues and at other times alone, proved effective in attracting African Americans, both slave and free, to the Wesleyan fold. The most prominent of these preachers were Harry Hoosier and Richard Allen, both of whom rose from slavery to freedom to become well-known itinerant ministers.

Hoosier was born in North Carolina around 1750, some years before Methodism arrived in colonial America. He was manumitted from slavery before the end of the American Revolution. Probably after he was free, Hoosier was converted and became a Methodist. He was authorized to preach some time in the early 1780s. Word of his proficiency in the pulpit spread rapidly in Wesleyan circles and soon he was accompanying Francis Asbury on various evangelistic tours. Other Methodist ministers, including Freeborn Garrettson, impressed by his ability to draw large crowds of blacks and whites, also invited Hoosier to travel with them. He died around 1806.

Richard Allen, like Hoosier, was born before Methodism spread to the British North American colonies. Allen was born in slavery on February 14, 1760 in Philadelphia and sold, with his family, to Stokeley Sturgis, a Delaware farmer of modest means. Methodists frequently preached to blacks and whites in the area where the Sturgis farm was located. Hence, Allen was converted to Christianity in 1777 under the preaching of Freeborn Garrettson. The Methodist meeting where Allen's religious awakening occurred was threaded with the rituals of Wesleyan conversion.

---

[2]   Winthrop S. Hudson, "The American Context as an Area for Research in Black Church Studies," *Church History* 52 (1983), 169.

Allen and other converts repeated words from Acts 12:7 and from the classic Wesley hymn, "And Can It Be That I Should Gain." The scripture recounted Peter's imprisonment and credited an angel with setting him free. Peter was directed to "Arise up quickly and his chains fell off from his hands." Drawing on this passage, Wesley's hymn declared "the dungeon flamed with light; my chains fell off, my heart was free." Allen joined many Methodist converts in using these words to memorialize his conversion: "my dungeon shook... and my chains flew off."[3]

According to David Hempton, Methodist conversion often coincided with some adolescent crisis.[4] Perhaps this was Allen's experience at age 17, and maybe the same was true for Hoosier, probably a young man in his twenties. The conversion freed Allen from sin and instilled in him a resolve to be free from slavery. He and Hoosier, from a distinctive black Methodist perspective, viewed their salvation as an emancipatory act freeing them from spiritual and servile bondage.

Allen's conversion also showed how this religious experience comforted him when his impecunious slave owner sold away his mother and some of his siblings. Hempton argues that conversions often gave cover to adolescent difficulties that many Methodist youth, especially those in slavery, confronted.[5] At a deeper level, Allen and other blacks construed their religious awakening as an emancipatory event which provided them with a greater appreciation for Methodism and its liberationist possibilities. Salvation from sin was only one component of this religious transaction. The process helped to move Allen toward liberation from slavery. Methodist evangelicalism became a conduit and catalyst for these salvific occurrences. The testimony of Hoosier and Allen, and their fealty to this evangelical and egalitarian movement, showed a depth of commitment and understanding that few Wesleyan whites experienced.

Hoosier and Allen were manumitted from slavery within a few years of each other. Allen had persuaded Sturgis to allow Methodists to preach in the slave owner's house and this paved the way for his master's conversion. Sturgis permitted Allen to purchase his freedom by working to save $2000, and accepted this amount from Allen in 1783. When the "Christmas Conference" convened in Baltimore in 1784, Hoosier and Allen, now free black preachers, were present as founding ministers of the Methodist Episcopal Church (MEC). Hoosier, however, bypassed the

---

[3]   See Dennis C. Dickerson, "Scripture and Hymnody in the Conversion Experience of Richard Allen," *A.M.E. Church Review* (Jan.–Mar. 2008), 57–60.

[4]   Hempton, *Methodism: Empire of the Spirit*, 65.

[5]   Ibid., 63.

formal institutional role that shaped Allen's subsequent ecclesiastical career.

EMERGENCE OF AUTONOMOUS AFRICAN METHODIST CHURCHES

Allen founded the Free African Society in 1787, built Bethel African Methodist Episcopal Church in Philadelphia in 1794, and was elected and consecrated as the first Bishop of the African Methodist Episcopal Church (AME) in 1816. Formally ordained and serving as the world's first black bishop, Allen had become a "quintessential Wesleyan."[6] Methodist doctrine and discipline shaped the structure and religious practices of this new denominational body. Methodist hymnody blended with black musical idioms and influenced its worship styles.[7] And Wesleyan "practical divinity" required AME members to fight slavery, defend the rights of free blacks, and oppose racist practices in both church and society.

The African Methodist Episcopal Church, as Allen envisaged it, embodied authentic Wesleyanism.[8] The racial incident at St. George's MEC church which precipitated the walkout of Allen and his followers has been viewed primarily as a racial protest. Actually, Allen (who later observed that the Christmas Conference showed Methodist clergy as increasingly pretentious and elitist) believed that declining spirituality pervaded the once evangelistic and egalitarian sect that awakened him to Christianity. The racist treatment that St. George's white officers imposed on black Methodist members in 1787 was evidence of this reduced religiosity. Even though the appeal of Methodism had reached across lines of class, region, and race, its ardent opposition to slavery had been abandoned. Diminished advocacy for these sacred tasks described an increasingly bourgeois Methodism which had departed from its insurgent social and religious origins. Perhaps African Methodism

---

[6] Charles H. Wesley, *Richard Allen: Apostle of Freedom* (1935) remains a useful biography; Richard S. Newman, *Freedom's Prophet: Bishop Richard Allen, the AME Church, and the Black Founding Fathers* (2008) offers a provocative interpretation that casts him in the context of the Atlantic world and in juxtaposition to white "founding fathers."

[7] See Dennis C. Dickerson, "Heritage and Hymnody: Richard Allen and the Making of African Methodism," in Mark Noll and Edith Blumhofer, eds., *Sing Them over again to Me: Hymns and Hymnbooks in America* (2006), 175–93.

[8] For more details and documentation on this summary of AME history, see Dennis C. Dickerson, *Religion, Race, and Region: Research Notes in A.M.E. Church History* (1995); and Dickerson, *A Liberated Past: Explorations in A.M.E. Church History* (2003).

could recover what Wesleyan whites had relinquished. A new Methodist denomination, albeit one populated mainly by blacks, seemed to be the answer. Francis Asbury said in 1796 that "I have thought if we had entered here to preach only to the Africans, we should probably have done better."[9] Methodism in America, Asbury believed, would have had greater spirituality if blacks had been the primary focus of Wesleyan evangelists. These sentiments, Allen believed, validated his founding of African Methodism.

If Hoosier had any grievances against Wesleyan whites, they are not cited in the few records that survive. Most black Methodists, however, affirmed that the self-determination that Allen championed also appealed to them. While the majority remained with the MEC, they formed separate churches and embraced a similar autonomy to that of Allen's (AME) Bethel church. Congregations in Oxon Hill, Maryland, founded in 1791; Zoar in Philadelphia, beginning in 1796; Bryan in Grasonville, Maryland, established in 1800; and innumerable others embraced the emancipationist ethos that Allen forged, even though they did not follow him into an independent ecclesiastical structure.[10]

James Varick (1750–1827) and Peter Spencer (1782–1843) resembled Allen more than Harry Hoosier and other blacks who stayed in the MEC. Born in Newburgh, New York, Varick's biographer claimed that either Philip Embury or Thomas Webb converted him and led him to John Street MEC church in New York City. Hence, Varick joined Hoosier and Allen as a part of the first generation of American Methodists. Though heralded as the founder of the African Methodist Episcopal Zion Church (AME Zion), one denominational historian declared that some Varick protégés played a similarly large role in starting this second black Wesleyan body.[11] Although Varick was older than Allen, he secured his ministerial credentials later than the AME founder. Allen was ordained as a deacon in 1799 and as an elder in 1816. The AME Zion leader was ordained a deacon in 1806 and an elder in 1820.

Although the dramatic encounter with racism that stirred Allen to action in Philadelphia was less salient with Varick and his colleagues in New York City, policies of segregation and subordination at John Street MEC church moved them to separate in 1796. In 1821, the New York group established the AME Zion Church. They rejected Allen, now

---

[9] *The Journal and Letters of Francis Asbury* (1958), 2:78.
[10] See J. Gordon Melton, *A Will to Choose: The Origins of African American Methodism* (2005), 139.
[11] See Reginald Broadnax, "Was James Varick the Founder of the A.M.E. Zion Church?" *A.M.E. Zion Quarterly Review* 109.1 (January 1997), 37–47.

a bishop, as a possible leader and eschewed white Methodist control. Skeptical of black episcopal authority and arbitrary white governance, the Zionites bypassed the bishopric during the first few decades of their institutional existence, in favor of superintendents who were elected for four-year terms.[12]

Peter Spencer, another African Methodist preacher who was born a slave in Delaware, led his followers out of Asbury MEC church in Wilmington, Delaware in 1805 for the same racial reasons that drove other Wesleyan blacks into separate congregations. Spencer's Union Church of Africans became a denomination in 1813 and, like the Zionites, initially eschewed the episcopacy. The Spencer churches split in 1848 and respectively developed as the African Union Methodist Protestant Church and the Union Methodist Episcopal Church, two religious bodies that eventually elected bishops.[13]

Despite the founding of black Wesleyan bodies, most black Methodists during the ante-bellum period remained members of the MEC. In 1816, for example, they numbered 42,304. After the sectional split in 1844, black membership in the MEC (North) reached 100,000 in 1856, whereas there were 200,000 in the MEC South in 1861. The three black Wesleyan bodies, with very few exceptions, were barred from the southern states. They spread primarily within the Northeast, the Chesapeake, the Midwest, and Canada. In 1837, the AME included 7,288 members, the AME Zion had 2,884 members, and the Union Church of Africans grew to 1,263 members. There were 20,000 members in the AME in 1856, and 4,600 members in the AME Zion in 1860.

THE WESLEYAN CHARACTER OF EARLY BLACK METHODISM

Wesleyan blacks embraced Methodism out of their experiences as slaves and as a racially proscribed population. Their understanding of Wesleyan doctrine drew from a deep well of insights that many Methodist whites could not fathom. "Practical divinity" and "the new creation," terms developed in the copious writings of later Wesleyan scholars,[14] reflected core facets of the Methodist message that blacks

---

[12] See William J. Walls, *The African Methodist Episcopal Zion Church* (1974).

[13] Lewis V. Baldwin, *"Invisible" Strands in African Methodism: A History of the African Union Methodist Protestant Church and Union American Methodist Episcopal Churches* (1983).

[14] Thomas A. Langford, *Practical Divinity*, esp. 7, 20; Randy L. Maddox, *Responsible Grace*, 16–17; and Richard P. Heitzenrater, "God With Us: Grace and the Spiritual

fully adopted. "Practical divinity" referred to John Wesley's blend of embodying God's love in service to people, especially the disadvantaged. "The new creation" posited God's commandment to renew both humankind and the earth. Blacks believed that these ideas – preached and communicated through sermons, hymns, and the abolitionist stands of Wesley and numerous Methodist preachers – required a vigorous practice of social holiness. Therefore, their churches explicitly fused salvation from sin with corresponding obligations to rescue blacks from slavery and white hegemony.

Perhaps Richard Allen and Sojourner Truth best exemplified these Wesleyan attributes. For example, despite the danger of disease, Allen volunteered (along with Absalom Jones) to bring relief to the victims of the 1793 yellow fever epidemic and to bury the dead. Allen's Bethel AME church provided economic, educational, and other social amenities to parishioners and others in Philadelphia. He participated in debates about emigration to Haiti, expatriation and trade with Africa, and strategies to achieve black advancement in the United States. Numerous efforts to undermine slavery and to assist those trying to escape it also marked Allen's "practical divinity" and his pursuit of "the new creation." Sojourner Truth became an influential abolitionist and women's rights advocate during the ante-bellum period. Although she had only a brief affiliation with the AME Zion Church in New York City, Wesleyan sanctification and perfectionism were foundational experiences in how Truth defined herself religiously. Born a slave in New York in 1797, and freed by the state's gradual emancipation law, Wesleyan ideas aided her identity transfer from being Isabella Hardenburgh to her invented identity as Sojourner Truth. Her best biographer, Nell Painter, noted that Truth remembered "being baptized in the Holy Spirit." Moreover, she had "a second birth of entire sanctification" and then gained "an assurance of salvation that gave her the self-confidence to oppose the rich and powerful of this world."[15]

Frederick Douglass was a premier abolitionist in the ante bellum period and the undisputed spokesman for African Americans in the post-bellum era. While he never identified himself as a devout Methodist, Douglass embodied the Wesleyan praxis of "practical divinity." His stubborn and unwavering advocacy of black civil rights drew in part from the public ministry of Richard Allen. Concerning the AME founder, Douglass acknowledged that he was an "ideal character" and deserved

Senses in John Wesley's Theology," in Robert K. Johnson et al., *Grace upon Grace* (1999), 87–97.
[15] Nell I. Painter, *Sojourner Truth: A Life, A Symbol* (1996), 30, 39.

credit for establishing African Methodism. During his experience in Baltimore as an urban slave, Douglass encountered the emancipationist ethos of African Methodism. He joined Bethel AME church and remembered with reverence "the quiet teaching" of Edward Waters, later the denomination's third bishop. After he escaped from slavery in 1838, Douglass settled in New Bedford, Massachusetts and attended the white MEC church. His disenchantment with the segregation and mistreatment of blacks in the congregation led him to join the local AME Zion church. His abolitionist pastor, Thomas James, exposed Douglass to church-based opposition to slavery and renewed his license to exhort. James, who promoted Douglass as a licensed preacher, recalled that:

> On one occasion, after I had addressed a white audience on the slavery question, I called on Fred Douglass, whom I saw among the auditors, to relate his story. He did so, and in a year from that time he was in the lecture field with Parker Pillsbury and other leading abolitionist orators.[16]

His affiliation with both AME and AME Zion churches demonstrates the Wesleyan influence upon Douglass. Though he forsook the ministry, Douglass's public involvement mirrored the same social holiness that Richard Allen and Sojourner Truth exhibited.

Wesleyan whites who were serious about the social insurgency that John Wesley espoused could empathize with black Methodists who saw much to correct in both church and society. They also discovered that their views about social holiness sometimes put them at odds with the increasingly institutionalized MEC, which frequently reflected the pernicious racist views of its secular environment. When the denomination split over the issue of slavery, the seeming abolitionism of the northern body did not prevent its ministers and members from practicing the same racial discrimination that afflicted the larger society. Hence, African Americans in both the MEC (North) and the MEC South, upon learning about black Wesleyan bodies, shifted their affiliation to these groups whenever they could. That Allen, Truth, and Douglass found support and like-minded activists in the AME and AME Zion churches showed that these religious bodies, despite organizational growth, retained an emancipationist ethos, which was more inviting to the few African American clergy and laity who could exercise these choices.

A good example is Dandridge Davis. Born free in Virginia in 1807, Davis migrated with his family to Kentucky where he joined the MEC.

16 Thomas James, *The Life of Rev. Thomas James* (1886).

He received a license to preach soon after his conversion. He was solicited to take a tour through Kentucky, Virginia, North and South Carolina, and Georgia to preach the glad tidings of salvation to blacks and whites. Though unfamiliar with African Methodism, Davis eventually "was directed by the Spirit to seek his oppressed brethren," not knowing that black Wesleyan bodies had been established to pursue this same objective. In 1834 he was invited to an AME camp meeting where he met Bishop Morris Brown and Reverend (later Bishop) William Paul Quinn. After several days at the meeting Davis was convinced that the Lord had called him "to unite with this people." He served as an AME pastor until his death in 1847.[17]

Similarly, Henry M. Turner, born free in 1834 in Newberry Courthouse, South Carolina, joined the MEC South in Abbeville in 1848. Between 1853 and 1858, he traveled as a licensed preacher to evangelize African Americans in South Carolina, Georgia, Alabama, and Louisiana. In New Orleans he learned about the AME. He united with the denomination in St. Louis at the Missouri Annual Conference and served as pastor to congregations in Baltimore and Washington, DC. In 1863 he became the nation's first black chaplain in the United States Army. After the Civil War he led the effort for AME expansion in Georgia. He held various political offices including a brief term in the state legislature where he was unjustly expelled in 1868 along with other black lawmakers. He was elected bishop in 1880.[18]

BLACK WESLEYANISM IN THE POST-WAR AND RECONSTRUCTION PERIOD

The era of the Civil War and Reconstruction could be construed as a jubilee period in the black Wesleyan experience. Proclamations from pulpits in African American Methodist churches in Philadelphia, New York City, and other urban venues, and in rural "brush arbors" in the slave-owning South, envisaged a "new creation" in which bondage would be abolished and the humanity of blacks would be affirmed. This vision of black Methodists, often expressed in the poignant lyrics of their sorrow songs and in the cadences of unlettered preachers, seemed to reach fruition in this era of black emancipation and enfranchisement. Just as the blood of Jesus Christ expiated the sins of humankind, blood that

---

[17] A. R. Green, *The Life of the Rev. Dandridge Davis of the African M. E. Church* (Pittsburgh: Benjamin F. Peterson, 1850), 20–23, 26–29.

[18] See Stephen W. Angell, *Bishop Henry McNeal Turner and African American Religion in the South* (1992).

was spilled on countless Civil War battlefields washed away the moral blight of slavery. AME Bishop Daniel A. Payne, when addressing emancipated blacks in 1862 in Washington, DC, rejoiced that freedom for a captive people was being accomplished and that God's judgment was being enacted upon a nation stained with race-based servitude.[19] Moreover, black Methodist preachers enlisted as chaplains in the Union Army and northern black parishes functioned as recruiting stations for African American soldiers. When the Civil War ended, a large harvest of new members in the former Confederacy awaited black Methodist groups. Missionaries from the MEC, the AME, and the AME Zion rushed to the southern states to evangelize the former slaves. The two African Methodist denominations had the greatest success. Between 1866 and 1876, for example, AME membership grew from 50,000 to 300,000.

Black Methodist clergy and laity pursued a Wesleyan witness in the civic arena. Attention to the spiritual needs of emancipated slaves without a joint effort to safeguard their citizenship rights and their economic interests would have lessened the loyalty of these new members in the Methodist fold. Despite their failure to curve the oppressive crop lien system, black politicians, including many African American Methodists, succeeded in establishing public schools and founding state-run orphanages, homes for the aged, asylums for the blind, and other social institutions to benefit the black population. In describing the AME mission to former slaves, Reginald F. Hildebrand characterized these blended church and civic involvements as pursuing a "gospel of freedom."[20]

As the work of African Methodists in the MEC, AME, and AME Zion expanded into the former Confederacy, whites in the MEC South feared that black communicants in this branch of Methodism would affiliate with one of these non-southern bodies. They preferred that blacks should form another black Methodist body that shared their sectional perspectives. While agreeing with their white counterparts about common ties of regional affinity, black ministers and members in the MEC South envied the independence and self-determination that the AME and AME Zion denominations represented. Both blacks and whites were conscious that black membership in the MEC South had dwindled from 200,000 to 70,000, largely because of aggressive recruitment from the three northern Methodist bodies. Hence, in 1870, bishops of the MEC South met with representatives of black conferences and congregations

[19] Daniel Alexander Payne, "Welcome to the Ransomed," in Milton C. Sernett, ed., *Afro-American Religious History* (1985), 217–28.
[20] Reginald F. Hildebrand, "Richard Harvey Cain, African Methodism and the Gospel of Freedom," *A.M.E. Church Review* (Jan.–Mar. 2001), 42–44.

in Jackson, Tennessee, and constituted them as the Colored Methodist Episcopal Church (CME). Despite the paternalistic intentions of CME benefactors, the denomination served the same constituency as its other black Methodist competitors and developed the same impatience toward the oppression of African Americans. The CME as much as the AME and AME Zion, and the Black jurisdictions within the MEC stood in the public square as advocates of social holiness in behalf of their aggrieved communities.[21]

Despite competition among the black Methodist groups, each connected its institutional identity with obligations to renew creation. Although mainly focused on the elevation of African Americans, black Methodists articulated their Wesleyan perspectives in broad terms. As full participants in London at the first ecumenical conference on Methodism in 1881, for example, they defined the raison d'etre of their denominations in familiar Wesleyan terminology. Lucius H. Holsey, a CME bishop, observed that "Methodism is peculiarly fitted to elevate and purify society because there is in pure Methodism much of the spirit of the blessed Christ, especially compassion on souls." Holsey lauded John Wesley because "he sought not only the elevation of society by evangelistic labors and evangelistic Christianity, but by every lawful and useful means that could instruct the minds and conditions of men." J. C. Price, an AME Zion minister and educator, agreed with Holsey. He acknowledged that Methodism was a purifying and elevating force "because Christianity, in the length and breadth of its effects upon man everywhere, not only in his religious state, but also in his social and civil state, has an influence which is for the glory of God and for the good of man everywhere." Price predicted that "Methodism is the great thing that will help us to solve the great American Negro problem." He added "wherever the name of Christ goes there is a general renovation of character and a corresponding renovation of action."[22]

INSTITUTIONALIZATION AT THE TURN OF THE TWENTIETH CENTURY

The Wesleyan influence purifying and elevating African Americans was harnessed in the late nineteenth century to enlarged efforts to establish black Methodist churches and schools throughout the Americas

---

[21] See Othal Lakey, *History of the CME Church* (1985); and Raymond R. Somerville, Jr., *An Ex-Colored Church: Social Activism in the CME Church, 1870–1970* (2004).

[22] *Proceedings of the Oecumenical Methodist Conference held in City Road, London, September 1881* (Nashville, 1882), 78–79, 81.

and into Africa. AME leaders (though burdened with assumptions about western civilization and its superiority to indigenous cultures in Africa) expanded to Sierra Leone and Liberia in 1891 and South Africa in 1896. A "millennial Ethiopianism" convinced AME thinkers about the important role of Africa in Biblical history and how it would define the destiny of people of color. Three bishops explored these millennial themes from an AME perspective. In 1893, Benjamin W. Arnett reviewed the participation of Africans in the New Testament. Two years later, Benjamin T. Tanner examined Solomon and his non-white origins. Then, in 1898, Henry M. Turner declared that "God is a Negro." Their works affirmed the humanity of blacks and offered African Methodism as an institutional vehicle to realize this objective.[23]

Charles Albert Tindley, a black pastor in the MEC, reflected a similar view in hymns he wrote in the early decades of the twentieth century. He spoke of a brighter future for black people and addressed the economic vulnerability of his African American parishioners in rural Maryland and Philadelphia. In "Take Your Burden to the Lord" and "We Are Tossed and Driven" Tindley presented God as their deliverer and emancipator.

Black Methodists developed deep loyalties toward the institutional structures they built in the African American jurisdictions in the MEC and in the independent black Wesleyan bodies. These entities nurtured black self-determination and emancipatory obligations toward the African American communities that they served. At the same time, the task of institutional preservation drew attention and resources away from black advancement activities. When the MEC merged with the MEC South and the Methodist Protestant Church, in 1939, to form the Methodist Church (MC), blacks in the MEC, some under duress, agreed to the creation of a Central Jurisdiction which segregated them into all black episcopal districts.[24] Despite the stigma of segregation, they retained pride in the heritage of autonomy and self-determination in governing black conferences and congregations, using them to benefit the black population. Their AME, AME Zion, and CME counterparts made the same boast about their glorious past, their respective heroes and heroines, and the freedom fighters who emerged out of their ranks.

Although claiming that their Wesleyan pursuit of spiritual and societal holiness had greater authenticity than what white Methodists practiced, black denominational leaders remained locked in intractable

---

[23] Dickerson, *Liberated Past*, 36–37, 44–48, 64.
[24] See Morris L. Davis, *The Methodist Unification: Christianity and the Politics of Race in the Jim Crow Era* (2008), esp. 127–28.

tensions between institutional preservation and insurgent liberationist activities. As a result, black Methodist institutions thinly sustained their emancipatory ethos through symbolic celebratory events and tangential involvements in black liberation initiatives. For example, AME churches kept the memory of Richard Allen alive with annual commemorations of his birthday. But, denominational leaders used these heritage activities to raise funds for various church projects – rather than underwriting major allocations to the NAACP, the National Urban League, and other black advancement organizations. Though bishops and leading pastors served these groups on the national and local levels, substantive funding from their religious bodies seldom followed them.

CIVIL RIGHTS ACTIVISM IN BLACK WESLEYANISM

Disappointed black activists in the former MEC condemned their spokesmen for their surrender to the sin of segregation. One of these activists, James L. Farmer, a founder of the Congress of Racial Equality (CORE) and a graduate of the School of Religion of Howard University, refused ordination to avoid serving in the Central Jurisdiction. Farmer's father, who knew that his son disdained the unification plan that segregated black Methodists, asked what he would do instead. "Destroy segregation" in the broader society was his answer![25]

Farmer's counterparts in both the merged MC and the black Methodist bodies recognized that institutional matters claimed the energies and attention of denominational leaders. Instead of depending on organizational support they became individual carriers of the emancipatory ethos of their respective religious bodies. James M. Lawson, Jr., a product of the MEC, like Farmer, drew upon their group's liberationist legacy to invigorate his civil rights activism. Such AME laity and clergy as A. Philip Randolph, Archibald J. Carey, Jr., J. A. De Laine, Oliver L. Brown, and Rosa Parks made indispensable contributions to the civil rights crusade from the 1940s through the 1960s. Each invoked Richard Allen as their model of spiritual and social holiness and considered his liberationist activities as core to their AME identity and insurgency. A similarly long roster of AME Zion and CME ministers and members became militant advocates of the black freedom struggle. S. S. Seay and Rufus E. Clement – Zion Methodists in Montgomery, Alabama and Atlanta, Georgia respectively – played crucial roles as activists against

[25] James L. Farmer, *Lay Bare the Heart: An Autobiography of the Civil Rights Movement* (1985), 143, 146.

segregation in the 1950s. Henry C. Bunton thrust Mt. Olive CME cathe-dral in Memphis, Tennessee as a conspicuous venue for local civil rights activities.

Scholars of the civil rights movement attribute the success in under-mining segregationist structures in American society to grassroots mobi-lization. But a black Wesleyan undercurrent provided crucial support to this strategy. Randolph, Farmer, and Lawson, all sons of black Methodist ministers, played critical roles in developing methodologies to destroy Jim Crow.

Randolph, the son of an AME pastor, fresh from winning recog-nition of the Brotherhood of Sleeping Car Porters in 1937, turned to the broader black struggle during the 1940s and beyond. Determined to prevent racial discrimination in employment in defense industries, Randolph mobilized thousands of blacks to march on Washington, DC, to press President Franklin D. Roosevelt to issue Executive Order 8802, in 1941, to end job discrimination. He maintained the March on Wash-ington Movement through the 1940s to keep up pressure for equity toward black laborers. Although he was not an avid churchgoer at this time, he invited ministerial participation in his grassroots efforts. His socialist ideas, however, interacted with his strong admiration of Richard Allen, Henry M. Turner, and other A.M.E. leaders who fought against the subjugation of African Americans.[26]

James Farmer belonged to an interracial group of divinity and grad-uate students who established CORE in 1942. He learned nonviolent direct action techniques from CORE's parent organization, the Fellow-ship of Reconciliation, but his black Methodist origins also energized his activism. Additionally, he and the other CORE founders were bene-ficiaries of Archibald J. Carey, Jr., an activist Chicago clergyman whose Woodlawn AME church served as the group's first headquarters and first national convention site. Carey, a conscious Allenite and Randolph ally, was a link to these two nonviolent direct action movements.

Rosa Parks, a stewardess at St. Paul AME church in Montgomery, Alabama, refused to relinquish her bus seat to a white man in 1955. Her act of defiance flowed from an understanding of Richard Allen and his liberationist ministry. Because her role in preparing the Eucharist at St. Paul church memorialized the Methodist call to holiness every first Sun-day, she believed this principle should be extended to the public arena.

James M. Lawson, Jr., whose father was a pastor in both the AME Zion and the Central Jurisdiction of the MC, learned the habits of

---

[26] See Cynthia Taylor, *A. Philip Randolph: The Religious Journey of an African American Labor Leader* (2006).

insurgency from his parents. A serious scholar of Gandhian *satyagraha* (non-violent resistance) and a participant in peace movements based in MC student organizations, Lawson became the architect of nonviolent workshops in the Nashville civil rights movement. He also provided founding documents reflecting his Gandhian principles in 1960, for the newly organized Student Nonviolent Coordinating Committee. The emancipatory ethos that pervaded black Methodism, no matter the denomination, provided a sub-text that helps to explain the individual activism of significant African American Methodists.

BLACK WESLEYAN ENGAGEMENT IN SYSTEMIC LIBERATION

The rise of Black Power in the late 1960s encouraged a new generation of black Wesleyan insurgents to criticize the lack of front-line activism in their denominations. The failure of black Methodist bodies to confront and condemn the raw exercise of white hegemony against the disadvantaged both in the United States and abroad was especially disturbing to these critics. Although the MC took steps starting in 1964 to dismantle the Central Jurisdiction and to merge in 1968 with the Evangelical United Brethren Church, black activists believed that the best Wesleyan witness lay in addressing societal injustices. Hence, several black Chicago area ministers urged the resulting United Methodist Church toward greater engagement with urban issues that negatively affected African American and Hispanic populations. Black Methodists for Church Renewal, organized in 1968, agitated for these objectives and aimed at greater empowerment for black ministers and members in this largely white denomination. In the last two decades of the twentieth century, several black male and female bishops were elected and innumerable district superintendents and agency officials were appointed. In 1984, Leontine T. C. Kelly became the first black female bishop in the United Methodist Church.

Theologians in the AME tradition – namely, James H. Cone, Cecil W. Cone, and Jacqueline Grant – urged their denomination to recover its emancipatory ethos and take seriously the ministry model that Richard Allen represented.[27] Their works in black theology, although arguing for

---

[27] James H. Cone, *My Soul Looks Back*, rev. ed. (1985), 64–92; Cecil W. Cone, "A Black Theology of Liberation: An African American Interpretation of the Christian Faith, Part I," *A.M.E. Church Review* (Oct.–Dec. 2003), 69–75; and Jacqueline Grant, "Black Theology and the Black Woman," in Wilmore and Cone, eds., *Black Theology: A Documentary History* (1979), 418–33.

a liberationist praxis against white hegemony, also called on black Wesleyan bodies to identify and struggle with the poor and empower women within the denomination. Cone's emphasis upon the Pan-African reach of African Methodism, and the push of those in Africa and the Caribbean, led to the election to the bishopric of additional indigenous leadership from these areas and to the first woman bishop, Vashti Murphy McKenzie, in 2000, and two others, Carolyn Tyler Guidry and Sarah F. Davis, in 2004. The AME Zion Church elected a second African bishop in 1988 and the first female bishop, Mildred B. Hines, in 2008.

Among contemporary black Methodists the most visible link with their Wesleyan heritage lies in their fealty to Methodist doctrine and hymnody. Whether in the regular publication of the *Book of Discipline*, in the ordination litanies and collects for clergy, or in the exuberant singing of Wesley's "And Are We Yet Alive" at opening services of annual conferences, the marks of Methodism remain conspicuous. Too little observed are regular recitations from John Wesley's copious writings on spiritual and social holiness. However, these core elements of the founder's "practical divinity" have been transmitted through the biographies and autobiographies of black Wesleyan ministers and members who blended spiritual and social holiness. These works, many of them hagiographies, have potential to invigorate the emancipationist heritage of black Methodists and to inform liberationist ministries badly needed in black communities. Although often enacted through the witness of individual black Methodists, this liberationist rhetoric and praxis require greater acknowledgment, commitment, and support from the institutional bodies that produced Hoosier, Allen, Douglass, Lawson, and Parks.

17 Current debates over Wesley's legacy among his progeny

SARAH H. LANCASTER

It is clear that the small movement called "Methodism" that began in the eighteenth century within the Church of England has had a lasting impact. Millions of Christians today identify with or can trace their roots to Methodism in some way. As the primary leader and organizer of the original Methodists, John Wesley has a place in the histories of many churches and movements within Christianity, and, in this sense, his legacy is quite impressive. His legacy as a theologian, though, is less clear. As Methodism spread and splintered, the theological views of each new body that formed were shaped by new contexts. Because each context is itself complex, a multiplicity of theological views are held by members within the same ecclesial body, and not simply across ecclesial bodies. The variety that exists among these descendants raises the question: Along with the historical legacy that ties many churches and movements to Wesley, is there also a legacy of shared theological commitments?

One way to think about this question is to start with the meaning of "legacy" itself. The word has several meanings in English usage, among the most common being "something handed down" or a "gift." In this case, a legacy is received by someone, was valued by the giver, and is probably valued by the recipient. But, in the world of technology, a somewhat different meaning has recently come into use. Here, a "legacy" is a system that has been standard, but is now considered basic, perhaps even outdated, compared to more enhanced systems. As technology advances, a legacy is destined to be left behind, or at least improved upon so that its present form becomes less and less useful. These different meanings of the word display the problem in asking about Wesley's theological legacy among his progeny. Are his theological ideas to be considered gifts, handed down from one generation to the next as valued markers of identity and guides for reflection? Or are they outdated, needing to be replaced by new and improved ways of thinking? As we shall see, both of these views have been present in responses to Wesley through time.

JOHN WESLEY AS THEOLOGIAN

The England into which Wesley was born had been the site of theological controversy for many years. Tied up with political fortunes, ecclesial fortunes had shifted sometimes drastically. Whether England was to be a Roman Catholic or Protestant country (and if Protestant, what kind) had been a central, sometimes bloody, question. Wesley's own familial background reflected some of the theological tension of the time. His grandparents had been nonconformists, but, his parents each committed themselves to the Church of England. John Wesley was reared in the Church of England and remained committed to its structure, worship, and theology. Even so, his childhood education included a wide variety of devotional and theological reading, from Puritans to Roman Catholics. Wesley continued to read broadly throughout his life and incorporated many different ideas into his theology.

During his years at Oxford University, Wesley engaged in serious study that included reading in theology (or "divinity" as it was known at the time), Greek and Latin classical literature, logic, languages, sciences, oratory, and poetry. Wesley enjoyed the scholarly life, and he pursued two degrees at Oxford, seeking ordination because it was required for the position of fellow and tutor (to which he aspired) at the University. Just as he was dedicated to his studies, Wesley also committed himself to a rigorous devotional life. His diaries from Oxford show regular self-examination, reading, and prayer.[1] Eventually, John and Charles Wesley began meeting with close associates in small groups to encourage one another in a disciplined Christian life. Through his formal studies and his serious devotional practices, Wesley's early adulthood was marked by a commitment to education and to holy living. These commitments characterized his theology throughout the rest of his life.

The emerging Methodist revival led Wesley to forego the option of spending his life teaching at Oxford University. In that sense, he did not become a "scholar" or "theologian" as we understand the profession today. Yet, he did continue to engage in study throughout his life, and he produced a large body of theological literature. His written material took different forms – including sermons, commentary notes, and edited versions of other authors' works – depending on what he perceived to be needed at the time in leading the revival. Such forms of theological expression were common in his time. Indeed, many Anglican "divines" (theologians) contributed to the church through sermons and liturgical

---

[1] See Richard P. Heitzenrater, *The Elusive Mr. Wesley*, 59–62.

resources. Wesley was making use of recognized forms to make theological ideas accessible and understandable.

Because his theological work was situational, and his active ministry was long, Wesley encountered and addressed many different situations over the span of his life. He also had some occasion to change his stance on certain issues. But, critics of Wesley and the early Methodist movement often charged him with more – they discerned major inconsistencies between his various writings, or unacknowledged reversals of earlier views. Wesley responded to these attacks by insisting that his position on key doctrines had remained consistent (at least after the significant reorientation of his theology at Aldersgate). He also stressed his training in logic, with its concern for the coherence of ideas.

But, Wesley's pressing concern was to bring theology in service to the needs of ordinary people, helping to revitalize their faith and practice in the world. He did not write works that were intended to be read primarily by scholars, and he was more concerned with affirming the whole of Christian faith in appropriate contexts than with arranging and connecting theological ideas in a coherent network. As such, he wrote nothing approximating a "systematic theology." If such a work is the assumed standard, then Wesley would not appear to have been a serious theologian.

One of the striking features of later Methodist history is how many of Wesley's ecclesial descendents reached this conclusion! They celebrated him as a pious Christian, an effective evangelist, and a brilliant organizer, while ignoring or betraying mild embarrassment about his contributions as a theologian. The reasons for this development are many. To begin in Britain, as Methodists sought to distance themselves from the Church of England following Wesley's death, they downplayed the characteristic forms of Wesley's work as an Anglican divine.[2] Methodists in the newly forming United States also sought independence from things Anglican. Francis Asbury set the tone for Methodism in this context, and he was neither inclined nor able to continue Wesley's model of bringing together scholarship with practical ministry.[3] Methodists in North America used materials that Wesley had produced to guide their preaching (his *Sermons* and *NT Notes*), but showed less interest in theological forms more characteristic of Anglicanism (like the *Sunday Service*, Wesley's revision of

---

[2] For examples of such "de-Anglicanization" of Wesley in the years following his death, see Randy L. Maddox, "Reclaiming an Inheritance: Wesley as Theologian in the History of Methodist Theology," in *Rethinking Wesley's Theology*, 214–16.

[3] Cf. Randy L. Maddox, "Respected Founder/Neglected Guide: The Role of Wesley in American Methodist Theology," *Methodist History* 37 (1999): 71–88.

the *Book of Common Prayer*). They also tended to look to Wesley's work more as a source or justification for certain debated Methodist teachings – such as universal atonement and Christian perfection – than as a model of the work of a theologian who reflected upon and could connect them with the breadth of Christian theology. Focused on the charge of spreading scriptural holiness through and reforming an entire continent, they sought Wesley's guidance most keenly for this evangelistic mission rather than for theological reflection or for a model of theological writing for a new generation.

The generations of Methodists immediately following Wesley did, of course, have theologians, but the changed contexts in which they did their work moved Methodist theology farther from Wesley's precedent. The polemic with Calvinism, which began in Wesley's lifetime continued to exert shaping pressure on Methodist theology, not only in substance, but also in form. Calvinists looked to Calvin's *Institutes of the Christian Religion* – a thorough, orderly exposition of theology – as the standard; in comparison, Wesley's short, practically oriented writings seemed unimpressive. Methodists who argued against Calvinists often found it more helpful to appeal to John Fletcher than to Wesley. Fletcher, an associate of Wesley who had earlier studied in the Reformed tradition in Geneva, published several apologetic treatises aimed at Calvinist and other scholars in defense of Wesley's positions on predestination and Christian perfection. His works were more systematic in treating these issues than anything from Wesley's hand.[4] Later Methodists advanced that systematizing process by writing compendiums of doctrine that could stand up to the accepted standard of their time for "real" theology.[5] These works retained a Methodist orientation on the disputed questions with Calvinists and others, but Wesley himself is rarely mentioned. The more that Methodist theologians adopted the current style of acceptable academic discourse, the less relevant Wesley seemed to be to their work.

Other developments in the nineteenth century also led Methodist theologians to look beyond Wesley for guidance. Wesley had stressed the importance of Scripture for Christian faith, and Methodists continued

---

[4] Ibid., 74–75.

[5] For accounts of how theology developed through the late eighteenth and the nineteenth centuries, see Maddox, "Respected Founder"; and Thomas A. Langford, *Practical Divinity*, 1:43–115. Examples of doctrinal expositions during this time in Great Britain include Richard Watson's *Theological Institutes* (1825–28; used in the course of study for many years on both sides of the Atlantic) and William Burt Pope's *Compendium of Christian Theology* (1875). In North America they include Samuel Wakefield's *Complete System of Christian Theology* (1862) and John Miley's two-volume *Systematic Theology* (1892–94).

to ground their beliefs in what they understood the Bible to say. But biblical scholarship was undergoing major changes in the late eighteenth and nineteenth centuries. Higher criticism was raising questions about the production of biblical texts. Meanwhile, geology and biology were developing an account of the origins of the world and its creatures that was quite different from the account in Genesis, raising acute doubts about the accuracy of biblical statements. These developments presented Methodists with questions for reflection that Wesley had barely imagined.

By the end of the nineteenth century, these questions could not be ignored. Some Methodists (for example, John Miley) addressed them by working within but adjusting the theological notion of the Holy Spirit's inspiration of Scripture to retain the special status of Scripture in the face of historical criticism of the Bible. Others (for example, Borden Parker Bowne) were not content to work within the framework of previous doctrines and looked instead for new ways of thinking about how God speaks through Scripture and works in the world. Moving forward meant engaging new questions with new resources, and, at the time, German scholarship was in ascendancy. Several leading Methodist scholars looked to German philosophy and biblical criticism to guide the way. In turning to the best thinkers of their time, Methodist scholars perhaps did what Wesley had done; but his direct influence was waning even more than it had before. Many themes of Methodism – such as the priority of grace and the freedom of the human being to respond to God – remained, but Wesley's own work was not used to develop them.

In other words, Wesley's theological "legacy" through this period was more akin to the technological use of the word than the idea of a valued gift. Both his theological materials and theological content seemed in need of updating, so he became less and less directly relevant to the work of Methodist theologians. A general orientation to certain problems remained, but Methodist scholars often looked to Germany rather than to eighteenth-century England for intellectual resources. When Wesley was remembered, it was more to acknowledge his position as founder and to follow his model of holiness than to seek his wisdom on how to think through theological problems.

RECOVERY OF APPRECIATION FOR WESLEY AS THEOLOGIAN

In the twentieth century, a new appreciation for Wesley's work in theology began to emerge. One reason for this renewed interest was the growing concern about the unity of the Church that had sparked the ecumenical movement. In the preface to his book *John Wesley's Theology Today* (1960), Colin Williams describes how the search for unity required churches to explain themselves to one another. Methodism had a hard time doing so, because it had lost touch with its roots. So Williams set out to present the distinctive emphases of Wesley's theology in a way that could contribute to Methodist self-understanding, and at the same time help ecumenical partners see what Methodism might be able to contribute to the larger Church.[6]

The year after Williams published his account of Wesley's theology, Albert C. Outler suggested the term "folk theologian" to describe Wesley.[7] As an ecumenist himself, Outler understood the value of clarifying Methodist theological identity, but he also knew that Wesley's work could not be compared straightforwardly to the grand systems of other theologians. The notion of "folk theologian" (of one whose primary interest is in taking great ideas and making them accessible to ordinary people) conveyed that Wesley was a man of learning, but that he used that learning in service of spreading the gospel. Recovery of Wesley's theology, then, started somewhat apologetically – carving out a place for Wesley without setting him up for a comparison with great theologians in which he would not fare well. As scholarship has gained greater contextual awareness of his work as an Anglican divine, though, and as the field of theology has retreated from grand speculative systems to explore models that attend to context and praxis, Wesley has come to be known and valued as a "practical theologian," that is, a theologian whose disciplined reflection addresses how faith is expressed in Christian life and worship.[8]

Wesley's theology is not only characterized by its practical nature, but also by the kind of synthesis it attempts. Outler noted that Wesley drew from many sources and held together ideas that were often taken to be competing with one another (such as faith and works). He described Wesley's organizing principle as "evangelical catholicism."[9] Randy L. Maddox has identified Wesley's "orienting concern" as

---

6 Williams, *John Wesley's Theology Today*, 5–10.
7 Outler used the term "folk theology" in his 1961 Presidential Address to the American Theological Society: "Towards a Re-Appraisal of John Wesley as a Theologian," in *Wesleyan Theological Heritage*, 39–54. See also his later essay "John Wesley: Folk Theologian," in ibid., 111–24.
8 See Randy L. Maddox, "John Wesley – Practical Theologian?" *Wesleyan Theological Journal* 23 (1988): 122–47; and Maddox, *Responsible Grace*.
9 Outler, "Towards a Re-Appraisal," 44.

"responsible grace."[10] In each case, these interpreters of Wesley are pointing to his ability to find a way to focus attention on Christian faith that not only brings clarity but also accounts for a range of concerns that have traditionally been set in opposition to one another. Even though his thinking was not captured in a grand system, Wesley was working with a sophisticated theological understanding that attempted to express the complexity of human experience before God.

DEBATES WITH THE RECOVERY

These features of Wesley's theology can be highly valued, but they also lend themselves to a variety of readings. Even grand systems can be interpreted in many ways, and the kind of work that Wesley did is more open to different directions for development than a tightly constructed system would be. A synthesis of ideas stated in different ways in different places can easily be broken apart. A practical theology that fits one context may not fit another. A situational writer, especially one who lived and wrote for many years and encountered many different kinds of situations, bequeaths the problem of how to discern consistency or development over time. The coherence of Wesley's ideas was not always stated in a formal way, and some issues are developed more fully than others. For these reasons, even as Wesley's theological "legacy" began to be taken as a valued gift, it was not always received and valued in the same way. Wesley's interpreters do not agree fully on how to read him. In particular, proponents on different sides of current theological debates have often cited Wesley to support their alternative positions. The following examples of debated appeals to Wesley's precedent within the broad Methodist or Wesleyan family can serve to illustrate this point.

Conversion

"Conversion" implies some kind of change. It is rooted in biblical notions of turning or returning to God. Although he did not use the word "conversion" often, Wesley's theology is full of images and concepts that show the importance of change – of waking up to the reality of sin, of being made a new creature, of no longer being considered guilty, of moving from sickness to health. But, how is change to take place? One of the persistent debates among the descendants of Wesley has been about whether the change that leads to new life with God is instantaneous or gradual. Or if both belong together, what their relationship to

[10] Maddox, *Responsible Grace*, 19.

one another might be. Is instantaneous change the norm, supported by gradual growth afterward? Or is gradual growth the norm, possibly punctuated by some instantaneous experience that may be desirable but is not necessary? The debate has many dimensions, ranging from different interpretations about Wesley's own "conversion" to different expectations about what ought to be happening in the lives of Christians today.

One of the most commonly known incidents in Wesley's life is his "heart-warming" experience at a meeting on Aldersgate Street, when during a reading from Luther's "Preface to Romans" he felt an assurance about his salvation that he had not felt before. The year was 1738, and it marked a significant shift in Wesley's preaching, particularly in his distinction between "almost" and "altogether" Christians.[11] He could even say that before this experience he was not himself a "real" Christian. Given its seeming importance at the time, one would expect that Wesley would consistently refer back to this experience in his subsequent theological reflection. But, mention of Aldersgate is noticeably absent in his later writings. Furthermore, he continued to ponder questions that one might expect to have been settled by such a powerful experience. It is this tension between pivotal moment and long-term reflection that has raised questions about the standard account of Aldersgate as the singular, defining experience of Wesley's life and the model for all "real" Christians.

The current debate on this issue is exemplified especially well in two books: *Aldersgate Reconsidered* and *Conversion in the Wesleyan Tradition*.[12] *Aldersgate Reconsidered* was written shortly after the 250th anniversary of Aldersgate had launched controversy over the event's interpretation. The introduction by Randy L. Maddox outlines the major points at issue and presents the essays as contributions to an alternative paradigm for understanding the importance and meaning of Aldersgate. Richard P. Heitzenrater's contribution to this book describes Aldersgate as a significant event in Wesley's spiritual pilgrimage, but it also explores how Wesley's ongoing theological reflection modified his understanding of the essential features of that experience in almost every important respect. Some years later, Kenneth J. Collins's introduction to *Conversion in the Wesleyan Tradition* lamented that many works since the 1990s had stressed gradual growth without also acknowledging the soteriological role of instantaneous change in Wesley's work. The essays

---

[11] See Sermon 2, "The Almost Christian," *Works*, 1:131–41.
[12] Randy L. Maddox, ed., *Aldersgate Reconsidered*; and Kenneth J. Collins and John H. Tyson, eds., *Conversion in the Wesleyan Tradition*.

in this latter book tend to stress the centrality of clear, decisive transformation, not only for Wesley's life but for Christian life itself.

The debate represented by these two books begins with the question of how to read Wesley's own account of his life, but the reading that one adopts has implications for practice. At issue are questions such as whether a vivid conversion moment should be considered the norm for Christian experience and its absence an exception, and whether ministry should be directed toward leading people to a vivid experience or forming them gradually in Christian life.

Baptism

Debate about conversion carries over into questions about how to understand baptism because both have been associated with justification (pardon) and regeneration (new birth). Wesley would have been well acquainted with debate about whether infants should be baptized or not. Anglicans practiced infant baptism and held a doctrine of baptismal regeneration, but some dissenters believed people should only be baptized when they could consciously respond to God in faith. Wesley continued to support infant baptism even as he preached about a conscious, adult experience of justification by faith and new birth. The tension between the focus on an adult experience and the practice of infant baptism has raised several questions for Wesley's descendants. The problem is not contained in or exemplified by a few sources but ranges across scholarship and practice. Two issues arise frequently: first, how might a vivid conscious experience of being "born again" be connected with the sacrament of baptism; and second, what practice of baptism best fits with Wesley's theology?

The materials that could be used to answer the first question pose particular interpretive challenges. Wesley's writings on baptism are few, and they consist not only of his own statements but also of material he edited and distributed. Much has to be inferred from what he chose to circulate, how he edited it, and when he distributed it. Randy Maddox has identified four different approaches to the question among scholars. One proposal, particularly suited to those who stress evangelical conversion, has been to say that Wesley retained the practice of infant baptism only out of his commitment to the Church of England, not because he affirmed baptismal regeneration. In contrast, another approach (suited to a high view of the sacraments) has been to see Wesley as clearly embracing baptismal regeneration. A few interpreters have believed that Wesley consciously held sacramental and evangelical regeneration in tension.

Other interpreters, though, simply acknowledge a certain ambiguity in Wesley's position that does not have an easy resolution.[13]

Because the theology can be read in different ways, Wesley's descendants were able to adopt different practices. Most Methodist denominations continued to uphold infant baptism, but some branches of the family, particularly holiness churches like the Nazarenes and Free Methodists, came to privilege baptism at the time of conscious belief.[14] Those who practice infant baptism regularly do not necessarily deny the option of a later baptism, and those who privilege a later baptism do not necessarily deny the option of infant baptism. But, their different preferences for practice are related to different theological understandings. Those descendants who now tend to delay baptism are breaking with Wesley's embrace of longstanding ecclesial practice to uphold a stress on the importance of conscious decision and experiential renewal that they find in Wesley's theology. They also tend to understand the act of baptism more as a "sign" of the renewal God has worked within the believer than as the "means" of that gracious renewal. By contrast, those descendents who practice infant baptism regularly are more likely to stress Wesley's affirmation that baptism is a true "means" of grace for the infant, and to highlight his insistence that all human works are in response to God's prevenient (or prior) grace. Although these differences may not rise to the level of active debate, they illustrate that Wesley's ecclesial descendants are not of one mind about how best to carry out his practical theology.

Communion

In the United Methodist context, another sacramental issue has sparked debate that has invoked Wesley in divergent ways: the question of "open table," or who may be admitted to communion. The specific question is whether baptism is required for admission. Those who argue that only baptized Christians should eat the Lord's Supper stress that this is longstanding Christian practice, including in the Church of England in Wesley's day. When John Wesley and his brother Charles speak of "all" being invited to the table, these interpreters note that in the eighteenth century the brothers could assume that their audience had been baptized

---

[13] Maddox, *Responsible Grace*, 221–22. The notes to these pages direct the reader to the relevant resources that exemplify the alternatives.

[14] An influential work that has challenged this tendency in the holiness tradition, arguing for a high view of the sacraments, is Rob L. Staples, *Outward Sign and Inward Grace: The Place of Sacraments in Wesleyan Spirituality* (1991).

as infants (or the few Baptists in the crowd as adults). More specifically, when John Wesley insists that communion can be a "converting ordinance," they stress that he is not referring to conversion to Christianity itself. Rather, he means the conversion from being a nominal or "almost" Christian to being an "altogether" Christian. Communion could function as a means of grace for those already in the Church to experience God's love so powerfully that they knew themselves to be children of God. Finally, proponents of offering communion only to the baptized argue that this restriction was assumed even in Methodist boasts about their "open table" in the changed context of the United States with its denominational pluralism. Unlike traditions that commune only their own membership, Methodists invited baptized members of all denominations to their table. The force of saying this is the "Lord's Table" was to assure that it was not the "Methodist Table."[15]

On the other side of this debate are those who believe the invitation to the Lord's Table should be for all who wish to come, whether baptized yet or not. They argue that God's love is not restricted to the baptized, so this important means by which that love may be experienced should not be restricted either. Because the current context is both secular and multi-religious, they believe the table must be as open as possible to show hospitality and to model the radically inclusive behavior of Jesus. Proponents of this view may concede the historical point about the difference between Wesley's context and ours, but they appeal to Wesley in a different way. His understanding of grace, his emphasis on experience, his conviction that communion is a means of grace to be used, and his willingness to depart from certain normative practices of the Church of England to spread the Gospel all present a model that we both can and should emulate in an open table. The force of saying this is the "Lord's Table," on this view, is to remind us that humans do not decide who belongs there.[16]

In the face of this disagreement, the official document of the United Methodist Church, *This Holy Mystery*, has attempted a mediating position. It affirms that baptism "normally precedes" the taking of communion; but it also affirms, "Nonbaptized people who respond in faith to the invitation in our liturgy will be welcomed to the Table." It then

---

[15] For representative arguments to restrict communion to baptized Christians, see Michael G. Cartwright and Gary R. Shiplett, "Closing Ranks on Open Communion: Two Views," *Quarterly Review* 8:1 (Spring 1988): 54–70.

[16] A representative argument on this side is Mark W. Stamm, "Open Communion as a United Methodist Exception," *Quarterly Review* 22:3 (Fall 2002): 261–72.

instructs that these persons should also be encouraged toward baptism.[17] By welcoming everyone, but also affirming the importance of baptism for communion, the United Methodist Church hopes to hold together both values that are expressed in the debate.

Christian perfection

The debate about instantaneous or gradual change that was discussed above in connection with conversion, or the beginning of the Christian journey, plays itself out in similar ways concerning the ideal or *telos* of this journey, the hope to be made perfect or holy in this life. This debate traces back to John and Charles Wesley. The brothers developed their respective models of sanctification over time, changing nuances along the way, but the eventual divergence between the two became clear. Early in the revival, both brothers maintained that it was possible for God (through a second, instantaneous, vivid experience of "hearing" God "speak") to root out sin so thoroughly *in this life* that one could enter into and manifest to others a state of perfect love of God and neighbor, or entire sanctification. Although John came to allow that this experience was rare, he continued to defend the possibility and to encourage Methodists to expect it, in part because the expectation opened them more fully to God's gradual transforming work.[18] By contrast, Charles became increasingly suspicious of those who claimed to have experienced entire sanctification instantaneously, particularly after the egregious antinomian examples in London in the early 1760s. From that point on, his hymns locate full deliverance into perfection at the point of death. He still exhorted the Methodists to pursue holiness in this life, but as a matter of gradual growth, not instantaneous cleansing.[19]

This disagreement revived among Methodists in the United States during the nineteenth century. Since the time of Wesley, holiness had been a hallmark of Methodism to be defended in the face of Calvinism. Methodist theologians argued for our human ability and need to respond to God's grace in contrast to the idea of God's foreordained, unconditional election. The commitment to growing in holiness through a disciplined life was deeply embedded in Methodist consciousness. But this emphasis on growth could easily eclipse the expectation of instantaneous perfection. Furthermore, whereas holiness remained a value in

---

[17] *This Holy Mystery: A United Methodist Understanding of Holy Communion* (2004), 14–15.

[18] See Sermon 14, "The Repentance of Believers," §I.20, *Works*, 1:346–47.

[19] See John R. Tyson, *Charles Wesley on Sanctification* (1986), esp., 248–52.

Methodist theology, Methodist practice began to slip away from some of the standards that had marked early Methodism. The tension between theology and practice began to prompt considerable controversy regarding the meaning of sanctification.

Those who were concerned about what they perceived as increasing accommodation to the surrounding culture began to call people back to lives of holiness. As they did so, many began to stress the notion of a "second blessing," that is, an instantaneous experience of entire sanctification by faith, available shortly after justification, which eliminated the inclination to sin. Although this emphasis was not the only issue of concern in the holiness movement, it drew much attention. By the late nineteenth century, the debate about whether sanctification occurred gradually or instantaneously had become divisive – both practically, because those who could say they had received a second blessing were divided from those who had not; and theologically, as pastors, bishops, and theologians took sides about the Methodist position. During this period, many Methodists left the dominant institutional expressions of Methodism to form or join various holiness churches (see Chapter 15 of this text).

With this background of division within Methodism, it is not surprising that renewed interest in John Wesley's theology would focus on his understanding of Christian perfection. The results have led to new insights and continued debate. Some scholars within holiness traditions have discerned that the way entire sanctification came to be understood in their traditions was a departure from Wesley's model. Rob L. Staples, for instance, points out that Phoebe Palmer stressed the "Word" as evidence for entire sanctification while Wesley understood that evidence to be from the "Spirit."[20] Thomas Jay Oord has argued for revisions in the Church of the Nazarene's article on "entire sanctification" to return to ideas closer to Wesley's own (for instance, Wesley saw entire sanctification as the work of God rather than a person's total commitment).[21] These instances show how a better understanding of Wesley's thinking can pose a challenge to common understandings among his descendents.

---

[20] Rob L. Staples, "John Wesley's Doctrine of the Holy Spirit," *Wesleyan Theological Journal* 21 (1986): 91–115.

[21] Thomas Jay Oord, "Revisioning Article X: Fifteen Changes in the Church of the Nazarene's Article on Entire Sanctification," paper delivered at the NNU Wesley Center conference "Revisioning Holiness: Looking Back and Pressing Forward," February 2007. Posted on http://wesley.nnu.edu/wesley_conferences/2007/ and accessed March 27, 2008.

Scholarly interest in Christian perfection has also opened interesting interpretive questions about how to understand John Wesley's commitment to instantaneous change within the gradual growth that he affirmed. Kenneth Collins argues that the force of Wesley's insisting on instantaneous change is to mark discontinuity with what has been before, a real death to sin that may not be dramatic but is nevertheless momentous.[22] This discontinuity defines entire sanctification. Randy Maddox, on the other hand, argues that Wesley could only maintain the idea of instantaneous change by modifying his understanding of entire sanctification to refer to a very specific understanding of sin that did not cover all possible sin. So, although he allowed that instantaneous change could happen, Wesley most often stressed growth. Even those who may have attained entire sanctification were to continue to grow, so entire sanctification, rather than being marked by utter discontinuity, finds a place within the overall pattern of God's grace and human responsive cooperation.[23]

Liberation

In 1977, the Sixth Oxford Institute of Methodist Theological Studies took the debate about sanctification in another direction. Whether talking about instantaneous or gradual perfection, Methodist theological discussion to that point had tended to be interested in what happened to individuals. Some of Wesley's descendants had caught more fully than others that social expression of inner sanctification was expected, but "perfection" still took place in one's inner life.[24] With the advent of liberation theology, this focus on the inner life of an individual became problematic. Liberation theologians were pushing Christians to see and to address problems caused by systemic oppression, a societal issue for which attention to individual sanctification was simply inadequate. The Sixth Oxford Institute offered a venue for scholars to explore whether and how the heritage could equip contemporary Methodists for liberating praxis.

Many of the papers presented at this Institute were published in a volume entitled *Sanctification and Liberation: Liberation Theologies in Light of the Wesleyan Tradition*.[25] These collected essays show the

---

[22] Collins, *John Wesley: A Theological Journey*, 194–195.

[23] Maddox, *Responsible Grace*, 180–90.

[24] Phoebe Palmer and Hugh Price Hughes, for instance, stressed matters of social conscience. The historically Black Methodist churches have always seen a connection between theology and social concerns.

[25] Theodore Runyon, ed., *Sanctification and Liberation*.

wrestling with Wesley that was taking place at the time. Was he hope-
lessly individualistic? Or did his concern for social religion make him
less individualistic than his interpreters in later generations? Would his
theology support revolution as a means of liberation? Or would his own
resistance to the American Revolution and his support of the monarchy
in his time limit Wesley's theology from being used to analyze the structural nature of oppression? Would his theological descendants have to
choose between faithfulness to the tradition and commitment to social
change? The essays do not present a point/counterpoint approach to
these questions. Rather, each author engages the connection between
liberation theology and the Wesleyan tradition from his or her unique
perspective. No attempt is made to settle these questions with a uni-
form answer; rather, the collection of distinct voices display "ambiguities and inconsistencies of the tradition" that can then be probed to
allow Wesley's theology to speak to a new time.[26]

The challenging engagement with Wesley's theology that was
prompted by liberation theology renewed the question of Wesley's
"legacy." Even in a time when certain members of the family were
reclaiming him as guide, others were showing how his theology did not
obviously fit the needs of their time and place. This creative tension
has continued to echo in subsequent meetings of the Oxford Institute of
Methodist Theological Studies.[27]

The "Wesleyan Quadrilateral"

The twentieth-century recovery of Wesley's theology was not limited to exploring specific theological ideas and their relevance for a new
time. It also included attention to Wesley's theological method. The
merger of the Methodist Church in the United States with the Evangelical United Brethren to form the United Methodist Church in 1968,
prompted reflection about how the new church ought to regard the official doctrinal documents of its predecessor bodies (the "Articles of Religion" for the MC, and the "Confession of Faith" for the EUB) as they
became a new institutional entity. A Theological Study Commission
was formed to consider the question of doctrine and doctrinal standards.
Even though the commission had the opportunity to do so, it decided not
to write a new creed or confession for the merged body, but instead to
suggest a method for reflection upon, not only the two official documents

---

[26] Ibid., p. 48.
[27] The list of presentations of the various meetings of the Oxford Institute, and copies of
many of the papers, are available at http://www.oxford-institute.org/archives.html.

in question, but also any matter of Christian teaching. Under the leadership of Albert Outler, the Commission produced a statement about the UMC's theological task that was informed by Outler's deep engagement with John Wesley's thinking. Outler had noticed practices in Wesley that were remarkably consistent, whether Wesley was self-conscious of them or not. In addressing any theological question Wesley would appeal first to Scripture; but because his opponents could and did also appeal to Scripture, Wesley would also look to "primitive" Christian tradition to see how Scripture had been understood on the point in question; the interpretation was then disciplined by reasoned argument; and finally the experience of knowing oneself to be a child of God would allow the theological point to come alive and matter for Christian living.[28] These four elements – Scripture, tradition, reason, and experience – became known as the "Wesleyan Quadrilateral." A description of how these four elements should work together in theological reflection began appearing in the *Book of Discipline of The United Methodist Church* in 1972.

Although the section in the *Book of Discipline* containing the description of the "quadrilateral" was approved quite easily by the General Conference in 1972 and gained rapid popular acceptance as a useful tool among members of the United Methodist Church, it soon began to be debated among scholars. A common concern was about authority and norms in the face of pluralism, especially the authority of Scripture itself.[29] Over time, more questions were raised about the status of Scripture in the quadrilateral, which many construed as an equilateral despite the clear reference to the primacy of Scripture in the disciplinary statement. These questions became forceful enough that the General Conference of 1984 formed a Committee on Our Theological Task (COTT) to review and revise this section of the *Book of Discipline*. Bishop Earl G. Hunt, Jr. chaired the COTT, and Richard P. Heitzenrater chaired the subcommittee that was responsible for drafting the new statement.

Neither the 1972 statement nor the revised statement (adopted in 1988) refer to Scripture, tradition, reason, and experience as the "Wesleyan Quadrilateral" (or even as the "Methodist Quadrilateral"). Nor do they make explicit claims that the method described in the *Book of Discipline* matches Wesley's practice in theological reflection. The 1988 statement does preface description of the four elements with

[28] See Albert C. Outler, "The Wesleyan Quadrilateral – in John Wesley," in *Doctrine and Theology in The United Methodist Church*, ed. by T. A. Langford (Nashville, 1991), 75–88.

[29] See chapters 2–5 of Langford, *Doctrine and Theology*, 26–74.

some historical reference to Wesley's thinking that includes this summary sentence: "Wesley believed that the living core of Christian faith was revealed in Scripture, illumined by tradition, vivified in personal experience, and confirmed by reason."[30] The language of this sentence (attributed to the United Methodist Church rather than Wesley) gets picked up in a question that candidates for probationary membership as elders must interpret as part of their examination by Boards of Ordained Ministry.[31] Other questions for candidates for ministry also require reflection regarding the section on "Our Theological Task." By incorporating this reflection into preparation for ordination, the United Methodist Church demonstrates that it values leaders who have learned how to be theologians with specific reference to the Wesleyan/Methodist tradition.

Although the "quadrilateral" was identified and came into prominent use within the particular context of the United Methodist Church, it has spread in use and popularity in other branches of Methodism. The question raised within the UMC about the authority of Scripture in the quadrilateral has been raised also in other branches of the Methodist family. Nazarene historian Timothy L. Smith raised an objection to the seeming diminishment of Scripture's role in a paper at the Seventh Oxford Institute.[32] In response, Donald Thorsen (Free Methodist) produced a study of Wesley's method in historical context that specifically sought to locate him in the tradition of evangelicalism, with a strong sense of the authority of Scripture, and argues that the "Wesleyan Quadrilateral" can provide a model of theological method for evangelicalism.[33]

The role of Scripture is not the only dimension of the "quadrilateral" that has sparked broader discussion. Brazilian Methodist theologian José Carlos de Souza argued in a paper presented at the Eleventh Oxford Institute (2002) that, in a time when ecological issues have such importance, theology has to consider the effect of any of its teachings on creation. This leads him to suggest (through an argument that shows Wesley himself was interested in the natural world) that "creation" should be a fifth factor in theological method in the Wesleyan tradition.[34]

---

[30] ¶104, *The Book of Discipline of the United Methodist Church 2004*, ed. by Harriet Jane Olsen (Nashville, 2004).

[31] ¶324, *2004 Book of Discipline*.

[32] Published as Timothy L. Smith, "John Wesley and the Wholeness of Scripture," *Interpretation* 39 (1985): 246–62.

[33] Donald A.D. Thorsen, *The Wesleyan Quadrilateral: Scripture, Tradition, Reason & Experience as a Model of Evangelical Theology* (1990).

[34] José Carlos de Souza, "Creation, New Creation, and Theological Method in Wesleyan Perspective," http://www.oxford-institute.org/docs/2002papers/2002–2Souza.pdf.

In describing the interaction of Scripture, tradition, reason, and experience, Outler was pointing to a method inspired by Wesley but not promoted by him. Further historical work has refined understanding of what Wesley understood about each of the four categories.[35] But the dynamic interaction that Outler first displayed and that Heitzenrater helped develop seems to reflect well the concerns that Wesley had for grounding theological reflection in Scripture, orienting it within theological values handed down by the Church, refining it through careful and logical thought, and linking any theological insight to lived experience. The method has proved useful beyond its original purpose and has elicited ongoing and fruitful dialogue about what it means to do theological reflection. As the use of the "quadrilateral" has taken hold in Methodism, Wesley's positive theological legacy has been broadened beyond individual concepts to promoting the life of reflection that Wesley himself led and that he wanted for others.

So has John Wesley left a legacy of ideas that is more than an outdated system? Although there was a period of neglect, current scholarship and ecclesial practice often look to Wesley for guidance, not only on particular issues, but also for how to think through questions as they arise. This legacy has not resulted in uniformity of ideas. Indeed, the legacy may lie in what descendants think it worth arguing about more than in their agreement. By extending the legacy to include the "quadrilateral," the legacy both calls for and provides a model for its own updating. I suspect that of most importance to Wesley himself would have been to leave a legacy of using theology to enliven Christian faith. So, as long as Methodism considers theology not as simply an intellectual exercise, but as a means of vital piety, Wesley's descendants will be honoring their founder as the theologian he wanted to be.

[35] See especially W. Stephen Gunter et al., *Wesley and the Quadrilateral*.

Select bibliography

Wesley's works

The Bicentennial Edition of the Works of John Wesley. General Editors, Frank Baker & Richard P. Heitzenrater. Nashville: Abingdon, 1984ff. [Volumes 7, 11, 25, and 26 appeared first as the *Oxford Edition of The Works of John Wesley.* Oxford: Clarendon, 1975–83.]

Vol. 1: *Sermons I,* Albert C. Outler, ed., 1984.

Vol. 2: *Sermons II,* Albert C. Outler, ed., 1985.

Vol. 3: *Sermons III,* Albert C. Outler, ed., 1986.

Vol. 4: *Sermons IV,* Albert C. Outler, ed., 1987.

Vols. 5–6: *Explanatory Notes upon the New Testament* (forthcoming).

Vol. 7: *A Collection of Hymns for the Use of the People Called Methodists,* Franz Hildebrandt & Oliver Beckerlegge, eds., 1983.

Vol. 8: *Worship and Prayer* (forthcoming).

Vol. 9: *The Methodist Societies I: History, Nature and Design,* Rupert E. Davies, ed., 1989.

Vol. 10: *Minutes* (forthcoming).

Vol. 11: *The Appeals to Men of Reason and Religion and Certain Related Open Letters,* Gerald R. Cragg, ed., 1975.

Vols. 12–13: *Doctrinal and Controversial Treatises* (forthcoming).

Vol. 14: *Social and Political Tracts* (forthcoming).

Vol. 15: *Catechetical and Educational Works* (forthcoming).

Vol. 16: *Editorial Works* (forthcoming).

Vol. 17: *Medical Treatises* (forthcoming).

Vol. 18: *Journals and Diaries I, 1735–38,* W. Reginald Ward & Richard P. Heitzenrater, eds., 1988.

Vol. 19: *Journals and Diaries II, 1738–43,* W. Reginald Ward & Richard P. Heitzenrater, eds., 1990.

Vol. 20: *Journals and Diaries III, 1743–54,* W. Reginald Ward & Richard P. Heitzenrater, eds., 1991.

Vol. 21: *Journals and Diaries IV, 1755–65,* W. Reginald Ward & Richard P. Heitzenrater, eds., 1992.

Vol. 22: *Journals and Diaries V, 1765–75,* W. Reginald Ward & Richard P. Heitzenrater, eds., 1993.

Vol. 23: *Journals and Diaries VI, 1776–86,* W. Reginald Ward & Richard P. Heitzenrater, eds., 1995.

Vol. 24: *Journal and Diaries VII*, 1787–91, W. Reginald Ward & Richard P. Heitzenrater, eds., 2003.
Vol. 25: *Letters I*, 1721–39, Frank Baker, ed., 1980.
Vol. 26: *Letters II*, 1740–55, Frank Baker, ed., 1982.
Vols. 27–31: *Letters III–VII* (forthcoming).
Vol. 32: *Oxford Diary* (forthcoming).
Vols. 33–34: Bibliography of Wesley's Publications

For material not (or not presently) included in *Bicentennial Edition*:

A Christian Library: Consisting of Extracts from and Abridgments of the Choicest Pieces of Practical Divinity Which have been Published in the English Tongue. 50 vols. Bristol: Farley, 1749–55 (2nd ed. 30 vols., edited by Thomas Jackson, including additional abridged items by Wesley; 1819–27).
Explanatory Notes Upon the New Testament. 3rd ed. 2 vols. Bristol: Graham and Pine, 1760–62 (many later reprints).
Explanatory Notes upon the Old Testament. 3 vols. Bristol: Pine, 1765; reprint ed., Salem, OH: Schmul, 1975.
John Wesley's Prayer Book: The Sunday Service of the Methodists in North America. Introduction, notes and commentary by James F. White. Akron, Ohio: OSL Publications, 1991, 1995.
The Letters of the Rev. John Wesley, A.M. 8 vols. Edited by John Telford. London: Epworth, 1931.
A Survey of the Wisdom of God in the Creation, or A Compendium of Natural Philosophy. 4th edition. London: J. Paramore, 1784.
The Works of John Wesley. 3rd ed. 14 vols. Edited by Thomas Jackson. London: J. Mason, 1829–31; reprint ed., Grand Rapids, MI: Baker, 1979.

Wesley's historical context

Campbell, Ted A. *The Religion of the Heart: A Study of European Religious Life in the Seventeenth and Eighteenth Centuries.* Columbia: University of South Carolina Press, 1991.
Clark, J. C. D. *English Society 1688–1832: Religion, Ideology, and Politics during the Ancien Regime.* Cambridge: Cambridge University Press, 2000.
Claydon, Tony. *Europe and the Making of England, 1660–1760.* Cambridge: Cambridge University Press, 2007.
Clifford, Alan Charles. *Atonement and Justification: English Evangelical Theology, 1640–1790.* Oxford: Clarendon Press, 1990.
Gibson, William. *The Church of England, 1688–1832: Unity and Accord.* London: Routledge, 2001.
Gregory, Jeremy and John Stevenson. *Britain in the Eighteenth Century, 1688–1820*, 2nd edn. London: Routledge, 2007.
Halevy, Elie. *The Birth of Methodism in England.* Chicago: University of Chicago Press, 1971.
Hempton, David. *Religion and Political Culture in Britain and Ireland: from the Glorious Revolution to the Decline of Empire.* Cambridge: Cambridge University Press, 1996.

O'Gorman, Frank. *The Long Eighteenth Century: British Political and Social History, 1688–1832.* London: Arnold, 1997.

Porter, Roy. *English Society in the Eighteenth Century.* London: Allen Lane, 1982.

Rivers, Isabel. *Reason, Grace and Sentiment: A Study of the Language of Religion and Ethics in England, 1660–1780.* 2 vols. New York: Cambridge University Press, 1991–2000.

Rupp, E. Gordon. *Religion in England, 1688–1791.* Oxford: Clarendon Press, 1986.

Sommerville, C. J. *The Secularization of Early Modern England: from Religious Culture to Religious Faith.* Oxford: Oxford University Press, 1992.

Suarez SJ, Michael F. and Michael Turner, eds., *The Cambridge History of the Book in Britain,* vol. 5, 1695–1830. New York: Cambridge University Press, 2009.

Walsh, John & Stephen Taylor, eds. *The Church of England, c. 1689–c. 1833.* New York: Cambridge University Press, 1993.

Ward, W. Reginald. *Religion and Society in England 1790–1850.* London: Batsford, 1972.

Ward, W. Reginald. *The Protestant Evangelical Awakening.* New York: Cambridge University Press, 1992.

Ward, W. Reginald. *Early Evangelicalism: A Global Intellectual History, 1670–1789.* New York: Cambridge University Press, 2006.

Young, B. W. *Religion and Enlightenment in Eighteenth-Century England.* Oxford: Clarendon, 1998.

Biographical studies

Baker, Frank. *John Wesley and the Church of England.* 2nd ed. London: Epworth, 2000.

Collins, Kenneth J. *A Real Christian: The Life of John Wesley.* Nashville: Abingdon, 1999.

Collins, Kenneth J. *John Wesley: A Theological Journey.* Nashville: Abingdon, 2003.

Heitzenrater, Richard P. *The Elusive Mr. Wesley.* 2nd ed. Nashville: Abingdon, 2003.

Heitzenrater, Richard P. *Mirror and Memory: Reflections on Early Methodism.* Nashville: Kingswood Books, 1989.

Heitzenrater, Richard P. *Wesley and the People Called Methodists.* Nashville: Abingdon, 1995.

Rack, Henry D. *Reasonable Enthusiast: John Wesley and the Rise of Methodism.* 3rd ed. London: Epworth Press, 2002.

Intellectual and Theological Studies

Abraham, William J. *Wesley for Armchair Theologians.* Louisville: Westminster John Knox, 2005.

Borgen, Ole Edvard. *John Wesley on the Sacraments: A Theological Study.* Nashville, TN: Abingdon, 1972; reprint ed., Grand Rapids: Zondervan, 1985.

Brendlinger, Irv A. *Social Justice Through the Eyes of Wesley: John Wesley's Theological Challenge to Slavery.* Ontario: Joshua Press, 2007.

Burdon, Adrian. *Authority and Order: John Wesley and His Preachers.* Burlington, VT: Ashgate, 2005.

Butler, David. *Methodists and Papists: John Wesley and the Catholic Church in the Eighteenth Century.* London: Darton, Longman & Todd, 1995.

Campbell, Ted A. *John Wesley and Christian Antiquity: Religious Vision and Cultural Change.* Nashville: Kingswood Books, 1991.

Chilcote, Paul Wesley. *John Wesley and the Women Preachers of Early Methodism.* Metuchen, NJ: Scarecrow Press, 1991.

Clapper, Gregory Scott. *John Wesley on Religious Affections: His Views on Experience and Emotion and Their Role in the Christian Life and Theology.* Metuchen, NJ: Scarecrow Press, 1989.

Collins, Kenneth Joseph. *The Theology of John Wesley: Holy Love and the Shape of Grace.* Nashville: Abingdon, 2007.

Deschner, John William. *Wesley's Christology: An Interpretation.* 2nd edition. Dallas, TX: Southern Methodist University Press, 1985.

Gunter, W. Stephen. *The Limits of "Love Divine": John Wesley's Response to Antinomianism and Enthusiasm.* Nashville: Kingswood Books, 1989.

Jennings, Theodore Wesley, Jr. *Good News to the Poor: John Wesley's Evangelical Economics.* Nashville: Abingdon, 1990.

Jones, Scott Jameson. *John Wesley's Conception and Use of Scripture.* Nashville: Kingswood Books, 1995.

Knight, Henry Hawthorne, III. *The Presence of God in the Christian Life: John Wesley and the Means of Grace.* Metuchen, NJ: Scarecrow Press, 1992.

Lawson, Albert Brown. *John Wesley and the Anglican Evangelicals of the Eighteenth Century: A Study in Cooperation and Separation with Special Reference to the Calvinistic Controversies.* Durham: Pentland Press, 1994.

Lee, Sung-Duk. *Der Deutsche Pietismus und John Wesley.* Giessen: Brunnen, 2003.

Lindström, Harald Gustaf. *Wesley and Sanctification.* Wilmore, KY: Francis Asbury, 1946.

Lodahl, Michael E. *God of Nature and of Grace: Reading the World in a Wesleyan Way.* Nashville: Kingswood Books, 2003.

Long, D. Stephen. *John Wesley's Moral Theology: The Quest for God and Goodness.* Nashville: Kingswood Books, 2005.

McGonigle, Herbert. *Sufficient Saving Grace: John Wesley's Evangelical Arminianism.* Carlisle: Paternoster, 2001.

Madden, Deborah. *"A Cheap, Safe and Natural Medicine": Religion, Medicine and Culture in John Wesley's "Primitive Physic."* Atlanta: Rodopi, 2007.

Maddox, Randy L. *Responsible Grace: John Wesley's Practical Theology.* Nashville: Kingswood Books, 1994.

Marquardt, Manfred. *John Wesley's Social Ethics: Praxis and Principles.* Nashville: Abingdon, 1992.

Outler, Albert Cook. *The Wesleyan Theological Heritage.* Edited by Thomas C. Oden & Leicester R. Longden. Grand Rapids: Zondervan, 1991.

Runyon, Theodore H. *The New Creation: John Wesley's Theology Today.* Nashville: Abingdon, 1998.

Steele, Richard Bruce. *"Gracious Affection" and "True Virtue" according to Jonathan Edwards and John Wesley*. Metuchen, NJ: Scarecrow Press, 1994.

Vickers, Jason E. *Wesley: A Guide for the Perplexed*. London: T&T Clark, 2009.

Weber, Theodore R. *Politics in the Order of Salvation: Transforming Wesleyan Political Ethics*. Nashville: Kingswood Books, 2001.

Williams, Colin Wilbur. *John Wesley's Theology Today*. Nashville: Abingdon, 1960.

Collections of essays on Wesley and Wesleyan theology

Chilcote, Paul, ed. *The Wesleyan Tradition: A Paradigm for Renewal*. Nashville: Abingdon, 2002.

Collins, Kenneth J. & John H. Tyson, eds. *Conversion in the Wesleyan Tradition*. Nashville: Abingdon, 2001.

Gunter, W. Stephen, ed. *Wesley and the Quadrilateral: Renewing the Conversation*. Nashville: Abingdon, 1997.

Heitzenrater, Richard, ed. *The Wesleys and the Poor: The Legacy and Development of Methodist Attitudes to Poverty, 1729–1999*. Nashville: Kingswood Books, 2002.

Kimbrough, S. T. Jr., ed. *Orthodox and Wesleyan Spirituality*. Crestwood, NY: St. Vladimir's Seminary Press, 2002.

Kimbrough, S. T. Jr., ed. *Orthodox and Wesleyan Scriptural Understanding and Practice*. Crestwood, NY: St. Vladimir's Seminary Press, 2005.

Kimbrough, S. T. Jr., ed. *Orthodox and Wesleyan Ecclesiology*. Crestwood, NY: St. Vladimir's Seminary Press, 2007.

Maddox, Randy L., ed. *Aldersgate Reconsidered*. Nashville: Kingswood Books, 1990.

Maddox, Randy L., ed. *Rethinking Wesley's Theology for Contemporary Methodism*. Nashville: Kingswood Books, 1998.

Meadows, Philip R., ed. *Windows on Wesley*. Oxford: Applied Theology Press, 1997.

Runyon, Theodore H., ed. *Sanctification and Liberation: Liberation Theologies in Light of the Wesleyan Tradition*. Nashville: Abingdon, 1981.

Runyon, Theodore H., ed. *Wesleyan Theology Today*. Nashville: Kingswood Books, 1985.

Stacey, John, ed. *John Wesley: Contemporary Perspectives*. London: Epworth, 1988.

Steele Richard B., ed. *"Heart Religion" in the Methodist Tradition and Related Movements*. Lanham, MD: Scarecrow Press, 2001.

Stone, Bryan P. & Thomas J. Oord, eds. *Thy Nature and Thy Name is Love: Wesleyan and Process Theologies in Dialogue*. Nashville: Kingswood Books, 2001.

Wesleyan/Methodist developments

Cracknell, Kenneth and Susan White. *An Introduction to World Methodism*. New York: Cambridge University Press, 2005.

Dayton, Donald W. *Theological Roots of Pentecostalism*. Metuchen, NJ: Scarecrow Press, 1987.

Dieter, Melvin Easterday. *The Holiness Revival of the Nineteenth Century*. Lanham, MD: Scarecrow Press, 1996.

Hempton, David Neil. *Methodism and Politics in British Society, 1750–1850*. Stanford: Stanford University Press, 1984.

Hempton, David. *The Religion of the People: Methodism and Popular Religion c.1750–1900*. London: Routledge, 1996.

Hempton, David. *Methodism: Empire of the Spirit*. New Haven: Yale University Press, 2005.

Langford, Thomas Anderson. *Practical Divinity: Theology in the Wesleyan Tradition*. 2 vols. Nashville: Abingdon, 1983.

Melton, J. Gordon. *A Will to Choose: The Origins of African American Methodism*. New York: Rowman & Littlefield, 2005.

Peters, John Leland. *Christian Perfection and American Methodism*. New York: Abingdon Press, 1956.

Stephens, Randall J. *The Fire Spreads: Holiness and Pentecostalism in the American South*. Cambridge, MA: Harvard University Press, 2008.

Synan, Vinson. *The Holiness-Pentecostal Tradition: Charismatic Movements in the Twentieth Century*. Grand Rapids: Eerdmans, 1997.

Tucker, Karen B. Westerfield. *American Methodist Worship*. New York: Oxford University Press, 2001.

Tucker, Karen B. Westerfield, ed. *The Sunday Service of the Methodists: Twentieth-Century Worship in Worldwide Methodism*. Nashville: Kingswood Books, 1996.

Turner, John Munsey. *Conflict and Reconciliation: Studies in Methodism and Ecumenism in England, 1740–1982*. London: Epworth, 1985.

Wainwright, Geoffrey. *Methodists in Dialog*. Nashville: Kingswood Books, 1995.

Yrigoyen, Charles Jr., ed. *The Global Impact of the Wesleyan Traditions and their Related Movements*. Metuchen, NJ: Scarecrow Press, 2002.

Index